TH
HI

OPERA

Edited by

ROGER PARKER

Oxford   New York

OXFORD UNIVERSITY PRESS

1996

Oxford University Press, Walton Street, Oxford OX2 6DP

Oxford New York

Athens Auckland Bangkok Bogota Bombay
Buenos Aires Calcutta Cape Town Dares Salaam
Delhi Florence Hong Kong Istanbul Karachi
Kuala Lumpur Madras Madrid Melbourne
Mexico City Nairobi Paris Singapore
Taipei Tokyo Toronto

and associated companies in
Berlin Ibadan

Oxford is a trade mark of Oxford University Press

British Library Cataloguing in Publication Data
Data available

Library of Congress Cataloging in Publication Data
The Oxford history of opera / [edited by] Roger Parker.
p. cm.
Includes bibliographical references (p.   )
1. Opera.   I. Parker, Roger, 1951-   .
ML1700.092   1996   782.1'09—dc20   96-2781
ISBN 0-19-284028-2

1 3 5 7 9 10 8 6 4 2

Datacapture by Puretech Corporation, Pondicherry, India
Typeset by Oxuniprint, Oxford University Press
Printed in Great Britain by
Biddles Ltd
Guildford and King's Lynn

CONTENTS

iv   *Contents*

LIST OF PLATES

The editor and publishers wish to thank those who have kindly given permission to reproduce their illustrations. In a few instances we have been unable to trace the copyright holder prior to publication. If notified the publishers will be pleased to amend the acknowledgements in any future imprint.

FOREWORD

ROGER PARKER

W ords about and around opera have never been lacking, if only for the simple reason that, of all events involving music, opera seems to produce the most abundant quantities of text. It is typically a collaborative enterprise, the product of composers, poets, scene designers, and interpreters of all kinds, and this fact—particularly in the last two centuries—has often given rise to a great deal of written communication between its various creators, a well-documented, sometimes even public genesis. Opera starts, of course, from a literary text, a libretto, itself usually drawn from earlier texts, and frequently centring on archetypal characters who go back even further, and who sometimes boast enormous literatures of their own. The operatic event is usually a grand public occasion, generating rich veins of public response: a reception history second to none. And finally, the peculiarly hybrid nature of opera, its strange amalgam of various systems of artistic communication, has continued to pose contentious aesthetic questions, causing a kind of age-old polemical war that may shift its fields of conflict but will never be finally resolved.

In the context of this mass of words, it may at first seem strange that there have been relatively few histories of opera. In the later eighteenth century, the first great general histories of music (the most famous of which is Charles Burney's *A General History of Music from the Earliest Ages to the Present*) of course included much about opera; inevitably so, as vocal music was still regarded as the mainstream, the essential line of musical development, and opera as its grandest manifestation. By the middle of the nineteenth century, however, the focus of historiography had shifted: in a great flowering of narrative biography, individual composers were now seen as *shaping* musical history, rather than merely illustrating its progress, and—with the notable exception of Wagner, whose biography and literary writings have spawned one of the largest bibliographies of modern times—these composers were mostly seen as pre-eminently the creators of 'pure' instrumental music.

Although one or two fine operatic histories have appeared in our own century, the best known in English being Donald Jay Grout's *Short History of Opera* (first published in 1947), this tendency to place opera on the sidelines of music history has continued until fairly recently. However, there are now strong signs of change. As musicology increasingly seems to be questioning the usefulness of purely formalistic modes of enquiry, and as it looks for inspiration and new methods among related disciplines, in particular literary studies and anthropology, operatic studies have become an ever more lively focus of scholarly interest. There have in the past few years been a number of significant landmarks in this shift of attention, perhaps most notably a new, multi-volume history of Italian opera, the *Storia dell'opera italiana* (edited by Lorenzo Bianconi and Giorgio Pestelli), which largely eschews musical analysis in favour of a broad cultural approach to the phenomenon. Much of the 'new' scholarship has now been collected and magnificently displayed in *The New Grove Dictionary of Opera* (edited by Stanley Sadie), four huge volumes that serve as a modern monument to this explosion of activity.

The present book is written by specialists who have been much involved in these recent developments (all of us, for example, have contributed extensively to *The New Grove Dictionary of Opera*), and it attempts to bring some of the new operatic scholarship to a broader audience. The bulk of the book is cast in the form of a loose historical narrative, dividing operatic history by chronological (and sometimes also national) boundaries. As befits a volume for the general reader, we have apportioned space roughly in line with the biases of the current repertoire, which means that the 'long nineteenth century', a period that includes a very large proportion of the operas in constant revival around the world, takes up more than half the available pages. Within the constraints of these broad chapter divisions, however, contributors were allowed a fair amount of freedom, both in method of approach and in content. This relative freedom has had the great advantage of allowing authors to find their own focus of attention—to develop an argument, or series of arguments, rather than to offer a mere roll-call of facts. But it has inevitably meant that the book's overall coverage is less than comprehensive. There is, for example, little mention of operatic composition in places such as Australia or South America or the Iberian peninsula; nor will devotees of, say, British opera in the nineteenth century find much to sustain them. Such lacunae (and there are others) are unfortunate, but we thought they were a fair price to pay for the increased focus on a discussion of the main centres of operatic activity.

The final chapters of the book deal with three aspects of opera that, although they are mentioned many times in the main narrative, seemed to demand special, and specialist, treatment. One chapter is devoted to opera singers. Performers are, of course, an essential part of most musical experience, but within this broad grouping, opera singers have very often played an unprecedentedly central role in their genre's history, and have sometimes been deeply involved in the creative phase of the works they perform, influencing substantially the broad outlines and the final shape of those works. One reason for this is that singers have usually been at the sharp end of public interest in opera, their successes and failures influencing considerably (and sometimes permanently) the fate of individual works. It is fashionable in some academic circles to look down on those who concern themselves with singers, but to do so is dangerous: most opera lovers (whether academics or not) have been lured into their obsession through a fascination with the human voice, and to downplay the centrality of singers to the operatic event is to deny a crucial element of the genre's extravagant charm.

Another 'specialist' chapter is concerned with opera as a social event, a further aspect of operatic history that can hardly be overestimated. Because of its conspicuous consumption, its lavish amalgam of theatrical and musical resources, opera has almost always been surrounded by elaborate social and political display, by demonstrations of economic power and cultural élitism. Though such manifestations may seem most obvious during the first two centuries of operatic history, in particular during the phase of so-called 'court' opera, they have continued with remarkable resilience during more recent, more democratic times. Opera as a social force may even have come to a peak in the nineteenth century, when the opera house was often the main social venue of the bourgeoisie, and—not surprisingly—often played an important role in that century's great bourgeois revolutions. Since then its influence has clearly diminished, but state-supported, twentieth-century opera has nevertheless proved extraordinarily adaptable to old, absolutist modes of behaviour.

The central chapter of these three, and quite properly the longest of the book, concerns the visual side of opera, and in particular the problems surrounding staging. There is at present no more contentious issue in operatic life, with many devotees—scholars and untutored enthusiasts alike—feeling that their beloved art is being taken over and gravely distorted by a group of 'modern' producers, those intent on making personal statements at the expense of the works they interpret. Wherever one stands in this debate, it seems certain that the level of argument would be enriched if more attention were paid to the history of staging, an area that has only recently begun to be explored. There is, for example, good historical evidence to suggest that staging has frequently existed in an uneasy relationship with musical drama, that fashions in the spoken theatre and those in the opera house were often at odds. True, we are at present attending an extreme moment in this disjunction, but the tension was always there: the laws that govern the various operatic systems of communication—words, music, the visual aspects—are very different; to give only the most obvious example of this, words and music may be captured on the page, recorded for posterity, while the theatrical gesture will die the moment it is created.

The current debate certainly admits of no easy answers, and the struggle between 'modern' and 'traditional' modes of operatic production seems bound to continue. However, just as historical awareness of various staging practices may broaden the aesthetic premises on which the debate takes place, it may also serve to reduce somewhat the rhetorical claims that so routinely issue from both camps. On the one hand, close historical study makes clear that today's 'traditional' stagings of nineteenth-century operas, though they often proclaim 'respect' for the original creators' intentions, are usually very far from those that would have been seen by contemporaneous audiences. A production of *Die Meistersinger* labelled 'traditional', for example, is more likely to take us back to the style of Germany in the 1930s than to that of the first performances. On the other hand, historical enquiry will also remind the most modern of modern producers that many of their creations will be far less shocking to today's audience than would aspects of a faithfully recreated, 'authentic' staging. The shock of the old could, in this particular context, be a great deal more violent that the shock of the new, and if such a conclusion spikes the odd ultra-modern and postmodern gun, then so much the better.

❦ 1 ❦

THE SEVENTEENTH CENTURY

Tim Carter

FEW genres in the history of music have their origins fixed with such apparent precision as opera: we know when and where the first through-composed music-dramas appeared on the stage—in Florence in the mid-1590s—and the precise political, social, and cultural contexts that gave them birth. Moreover, few genres were from the outset subject to such intense theorizing about their *raison d'être*: the self-examination, at times violent polemic, characteristic of opera up to the present day began early in its history. In part this was because the academic orientation of intellectual life in the courts of late Renaissance Italy generated an almost obsessive need to document, explain, and debate—hence validate—the issues at the heart of contemporary cultural endeavour. But also, opera, that most difficult of genres, raised crucial problems concerning the aims and effects of music, drama, and indeed the arts in general that could not be ignored. These problems remain as valid today as they were to the first composers, librettists, and patrons of opera; and the history of opera is a history of repeated attempts, variously conditioned by time, place, and circumstance, to find their solutions. At the heart of the matter lies a fundamental question. What makes opera anything more than, as Dr Johnson famously claimed, 'an exotick and irrational entertainment'?

Of course, music was used in the theatre long before opera took the stage: it had a crucial role to play within the politics of splendour that lay at the heart of courtly endeavour. In the fifteenth and sixteenth centuries, the north Italian courts had well-established ways of articulating moments of princely celebration. The birth of an heir, the wedding of a prince, the death of a duke were all key moments in courtly life that required due emphasis on both private and public platforms: indeed, the cohesiveness of the political and social fabric crucially depended on the articulation and consequent control of moments of both celebration and crisis as manifestations of the glory and permanence of the ducal state. Theatrical entertainments provided one means for this articulation and control.

Various forms of entertainment were available to the Renaissance court and academy. Tragedies and comedies, whether classical or classically inspired, gave vent to the Humanist-inspired emulation of ancient Greece and Rome that was so powerful a force in the Renaissance as a whole: given the acknowledged place of music on the classical stage, they also allowed composers to emulate the renowned music of antiquity (hence Andrea Gabrieli's choruses for the translation of Sophocles' *Oedipus tyrannus* performed at the opening of the Palladio's Teatro Olimpico in Vicenza in 1585). Pastoral plays, too, displayed the trappings of classical authority: important precedents were set by two entertainments staged in Mantua in the late fifteenth century, Angelo Poliziano's *Orfeo* (?1480) and Niccolò da Correggio's *Il rapimento di Cefalo* (1487). But doubtless more important was the fact that the pastoral's celebration of the Age of Gold—that idyllic time of prosperity and peace—was readily susceptible to allegorical interpretation: Tasso's *Aminta* (1573) proved the point. This made it a powerful tool in the hands of Renaissance princes and their propagandists. More effective still as propaganda were the entr'acte entertainments, known as the intermedi, performed with tragedies and, more frequently, comedies. In part, they provided light relief from the drama: in 1536, Bernardino Daniello reported that between the acts of a play, 'so that the stage will not remain empty, music and songs, and morescas and buffoons are usually brought in mixed together'. They also served to define the temporal perspective of the action. But the intermedi soon assumed a much grander function, particularly in Florence.

According to the Florentine playwright Alessandro Ceccherelli, writing in 1566:

It is commonly held amongst those who know best . . . that of all the spectacles that are performed, the most worthwhile and worth listening to and seeing is the comedy . . . especially as for some time it has become usual to make them [more] attractive and ornate, by performing wonderfully inventive and skilfully contrived intermedi between their acts.

Not for nothing did his colleague Antonfrancesco Grazzini comment bitterly, 'Once intermedi were made to serve the comedy, but now comedies are made to serve the intermedi.' For example, in the first of the intermedi for Francesco d'Ambra's *La cofanaria*, performed in 1565 for the wedding of Prince Francesco de' Medici and Johanna of Austria:

Accordingly, a brief space after the descent of the curtains which conceal from the eyes of the spectators the perspective of the concave heavens of the opening scene, there is seen to appear a second, most ingeniously contrived heaven wherefrom, little by little, a cloud is perceived approaching, in which there is set with singular ingenuity a gilded and gem-encrusted car, recognized as that of Venus, because it is seen to be drawn by two snow-white swans, and in which, as mistress and charioteer, is most majestically seated that loveliest of goddesses, entirely nude, engarlanded with roses and immortelles and, reins in hand, adorned with the beautiful girdle called Cestus by the ancients. In her train follow the three Graces, likewise recognizable by appearing wholly nude, by their brilliantly blond tresses falling free over their shoulders, but still more by the manner in which they hold each other's hands.... [The cloud,] descending little by little, seemed to leave behind it in heaven Jove, Juno, Saturn, Mars, Mercury and the other gods, from whose midst is nevertheless heard to issue a harmony passing sweet, seemingly a thing divine rather than human, while the entire great, dark hall is filled with the sweetest and most precious odours.

This rich display and erudite symbolism made the intermedi an ideal projection of princely magnificence. The Medici dukes and grand dukes of Florence clearly exploited such entertainments for political ends.

The pastoral play and the intermedi provided two immediate predecessors for the first Florentine operas. Giovan Battista Guarini's *Il pastor fido* (completed in the 1580s) was given a magnificent performance in Mantua to celebrate the wedding of Philip III of Spain and Margaret of Austria in 1598. The play itself—and the academic scandal prompted by its ostensibly irregular form and content—provided an important context for early operatic endeavour. For the intermedi, the genre culminated in the magnificent set performed at the festivities for the wedding of Grand Duke Ferdinando de' Medici and Christine of Lorraine in Florence in 1589. Ferdinando had good reason for lavish celebrations—his succession on the death of his unpopular brother, Grand Duke Francesco, ushered in a bright period in Florentine history—and the wedding was celebrated by spectacular jousts and tournaments, a naval battle in the flooded courtyard of the Pitti Palace, a *sacra rappresentazione*, and several other theatrical entertainments, at the head of which stood a comedy (Girolamo Bargagli's *La pellegrina*) with magnificent intermedi. Significantly, these intermedi focused on various aspects of the power of music (the third and fifth dealt specifically with the mythological musicians Apollo and Arion) and, to match the theme, the composers involved in the production produced a rich musical display. Thus in the first intermedio ('The Harmony of the Spheres'), Harmony descends on a cloud and sings a solo song accompanied by lute; the Sirens and Planets have a five-part chorus, followed by a sinfonia for lutes, viols, trombones, flute(s), and harps; the Fates and the Sirens then sing a dialogue (in two five-part choirs); and the entire body of musicians on stage sings and plays a thirty-part madrigal praising the grand duke and the new grand duchess. So the entertainment continues to the final dance at the end of the sixth intermedio, the celebrated 'Ballo del Granduca', where the gods pay homage to Florence and its court.

Early Opera in Florence

Those in charge of the 1589 intermedi included Giovanni de' Bardi (1534–1612; he also wrote some of the words and music), the architect and scene-designer Bernardo Buontalenti, and Emilio de' Cavalieri (*c.*1550–1602), a Roman musician who had come to Florence with Ferdinando and was now head of the court musical establishment. The texts for the six intermedi were provided in the main by Giovanni Battista Strozzi and Ottavio Rinuccini, while the bulk of the music was composed by Grand Duke Ferdinando's *maestro di cappella*, Cristofano Malvezzi, and by the renowned madrigalist Luca Marenzio (brought specially to Florence for the occasion); individual pieces were also supplied by Cavalieri, Jacopo Peri, Giulio Caccini, and others. A good number of these artists were variously involved in the experiments that led to the emergence of opera in the next decade. For example, Bardi's so-called 'Camerata'—a group of artists and dilettantes who met in the 1570s and 1580s to discuss the state of the arts, particularly music—articulated a general dissatisfaction with the failure of modern music to achieve the emotional power reputed to music in classical antiquity. Emilio de' Cavalieri's music (now lost) for pastoral entertainments in Florence in the 1590s, including *Il satiro* and *La disperatione di Fileno* (1590) and *Il giuoco della cieca* (1595, drawing on Guarini's *Il pastor fido*), established significant dramatic and musical precedents. And Ottavio Rinuccini was the librettist of a significant number of early operas with music by Peri, Caccini, and, later, Claudio Monteverdi.

However, Bardi left Florence for Rome in 1592. His place as the chief patron of the arts in Florence was taken by the younger Jacopo Corsi (1561–1602). Corsi was effectively a new arrival on the Florentine political scene, and he epitomized the generation of younger, more entrepreneurial noblemen with whom Grand Duke Ferdinando surrounded himself at the expense of the rather crusty patricians (Bardi included) who had dominated Florentine political life during the unpopular reign of Grand Duke Francesco I. Corsi's mercantile interests in wool, silk (a rising industry in Florence), and banking created considerable wealth.

He also became heavily involved in affairs of state and surrounded himself with the trappings of nobility: a well-furnished residence in the city, two country villas, an extensive collection of sculptures, paintings, and books, and a coterie of artists, poets, and musicians.

The poet Ottavio Rinuccini (1562–1621) and the musician Jacopo Peri (1561–1633) were closely associated with Corsi (in business as well as in the arts). Their idea of applying music to drama in the manner of the reputed performances of Greek tragedy seems to have taken root in the mid-1590s (Peri claimed 1594). The first result of their collaboration was *Dafne*—the subject-matter harks back to the third of the 1589 intermedi—which was performed in early 1598 and repeated in 1599 and once (perhaps twice) in 1600 (the music is almost entirely lost). Then Corsi offered a second music-drama to the court for the celebrations of a wedding which he had played a considerable part in organizing, that of Maria de' Medici and Henri IV of France in October 1600: *Euridice* was performed in the Pitti Palace on 6 October, and Peri's score was published in February 1601.

The subject-matter of the first operas is significant. The Florentines, like a good number of their successors through the centuries, turned to classical myth both as a source of inspiration (it had long been thus for the Renaissance Humanists) and as an attempt to justify their new revelation of music's power: Apollo and Orpheus, the protagonists of the first operas, were renowned for their musical prowess. Such subjects could also counter the accusation that having characters sing, rather than speak, was essentially irrational: verse, not prose, and music, not speech, formed the natural language of the gods. But the use of myth also made early opera more than mere entertainment. Those involved in the first operas believed that they were making a powerful statement both about their times—when the arts had reached such a peak that Orpheus himself could be brought back to life—and about their princely patron, the Apollo / Sun-King around whom the political, social, and cultural world revolved.

Peri's chief problem was to devise a musical style that would cope with the demands of clear diction and dramatic flexibility while retaining at least a degree of structural coherence and musical integrity. As he explained in the preface to *Euridice*:

seeing that it was a question of dramatic poetry and that therefore one should imitate with song him who speaks...I judged that the ancient Greeks and Romans (who, according to the opinion of many, sang their tragedies throughout on the stage) used a harmony which, going beyond that of ordinary speech, fell so short of the melody of song that it assumed an intermediate form.... Therefore, rejecting every other type of song heard up to now, I set myself to discovering the imitation necessary for these poems, and I considered that that type of voice assigned to singing by the ancients, which they called Diastematic (as it were, sustained and suspended) could in part speed up and take an intermediate path between the suspended and slow movements of song and the fluent, rapid ones of speech, thus suiting my intention (just as they, too, adapted it in reading their poetry and epic verse), approaching the other [voice] of speech, which they called Continuous.... Similarly, I realized that in our speech some words are intoned in such a manner that harmony can be founded upon them, and that while speaking one passes through many others which are not intoned, until one returns to another capable of movement through a new consonance. Taking note of these manners and those accents that serve us in grief, joy, and in similar states, I made the bass move in time to these, now faster, now slower, according to the affections, and I held it firm through the dissonances and consonances until the voice of the speaker, passing through various notes, arrived at that which, being intoned in ordinary speech, opens the way to a new harmony. I did this not only so that the flow of the speech would not offend the ear (as if stumbling in encountering the repeated notes because of the more frequent consonances) or that it might not seem in a way to dance to the movement of the bass, and especially in sad or serious subjects, since happier subjects require by their nature more frequent movements, but [I did this] also because the use of dissonances would either diminish or mask the advantage thereby gained because of the necessity of intoning every note, which the ancient musics perhaps had less need of doing. And so (even though I would be reluctant to claim that this was the type of song used in Greek and Roman plays), I have thus believed it to be the only type that our music can give us to suit our speech.

That final sentence undercuts the oft-presumed antiquarian tendencies of early opera. Certainly Peri and Rinuccini, like Cavalieri, were anxious to associate their endeavours with the classical revival, but these Humanist overtones seem designed more to give a veneer of academic respectability to an essentially modern (and modernist) enterprise. Indeed, in the prologue to *Euridice*, the allegorical figure Tragedy admits that she is here not to sing of typically tragic events: instead, 'Behold, I change my gloomy buskins and dark robes to awaken in the heart sweeter emotions'. Of course, this was entirely appropriate for the occasion of the performance (similarly, Rinuccini modifies the outcome of the myth as Orfeo successfully leads Euridice from Hades). But *Euridice* owes more to the pastoral than to classical tragedy. Similarly, it sits squarely in the tradition of the Florentine intermedi, even if its staging was on a smaller scale and without elaborate machines.

Euridice owes a great deal to Rinuccini's fine libretto. Here structural paradigms are established that were to last in Italian opera through the nineteenth century and beyond. Recitative verse—for action, dialogue, and some soliloquies—is in free rhyming seven- and eleven-syllable lines: the flexible poetic structure has clear implications both for the musical setting and for the pacing of the dramatic action. At key points, however, Rinuccini adopts different poetic structures (if the drama calls for a formal song or if a character or group of characters is commenting on a particular situation), exploiting more regular rhymes and sometimes different line-lengths (for example, four- or eight-syllable lines). This more structured verse requires a more structured musical style, which Peri matches by formal arias (duets, choruses, etc.) where a flexible declamation is abandoned in favour of more inherently musical concerns (clear melodic and harmonic patterns, regular periodic phrases, etc.). The distinction between recitative and aria styles remains crucial for opera, although, as we shall see, their relative dramatic and emotional weights shift significantly in the first half of the seventeenth century.

The wedding of Maria de' Medici and Henri IV of France emphasized a reorientation of Florentine foreign policy away from Spain and the Empire—it was a considerable political coup—and presumably the court was attracted by the association of this new policy with a new musico-dramatic genre. But *Euridice* was not the most important entertainment staged during the 1600 festivities: that honour went to Gabriello Chiabrera's *Il rapimento di Cefalo*, with music in the main by Giulio Caccini (1551–1618). *Il rapimento* also seems to have been set entirely to music (only a section survives in Caccini's collection of solo songs, *Le nuove musiche*, 1602), although the libretto suggests that it was more akin to a string of spectacular intermedi loosely linked by a dramatic thread. In contrast, *Euridice* was staged on a small scale. Indeed, that it was presented at all was probably due more to Jacopo Corsi than to the court: Corsi paid most of the costs for the performance and even took part in it himself (at the harpsichord). The audience was unimpressed: one eyewitness account ignored it altogether; others found the recitative 'like the chanting of the Passion'; and Bardi commented that Rinuccini and Peri 'should not have gone into tragic texts and objectionable subjects'.

Euridice was eclipsed by the court-sponsored entertainments mounted in 1600. Moreover, its staging was marred by squabbles between the court artists. Caccini insisted that his singers should sing his and not Peri's music, and he also raced Peri to the press, publishing his own setting of *Euridice* some six weeks before Peri's appeared (although it was not performed complete until December 1602). But there were more fundamental problems: *Euridice*, essentially a private entertainment, was wholly ill suited to a public ceremony intended to glorify the Medici in the national and international arena. Significantly, at the wedding of Prince Cosimo de' Medici to Maria Magdalena of Austria in 1608, the Florentines turned their backs on opera and reverted to the traditional format of a comedy with intermedi (Michelangelo Buonarroti's *Il giudizio di Paride*)—the 1589 festivities were used as a model—wishing, they said, to avoid the mistakes so clearly made in 1600.

Mantua

Vincenzo Gonzaga, duke of Mantua, attended the wedding of Maria de' Medici and Henri IV in Florence in 1600: among his retinue was the court secretary and sometime poet, Alessandro Striggio (?1573–1630). Seven years later, Striggio collaborated with the duke's *maestro di cappella*, Claudio Monteverdi (1567–1643), on a new opera, *Orfeo*. This was doubtless a deliberate attempt to compete with Florence in the theatrical arena: there were close political and artistic connections between the two cities. *Orfeo*—called a *favola in musica* ('play in music')—was certainly a court entertainment (sponsored by Prince Francesco Gonzaga, heir to the throne). But significantly, it first appeared within the confines of an academy, the Accademia degli Invaghiti, and thus in an atmosphere more amenable to its Humanist pretensions.

Striggio and Monteverdi clearly had access to the printed libretto and score of *Euridice*: *Orfeo* puts to good advantage lessons learnt from Rinuccini and Peri. But the opera surpasses its Florentine predecessor at almost every turn. In part, this is because Striggio is a better librettist than poet: the advantage is that he provides clearer, less involved verse that gives the composer more flexibility. But still more, it is due to Monteverdi's skill in dramatic music, already cultivated within his polyphonic madrigals.

Orfeo refers back to other Florentine models, particularly the intermedi: witness the spectacular stage effects, the mythological subject-matter, the allegorical figures, the use of the instruments, and the extended choruses. There are also obvious connections with classical tragedy and, as with *Euridice*, the recent pastoral dramas of Tasso and Guarini. Similarly, Monteverdi's music is redolent of older techniques: even in the 'new'-style recitative, he exploits expressive devices first explored in his 'old'-style five-part madrigals, including carefully crafted dissonances and chromaticism. These backward-looking, 'Renaissance' aspects of the opera are reinforced by its various Humanist messages about the power of man and music.

But *Orfeo* also looks forward. Monteverdi demonstrates his openness to the styles developed by his contemporaries, particularly in his use of new kinds of aria and duet writing. The opening of Act 2, for example, has a succession of arias (for Orfeo), duets, and choruses—cued by changing metres and rhyme-schemes in Striggio's verse—that serve to highlight the dramatic reversal at the arrival of the messenger to announce the death of Euridice. Moreover, Orfeo's set-piece lament (in Dante-like *terza rima* stanzas) at the gates of Hades in Act 3, the centre of the opera, is an elaborate set of strophic variations with instrumental accompaniment, exploiting vocal virtuosity to evoke Orfeo's magical powers (there is a precedent by Peri in the 1589 intermedi). Then in Act 4 Orfeo has an aria of celebration, 'Qual onor di te fia degno' (with obbligato parts for two violins over a 'walking bass'), reminiscent of the modern settings that Monteverdi included in his *Scherzi musicali* (also 1607). Other novel aspects of Monteverdi's score are his obvious concern for large-scale formal planning (with ritornello and refrain patterns) and the detail with which he notes his intentions in matters of scoring and ornamentation. Thus *Orfeo* contains an intriguing mixture of old and new elements. Rather than rejecting previously perfected techniques in an iconoclastic search for novelty, Monteverdi reinterprets the old in the light of the new (and vice versa) to achieve a synthesis of undeniable dramatic force. He also produces what is arguably the first great opera.

Mantua continued to support opera in a courtly context. Shortly after the first performances of *Orfeo* (on 24 February and 1 March 1607) plans were initiated for the wedding festivities of Francesco Gonzaga and Margherita of Savoy. Rinuccini and—much to Monteverdi's annoyance—the Florentine composer Marco da Gagliano (1582–1643) were brought to Mantua to provide entertainments for the festivities. The wedding, however, was delayed for political reasons, and so Gagliano's *Dafne* was performed in advance—to a revised and expanded version of Rinuccini's first libretto—in late February 1608. Eventually, Margherita of Savoy made her triumphal entry into the city on 24 May; on the 28th the opera *Arianna*, by Monteverdi and Rinuccini, was staged; the 31st saw a grand naval battle on the lagoon; the centre-piece of the festivities was on 2 June, a performance of Giovan Battista Guarini's *L'idropica*, with spectacular intermedi by Chiabrera; and on the 4th, Monteverdi's dramatic ballet, the *Ballo delle ingrate*, was performed (a revised version was later published in the composer's *Madrigali guerrieri, et amorosi* of 1638). The festivities also included other comedies, ballets, and tournaments. The audience at the performance of *Arianna* was particularly moved by Arianna's lament at her desertion by Teseo, the only section of the opera to survive. *L'idropica*, on the other hand, made its effect by its spectacular staging, particularly in its splendid intermedi: indeed, Federico Zuccaro reported that although the play 'was beautiful and well performed...it served merely as intermedi to the intermedi'.

Arianna is called a 'tragedia in musica', and the lament certainly conveys a tragic spirit commensurate, it would seem, with the serious ideals of early opera. But when Rinuccini first presented his libretto to the duchess of Mantua (in February 1608), she found it 'rather dry', and the poet was ordered to 'enrich it with some action'. As a result, *Arianna* has many elements more in keeping with the intermedi than with high-minded opera. Again, a court opera seems to have been compromised by the need to conform to long-established archetypes still retaining their potency to articulate power and sovereignty. In turn, opera composers resented the demands made upon them by their patrons: Monteverdi was adamant over the impossibility of producing an opera from a typical courtly *favola marittima*, Scipione Agnelli's *Le nozze di Tetide*: '*Arianna* led me to a just lament, and *Orfeo* to a righteous prayer, but this fable leads me I don't know to what end' (significantly, however, he was happier when he discovered that Agnelli's text was to be performed as intermedi). The apparent problems of reconciling early opera with courtly requirements go a good way to explaining its fluctuating fortunes in the first half of the seventeenth century.

Not for nothing did many north Italian duchies avoid opera altogether, or else keep it as just one of several possibilities for court entertainment. Intermedi remained popular, especially in Florence, while a number of courts—Savoy is a good example—focused on tournaments and ballets. Here princely messages could more easily be conveyed, not least by the active participation of courtiers displaying their military skills in battle and their social skills in dance. For indoor entertainments, the point was emphasized by theatres that somehow established a free passage from stage to auditorium. Opera, however, threatened to erect a conceptual, if not physical, barrier between the stage action and the audience, negating the merging of life and art that was so central to the courtly ethos. On the whole, the north Italian courts felt little sympathy with musico-dramatic experiments. New types of entertainment were fundamentally ill-equipped to cope with traditional modes of princely celebration.

Rome

Emilio de' Cavalieri was unpopular in Florence, but he found more favour in his native Rome: his sacred opera, *Rappresentatione di Anima, et di Corpo*, was first staged there in the Oratorio di Santa Maria in Vallicella in February 1600. The Roman oratories, under the influence of Saint Filippo Neri, embraced the function of confraternities, working for the spiritual benefit of their members, and, as the Jesuits well knew, theatrical entertainments, for all their apparent worldliness, could act as powerful propaganda for the Church. But inevitably the *Rappresentatione* is full of 'soft' morality, and the music is more tuneful than dramatic. Its main influence was on Agostino Agazzari's *Eumelio*, a rather insipid school-opera staged at the Roman Seminary in 1606.

The lack of a central court in Rome meant that the patronage of opera, such as it was, was limited to individuals and a few institutions. Stefano Landi's (1587–1639) *La morte d'Orfeo*, another treatment of the Orpheus myth, was possibly staged in 1619 (but not necessarily in Rome); the Florentine Filippo Vitali's *Aretusa*—a feeble imitation of Peri—was performed by Ottavio Corsini in honour of Cardinal Scipione Borghese in February 1620; and Domenico Mazzocchi's (1592–1665) *La catena d'Adone* (text by Ottavio Tronsarelli, after Giambattista Marino) was produced in February 1626 by Marquis Evandro Conti. These few examples seem scarcely enough to foster a continuing tradition. But the election of Maffeo Barberini as Pope Urban VIII in 1623, and the general commitment of the Barberini family to theatrical entertainments for political expediency, offered opera at least potential stability, and the performance of Landi's *Sant'Alessio* (1631; libretto by Giulio Rospigliosi) at the 3000-seat theatre within the Barberini's Palazzo alle Quattro Fontane on 18 February 1632 initiated a regular series of operas performed under their aegis.

The subjects of Roman operas were typically chosen with spectacle in mind, but now they ranged from pastoral to epic—Michelangelo Rossi's *Erminia sul giordano* (1633; libretto by Rospigliosi) draws on Tasso's *Gerusalemme liberata*, and Luigi Rossi's (1597/8–1653) *Il palazzo incantato, overo La guerriera amante* (1642, Rospigliosi) on Ariosto's *Orlando furioso*—to the lives of the saints (*Sant'Alessio*, *Santa Teodora* (1635), and *San Bonifatio* (1638)). The evident broadening of subject-matter is matched by a receptiveness to models essentially foreign to opera as developed in the north Italian courts. For example, techniques drawn from the *commedia dell'arte* inspire the first comic opera, Virgilio Mazzocchi's and Marco Marazzoli's (*c*.1602 or 1608–62) *Chi soffre speri* of 1637 (it survives in a revision for 1639; the text is by Rospigliosi, after Boccaccio). No less significant is the evident influence of Spanish drama apparent in the abandoning of the classical unities, the mixing of serious and comic elements, and (later) the use of three-act rather than five-act structures.

Roman opera of the second quarter of the century exploited similar musical resources to those of earlier court operas (the main vehicle for furthering the action remained recitative), and even the prominent use of the chorus often deemed characteristic of this repertory was not without precedent. However, there is some evidence to suggest that as in Florence in 1600 simple recitative was deemed thoroughly tedious by contemporary audiences, and fully-fledged arias, or for that matter *mezz'arie* ('half-arias')—the term appears in the preface to *La catena d'Adone*—were becoming essential to maintain the interest of the spectators. This is a significant indication of things to come.

However, Rome remained ambivalent about opera—still more about the use of female singers therein (women's roles were often left to castrati)—and the genre remained subject to the whims of individual patrons. On the death of Urban VIII in 1644, the Barberini were banished from Rome on account of their profligate use of papal funds for these entertainments. When they returned, opera was re-established from 1653 to 1656—productions included Marazzoli's magnificent *La Vita humana, ovvero Il trionfo della pietà* (1656) in honour of Queen Christina of Sweden—but the Barberini theatre was closed again during the reign of Pope Alexander VII. Similarly, when Giulio Rospigliosi (1600–69), librettist of a number of the Barberini operas, was elected Pope Clement IX, he encouraged the foundation of the Teatro Tordinona as a public opera house. It opened in 1671 with a revival of Francesco Cavalli's *Scipione affricano* (with a prologue and additional music by Alessandro Stradella), but it was closed (like all Roman theatres) in 1675 for the Holy Year, and it did not reopen until 1690 because of opposition from Clement IX's successors.

It is now clear that musicians somehow associated with Rome had a significant influence on the emergence of 'public' opera in Venice. For example, the composer and singer Francesco Manelli (d. 1667) and his wife Maddalena, herself a virtuoso singer, lodged in the house of Stefano Landi around 1630: Maddalena was later involved in the tournament

Ermiona performed (with music by Giovanni Felice Sances) in Padua in 1636. Similarly, Francesco Manelli's later collaborator, the poet, composer, and lutenist Benedetto Ferrari (1603 or 1604–81), was trained in Rome, even if he later found employment (at least from 1619 to 1623) in Parma. Manelli, as composer, and Ferrari, as librettist, provided the first operas staged at the Teatro San Cassiano in Venice, *Andromeda* (1637) and *La maga fulminata* (1638). Significantly, opera now came to depend on newer patronage systems, finding a home in different political institutions and social and cultural environments. One might even argue that this is where the history of opera really begins.

Venice

Venice, always and on every occasion extraordinary, and never tired of displaying her greatness, has discovered the remarkable also in virtuoso entertainment, having introduced a few years ago the presentation in music of grand drama with such sets and stage-machines that they surpass all belief; and what the richest treasuries can produce only with difficulty (and only rarely) in royal halls here we see easily achieved with private resources, not only in one, but in three theatres at once; and competing with each other for the greatest perfections, they each draw spectators from the most remote parts of Italy. (Maiolino Bisaccioni, *Apparati scenici per lo Teatro Novissimo*, 1644)

The rapid success of the new genre brought to Venice by Ferrari and Manelli is remarkable. Venice certainly had strong theatrical traditions, whether in private houses (witness Monteverdi's two musical entertainments, the *Combattimento di Tancredi et Clorinda* and *Proserpina rapita*, performed at the Mocenigo palace in 1624 and 1630 respectively) or in the more public forum of the *commedia dell'arte*. Moreover, the civic and ceremonial life of the city always took on a theatrical aspect, especially during carnival. But opera seems to have struck a particular chord with the Venetian public. The Teatro San Cassiano opened for opera in 1637, and it was quickly followed by the Teatro SS Giovanni e Paolo (1639), the Teatro San Moisè (1640), and the Teatro Novissimo (1641). For the first time, these opera houses catered for a paying public. Five new operas were performed in the three seasons following the opening of the Teatro San Cassiano; some fifty had been performed by 1650.

Opera entertained both the city's leisured classes and the steady stream of tourists who saw Venice as an essential stop on the 'grand tour'. John Evelyn, for example, was mightily impressed by Giovanni Rovetta's *Ercole in Lidia* (1645):

This night…we went to the Opera, which are Comedies & other plays repre-sented in Recitative Music by the most excellent Musitians vocal & Instrumen-tal, together with variety of Seeanes painted & contrived with no lesse art of Perspective, and Machines, for flying in the aire, & other wonderfull motions. So taken together it is doubtlesse one of the most magnificent & expensfull diver-sions the Wit of Men can invent: The historie was *Hercules* in Lydia, the Seanes chang'd 13 times, The famous Voices *Anna Rencia* a Roman, & reputed the best treble of Women; but there was an *Eunuch*, that in my opinion surpass'd her, and a *Genoveze* that sung an incomparable Base: This held us by the Eyes and Eares til two in the Morning…

But there was more: the genre remained a powerful political tool even in the ostensibly more democratic environment of a republic rather than a duchy. Like all the arts, opera was fast drawn into the service of articulat-ing the so-called 'myth of Venice', emphasizing greatness, magnificence, and luxury. This had its most obvious impact on the kinds of subject-matter now adopted for opera. As in Rome, mythological subjects remained popular, also tales of romance epic, with their obvious possi-bilities for spectacular scenic effects. But the classical histories of Troy and its offspring, Rome, had special resonance for the inhabitants of the 'new Rome', Venice: Monteverdi's three new operas for Venice—*Il ritorno d'Ulisse in patria* (1640), *Le nozze d'Enea in Lavinia* (1641, now lost), and *L'incoronazione di Poppea* (1643)—reveal the trend. Heroic historical tales could take on even more significance during Venice's long wars against the Ottoman empire that dominated the mid-century and beyond.

The new social and economic contexts for 'public' opera established different mechanisms—and different priorities—for opera production. Opera still catered for the upper echelons of society: it was by no means as 'popular' as some have assumed. But the rise of the impresario (some-times a theatre owner, sometimes a freelance agent) is symptomatic of a new commercial orientation, as is the emergence of the 'star system' for virtuoso singers, the successful hiring of whom could often make or break a production. Similarly, the steady stream of new works for which contemporary audiences clamoured, coupled with the growth of fixed conventions that make many of them variations on a basic theme, also gave opera, for better or for worse, a permanence and a tradition that had been so sorely lacking before. The Venetian theatres found a recipe for success that, while not without risk, could work for profit. Indeed, one can speak of a veritable opera factory, with impresarios, librettists, singers, stage and costume designers, and—probably last in the pecking order—composers all earning something of a living from what was clearly a growth industry.

Monteverdi's ability to adapt to the new demands of the 'public' opera house bears striking witness to his skill and sensitivity to the theatrical world. He had moved to Venice in 1613 to take up the prestigious post of *maestro di cappella* at the Basilica of St Mark, the focal point of Venice's sacred and civic liturgies. Now in his seventies, one might expect him to have opted for a peaceful retirement. But younger figures were fast making their mark, and Monteverdi made a concerted effort to reassert his considerable musical presence. Reviving his renowned *Arianna* in early 1640 clearly served the purpose—it also allowed him to test the water—but the opera, even with revision, was scarcely right for the times. *Il ritorno d'Ulisse in patria* (to a libretto by Giacomo Badoaro) is, on the other hand, an accomplished bow to the new musical market-place. While scarcely as spectacular as some operas staged in Venice—notably at the Teatro Novissimo under the influence of the stage designer Giacomo Torelli (1608–78)—there is a fair amount of stage business designed to amaze the audience: gods emerging from the sea and seated in the heavens; the Phaeacian ship turned into a rock; Telemachus and Minerva on a chariot flying through the air; Ulysses struck by heavenly fire and disappearing beneath the earth; and Jove's eagle flying through the air. We also find other devices now standard in Venetian opera: the prologue framing the moral and emotional issues to be worked through in the drama to follow, scurrilous and comic characters (here Iro, the social parasite), nagging nurses (often played by men in transvestite garb), flirtatious servants, and regular recourse to magic and disguise.

The characters of *Il ritorno d'Ulisse* may still invoke the power of myth, but their concerns are more human than divine, exploring emotional issues—Penelope awaiting the return of her long-lost husband Ulysses from the Trojan Wars—close to the heart of contemporaneous, and for that matter modern, audiences. The immediacy of these issues places even more strain on conventions traditionally used to justify song on the stage. Orpheus sings as a natural part of his daily existence; whether singing is a similarly natural part of the existence of Penelope and Ulysses (or Nero and Poppaea) is quite another matter. As the anonymous author of *Il corago*, a Florentine treatise on opera written around 1630, said: 'If we take as characters people close to our times, and of manners more obviously similar to ours, all too clearly this manner of sung speech soon presents itself to us as improbable and not lifelike [*inverisimile*].'

It is significant in the light of the new contexts for opera that academic debate (with the exception of the conservative Giovanni Battista Doni) now focused less on the pseudo-classical origins of opera than on the more immediate problems of verisimilitude, and of whether opera should adhere to the rules normally applicable to spoken drama. The simplest—and probably the best—tack was to accept the irrationality of opera as inevitable and be done with it. As Giacomo Badoaro said in the preface to his *L'Ulisse errante* (1644), a 'prequel' to *Il ritorno d'Ulisse* set to music by Francesco Sacrati:

Today, no one worries, to increase the delight of the spectators, about giving way to something not lifelike, which does not damage the action. Thus we see that to give more time for the changes of scene, we have introduced music, in which we cannot avoid something not lifelike—that men should carry out their most important business in song. Moreover, so as to enjoy all kinds of music in the theatre, we are accustomed to hearing pieces for two, three and more voices: this produces something else not lifelike—that talking together men should without thinking happen to say the same things. Therefore it is no wonder that, devoting ourselves to pleasing modern taste, we have rightly moved away from the ancient rules.

Similarly, Vincenzo Nolfi admitted in the preface to his *Bellerofonte* (1642):

You waste your time, O reader, if, with the *Poetics* of the *Stagirita* [Aristotle] in hand you go tracking down the errors in this work, because I freely confess that in composing it I observed no other precepts than the desires of the inventor of the machines, nor had I any other aim than the pleasure of that audience for which it was to be performed.

As a result, opera was left to be judged only by the criterion of plausibility ('probability' is the more authentic term) in the context of convention.

The problems were exacerbated—but in the end solved—by radical changes in musical style. In one sense, Venetian opera of the late 1630s and 1640s marked a reduction in musical possibilities for the composer. The commercial exigencies of the public opera house prohibited the extensive choruses and large-scale instrumental participation characteristic of, say, *Orfeo*: witness the near total absence of choruses in *Il ritorno d'Ulisse*, and the use of only a small-scale string ensemble and a few continuo instruments. Nevertheless, the expressive potential of operatic music was vastly expanded. By the 1630s, more structured—and more tuneful—musical styles and forms were coming to the fore, in the manner popularized by the arias in contemporary songbooks. These arias are strophic settings of strophic poems: the regular poetic structure also establishes standard musical characteristics—clear-cut melodies, strong harmonic support, and rhythmic drive. The development of newly sensuous forms of triple- and duple-time writing is one of the most striking features of the 1620s and 1630s (witness Monteverdi's Eighth Book of Madrigals). But more to the point, in both songbooks and (later) operas, such structured melodies were increasingly usurping the place of recitative—so carefully established by Peri as a 'natural' (and naturalistic) mode of musical discourse—to signify serious musico-dramatic statement. This is not necessarily evidence of composers pandering to bourgeois taste. Rather, they seem to have realized that the formal distancing of the aria engages—perhaps paradoxically—far more closely with the emotions in hand. It also reclaims the ground for music as music, rather than as some spurious form of speech. Triple-time love songs and laments offer the key to a new operatic aesthetic of profound consequence for the development of the genre.

But even if musical recitative could be accepted as a plausible representation of speech, what about aria? There were various attempts to establish reasonable principles whereby song (aria), not just 'speech' (recitative), could be allowed in opera—particularly 'historical' opera—without impropriety. Gods and allegorical figures can sing rather than speak by virtue of their superhuman powers: indeed, song signifies such powers, especially when joined with virtuoso ornamentation (a convention lasting through to the twentieth century). Shepherds can sing by virtue of the pastoral convention, as can 'low' characters such as nurses and servants: their social status is not at issue, and for that matter such characters were often heard singing in contemporary comic theatre. Arias are acceptable for noble characters in disguise (where the constraints are loosened and indeed the deception enhanced). And librettists could always helpfully provide an excuse for formal songs in a somehow natural setting (drinking songs, lullabies, and the like). For the rest, contemporary librettists were forced to make the best of a bad job. As Francesco Sbarra admitted in the preface to his *Alessandro vincitor di se stesso* (1651):

I know that some people will consider the *ariette* sung by Alexander and Aristotle unfit for the dignity of such great characters...nevertheless it is not only permitted but even accepted with praise....If the recitative style were not mingled with such *scherzi*, it would give more annoyance than pleasure. Pardon me this licence, which I have taken only in order to make it less tiresome for you.

Monteverdi made some sense of the problem in *Il ritorno d'Ulisse*: Penelope is effectively imprisoned in recitative throughout the opera until the point where she finally acknowledges Ulisse; her final, triple-time aria is a glorious moment of emotional, nay sexual, release as she finally learns to sing the language of love. But for many modern critics, the issue proves to be the downfall of his last opera, *L'incoronazione di Poppea*, a story that glorifies the illicit affair of a Roman emperor and his mistress at the expense of virtue and honour (the wise Seneca commits suicide and Empress Ottavia is sent to exile). Here the sensuous arias and duets for Nerone and Poppea seemingly violate all bounds of decorum (moral or otherwise).

Questions of ethics aside, *Poppea* is problematic on the grounds of its sources. These problems, however, are typical of Venetian opera and reveal much of its workings. For example, the two scores that survive both date from the 1650s, and they transmit musical texts reflecting the work of one or more other composers (whose music may or may not have been used at the première). The prime candidate for the music of the final scene—with its ravishing love-duet for Nerone and Poppea—now seems to be Monteverdi's younger contemporary Francesco Sacrati (1605–50), whose recently rediscovered *La finta pazza* (1641) was one of the first great successes of the Venetian operatic stage. The issue is troublesome for critics fixed on the nineteenth-century notion of a single-composer masterpiece. But it is entirely consistent with working practices in seventeenth-century theatres.

The librettists of *Il ritorno d'Ulisse* and *Poppea*, Giacomo Badoaro (1602–54) and Giovanni Francesco Busenello (1598–1659), were both members of the Accademia degli Incogniti (which in turn was a chief patron of the Teatro Novissimo): the libertine scepticism cultivated by the academy may have affected the subject-matter of operas produced under its influence (this, at least, is one presumed explanation for the 'immorality' of *Poppea*). But as literary dilettantes—a nobleman and a lawyer respectively—Badoaro and Busenello soon yielded their place to what might as well be called professional librettists whose task, it seems in retrospect, was to give some stability to Venetian opera in what was still a formative decade. Thus the eleven opera texts of librettist, and later impresario, Giovanni Faustini (1615–51) establish dramatic and formal characteristics—an exotic location, two entangled pairs of lovers, comic servants, conventional stage business (disguises, letters, sleeping potions) to knot, and at the very last moment unknot, the action—that were to sustain librettists for a good many years to come. These principles—relying heavily both on the Italian *commedia dell'arte* and on Spanish theatre—were further codified by Faustini's successors, including Giacinto Andrea Cicognini (1606–*c*.1650), Nicolò Minato (*c*.1627–98), and Aurelio Aureli (*fl.* 1652–1708). Cicognini's *Giasone*, for example, with its faintly ludicrous mixture of serious and comic elements, its emphasis on the extravagant and outrageous (one of the servants is a stuttering hunchback), its hopelessly unrealistic combination of stage-settings and its mixture of philosophical moralizing and pragmatic amorality, is entirely typical of the genre. Moreover, *Giasone* reveals opera's coming of age: jokes about castrati and the inclusion of at least one Venetian popular song suggest that the genre had gained in maturity to the extent of not having to take itself too seriously.

For music, a similar stability seems to have been granted by Faustini's chief musical collaborator, Francesco Cavalli (1602–76), organist at St Mark's but essentially the pre-eminent theatre musician of the mid-century. He wrote almost thirty operas for Venetian theatres—many were also taken on tour—and works such as *Egisto* (1643), *Ormindo* (1644), and *Calisto* (1651) fix musical characteristics in much the same way as their librettos by Faustini. Typical of the earlier works (and like Monteverdi) is a flexible shifting between recitative and aria styles, sometimes within the space of only a few bars. Such shifts will generally be prompted by one or more textual cues concerning either content (the need to 'paint' a particular image or to establish a particular idea) or structure (a shift from free-rhyming seven- and eleven-syllable lines to more regularly structured verse, perhaps using other line-lengths). But recitative gradually becomes rather more stereotyped in structure and expression, and arias more fully formed and structurally discrete. The move is even clearer in two of Cavalli's operas to texts by other librettists, *Giasone* (1649; Cicognini)—which to judge by its some twenty revivals up to the late 1680s was his best-known opera—and the popular *Xerse* (1655; Minato). These arias, in turn, draw on certain duple-and triple-time conventions that become associated with specific dramatic situations: the 'chattering' duple-time aria over a 'walking bass' for comic characters, the triple-time lament over an ostinato ground bass descending through a fourth (whether diatonically or chromatically), the incantation aria often exploiting patterns with the accent on the antepenultimate syllable (Medea's 'Dell'antro magico' in *Giasone* is typical, although there are earlier examples). If Cavalli sometimes resorted to routine, that is in the nature of the genre; but when his lyric inspiration took flight he could produce music of remarkable poise and dramatic effectiveness.

Opera on Tour

In his *Della cristiana moderatione del teatro* (1652), the Jesuit Giovan Domenico Ottonelli divided musical spectacles into three categories, in order of those 'performed in the palaces of great princes and other secular or ecclesiastical lords', those 'put on sometimes by certain gentlemen or talented citizens or learned academicians', and those 'done by mercenary musicians who are players [*comedianti*] by profession and who, gathered in a company, are directed or controlled by one of their number'. He would doubtless have included Venetian opera in the third category, the one most open to moral concern. But in fact, the organization of opera in Venice merged Ottonelli's second and third categories, and the influence of the Accademia degli Incogniti, for example, suggests that even in the world of 'public' opera, academies still had a part to play in the production and reception of these works. This was still more the case in centres deprived of established mechanisms for public performance. In mid-seventeenth-century Florence, for example, opera was largely in the hands of the Accademia degli Immobili and Accademia dei Sorgenti. The Immobili inaugurated their theatre in the Via della Pergola in early 1657 with Jacopo Melani's (1623–76) *La Tancia* (or *Il potestà di Colognole*; libretto by Giovanni Andrea Moniglia) and performed another six operas, including a number of rustic comedies in dialect, until its closure in 1663. Significantly, however, the Sorgenti achieved more commercial success with their productions of Venetian 'standards'. But as for Ottonelli's third category, this is better represented by the touring companies moving from town to town, forming various attachments (for varying lengths of time) with local patrons and institutions. For all the taint of commercialism (and of dubious morals), such companies played a key role in disseminating the repertory throughout Italy and establishing something of a national style, for all its potential regional variants.

The fairly short seasons for opera in Venice (the main one was carnival, traditionally from 26 December, St Stephen's Day, to Shrove Tuesday) left time for touring: the performances of Monteverdi's *Il ritorno d'Ulisse in patria* and other operas in Bologna from 1640 onwards are significant early examples. Touring companies were by no means new. They had their roots in the *comici dell'arte*, touring bands of players who made themselves available for hire to perform improvised, semi-improvised, and formally written plays, often with music. The best-known example is the *Comici gelosi* and its successor, the *Comici fedeli*, headed by the actor, dramatist, and poet Giovanni Battista Andreini (1579–1654), which served the dukes of Mantua, with brief interruptions, until about 1647–50, playing throughout northern and central Italy (they also toured to France, Prague, and Vienna). Andreini's plays often included music, sometimes to a considerable degree, not least to exploit the talents of his wife Virginia Ramponi (1583–?1630), who was enough of a virtuoso singer to take the title role of Monteverdi's *Arianna* (1608) at short notice after the untimely death of the young Caterina Martinelli.

Such troupes provided a model for touring opera companies. By the mid-1640s a group known as the Febiarmonici ('Musicians of Apollo') was performing operas in northern Italy (for example, Sacrati's *La finta pazza* in Piacenza in 1644) and possibly in Paris (in early 1645). The closure of the opera houses in Venice in 1645–7 due to sumptuary legislation on account of the War of Candia (between Venice and the Turks) further encouraged touring. Performances by the Febiarmonici—there may have been several companies with the name—are recorded in Genoa (1644), Florence and Lucca (1645), Genoa and Florence (1646), Genoa, Bologna, and Milan (1647), Bologna, Turin, Reggio Emilia, Ferrara, and Rimini (1648), Milan (1649), and Lucca (1650), with operas such as *La finta pazza* and Cavalli's *Egisto* and *Giasone*. In early 1650, the company was brought to Naples by the viceroy, Count d'Oñate, who was anxious to exploit theatrical entertainments as a means of restoring normality after the Masaniello uprising of 1647–8. Cavalli's *Didone* was staged in October, and in 1651 the Febiarmonici performed *Egisto* and *Giasone*, and also Monteverdi's *L'incoronazione di Poppea* (as *Nerone*). They also gave the première of Cavalli's *Veremonda* to celebrate the Spanish victory in Catalonia (and also the queen's birthday) in December 1652. With the departure of Count Oñate in late 1653, the company transferred to the Teatro San Bartolomeo (from April 1654). Their precarious financial position was exacerbated by the plague of 1656, but performances resumed in 1657, largely of revised Venetian operas, and are recorded through to 1668.

For that matter, individual composers could tote their skills from city to city. For example, the rather chequered career of Antonio Cesti (1623–69) took him from his native Arezzo through Volterra, Florence, Venice, Innsbruck, Rome, Vienna, and back to Florence, where he met an untimely death (he may have been poisoned by his rivals) at the age of 46. He was a tenor, an organist, and above all a composer of cantatas and of operas for the theatres of Venice, Innsbruck, and Vienna. His works include the sumptuous court opera *Il pomo d'oro*, with twenty-four different stage sets and a large-scale orchestra, staged in Vienna in 1668 (it was originally intended to celebrate the marriage of Emperor Leopold I in 1666). More typical of current trends, however, were his operas for Venice (including his setting of Sbarra's *Alessandro vincitor di se stesso*, 1651) and Innsbruck, including *L'Argia* (1655), *Orontea* (1656), and *La Dori* (1657). To judge by its number of performances, *Orontea* (to a libretto by Giacinto Andrea Cicognini) was one of the most successful operas of its time: it was performed in Genoa (1660, 1661), Rome and Florence (1661), Turin (1662), Ferrara (1663), Milan (1664), Macerata (1665), Bologna (1665, 1669), Venice (1666), Bergamo, Brescia, and Palermo (1667), Lucca (1668), Portomaggiore (1670), Naples (1674), Reggio Emilia (1674), Hanover (1678), and Venice (1683).

The spread of opera through Italy from mid-century on bears witness to the versatility of a genre that could now adapt itself to very different social and political environments. In part, this is the result of the typical subjects of seventeenth-century opera, which were amenable to a wide variety of symbolic interpretations—should interpretations be needed—but it also reflects the strengths, and the popularity, of contemporary operatic musical styles. Of course, taking a work from one city to another could prompt changes and revisions to suit the new context (substitute prologues could be particularly useful in this light) and different audience expectations. For example, when Jacopo Melani's *Ercole in Tebe*, staged by the Accademia degli Immobili in Florence to celebrate the wedding of Cosimo III and Marguerite Louise of Orléans in 1661, was revived in Venice a decade later, the plot was reworked, the intermedi removed, the spectacular stage effects cut down, recitatives shortened or omitted, and the whole compressed from five to three acts. However, the mere possibility of such changes is witness to the increasing solidity of the genre: the codification of literary and musical conventions, and the stabilizing of fixed textual and musical forms, permitted the easy and effective interpolation or substitution of discrete units within the whole without necessarily affecting its integrity.

This also eased the transmission of Italian opera to northern Europe. Cesti's contribution to opera in Innsbruck and Vienna reveals the domination of Italian or Italian-trained composers north of the Alps: the only important exceptions are offered by France and England. The arm of Italian opera stretched widely through Germany, and even east to Poland (at least from 1635 to 1648 under the influence of the secretary to the royal court, Virgilio Puccitelli). In part, this reflects the interests of northern princes—frequent visitors to Venice during carnival—and later, political alliances in the wars against the Turks. True, in Germany native composers did have a part to play. Heinrich Schütz (1585–1672) provided the first German 'opera', *Dafne* (to a translation of Rinuccini's libretto by Martin Opitz), performed in Torgau in 1627 for the marriage of Landgrave Georg II of Hessen-Darmstadt and Princess Sophia Eleonora of Saxony (in fact, it is a spoken play with musical interpolations). Sigmund Theophil Staden's *Seelewig* (1644) was a Singspiel modelled on contemporary school-dramas: as such it is more a moral allegory than an opera. And after the horrors of the Thirty Years War, the newly opened grand opera house in Munich saw the splendid *Oronte* (1657) by Johann Caspar Kerll (1627–93). But both Schütz and Kerll had studied in Italy, and, typically, the first 'opera' performed in Munich was Giovanni Battista Maccioni's brief allegorical *L'arpa festante* in 1653. Benedetto Ferrari had preceded Cesti to the imperial court, arranging tournaments and ballets, and providing the libretto for *L'inganno d'amore* (Regensburg, 1653; music by Antonio Bertali, court Kapellmeister). Agostino Steffani (1654–1728), Kammermusikdirektor of the Bavarian court from 1681 to 1688, composed five operas for Munich—including *Servio Tullio* to celebrate the wedding of Elector Maximilian II Emanuel to Maria Antonia, archduchess of Austria, in 1686—before moving to Hanover (from 1688 to 1703), where he produced some eight operas to librettos by Ortensio Mauro for the permanent Italian opera company there founded by Duke Ernst August. Similarly, opera in Dresden was in the hands of Giovanni Andrea Bontempi (1625–1705)—whose grand *Il Paride* was staged for the wedding of Christian Ernst, Margrave of Brandenburg, and Erdmunde Sophia, Princess of Saxony, in 1662—and later, Carlo Pallavicino (c.1640–88), who as musical director of the Ospedale degli Incurabili in Venice from 1674 to 1685 had made a name for himself as a leading composer of Venetian operas. The only consolidated moves towards a native opera were made in Hamburg, where the important Theater am Gänsemarkt was founded on the Venetian model, presenting year-round performances of opera in German. The theatre opened in 1678 with Johann Theile's *Der erschaffene, gefallene und auffgerichtete Mensch*, based on the Adam and Eve story, inaugurating a rich tradition that was to extend through the operas of Reinhard Keiser, Handel, and Telemann.

Paris

Italian opera was also exported to France, but to considerably less effect. Here, as always, matters cultural revolved almost entirely around the royal court at Versailles and associate institutions in Paris. Louis XIV had a clear perception of the political usefulness of entertainments as a means of amusing and controlling his subjects, of impressing foreigners, of developing and demonstrating physical dexterity among his courtiers, and of displaying at every opportunity his personal emblem, the sun, as a symbol of enlightened rule (see his *Mémoires pour l'instruction du Dauphin*). Some of these entertainments went back to late Renaissance models, such as the tournament and the ballet de cour. The latter typically consisted of a series of *entrées* and dances in spectacular scenery and costumes more or (often) less linked by a dramatic thread: the archetype was the magnificent *Circé, ou Le Balet comique de la royne* for the wedding of the Duc de Joyeuse and Marguerite de Vaudemont in 1581; and some of the examples of the 1610s, based on mythological and chivalric themes— *Le Triomphe de Minerve* (1615), *La Délivrance de Renaud* (1617), the *Ballet de Tancrède*, and the *Ballet de Psyché* (both 1619)—established important topical precedents for later theatrical endeavours. Other entertainments merged older types with newer tendencies, also taking advantage of the rich developments in French spoken drama (both comedies and tragedies) in the seventeenth century. One example is the comédie-ballet established by Molière and Jean-Baptiste Lully (1632–87), an expatriate Italian (he arrived in Paris in 1646) and from 1661 Louis's *Surintendant de la musique et compositeur de la musique de la chambre*. They sought a fusion of spoken comedy with a series of sung and danced *entrées* both between and sometimes within the acts; the whole could also be framed by a spectacular prologue and finale. The best example is Molière's well-known *Le Bourgeois Gentilhomme* (1670), often performed as a play but making its true effect only when joined with dance and with Lully's rich music.

Inevitably, the fate of Italian opera in France was inextricably linked with political issues. The performances in Paris of Sacrati's *La finta pazza*, Cavalli's *Egisto*, and Luigi Rossi's magnificent *Orfeo* (libretto by Francesco Buti) in 1645, 1646, and 1647 respectively were promoted by Cardinal Mazarin (1602–61), French first minister and himself an Italian. But despite the fact that these works were specially adapted for French tastes, with ballets and spectacular stage effects (the latter designed by the newly arrived Giacomo Torelli), the general reaction was mixed. Moreover, Mazarin's involvement proved a liability, and Italian opera— felt by many to be a profligate use of public funds—fell victim to the anti-Mazarin (and anti-Italian) sentiments that exploded during the Fronde (1648–53). On Mazarin's return to Paris, he engaged Carlo Caproli to compose *Le nozze di Peleo e di Theti* (1654; libretto by Buti), and for the celebrations for the marriage of Louis XIV in 1660 he commissioned a grand court-opera from Cavalli, *Ercole amante* (again to a libretto by Buti). The production was not ready for the wedding—Cavalli substituted his *Xerse*, expanded as usual with ballets (with music by Lully)—and *Ercole amante* was staged only in February 1662. Both flopped.

But anti-Mazarin sentiment is not enough to explain the ambivalence of the French towards Italian opera: general cultural chauvinism also had its part to play. Torelli's spectacular designs were certainly appreciated, and they had a significant influence on native theatrical endeavour, notably the so-called *tragédie à machines* that achieved some popularity in mid-century (Corneille's *Andromède* of 1650, with music by Charles Dassoucy, is a good example). Moreover, the need to emulate, nay surpass, the Italians was a strong force in French culture: this was doubtless one impetus behind the pastorals with music that appear in the 1650s, including Dassoucy's *Les Amours d'Apollon et de Daphné*, written during the Fronde in 1650, and *Le Triomphe de l'Amour sur les bergers et bergères* (text by Charles de Bey, music by Michel de la Guerre), a 'French comedy in music' performed before the king at the Louvre in 1655. Similarly, Pierre Perrin (*c*.1620–75), the author of the *Pastorale d'Issy* (1659), was motivated by 'the keenness to see our language, our poetry and our music triumph over a foreign language, poetry and music'. Nevertheless, many aspects of Italian opera—especially in its baroque, anti-classical guise—scarcely suited French tastes. Thus Perrin prefaced his play (wrongly called 'the first French comedy in music performed in France') with a lengthy critique of Italian opera, covering defects in librettos (too long, too much like spoken plays and therefore ill suited to music, poetry too overblown and archaic), music (tedious recitative, too little variety in the use of voices, the use of castrati), and staging.

The music (now lost) for the *Pastorale d'Issy* was by Robert Cambert (*c*.1627–77), who seems to have gone some way towards establishing an effective French operatic style. Perrin also had plans for other works to establish his precedence not only in pastoral, but also in comedy (*Ariane, ou Le Mariage de Bacchus*, possibly written in 1659; it was revived by Luis Grabu in London in 1674, but the music is now lost) and tragedy. Certainly Perrin and Cambert did enough to convince Louis XIV of the viability of French opera, to the extent that on 28 June 1669 he granted them a twelve-year patent exclusively to establish an Académie d'Opéra (specifically on the Italian model) for performance of such works: such academies—witness the Académies Royales de Danse, des Inscriptions, Médailles et Belles Lettres, and de Peinture et Sculpture (also founded or reorganized in the 1660s)—were becoming an increasingly important institutional feature of French cultural life under Louis's controller-general of finances, Jean-Baptiste Colbert. The Académie d'Opéra was inaugurated on 3 March 1671 with the pastoral *Pomone* (again revived by Grabu in London in 1674), of which only fragments survive: it ran for 146 performances. However, Perrin was fleeced by his unscrupulous theatre managers and ended up in a debtors' prison. Despite an attempt to revive the Académie in early 1672 with *Les Peines et les plaisirs de l'amour* (music by Cambert, libretto by Gabriel Gilbert), Perrin's monopoly was passed over to Lully, who established his new position at the head of the Académie Royale de Musique with the hastily compiled *Les Fêtes de l'Amour et de Bacchus* (November 1672). Thereafter Lully produced a new opera almost every year until his death, beginning with *Cadmus et Hermione* (1673) and ending with *Armide* and *Acis et Galatée* (1686). Most were to librettos by the skilled poet and playwright Philippe Quinault (1635–88).

Lully and Quinault relied heavily on earlier traditions of French court entertainment in terms of subject-matter (classical mythology or medieval romance), structure (action mixed with prominent dance episodes), and stage design: indeed *Psyché* (1678) was a straightforward reworking of a tragédie-ballet first staged in 1671. But these tragédies lyriques—a resonant term for those French academicians who distrusted Italian opera for its frivolity and anti-classical tendencies—were sung throughout. Lully effectively proved that French verse was amenable to sung recitation—despite his own early fears that such a task was impossible—reportedly following the example of the actress La Champmeslé, famous for her declamation of Racine. He also integrated spectacle, instrumental music, and dance into the drama. Most of all, he confounded those who, like Corneille (witness the preface to his *Andromède*), felt that music could only obscure dramatic action and thus should be restricted to the incidentals of any theatrical endeavour.

Although Lully's patent allowed him to perform his operas before a paying public, they are indelibly stamped with a courtly ethos: the focus on glorifying the Roi-soleil was inevitable. In the prologue to *Alceste* (1674), the Nymphe de la Seine laments Louis's absence on military campaigns in the Netherlands: the opera itself equates his return with the Louis/Apollo who provides the happy ending. No less typical in *Alceste* is the emphasis on spectacular *divertissements* and the *merveilleux* variously integrated into the action: a nautical pageant in Act 1, the siege and capture of Scyros in Act 2, the funeral of Alceste in Act 3, an inferno scene in Act 4, not to mention the appearance of various gods at the end of each act and the final descent of Apollo and the Muses to bring the drama to a close. This rich spectacle frames noble characters whose actions and dilemmas ape the high drama of spoken theatre, plus flirtatious servants and comic characters (not least the hilarious Charon) in the Venetian mould. Thus Lully and Quinault attempt to marry tragedy with comedy, and academic sensibilities with operatic requirements.

Musically, too, Lully mixes elements drawn from Venetian opera and earlier courtly models. He follows (in principle, at least) the shifting verse-structures to move in and out of recitative, evoking the Italian style of some twenty or thirty years before. His short-breathed arias, more often in open than in closed forms, may reflect an inherent conservatism, but this is probably an attempt to neutralize their threat to verisimilitude. Moreover, his powerful choruses and rich instrumental writing, typically in five parts, add a musical depth that many found lacking in contemporary Italian opera: it was perhaps for this reason that Lullian techniques also found favour elsewhere in northern Europe. So successful, and unique, were Lully's solutions to the problems of establishing a French opera, and so powerful his own control of the theatre, that he effectively established an operatic canon, fixing a tradition, and specific techniques, that were to dictate the course of opera in France for the next half-century and more. His works were published—something almost unheard of in Italy since the 1630s—and were regularly revived well into the second half of the eighteenth century.

London

After the débâcle of the Perrin–Cambert Académie, Cambert moved to England to join his former pupil, the composer Luis Grabu (*fl.* 1665–94). The London of the Restoration offered a welcome home to French artists, not least because Charles II had himself spent much of the Commonwealth in exile in Paris. Thus French models provided the most immediate influence on early English opera. However, London was also a cosmopolitan city, and English musicians were well aware of Italian styles in vocal and instrumental music: for example, Cavalli's *Erismena* (1655) seems to have been known there. Dryden and Purcell claimed in the preface to the score of *The Prophetess, or The History of Dioclesian* (pub. 1691) that English music is 'now learning Italian which is its best master, and studying a little of the French ayre, to give it somewhat more of gayety and fashion'. The English, 'being farther from the Sun', are 'of later growth' and so must 'shake off [their] barbarity by degrees'. Nevertheless, 'The present age seems already dispos'd to be refin'd, and to distinguish betwixt wild fancy, and a just, numerous composition.' As a result, in English opera and related genres both French and Italian traits merge with native traditions in intriguing and perhaps unique ways.

As in France and Italy, the Jacobean and Caroline courts (and their satellite institutions) in London in the first half of the century had well-established ways of articulating princely celebration, notably in the form of the masque (a genre mixing dance with scenic spectacle, sometimes with a dramatic thread): the masques by Ben Jonson, with stage designs by Inigo Jones, established important archetypes. These entertainments drew on both French (the ballet de cour) and Italian (the intermedi) models—with (later) some experiments in the Italian recitative—even to the extent of reworking specific foreign works. The Civil War and Commonwealth necessarily restricted the opportunities for such lavish displays, although diplomatic niceties could still provide an excuse for grand entertainments, as with James Shirley's *Cupid and Death* performed in honour of the Portuguese ambassador in 1653 (it was revived in 1659, and the music by Matthew Locke and Christopher Gibbons survives). Similarly, in the 1650s the poet William Davenant (1606–67), who had provided texts for a number of Caroline masques, sought to maintain English theatrical traditions (and his own flagging fortunes) with a number of entertainments with music, thereby circumventing the Puritan ban on stage plays (masques, operas, and 'moral representations' were excluded). Davenant's *The Siege of Rhodes* (1656) was set to music (now lost) throughout—the vocal music was by Henry Lawes, Henry Cooke, and Matthew Locke, and the instrumental music by Charles Coleman and George Hudson—and was followed by two propaganda pieces, *The Cruelty of the Spaniards in Peru* (1658) and *The History of Sir Francis Drake* (1659), again with music by Locke.

At the Restoration (1660), Davenant became manager of the Duke's Company. Opera as such was not an issue (indeed *The Siege of Rhodes* was revived as a spoken play), but the company's repertory included plays with (often extensive) music, and also with masques incorporated in the action on the Elizabethan model (compare the masque-scenes in Shakespeare's *A Midsummer Night's Dream* and *The Tempest*). In particular, Davenant's revivals of *Macbeth* (1663) and *The Tempest* (1667, with Dryden) had extensive scenes set to music. The trend continued in the hands of Davenant's successors, Thomas Betterton and Henry Harris, whose spectacular semi-operas performed at the Dorset Garden Theatre included another revival of *The Tempest* (1674), Shadwell's tragedy *Psyche* (1675, with music by Locke and Giovanni Battista Draghi), and *Circe*

(1677). Here French models are particularly apparent: indeed *Psyche* seems to have been directly modelled on Lully's and Molière's tragédie-ballet of 1671.

The performance of Perrin's and Cambert's *Ariane, ou L'Amour de Bacchus* (sung in French) in 1674 for the wedding of the duke of York (later James II) and Mary of Modena suggests the court's interest in opera in the French style (Lully's *Cadmus et Hermione* was similarly performed in London in 1686). But opera repeatedly met with resistance from (and preference for) more native traditions of music-theatre. John Blow's (1649–1708) *Venus and Adonis* (c.1683), in effect a miniature opera, is still entitled 'A Masque for ye Entertainment of the King'—it may have been staged as a private entertainment for Charles II by his former mistress, Mary Davies (who sang in the performance)—and it includes a number of masque-like scenes and dances. Similarly, the poet John Dryden's (1631–1700) *Albion and Albanius* (originally designed as a prologue to his *King Arthur* but then expanded) has a lengthy preface discussing the problems of opera for English tastes, and indeed for the English language. Dryden's text was set to music by Luis Grabu—much to the annoyance of native musicians—and was in rehearsal in early 1685, although it was staged only in June because of the death of Charles II.

Venus and Adonis provided direct precedents for Henry Purcell's (1659–95) *Dido and Aeneas*, undoubtedly the greatest English opera to emerge from this period. It was performed in 1689 at a girls' school in Chelsea run by Josias Priest, also a professional dancer involved with the London theatres. School-plays and masques were not unusual in this period, although there is some (as yet inconclusive) evidence to suggest that Purcell's opera was in fact designed for (and had been staged at) court earlier in the decade, perhaps just after *Venus and Adonis* (which, in turn, was staged at Priest's school in 1684). The libretto by Nahum Tate draws on a number of models: his own spoken play *Brutus of Alba, or The Enchanted Lovers* (1678), the allegorical prologues of French drama (but the music of the prologue to *Dido and Aeneas* is now lost), the witches' scenes so popular in Restoration revivals of *Macbeth*, and the scenic spectacle and dance typical of the masque. Purcell's superb music is also highly eclectic, with a typical French overture and French-style songs, choruses, and dances, a recitative style drawing primarily on English declamatory traditions, and Italianate formal arias over a ground bass, including Dido's heart-rending lament over the emblematic descending chromatic tetrachord.

Dido and Aeneas may have fallen victim to political circumstances: its tale of a queen abandoned by her royal lover was hardly suited to the new reign of William and Mary. Purcell instead began to concentrate on music for the mainstream public theatre, producing a splendid series of semi-operas for the London stage: his contribution to *The Prophetess, or The History of Dioclesian* (1690) encouraged Dryden to use Purcell for a revised *King Arthur, or The British Worthy* (1691), while the play-with-masque tradition continued with *The Fairy-Queen* (1692), a splendid adaptation of *A Midsummer Night's Dream* with end-of-act masques on the model of the French comédie-ballet. Even *Dido and Aeneas* succumbed: in 1700 (five years after Purcell's death) it was revised and inserted into an adaptation of *Measure for Measure*, and in 1704 it was attached both to Edward Ravenscroft's three-act farce, *The Anatomist*, and to George Etherege's *The Man of Mode*.

The Path to Reform

In contrast to the evident fluidity of (and between) opera and related genres in France and England, opera in Italy, particularly Venice, in the third quarter of the century was tending increasingly towards the codification of fixed forms and conventions both for librettos (in terms of content and structure) and for their music. The authority granted by convention meant, at least for the time being, that there was little need for academic debate about opera and its component parts: the genre (and audience demand for it) perpetuated itself. This offered a perhaps welcome break from self-questioning that in turn permitted the exploration of various facets of the genre within securely defined parameters: witness the aria, where composers could experiment with a range of strategies, whether formal (e.g. strophic, da capo, and other structures), harmonic ('tonal' articulations, say by way of ritornellos), or textural (handling instrumental accompaniments in various ways). The operas of Carlo Pallavicino merit close study in this light. But the self-satisfaction, so to speak, generated by convention could all too easily foster arid, sometimes fatuous, approaches to the genre.

For example, Antonio Sartorio's *Orfeo* (1672; libretto by Aurelio Aureli) is a fairly dismal example of a genre with all the symptoms of terminal decline. Sartorio (1630–80) was an important composer of opera in Venice in the 1660s and 1670s; he was also associated with Hanover. But this Orpheus is no noble heir to the tradition established in Florence and Mantua in the first years of the century. He takes the stage with Aristeo (his rival for Euridice's affections), Autonoe (in love with Aristeo), a comic nurse and servant, and Achille, Chirone, Ercole, and Esculapio (plus various gods) for a series of irrelevant sub-plots. Orfeo is scarcely in a state of wedded bliss, and his journey to Hades seems almost a Sunday-school outing: moreover, his final renunciation of women is little more than comic chatter. No longer the hero-musician of antiquity, Orfeo does not even sing his prayer to the underworld. Whether satire or not, this is indeed a sorry tale.

Even Venetian opera's great apologist and chronicler Cristoforo Ivanovich used his historical account, *Minerva al tavolino* (1681), to lament the decline of the genre at the hands of unscrupulous librettists and composers, and of impresarios (not, he hastens to add, his patrons the Grimani) happy to lower their ticket prices and thereby open opera to the lower classes. Francesco Fulvio Frugoni had already noted (in the preface to his *Epulone*, 1675) that 'the art of producing dramas has become nothing but the art of ruining human society. Instead of imitating nature for the ethical betterment of mankind, literature, painting, and the theatre have become monstrous fantasies which corrupt.' And in his *La bellezza della volgar poesia* (1700), Giovanni Maria Crescimbeni—speaking for the Arcadian Academy—made an eloquent attack on the sins of opera stemming, he claimed, from Giacinto Andrea Cicognini's *Giasone*:

with it he brought the end of acting, and consequently, of true and good comedy as well as tragedy. Since to stimulate to a greater degree with novelty the jaded taste of the spectators, equally nauseated by the vileness of comic things and the seriousness of tragic ones...[he] united them, mixing kings and heroes and other illustrious personages with buffoons and servants and the lowest men with unheard of monstrousness. This concoction of characters was the reason for the complete ruin of the rules of poetry, which went so far into disuse that not even locution was considered, which, forced to serve music, lost its purity, and became filled with idiocies. The careful deployment of figures that ennobles oratory was neglected, and language was restricted to terms of common speech, which is more appropriate for music; and finally the series of those short metres, commonly called *ariette*, which with a generous hand are sprinkled over the scenes, and the overwhelming impropriety of having characters speak in song completely removed from the compositions the power of the affections, and the means of moving them in the listeners.

The stage was set for reform.

✎ 2 ✎

THE EIGHTEENTH CENTURY: SERIOUS OPERA

Thomas Bauman

Opera Seria in the Age of Metastasio

'ITALIAN, not German; seria, not buffa', wrote Mozart to his father in early 1778 about his keen wish to be writing an opera. His passing remark could well stand as the signature of the entire century, for from beginning to end Italian opera's European-wide influence remained paramount despite growth and innovation in other vernacular traditions. And within the world of Italian opera the summit of prestige (and remuneration) for composer, librettist, and performer was occupied throughout the epoch by opera seria. For much of the eighteenth century, opera seria as an institution was maintained by court cultures, from Naples to St Petersburg and from Lisbon to Vienna, or by associations of aristocrats at centres such as Venice, Milan, or London. Opera seria was seldom subject to the censorship that worried rulers imposed on the spoken stage and on the printing press, for in every respect the genre upheld a sense of dignity, stability, and decorum that lay at the heart of the culture sustained by the ruling class. The literary reform that brought opera seria into existence during the decades around 1700 was initiated by aristocrats, and in the course of the century the excesses to which the genre sometimes succumbed were never ones of literary impropriety.

Opera seria was typically performed in large, well-appointed theatres, and the construction of costly new edifices devoted specifically to its cultivation continued throughout the century, both within Italy and abroad. At Naples the old San Bartolomeo theatre was replaced in 1737 by the Teatro di San Carlo as the site of court-sponsored opera seria. When the Regio Ducal Teatro at Milan burnt down in 1776, its aristocratic box-holders set about building a new and larger edifice, the Teatro alla Scala, and when a group of patrician box-holders at Venice lost the San Benedetto in a legal battle, the Republic waived a prohibition on new theatres in Venice and allowed them to build the Teatro La Fenice in 1792 for the exclusive performance of opera seria and ballet. At Dresden a new opera house, built near the Zwinger's pavilion at a cost of nearly 150,000 Thaler, opened in 1719. It was one of the largest in Europe, with seating for 2,000 spectators. On succeeding to the Prussian throne in 1740, one of the first acts of Frederick the Great was to order the building of a lavish opera house on the present avenue Unter den Linden. Inaugurated at the end of 1742, it included a canal system for cascades and waterfalls that also provided fire protection.

Administrative arrangements varied somewhat from place to place. Especially in Italy, an impresario was normally hired to manage affairs, particularly by those theatres owned by their box-holders. At court-owned theatres an aristocratic administrator usually supervised theatrical activities, often with such a title as *Directeur des spectacles* or intendant. Operatic seasons also varied to some extent, although the proscription of all stage representations during Lent and also during periods of official mourning was recognized everywhere. Opera seria was seldom performed between May and October, since its patrician sponsors tended to spend summers at their country estates (supervising the agricultural activities on which their incomes typically depended). An autumn season, lasting one or two months, was less important in Catholic lands than carnival, the main operatic season running from 26 December to Shrove Tuesday. At Naples carnival was divided into two segments, each featuring a new opera. The *seconda opera di Carnevale* tended to be the more important, both because the audience was more plentiful and because the singers had more time to prepare. After Easter there was sometimes a brief opera season, often favoured by theatres at smaller courts and municipalities, since it offered the opportunity to secure the first-rate singers who sang at the big houses during carnival. The opera season at the non-Catholic court at Berlin ran from November to March, with performances twice a week. Admission, limited to members of the court, army officers, and the higher strata of society, was free—the normal practice at court-sponsored theatres. A typical season included two new operas, in addition to shorter works such as intermezzi, pastorales, and serenatas. New operas routinely marked the birthdays of the king and the queen mother, a practice also followed at Vienna by Charles VI and Empress Elizabeth Christina for her birthday and his name day.

The primacy of opera seria's highly regular and stylized verbal and dramatic structure in the eighteenth century is reflected in the widespread use of the term 'Metastasian opera'. None the less, despite Pietro

Metastasio's unique importance, in operatic practice the new phenomenon wove a complex texture of cultural interdependencies between, on
the one hand, librettists, aristocratic connoisseurs, and the patrician
world they lived in, and, on the other, composers, singers, and the institutional structures that trained and employed them. Eighteenth-century
opera seria is also sometimes referred to as 'Neapolitan opera'. While no
single centre can claim to be the new genre's birthplace, Naples did provide the formative cultural and musical environment in which the literary and intellectual achievements fostered at Venice and Rome could be
put into practice and thrive.

The problem posed at the end of the seventeenth century by the
excesses of Italian opera—low farcical comic scenes, plots complicated
to the point of incomprehension, reliance on the supernatural or the
marvellous and anything that might serve as an excuse for a spectacular
visual effect—occupied a prominent place in the discussions of Italian
literati at the Arcadian academies at Rome and elsewhere initiated by
Crescimbeni. Attempts at a literary reform of opera soon emerged from
a generation of librettists headed by the Venetian patrician and scholar
Apostolo Zeno (1668–1750). His early librettos are in five acts, a sign of the
deep debt they owe to the example of Corneille and Racine. Plots, drawn
from ancient history rather than mythology, proceed along rational lines
and involve a cast reduced from earlier practice to around seven. Zeno,
himself unmusical, showed little interest in the musical possibilities of his
texts. His numerous short arias are placed with little care or consistency,
and he encouraged performances of his dramas without music, in which
case the aria texts, which all purvey generalities at moments of ethical or
emotional reflection, were simply omitted. Later, when he collaborated
with Pietro Pariati, Zeno turned the task of writing the aria texts over to
him.

Zeno's first libretto, *Gli inganni felici*, was produced at the Teatro S.
Angelo in Venice in 1695, with music by Carlo Francesco Pollarolo
(*c*.1653–1723). A pastoral setting, such as the Arcadian one encountered
here, allowed for a simpler plot than those typical of operas dealing in
political or heroic themes, and its avoidance of extreme situations promoted a more familiar emotional palette. Pollarolo, a prolific composer,
made no special departure from his musical routine for the newer texts
of Zeno and others in his camp. In all his works he shared with other Italian composers a growing tendency towards a more homophonic texture
and a clearer distinction between simple recitative and aria.

More prolific than the Venetian Pollarolo, and highly esteemed even after his death, Alessandro Scarlatti (1660–1725) wrote most of his sixty-nine operas as well as many other stage works either for Rome, where his patrician support was based, or more especially for Naples, where he served as the viceroy's *maestro di cappella* from 1684 to 1702. During these years Naples rose to national and international significance as a centre for the cultivation of Italian opera and also for the training of singers, composers, and instrumentalists at its four conservatories. Scarlatti is sometimes described as the father of a Neapolitan school of composers who rose to prominence in the first decades of the eighteenth century, but there are neither stylistic nor historical grounds for such a claim. Despite his enormous productivity at Naples, Scarlatti's sense of opera seria changed little during his eighteen years there, even in the new Venetian librettos by Zeno and others that he began setting in 1699 (with comic scenes added, as was the custom at Naples). Like others, he gradually abandoned the strophic aria and reduced the number that were accompanied only by the continuo group, but his idiom remained contrapuntal. He does not seem to have been connected with the Neapolitan conservatories for more than a month or two, and among later composers only Hasse claimed to have studied with him. Scarlatti's duties as director of the San Bartolomeo for the entire period no doubt took up much of his energy: he supervised rehearsals, conducted new works for their first few performances and composed virtually every other opera that was produced there.

His late operas, written for both Naples and Rome, show a deepening mastery but no fundamental changes even when compared with his first opera, which was also one of his most successful, *Gli equivoci nel sembiante* (1679). His valedictory work, *Griselda* (1721), was adapted from one of Zeno's most prolix and retrospective texts and even with the wholesale revision undertaken by Prince Ruspoli still contains forty-seven numbers. Like Scarlatti's other operas written during his last two decades it met with very little enthusiasm outside the circle of Roman patrons who continued to support him.

Pietro Metastasio (1698–1782), patrician only by adoption, differed significantly from Zeno and his generation. His commitment was to a musical as well as literary conception of opera seria, and to that end he consorted and corresponded throughout his life with composers and singers as well as with patrons and patrician men of letters. He also routinely took upon himself the role of stage director for his dramas. The features he settled on in his librettos were all shaped with an ear to their musical realization. Aria texts were disposed in two stanzas, whose contrasting or complementary sentiments lent themselves to the da capo pattern favoured by composers until mid-century. Unlike Zeno, Metastasio came to place his arias at the end of scenes, where they not only crystallize the emotional situation developed in the preceding recitative but also articulate musically the singer's departure from the stage. He inserted verbs of motion where movement to a new key is likely to occur, and avoided the vowel sounds 'i' and 'e' where the singer normally embellished a cadence. And Metastasio nearly always ended each stanza with a *verso tronco* (in which the last syllable is accented), anticipating the strong tonic accent of the vocal part's final, emphatic cadence that rounded off each segment of an aria.

Metastasio showed little interest in ensemble numbers. To his mind, the two-stanza aria provided a perfect forum for the inner psychological struggles between duty and inclination, between reason and desire, that constitute the central moral conflict in nearly all of his libretti. In the mellifluousness of his verses, the stylized decorum of his poetic lexicon, and the finesse of his emotional palette Metastasio has never had his equal in the history of opera. His texts were set over 800 times in the course of the eighteenth century, but not simply because composers were attracted to their musical merits (composers seldom had a completely free hand in deciding which librettos they were to set). More importantly, Metastasio articulated with a gratifying and refined sensuality the essential qualities that ought to define nobility and the exercise of authority in an age of reason.

The eight 'drammi per musica' Metastasio completed in Italy between 1723 and 1730 established him as by far the most sought-after librettist of serious opera. They were the proving ground for a young generation of composers, all trained at Naples, who brought to fruition a new musical language attuned to the aesthetic these texts embody. Elegant, concise, and uncluttered, a new kind of musical texture reduced and simplified harmonic motion so that emphasis fell more fully on the voice than it had in the works of Scarlatti and Pollarolo. Carefully wrought melodies develop clear, long-range trajectories out of short, suave phrases in perfect syntactic and expressive harmony with each poetic line. Chief among these young composers was Leonardo Vinci (1690–1730), whose settings of Metastasio's early texts, especially his *Didone abbandonata* (1726), were so widely admired that performances continued after Vinci's early death for more than a decade. At mid-century Francesco Algarotti was still enthusing about the impressive obbligato recitative with which Vinci closed *Didone*: 'Vergil himself would have been pleased to hear a composition so animated and so terrible, in which the heart and soul were at once assailed by all the powers of Music.'

Didone, Metastasio's first dramma per musica, is an unusual work— one of only two tragedies among his twenty-seven three-act serious operas—and Vinci's recourse to a highly charged obbligato recitative for Dido's suicide scene was also unusual. At the other extreme, his limpid and pliant melodic style is one of the first to merit the term 'galant', a manner that Tartini was to define as a happy combination of 'chiarezza, vaghezza e buona modulazione' ('clarity, charm, and good modulation'). It owed much to Vinci's journeyman years as a composer of Neapolitan dialect comedies from 1719 to 1724. His career—beginning as a pupil at one of the four Neapolitan conservatories, then writing comic operas for the city's smaller theatres, and eventually attracting commissions for serious operas from the San Bartolomeo and later the big houses at Rome and Venice—established a pattern followed by the great majority of Italian composers throughout the century.

In early 1730 Metastasio moved to Vienna, where he took up the post of imperial poet, succeeding Zeno. Emperor Charles VI, who himself composed, was the last of the Habsburg dynasty to devote lavish resources to the cultivation of opera seria. He favoured a ponderous and at times learned style, such as his Kapellmeisters M. A. Ziani and J. J. Fux (1660–1741) were willing to supply. For the coronation of Charles at Prague as king of Bohemia in 1723, Fux wrote the music for one of the most extravagant operatic productions ever, *Costanza e fortezza* (the title was the Habsburg motto). After mid-century his score was still remembered as an example of the old learned style that had disappeared from opera by around 1740. The emperor's particular favourite was Antonio Caldara (*c*.1670–1736), vice-Kapellmeister from his appointment in 1717 to his death. It was with Caldara that Metastasio had to collaborate on the new dramas and occasional pieces that were demanded of him, although he had little good to say about the composer's insensitivity to the affective content of his aria texts.

Metastasio's Viennese texts were as much sought after as his earlier ones in Italy. Giovanni Battista Pergolesi (1710–36) attempted to establish himself as a successor to his teacher Vinci with impressive settings of Metastasio's *Adriano in Siria* (1734) and *L'Olimpiade* (1735), both composed earlier by Caldara, but fame came only posthumously, beginning with revivals of the latter work in 1738 at Venice and Munich.

The young German Johann Adolf Hasse (1699–1783), after having studied and sung at Hamburg, came to Italy in 1722 and eventually began composing serious operas for the San Bartolomeo. But it was his setting of Metastasio's *Artaserse* for Venice in 1730 that earned him international attention. He was appointed Kapellmeister to the Elector of Saxony Friedrich August I and also established contact with the Habsburg court, where he became a favourite of the future empress Maria Theresa. Another young German who spent formative years in Italy, George Frideric Handel (1685–1759), scored a decisive triumph on his first visit to London in 1711 with his *Rinaldo*. This opera was revived many times during Handel's years in London. The abiding emphasis there on machinery, costume, dance, and the ravishing voices of Italy's greatest castrati favoured operas with plots dealing in the magical or supernatural.

Opera seria became a fixed part of London's cultural life with the opening of the Royal Academy of Music at the King's Theatre in the Haymarket in 1720, with Handel as its music director. Its first eight years were filled with activity and high points, not simply because Handel's finest operas date from that period (*Giulio Cesare*, *Tamerlano*, *Rodelinda*, and *Admeto*, all four on librettos adapted by Nicola Haym) but more especially owing to the presence of three great singers, the castrato Senesino and the rival prima donnas Cuzzoni and Bordoni. Open hostilities between the latter two and squabbles among the members of the nobility who had established the enterprise led to its demise in 1728. Handel and J. J. Heidegger, the skilled theatre manager of the undertaking, contracted to carry on a 'Second Academy' at the King's Theatre for a five-year period. But with distressing frequency the new operas they mounted failed, so revivals of popular works and pasticci came to dominate. Matters worsened when the Opera of the Nobility was formed in 1733. The rivalry of the companies rose as public interest in Italian opera plummeted. Handel kept stubbornly at it until 1740, although other musical activities including the English oratorio, which had been flourishing since 1732, provided more secure avenues to public favour.

Like Scarlatti before him, Handel quickly established a mature operatic style and never forsook it. He stands out in the history of Italian opera before Mozart for the psychological penetration and strongly expressive musical cast of his arias, which sometimes move far beyond what either the text or the dramatic situation suggest. Like the Viennese composers favoured by Charles VI he maintained a strongly contrapuntal style within the structural confines of the da capo aria, but the ingeniousness and strength of his ritornellos, with their artful recombination of an aria's basic motives, and his experiments with thematic connections and requotations of earlier material were altogether unusual. Three times he set adaptations of librettos by Metastasio, but despite his years in Italy he kept the fashionable 'galant' style of young Italians like Vinci at a distance (although he incorporated some of their music into the *pasticci* he put together). Although the full scores (without the simple recitative) or at least the 'Favourite Airs' from many of his operas were published in London, his operas remained by and large unknown on the continent except in his native Lower Saxony.

The international prestige denied Handel continued to accrue to Hasse even after he had settled at Dresden. An era of unstinted support for Italian opera had commenced there with the accession of Friedrich August II. He and his wife, the Austrian archduchess Maria Josepha, took a keen and detailed interest in operatic affairs, as did their daughter-in-law, Maria Antonia Walpurgis, eldest daughter of Charles VII, Elector of Bavaria: she not only wrote both text and music of *Il trionfo della fedeltà*, produced in 1754 for a small circle of courtiers, but also sang the principal role. The work is written wholly in the spirit of Hasse and Metastasio, both of whom dominated at Dresden, Vienna, and Venice. From 1734 until the start of the Seven Years War in 1756 Hasse wrote, rehearsed, and conducted a new opera for carnival at Dresden nearly every year, sometimes two, in ever more lavish productions. Rousseau, in his *Dictionnaire de musique*, praised the Dresden opera orchestra and Hasse's arrangement of it. Little store was set by the chorus, however; it continued to be made up of students from a local school.

During the 1740s Hasse's waxing enthusiasm for Metastasio, kindled by Algarotti, grew into a close personal friendship. This may in part account for his gradual withdrawal from the practice, ever more frequent at the time, of altering the imperial poet's texts. Singers—including Hasse's wife Faustina Bordoni—were demanding ever longer and more challenging virtuoso arias. It was also common practice to substitute arias from other operas or *arie di baule* ('suitcase arias') that had been written expressly for a particular singer to carry around and insert into any number of operas. As arias grew in length, the old da capo pattern (in which an opening section, A, was followed by a contrasting section, B, and then an ornamented return of A) tended to be shortened by truncating the 'A' section, but even so a reduction in the overall number of arias an opera could accommodate became necessary, either through omission or in some cases by combining several arias into a trio or quartet. Baldassare Galuppi (1706–85) dared such an alteration under Metastasio's own nose with the Act 2 quartet in his setting of *Artaserse* for Vienna in

1749. Hasse, by contrast, produced during the 1750s new settings of Metastasian librettos he had already composed earlier that now followed the original texts far more closely, which earned him the poet's praise as the ideal composer of his librettos.

At Berlin Frederick the Great's cultivation of opera seria proceeded in parallel with Hasse's career at Dresden. Most of the operas produced at Berlin were either Hasse's or those of Frederick's Kapellmeister, Carl Heinrich Graun (1703/4–59), whose style was modelled on that of Hasse. The king exercised unprecedented control over every aspect of operatic production. In 1743 he created an international incident in demanding that the dancer La Barbarina honour her contract with Berlin despite her marriage to Lord Stuart Mackenzie. The king was always involved in the selection of librettos, and in 1749 began sketching opera plots himself, in French prose, which his court poet put into Italian verse for Graun. The king also supervised set and costume design, attended rehearsals, and insisted on a rather strict adherence to the written score by his singers. A high point came in 1755 with *Montezuma*, the twenty-fourth of Graun's twenty-seven operas for Berlin. Frederick, a foe of Christianity, chose this unusual subject of cultural collision between the Spaniards and Aztecs largely for ideological reasons. He ordered that wherever possible Graun use the shorter cavatina (the equivalent of just the first part of the old da capo form) in place of da capo or dal segno arias (of which only four remain). In 1756 Graun mounted his last opera, *Merope*. During the Seven Years War (1756–63) nearly all the opera personnel were dismissed and Berlin's creative contribution to opera seria ceased.

Rameau and the Tragédie Lyrique

After the death of Louis XIV in 1715 the distinctive corpus of tragédies lyriques left by Lully and Quinault continued to assert its right to give operatic definition to Absolutism's self-image in France. In its curatorial role, the Académie Royale de Musique sought to preserve the dignity of the Lullian style, but it also found itself freer to absorb significant new works that modified some of its central features. At the same time, the institution looked with concern on the alternatives offered at other Parisian theatres—the coalescence of opéra comique out of the low-comic vaudeville comedies acted at the Foire theatres and the return of Italian opera to Paris. On both fronts, spirited partisanship took the form of heated debates, pamphlet wars, and even fist fights on occasion. The high passions aroused indicate the importance to national identity of a distinctively French style of serious opera, at least to the community of opera lovers and intellectuals who frequented the cafés near the Opéra. But the genre's significance was by no means confined to Paris and its environs. As a well-defined, established alternative to the ever more palpable international ascendancy of opera seria, the tragédie lyrique exerted a European-wide influence on musical and literary practice as well as on aesthetic thought throughout the century. After mid-century, French tradition stood as the direct inspiration for the thoroughgoing changes that began to appear in opera seria, whereas Italian opera, serious or comic, played only a partial and attenuated role in the modifications to Lulliste and Rameauiste opera prior to the Revolution.

The tragédie lyrique, while unchallenged in its prestige, was not the only kind of spectacle cultivated at the Opéra and at court. During the Regency of Philippe of Orléans the most characteristic form of entertainment was something much closer to fashionable trends in poetry and the visual arts—the opéra-ballet. It consisted of a mythological or allegorical prologue (often a flattering address to a patron or protector in attendance) followed by three or four acts that are better called *entrées*, since the operatic portion that each contained served as a mere pretext for a dominating *divertissement*. The genre was the creation of André Campra (1660–1744), who as early as 1697 in *L'Europe galant* had initiated its characteristic substitution of a series of more or less independent comic intrigues set in a modern petit bourgeois or exotic milieu in place of the stylized, mythological world of the tragédie lyrique.

The central figure in French opera between Lully and the Revolution was Jean-Philippe Rameau (1683–1764). Having decided on a career in music rather than law when he turned 18, Rameau studied briefly in Milan before taking up a succession of appointments as an organist in France. His operatic career began humbly when he started composing and arranging for the Foire theatres at age 43 in 1726. At that time he was already known in intellectual circles for his influential *Traité de l'harmonie*, published in 1722, whose claim that the structural basis of melody is harmonic was intimately linked to his own musical style. In the 1730s, when already in his fifties, Rameau turned to the tragédie lyrique and to ballet. Between 1733 and 1760 twenty-four of his dramatic works found their way to stages at the Opéra, Versailles, and Fontainebleau. Only four of these are tragédies lyriques, but together they established Rameau as the first composer successfully to challenge Lully's heritage on its own ground. Old Campra identified the basis for both admiration and condemnation of this new musical phenomenon. When he heard Rameau's

Hippolyte et Aricie at the Opéra in 1733 he declared that it contained enough music for ten operas, and he predicted that its composer would soon eclipse everyone else.

Rameau did not forsake the middle ground between aria and recitative that Lully's style occupied, nor the dramatic use of choral resources, nor the integration of ballets d'action into his scores. But unlike Lully and the Lullistes he conceived of music as the primary agent in French opera. In consequence, he contented himself with texts written by over a dozen collaborators that make haphazard and opportunistic use of these traditional ingredients, texts that in both tone and construction represent a sharp decline from Quinault. One of the best, P.-J. Bernard's *Castor et Pollux*, stunned audiences in 1737 at the very opening of the opera with a scene of lamentation at Castor's tomb that sets the elegiac mood of the work as a whole. (Gluck's *Orfeo* of 1762 is just one work beholden to this example.) The success of *Castor* not only secured Rameau's reputation but initiated sustained hostilities between the adherents of Lully and a camp of his own supporters. The battle reached its highest pitch as a part of the intense excitement stirred up in 1739 by Rameau's third and most powerful tragédie en musique, *Dardanus* (made even more powerful when the composer revised it five years later). The last of Rameau's tragedies produced at the Opéra, *Zoroastre* (1749), marks a turn from the myths of antiquity to an oriental theme of the kind he had explored a year earlier in the ballet-héroïque *Zaïs*. Louis de Cahusac, who wrote both librettos, seems to have inspired Rameau in these works to an especially fluid interchange of singing, declamation, spectacle, and dance that was the strength of French opera at its best. The score also embodies the features of Rameau's style that distressed some of his detractors— complex, 'learned', incessantly modulating, abandoning melodies as quickly as it takes them up, with an orchestra that competes with the singers rather than supports them.

One advantage Rameau, with his natural bent towards flights of inventiveness, enjoyed over Lully was the muted interest Louis XV expressed for music. The queen, it is true, had a great fondness for Italian opera and initiated the Concerts de la Reine, held twice each week at Versailles, at which some of Italy's greatest singers appeared. Further, during her ascendancy Madame de Pompadour encouraged lavish expenditures on opera and instigated the building of two new theatres at Versailles. But in town the Académie could go its own way, which by mid-century involved less emphasis on Lullian tragedies and greater experimentation with the opéra-ballet, ballet-héroïque, and the pastorale-héroïque.

In 1763 the Grande Salle du Palais Royal, at which the Académie had been putting on operas and ballets for ninety years, burnt to the ground. It had been one of the most cramped stages for serious opera in Europe, although visitors remarked on the excellence of its machinery. A new theatre was planned for the same site, one that for the first time was to be built on the Italian 'teardrop' plan rather than the rectangular pattern common in France. Meanwhile, activity shifted to the Salle des Machines in the Tuileries. Here François-André Danican Philidor's (1726–95) impressive tragédie lyrique *Ernelinde* saw its première in 1767. Poinsinet's libretto, set in medieval Norway, is actually an adaptation of an old Italian text (Matteo Noris's *Ricimero*), and Philidor's music owes far more to Italian example than anything Rameau had written. In addition to its ample arias, it contains passages so close to ones in operas by Gluck and Jommelli that later ages have tarnished Philidor's memory with charges of plagiarism. The opera, none the less, is a high point in the years between Rameau's death in 1764 and Gluck's arrival at Paris in 1772—an era otherwise wholly dominated by developments at the Opéra-Comique.

So meagre was the harvest of serious operas in France during these years that the Académie decided to inaugurate the new and much enlarged Grande Salle at the Palais Royal in 1770 with a new production of Rameau's *Zoroastre*. The new theatre, which lasted only until 1781 when it, too, was destroyed by fire, seated over 2,000. Louis and his entourage occasionally attended performances given there, but he was not interested in making it a court-subsidized operation. His funds supported more exclusive performances of both serious and comic works at the theatres at Versailles and Fontainebleau. As at the former Grande Salle, all seats and boxes had to be purchased or subscribed for, and prices doubled for the première of a new work, and quadrupled if the king himself attended. Thought had been given as well to the reality that attendance at the Opéra was as much a performance as what took place on stage. A foyer was provided and no expense was spared in decorating the hall.

For those who went to the theatre for the opera rather than for the society, 1770 offered an intellectual and aesthetic climate very different from the one that had greeted Rameau's *Hippolyte* in 1733. The debate between the Lullistes and Rameauistes had acclimatized Parisians to the possibility of something more complex and rich than Lully's austerities. A little later, the merits of the underlying structure of tragédie lyrique, which Rameau did not change, came under critical scrutiny through the peculiar controversy that came to be known as the Querelle des Bouf-fons. Baron von Grimm, a German diplomat resident in Paris since 1749, used a revival of Destouches's *Omphale* as an excuse to attack French opera in early 1752. Grimm had in mind as an alternative the kind of opera seria he had heard at the Dresden Opera under Hasse, music with which French audiences had no experience. The groundwork was laid later that year when an Italian company performed Pergolesi's inter-mezzo *La serva padrona* between the acts of Lully's *Acis et Galatée*. Initial response was positive, and it was not until a new tragédie lyrique at the Opéra (Mondonville's *Titon et l'Aurore*) provided Grimm with the oppor-tunity for an even more sarcastic pamphlet that formal hostilities com-menced. The Encyclopédistes and especially Rousseau threw in with Grimm. The insouciance of Rousseau's wholesale denigration of all French opera in his *Lettre sur la musique française* (1753) hardened senti-ments of patriotic allegiance in certain quarters, but it also prepared the way for more thoughtful and moderate reflection on the single concept that was to dominate criticism of serious opera for the rest of the cen-tury—verisimilitude.

Neo-classicism and Reform

Two Italian writers who experienced French opera first-hand took important practical and theoretical steps towards a reorientation of opera seria in the 1750s and 1760s. As cultured men of letters, both Francesco Algarotti (1712–64) and Ranieri de' Calzabigi (1714–95) were in close touch with the intellectual currents that after mid-century began urging all of the arts towards a new spirit of naturalness, directness, and simplicity. The artificiality and rococo preciosity established during the Regency in France along with their counterparts elsewhere began to yield to this new spirit in the theatre, in painting, and in costume and con-versation. An imaginary Arcadia faded before catastrophes like the Lis-bon earthquake of 1753 and the rediscovery through archaeological investigation of the 'noble simplicity and quiet grandeur' of the ancient world.

To writers like Algarotti and Calzabigi, reconciling opera seria to the changes animating its sister arts presented an interesting problem. Metastasio had attained a European stature akin to that of Petrarch, and even his worst detractors did not deny the gracious precision and econ-omy of his language nor the simple yet satisfying structural rhythm created by the recitative-aria pattern of his scenes. But the metaphor arias and lengthy ratiocinations that accompanied the inner struggles of his characters, when stripped of their elegant verbal dress, seemed cold and stinted. And as the extremes of situation and emotion to which the seventeenth century had been partial faded from memory Metastasio's self-imposed limits seemed to restrict expressive possibilities.

Still, the abiding popularity of his texts counselled against a frontal assault. Musical practice was another matter. Under pressure from singers and audiences, composers had forsaken the balance between poetic and musical syntax that had been the hallmark of Vinci's generation. Now the same elegant eight or ten verses were stretched across grand da capo and dal segno arias introduced by lengthy ritornellos and punctuated by roulades and cadenzas that scorned the earlier practice of limiting such embellishments to a single breath. Acting standards, especially in Italy, were a scandal. As a counterpoise, the French operatic stage had several points in its favour. To be sure, no one seriously believed that the French style of singing was the technical equal of Italian bel canto, and some visitors to Paris found the French preference for a middle ground between simple recitative and grand aria disconcerting (Rousseau had reviled it as 'a kind of psalmody without melody or rhythm'). But others noted with approval the absence of *ad libitum* ornamentation in the tragédie lyrique and many, including David Garrick, praised the powerful sense of dramatic illusion created through the high standards of acting and the precise co-ordination of all components of the drama—action, declamation, ballet, chorus, descriptive music, and visual effects.

The Venetian Algarotti, after receiving a classical education in Italy, travelled to London and Paris, lived for a while with Voltaire, served Frederick the Great, advised the Dresden opera, and finally returned to Italy where he published one of the most influential and widely disseminated critical essays on opera, his *Saggio sopra l'opera in musica* (1755). With his experiences in France and Germany clearly in mind, Algarotti attacked not just the swaggering stars of the modern Italian system but also the unruly and hedonistic audiences who flocked to hear them. After perfunctory words of admiration for Metastasio's art, Algarotti offered a libretto of his own—in French—at the end of his essay, *Iphigénie en Aulide*. It illustrates his desire for more spectacle, stronger situations, and a more direct confrontation with the tragic in opera plots. Most of all, Algarotti found in the theme of Agamemnon's sacrifice of his daugh-

ter a vehicle for the union of opera's many constituent elements under a
single stark and compelling poetic force.

On a visit to the Bourbon court at Parma in 1759 Algarotti must have
been pleased to discover the enlightened intendant Guillaume du Tillot
working with the gifted singer-actress Catterina Gabrielli, the poet Carlo
Frugoni, and the young composer Tommaso Traetta (1727–79) on an Italian counterpart to Rameau's first great tragédie lyrique, *Ippolito ed Aricia*.
This early attempt at reconciling the two national traditions shares several features with later efforts in the same direction: it took place entirely
within the court system of patronage, for one thing, and at a centre of
cosmopolitan intellectual ferment (Parma was called 'the Athens of
Italy' at the time); furthermore, inspiration and guidance came not from
a reform-minded composer but from the theatrical administration in a
co-operative undertaking touching all aspects of the presentation. While
the ideals of simplification and greater verisimilitude were pursued as
aesthetic ends (bringing opera seria into line with a turn from the orna-
mental and artificial already well along in the genre's individual components), the literary reorientation towards dramas of sacrifice,
supernatural intervention, and visits to the underworld opened the way
to more human protagonists as forces beyond even the most enlightened
ruler's control thwarted his ability to contrive an ordered world dispens-
ing the greatest good to the greatest number.

Calzabigi, like many librettists before him, came from circumstances
that made it natural for him to identify with the élite that still controlled
the cultivation of opera seria. His early Neapolitan opera texts, while
they found little favour, already show his characteristic severity of style.
He spent an important decade at Paris from 1750 to 1760, where he saw
through the press a complete edition of Metastasio's works. In a prefa-
tory *Dissertazione* Calzabigi praises Metastasio warmly but also voices
admiration for some of the traits of tragédie lyrique, even though in the
heat of the Querelle he had joined other impudent foreigners like
Grimm and Rousseau in attacking the genre as a whole and in questioning the fitness of French as a musical language.

In 1761 Calzabigi settled in Vienna. Here he was able to put his ideas
on opera into practice as part of a collaborative team that included a
composer with international experience in Christoph Willibald von
Gluck (1714–87), an energetic intendent in Giacomo Durazzo, a leading
castrato who had studied acting with Garrick in Gaetano Guadagni, a
Viennese counterpart to Noverre in the choreographer Gaspero Angiolini, and a seasoned set designer with a flair for combining the formal

with the natural in Giovanni Maria Quaglio. Their first effort, *Orfeo ed Euridice* (1762), belongs to a genre that Metastasio himself had actively cultivated during his later years at Vienna—the 'azione teatrale' or 'festa teatrale'. These celebratory pieces departed from the norms Metastasio had established for opera seria in that mythological rather than historical subjects were the rule, and more use was made of the chorus, ballet, and even spectacle. *Orfeo* was first performed to celebrate the name day of Maria Theresa's husband Franz Stefan. It included an unusual amount of dancing (four ballets) and choral participation, for which the resources of the French troupe who performed opéra comique and ballet at the Burgtheater were enlisted. Everyone had a different idea about why the new work made such a deep impression—Calzabigi's Greek-influenced choral tableaux, Guadagni's voice and stage presence, Gluck's 'divine' music, the beautiful stage designs. Durazzo made the most of the moment and, through a series of shrewd manœuvres that included arranging for Gluck's score to be published at Paris, focused international attention on the innovative activities involving ballet, Italian opera, and even opéra comique at the imperial capital.

The following year Traetta came to Vienna. He had written an *Armida* for the Burgtheater (and for Catterina Gabrielli) in 1761, its libretto adapted from Quinault, and a *Sophonisbe* the following year for the electoral court at Mannheim, with a tragic ending whose effect was likened to the legendary power of Greek tragedy. His poet for the latter work was another remarkable Italian, Mattia Verazi, who with the composer Niccolò Jommelli (1714–74) had created several powerful French-inspired works for Duke Karl Eugen at Stuttgart. Jommelli, who served Karl Eugen from 1753 to 1769, made brilliant use of the orchestral resources there, which he himself had built up. Yet despite the duke's fondness for French opera, which he had heard at Paris and Versailles, Jommelli and Verazi avoided direct emulation and sought instead to enhance the dramatic force of opera seria through greater reliance on obbligato recitative. Tellingly, even these innovations Jommelli was forced to abjure when he returned periodically to compose new operas for Naples and Rome.

At Vienna Traetta was asked to set a libretto by Calzabigi's fellow Livornese Marco Coltellini based on one of the great sacrifice dramas of ancient Greek tragedy, *Ifigenia in Tauride*. It was the first in a series of full-length serious operas that took *Orfeo* as a point of departure, even to the extent of direct imitations of its most memorable tableaux. Orestes' scene with the Furies was conceived by virtually the same group of innovators who had collaborated with Gluck on Orpheus's parallel scene, including Guadagni. *Ifigenia* was also commissioned to mark the name day of the emperor, which *Orfeo* had helped celebrate a year earlier. Although there is reason to credit Gluck's radical musical departures in *Orfeo* for the greater renown achieved by his opera, he himself was deeply impressed by Traetta's music, conducted the opera at Florence in 1767 with his own prologue added, and seems not to have forgotten *Ifigenia* when he composed his own opera on the same subject in 1778.

It is useful to stress three points concerning these two operas. First, neither was principally its composer's doing, but rather came into being through the efforts of a constellation of experimenters at Vienna who enjoyed the full support of the imperial court (even the empress, contrary to her custom, visited the theatre for virtually all of the early performances of *Orfeo*). Second, their appearance did not betoken a direct repudiation of the Metastasian heritage. The same year that Vienna saw Gluck's new opera the city also enjoyed twenty-one performances of Hasse's setting of Metastasio's newest libretto, *Il trionfo di Clelia*; moreover, the following year Gluck himself set this same text as the inaugural opera of the new Teatro Comunale in Bologna. And finally, although the tragédie lyrique was clearly a model for many of the structural innovations in both *Orfeo* and *Ifigenia*, to contemporary minds the spiritual source of their aesthetic power lay in Greek tragedy.

The lugubrious and austere atmosphere of the new operas and ballets created by Gluck, Calzabigi, and Angiolini further cemented connections with the ancient world that Winckelmann and others were recovering, but it also created a certain difficulty for Viennese audiences. The tragic darkness of the ballet *Semiramis* was scarcely an appropriate subject to celebrate the second marriage of Joseph II in 1765; and two years later, Gluck's new Italian opera *Alceste*, based on Euripides' tragedy of a wife who dies in her mortally ill spouse's stead, was brought to the stage just after the death of Franz Stefan. The opera gained critical favour slowly; and a third collaboration of Calzabigi and Gluck, *Paride ed Elena*, failed in 1770 'owing to its uneven and rather bizarre manner', according to one witness, despite ballets by Noverre and the participation of the famed castrato Giuseppe Millico.

Fittingly, there has been some dispute over the authorship of the famous preface to the first edition of the full score of *Alceste*, which was brought out at Vienna in 1769. It carries Gluck's name only, but it is widely surmised that Calzabigi and perhaps Durazzo as well had a hand in drafting it. Composers were not as a rule men of letters and only exceptionally had recourse to the printed word as a polemic tool. The protests against the abuses of vainglorious singers had long been common coin among *literati*, and the preface's new musical principles that promise to correct these abuses all share a common trait—to restrict music to the role of colouring and enlivening what the poet has already created. The preface nowhere suggests that music's role in opera is formative or that poetry's role is not.

A year later the young Antonio Salieri (1750–1825) collaborated with Coltellini on a new opera for Vienna based on Tasso's story of Rinaldo and Armida. Salieri's *Armida* struck a happy compromise between Gluck's manner and the bel canto tradition, and established his reputation in Vienna. One important point of contact between Salieri and Gluck (who may well have aided the younger composer) was stressed by Salieri's pupil Mosel in his biography of the composer—'the thoroughly *scenic* construction of the whole'.

In 1773 Gluck made the first of several trips to Paris. His determination, late in life, to conquer the French capital and to leave his mark on French opera is a singular occurrence in the history of eighteenth-century opera. Although the poet Du Roullet had offered him a libretto based on Racine's *Iphigénie en Aulide*, Gluck had no fixed commission from the Paris Opéra when he began setting the text. A carefully orchestrated series of manœuvres brought about a triumph at the work's première in 1774. Another curiosity provided by the 1770s is the counter-strategem of the Neapolitan ambassador to have the composer Piccinni brought to Paris as an explicit rival to Gluck, for—unlike Gluck—Piccinni knew nothing of either the French language or French opera. His innocence of the deep play indulged in by the 'Gluckistes' and 'Piccinnistes' did him credit, as did his remarkable adaptation to French sensibility with *Roland* (1778), reworked from Quinault by Marmontel. Four months earlier, Gluck had stirred up heated debate with his setting of Quinault's *Armide*, but he discreetly dropped plans to set a *Roland* libretto on learning of Piccinni's plans, just as Piccinni deferred completion of his *Iphigénie en Tauride* when Gluck produced an opera on the same subject.

Gluck's *Iphigénie en Tauride* (1779) was the last and greatest triumph of a remarkable career. Never had Gluck integrated aria, chorus, and ballet into tableaux of greater plasticity and dramatic point. The individual elements do not differ greatly from the ingredients of the operas Gluck composed in collaboration with Calzabigi at Vienna, but the simplicity of a choral prayer such as 'Chaste fille de Latona' derives its expressive power not from its own musical structure but its disposition within scene, act and, ultimately, the entire drama.

Gluck's remark that in *Armide* (which he considered the best of his works) he had striven to be more painter and poet than musician speaks directly to the role of the composer promulgated in the preface to *Alceste*, and in addition suggests the common ground Gluck's neo-classical operas share with Lully, whose scores Gluck is reported to have studied in the 1770s. The impact of both Gluck and Piccinni on French opera differs markedly from the direction taken by Rameau, who saw poetry's role as subordinate. What is more, Rameau had no successors. Gluck and Piccinni, on the other hand, stand at the beginning of a long chain of foreign, Italian-trained composers who dominated French opera into the age of Meyerbeer. Salieri was ceremoniously anointed as Gluck's heir when the old composer allowed *Les Danaïdes* to be bruited in advance as his own work and only revealed as Salieri's after its successful launching at the Opéra.

Without ever declaring discipleship, Wolfgang Amadeus Mozart (1756–91) absorbed some of the neo-classical principles preached and practised by Gluck into his own more Italianate, music-centred conception of opera. *Idomeneo* (1781) provided him with a singular opportunity to challenge the literary bias that subordinated music's role to the colouring of an essentially poetico-dramatic structure. From the start Mozart took control of the conceptual shaping of the drama and in the end created a music-dramatic synthesis that drew on the strengths of French, Italian, and German practice. As Traetta had done at Vienna, he incorporated elements of the tragédie lyrique into a French sacrifice drama essentially governed by Italian principles. Acts 1 and 2 end with impressive choral tableaux directly inspired by both Rameau and Gluck: the act-ending chaconnes of the former and particularly the choral complexes in the *Iphigénie en Aulide* of the latter, where a father also seeks to escape propitiatory sacrifice of his own child brought on by navigational difficulties. Prior to these act-ending scenes, none the less, Italian ideals prevail in *Idomeneo*. Ritornello, aria, both orchestrally accompanied and simple recitative, still articulate the dramatic rhythm. And at times a sensuous and even playful tone lightens the dark proceedings. But points of musical rest are no longer determined by the individual numbers but rather by the dramatic situation. Although traditionally structured, numbers are now linked together, and a network of recurring motives helps subordinate both singer and character to forces beyond human control. To effect this kind of continuity

Mozart relied on the famous Mannheim orchestra, which Karl Theodor had brought with him to Munich. He wrote for these players much as he wrote for his singers, creating an orchestral voice with the ability to speak of the human tragedy both from within and beyond the perspective of its participants.

German Opera and the Melodrama

During most of the eighteenth century, serious opera in German-speaking lands found its characteristic niche at court-sponsored theatres devoted to opera seria in Italian. For the first third of the century, Germany's most important civic stage, established at Hamburg in 1678, was also the major centre for German-language opera. Although local diplomats and nobles involved themselves sporadically, the undertaking was essentially public in nature. It sustained itself by tailoring its repertory to Hamburg's middle class, one of the largest and most prosperous in Germany. None the less, there were frequent changes of management and eventually the opera closed its door in 1738. The composers who lent their skills to the enterprise were typically hired in some other capacity. Johann Mattheson (1681–1764), for example, joined the Hamburg Opera as a singer, and Handel served as second violinist and cembalist. It was only by virtue of his exceptional productivity and talent that Reinhard Keiser (1674–1739), after managing the Theater am Gänsemarkt from 1702 to 1707, was able to pursue a career as a more or less independent composer.

Prior to the turn of the century new operas at Hamburg had concentrated on the kinds of biblical themes typical of early German opera, apparently to mollify the angry opposition of church authorities to opera in any form. But by the time Keiser moved there in 1695 Italian models had begun to figure more prominently. In 1703 Keiser took the novel step of intermixing Italian-language arias with German ones in *Der verführte Claudius*, and their number increased thereafter. Whoever the composer was, the emphasis fell on an eclectic variety in style and expression, ranging from militantly simple German songs through the pathos of accompanied recitative to the breathtaking virtuosity of the bravura aria. Plots drawn from ancient history and mythology joined biblical ones, as did stories—historical or otherwise—from every corner of Europe (Mattheson composed a *Boris Goudenow* in 1710). The reforms associated with Zeno and Metastasio were all but ignored. Librettists, most of whom were local, scattered a profusion of arias here and there, and spectacle was an essential ingredient, especially in the last decades. Although a more or less serious tone was typical, especially of Keiser's works, comic scenes were not eliminated: the triumph Keiser scored with *Der Carneval von Venedig* in 1707 rested partly on the folk-like arias in its comic scenes, sung in the local Lower Saxon dialect.

The better singers were asked to manage some dazzling florid passages, but nothing like Italian bel canto was to be heard. Mattheson, himself a tenor, could write fluent lyric melodies, but Keiser's high reputation sprang from startling and ingenious ideas with active participation of the orchestra. Young Handel's vocal writing is even more ruthlessly instrumental, apart from the few comic scenes in his one successful opera, *Almira* (1705). Christoph Graupner's (1683–1760) *Dido, Königin von Carthago*, a 'Singe-Spiel' in three acts to a libretto by Heinrich Hinsch first performed in the spring of 1707, offers a useful point of contrast with Italian practice. Hinsch's libretto is rife with sub-plots and supernatural visitations, although it does not contain any comic scenes. Graupner's score, his first for Hamburg, mixes twenty-nine German and sixteen Italian arias with twelve ensembles. Dido sings for the most part in the minor mode, and her suicide takes place on stage.

After the collapse of the Hamburg enterprise a serious opera in German was scarcely to be heard for the next thirty-five years. The system of private entrepreneurship that prevailed in German theatres during those years did bring forth the popular Singspiele of Weisse and Hiller after the Seven Years War, but serious opera was left to the big court theatres and their Italian singers. A fortuitous combination of circumstances at the small ducal court of Weimar led to the surprising appearance of an opera seria with a German text in 1773. The creation of *Alceste*, instigated by its poet Christoph Martin Wieland, an ardent admirer of Metastasio, enjoyed the full support of Duchess Anna Amalia, who had grown up on Italian opera seria at Brunswick. The German *Alceste* had almost nothing to do with Gluck's reform opera, which had been the subject of a severe review by Frederick the Great's Kapellmeister, J. F. Agricola. Wieland's musical collaborator, Anton Schweitzer, showed little interest in emulating the neo-classical restraint of Gluck's music, although he shared fully his penchant for the dark and severe. Musically, the opera is dominated by its extensive, heavy-textured arias (twelve of its sixteen numbers) and two massive obbligato recitatives rich in harmonic and melodic surprises. As music director of the Seyler theatrical company, Schweitzer had engaged several outstanding singers, without whom his demanding arias would have been unthinkable.

Alceste achieved an immediate and surprising popularity, not just at Weimar and other German courts but also on civic stages. Troupes that had improved their musical resources beyond what Hiller's Singspiele demanded took it up, and in cities where this was not possible it was often given in concert performances. One of its most brilliant productions came at the hands of a group of outstanding German singers, performing before the Palatine Court of Karl Theodore at Schwetzingen and Mannheim. Promptly the local poet Anton Klein (founder of a society to purify the German language) set about writing another German serious opera, *Günther von Schwarzburg*, that took Wieland's patriotic exertions a step further by exploring a subject from German history. Holzbauer's music follows closely the manner of Jommelli, whose influence was considerable in southern Germany. The strong passions of the heroine Asberta and the death-scene of Günther elicited a score from the ageing composer far more animated than Schweitzer's 'mournful *Alceste*' (as Mozart called it).

There were several other Italianate serious operas in German that followed the paths marked out by these two (including two further settings of Wieland's libretto). But none of them approached the originality of the serious German works written for the court theatre at Gotha by its Kapellmeister, Georg Anton Benda (1722–95) during the mid-1770s. As part of his campaign against French as an operatic language, Rousseau had invented an experimental new genre of music drama in which spoken declamation alternates with orchestral interludes. The one specimen he produced, *Pygmalion*, was produced first at Lyons in 1770 and later at Paris. The French showed no interest in Rousseau's 'mélodrame', but in Germany, where anything he wrote was taken seriously, imitations sprang up. Schweitzer composed music to a translation of Rousseau's text, produced at Weimar in 1772. The melodrama exploited the strengths of both sides of a German theatrical company, combining the high art of the tragic monologue with the musical technique serious opera reserved for its most impassioned scenes, the obbligato recitative.

When the Seyler company moved to Gotha in late 1774 Benda produced two new melodramas, *Ariadne auf Naxos* and *Medea*, that established the new genre and his own fame at a stroke. Written for a leading tragedienne in the troupe, each unfolds as if it were a single, culminating act of a Greek drama. Audiences, who considered the innovation a theoretical absurdity, were stunned by its compelling realism and sweep, effects enhanced in the case of *Ariadne* by the first use of historical costuming on the German stage. Benda's epoch-making scores swept triumphantly across every stage in Germany and travelled as far as France and Italy. Their varied musical language includes much text painting, but also a firm consciousness of overall design. Benda embarked on a second experiment in 1776 that equalled the sensation created by his melodramas with his three-act serious opera *Romeo und Julie*. The score is completely in the style of opera seria except that spoken dialogue is used instead of simple recitative, a decision Benda pointedly defended in print. The capital scene, a solemn funeral chorus at the beginning of act three, offers a Northern counterpart to Gluck's sublime choral tableaux. The idea apparently came from David Garrick's 1750 production of Shakespeare's play.

Opera Seria in the Shadow of the Revolution

After Metastasio's death in 1782 his texts continued to hold their own on stages devoted to opera seria, both in Italy and abroad. Wholesale changes and in particular reductions in the number of arias continued to be the rule, but even where the excisions and substitutions were at their most ruthless the essential plot structure remained unaltered. The best-known setting of a Metastasian text in the late eighteenth century is of course Mozart's *La clemenza di Tito*, composed in great haste for the coronation of Leopold II at Prague in 1791. Leopold's ascension to the Habsburg throne and to that of the Holy Roman Empire also signalled the return of opera seria to Vienna after the Josephine era, in which it had been confined to the performance of excerpts in concert. Leopold reinstated both opera seria and ballet at the Burgtheater as he had known and cultivated them while Grand Duke of Tuscany at Florence, one of the major centres of both genres during the last quarter of the century.

Mozart's *La clemenza di Tito* brings together many, but certainly not all of the new features that opera seria had acquired during that time. Acts 2 and 3 have been conflated, the first act's conclusion has been restructured into a true finale, the number of exit arias has dwindled and in the penultimate scenes the primo uomo and prima donna each sing a two-tempo aria, usually called a rondò. Mozart's catalogue entry for the work, which reads 'opera seria...ridotta a vera opera dal Signor Mazzolà', suggests not only that the transmutations undergone by the old genre were thoroughgoing enough to merit a new designation, but also that these changes were in part literary, the work of his collaborator Caterino Mazzolà, court poet at Dresden.

As a celebration of dynastic continuity and enlightened leadership, *La clemenza di Tito* occupied a fairly conservative position in the seria world of the 1790s. In a reversal of the situation in the age of Gluck, after Mozart's death Vienna and the other transalpine courts that continued to cultivate serious opera in Italian took up the rear-guard, while Italian stages assumed the lead in the transformation of Metastasian opera into the *melodramma tragico* of the nineteenth century. Naples, Milan, Turin, and Florence all played significant roles, but leadership returned to where it had been at the beginning of the century, to Venice. At all these centres, new and forward-looking works coexisted with the continued cultivation of Metastasian opera, along with the occasional appearance of a neo-classical opera of more or less Gluckian stamp.

The two-tempo rondò, which Mozart exploited throughout the 1780s, was just one feature that opera seria and opera buffa shared. It allowed for an exploration of the full range of a singer's voice in a single aria and invited an emotional engagement by the audience in its slow part that may serve as an index of many other changes in the structure of opera seria. The chorus, for example, appears more frequently, especially in finales (which are beholden as much to French example as to opera buffa); and plays a role that is less formal-architectonic and more interactive. The two-tempo duet, which will see expansion in the coming century, also gains in fluidity, with each of its parts divided into interactive and reflective sections.

Most striking, however, is the marked rise in the amount of spectacle and violence introduced by a new generation of librettists, which at its extreme undermined one of the hallmarks of Metastasian opera, the 'lieto fine'. In 1772 Antonio Planelli had defended the happy ending of opera seria as a welcome sign of the modern world's commitment to 'gentility, urbanity and clemency'. By the 1790s, however, a whole generation of 'morte' operas was enjoying widespread popularity. The Venetian librettists Giuseppe Foppa and Antonio Sografi, following the example of the eccentric count Alessandro Pepoli, spearheaded the sustained exploration of the tragic ending. As early as 1786 Abate Pietro Giovannini had reworked Voltaire's *Semiramis* into a bloody tragedy, *La vendetta di Nino* (produced at Florence with music by Alessio Prati), in which a son unwittingly caught in an incestuous entanglement with his mother murders her before not only the horror-struck audience but also the ghost of the husband she had conspired to kill.

At Milan La Scala produced a *tragedia per musica* based on Shakespeare during the carnival season of 1796—Niccolò Zingarelli's (1752–1837) *Giulietta e Romeo*. Foppa's libretto, derived from Shakespeare by way of the

French translation of Ducis, employs an especially effective variant of the Garrick ending in which Romeo dies in Juliet's arms. The opera centres on Romeo, who is shown in heroic as well as amorous guise. The part was written to set off the artistry of the great castrato Giuseppe Crescentini, known across Europe as 'l'Orfeo italiano'. So great was the éclat both of the opera's music and of Crescentini's singing that both were brought to Venice that same year (where another drama on interfamilial strife, Cimarosa's *Orazi e Curiazi*, was just going into rehearsal). A local critic testified to the new spirit that tragedies in music like these were beginning to create in audiences. 'The gloominess of the story', he reported of Zingarelli's *Giulietta e Romeo*, 'which reserves all its horrors for the third act, appears somewhat weighty to those who do not have a spirit inclined to melancholy, and who are used to going to the theatre to be entertained and not distressed. But if the action demands it, if the music responds to the text, one cannot but praise the poetry and the composer who has dressed it with such beautiful and expressive notes.'

The combination of cumulative tragic power and bel canto described here required singers who were willing to devote at least some thought and effort to acting standards. It also summarizes the post-Metastasian legacy of Italian serious opera inherited by the age of Rossini and Verdi.

❧ 3 ❧

THE EIGHTEENTH CENTURY: COMIC OPERA

Thomas Bauman

Italy to 1770

THE political, cultural, and economic factors that distinguished life in northern Italy from that in southern Italy paralleled to some extent the cultivation of various strains of comic opera during the first half of the eighteenth century. But the differences did not run deep, and by the end of the century they had all but disappeared. A larger gulf separated comic opera from serious opera, one that was only partially bridged by 1800. The distance between these genres made itself felt on nearly every front—their subject-matter and literary tone, the skills and training of their executants, their audiences and relative engagement with contemporary society, the cost and institutional structure of each, and, not least, their diverging dramaturgical ideals and musical means.

Whereas the dynastic dimension of serious opera inclined it to seek a seemingly timeless stabilization of the more exalted human passions in figures from ancient history, comic opera sought out a typology of human nature in the more familiar surroundings of contemporary domestic life, which needed no translation into a remote past. The language of comic opera was up to date as well, employing a far broader, less 'literary' vocabulary than serious opera, and in some cases included local dialect. Librettists, not surprisingly, tended to specialize in one genre or the other. Before 1770 Italian singers, too, did not move very freely between the two worlds, once having established a reputation in either. An ability to act well was as important as a good voice on the comic stage. The development of ensemble skills that the plots of comic operas demanded was facilitated by a tendency for comic troupes to remain together under an impresario. (In the world of opera seria, singers were ordinarily engaged for a single season, and the impresario's primary relationship was to the theatre and its owners.)

Comic opera was less expensive to produce than serious opera, and cost much less to attend. Southern Italy's agrarian economy tended to inhibit the development of a sizeable middle class, and its comic operas inclined to cater to upper-class theatre-goers who looked with amused detachment on the antics of the lower-class personages who peopled the comic entertainments in its smaller theatres. In the North, a broader cultural basis of bourgeois support for comedy, both spoken and sung, existed by the time of the relative peace and prosperity under Austrian rule during the age of Maria Theresa. By mid-century a distinctive tone in Venetian comedies and comic operas appealed to a gentler and more sympathetic rapport between audience and drama.

Unlike librettists, most Italian composers moved freely between the serious and comic operatic worlds. A young composer upon leaving the conservatory at Naples might serve a journeyman period writing for a comic company in one of the city's smaller theatres before securing a commission for an opera seria for one of Italy's big opera houses. Elsewhere, the typical employment opportunity the eighteenth century offered a composer—as head of a court or civic musical establishment—usually carried with it a demand for new music of all kinds, including different categories of opera. The operatic season for theatres specializing in comic opera differed somewhat from the 'stagione' system practised by the bigger seria houses. As in all Catholic lands, stage representations were proscribed in Italy for all of Lent, but performances of comic opera could reasonably and profitably be undertaken for nearly all of the balance of a year. Where comic opera did not depend on the same affluent, patrician audience that opera seria did, its cultivation was not as severely restricted by their habit of spending summers at their country estates (the so-called 'villeggiatura').

The modifications of seventeenth-century operatic practices in Italy that created opera seria as a literary, musical, and institutional phenomenon included the banishing of comic episodes. These had by convention involved a sub-plot carried on among a few servants in scenes most often placed at the ends of the first two acts. The plot in these 'scene buffe' tended to have little if any connection with the main story and eventually became detached in performance as well. As early as 1706, the Teatro San Angelo in Venice was presenting such scenes as separate two- or three-act musical comedies. Each act was performed in front of the curtain in alternation with the three acts of the serious operas given at the same theatre, and together these comic interpolations came to be called 'intermezzi'. The San Cassiano took up the practice the following year, and soon the intermezzi were a common feature throughout northern Italy.

The new genre became the speciality of male-female pairs of actor-singers, who frequently travelled from stage to stage. The stories involved low-comic domestic squabbles, and incorporated features of the *commedia dell'arte* to some degree. Few musical texts survive, and in all probability were subject to modification as they migrated from city to city. By the 1720s, major composers of opera seria were also providing intermezzi. Johann Adolf Hasse, for example, composed intermezzi for two of the opere serie he provided for the San Bartolomeo at Naples in 1726. One of these, *L'artigiano gentiluomo*, is based on Molière (*Le Bourgeois Gentilhomme*, 1670). Its text, by Antonio Salvi, had already been set in 1722 by Salvi's fellow Florentine G. M. Orlandini. Characteristically, it underwent some major alterations in Hasse's setting. Its three acts include eight numbers, only three of them from the original version—five arias (three for the astute Larinda, two for the gullible buffoon Vanesio), and three duets, each concluding an act.

The best-known of all intermezzi was *La serva padrona*, composed by the young Giovanni Battista Pergolesi (1710–36) and first performed between the acts of his opera seria *Il prigioniero superbo* at Naples in 1733. Not much noted at the time, it later gained national and international recognition as a stylish exemplar of a new comic manner, one of spare textures, witty motivic play in both voice and accompaniment, and an overall vivacity suggestive of on-stage gestures at every turn. Its plot, like that of *L'artigiano gentiluomo*, is built out of the series of stratagems through which the servant girl Serpina coaxes a proposal of marriage from her master Uberto. *La serva padrona* and other successful intermezzi eventually shrugged off their opera seria surroundings and were performed as independent works. By mid-century, in fact, ballets had largely replaced the intermezzi between the acts of serious operas throughout Italy.

Full-length comic opera developed alongside the intermezzi, but differed in several important respects. At Naples, the commedia per musica appeared shortly after the turn of the century, first in private homes of local aristocrats, then in the city's smaller theatres. The genre came to focus on the Teatro dei Fiorentini and, after 1724, the Teatro Nuovo and Teatro della Pace. Its texts were often partly or wholly in Neapolitan dialect, depending on the dramatis personae, which normally included artisans and members of the lower middle class. An initial high point in the cultivation of Neapolitan comic opera came with Alessandro Scarlatti's *Il trionfo dell'onore* (1718). Later masters of Neapolitan opera seria also contributed. Leonardo Vinci's *Li zite 'ngalera* (1722) illustrates the variety of vocal types the new genre admitted (castrato, trouser, and falsetto roles) and the larger ensembles absent from both the intermezzi and opera seria of the day. Leonardo Leo's *Amor vuol sofferenze* (1739) introduced a sentimental strain alongside the low comic tone that had dominated the commedia per musica.

Pergolesi's *Lo frate 'nnamorato* (1732) illustrates just how early the traits that were to inform Italian comic opera for much of the century found steady and fruitful employment. Class distinctions are delineated both linguistically and musically, from the seria accents of the Roman visitors to the brisk comic tone tinged with folk elements of the local inhabitants of the Neapolitan suburb Capodimonte, who sing in dialect. In between is Don Pietro, a young eccentric of uncertain pedigree. A simple orchestra of strings only (a flute materializes in one aria) supports over two dozen numbers spread across a broad emotional and psychological spectrum. But the overriding tone is the cheerful, short-breathed manner of the intermezzi. (Pergolesi's commedia per musica was in fact performed, like contemporaneous opera seria, with an intermezzo and a ballet between its acts.)

The next significant developments in the formation of eighteenth-century comic opera in Italy occurred not at Naples but at Venice. Throughout its long history, Venice had always allowed varied cultural practices to coexist peacefully, and did as much for the different forms that comic entertainments with music took in the early eighteenth century. Around 1740, there coalesced from these varied sources a new kind of comic opera that has come to be called 'opera buffa' (although the term stabilized some time after the genre itself). Its chief literary architect was also the main figure in the elevation of Italian spoken comedy during the same era, Carlo Goldoni (1707–93). After an ill-fated attempt at opera seria, Goldoni had turned to writing intermezzi during his tenure at Venice's San Giovanni Grisostomo from 1734 to 1741. But it was between 1748 and his departure from Venice in 1762 that Goldoni gave definitive form to the new Venetian counterpart to Neapolitan comic opera (which had arrived there in 1743). Like his spoken comedies of the same years, his full-length opera buffa librettos (all in three acts) explore a cast of characters drawn from a broad social spectrum—by convention seven singing roles in all, sometimes explicitly divided by Goldoni into 'parti buffe' and 'parti serie', to which he occasionally added 'parti di mezzo carrattere'.

A typical Goldoni libretto also made due allowance for the visual and musical variety Italian audiences had come to expect of their musical theatre, comic or serious. Several scene changes, using both half and full stage, occur in each act. Musical numbers, from twenty-five to twenty-eight of them, alternate with simple recitative, which Goldoni kept far shorter than in earlier practice. As with opera seria of the day, ballets were danced between the acts (all his full-length librettos are in three acts). In his sharpest departure from earlier structural practices, Goldoni placed great weight on the musical resources deployed at the ends of acts. The outer ones were less important: a static ensemble concluded the first act, and usually a duet of reconciliation between the principals and a final 'coro' (a brief, homophonic ensemble sung by all the soloists) ended the third. In 1749, at the end of the second act of *L'Arcadia in Brenta*, Goldoni introduced one of the most important innovations in the genre's history—a multi-sectional action ensemble that came to be called a 'finale'. This first effort was among his most ingenious, a play within the play in which the principals amuse themselves at Fabrizio's country estate on the Brenta by assuming various masks of the *commedia dell'arte* and acting out a little self-contained drama.

Goldoni's chief musical collaborator was Baldassare Galuppi (1706–85), a native of the island of Burano (and hence often called 'il Buranello') who turned to writing opera buffa only after having established himself among the foremost composers of opera seria. Galuppi, following Neapolitan practice, deployed distinctive idioms for each genre. In length, formal structure, and emotional range his comic arias show far greater variety than his serious arias. Short phrases arranged in fluid patterns dominate his larger ensembles as well as his arias and duets. At times a sharply etched motivic style allows for an engaging give and take between the vocal parts and the orchestra; at others, a gentler, more mellifluous lyric tone of a specifically Venetian stamp settles over a scene. The seria style appears in some of his earlier comic operas for the important arias of the 'parti serie'.

Taken as a whole, the corpus of operas created by these men established a new relationship between music and text that was able to bring vividly to life the multicoloured contemporary world familiar to eighteenth-century audiences, and did so with ease, elegance, and wit. Galuppi became the first composer to gain an international reputation primarily through comic opera, and Goldoni's crucial technical innovations laid the foundation for the cultivation of opera buffa into the next century. Many of the plots Goldoni created in his comic operas explore domestic situations and problems of a lighter sort, while a few others concoct fanciful worlds in order to satirize contemporary mores. During a sojourn at the court of Parma in 1756, he added a third category, a musical equivalent of the French 'comédie larmoyante', with *La buona figliuola*, an adaptation of Richardson's *Pamela* (on which he had already based a spoken comedy in 1750) for the composer E. G. Duni. The poignant, tuneful setting of the same text by Niccolò Piccinni for Rome four years later captured the simple goodness of its heroine so aptly that the opera quickly became an international sensation.

Galuppi's success with opera buffa during the 1750s had for the most part been confined to Italian stages, but during the 1760s the best new comic operas emanating from Italy, such as his setting of Pietro Chiari's *Il marchese villano* (1762), spread quickly to foreign theatres, especially those in Central Europe. Sometimes these works were performed in Italian, but just as often they were translated into the language of the local audience. Sacchini's most popular opera buffa, *L'isola d'amore* (Rome, 1766) was given abroad in French, German, Spanish, Danish, Polish, Dutch, Swedish, and Russian.

Italian buffa companies soon established themselves at courts abroad that had previously cultivated opera seria, and both Italian and non-Italian composers at these courts contributed important new works to the genre. Florian Gassmann's setting of Goldoni's *L'amore artigiano* for Vienna in 1767 enjoyed the same international success achieved by the best works of Galuppi, Sacchini, and Piccinni. But, more typically, even very fine contributions such as the comic operas Joseph Haydn (1732–1809) composed at Eszterháza, beginning with his setting of Goldoni's *Lo speziale* in 1768, did not circulate as readily as works emanating from Italy.

France before Grétry

At the start of the eighteenth century, comic opera at Paris consisted of an indigenous form of popular entertainment at the small theatres active at the city's two annual fairs, the St Germain (3 February to Palm Sunday) and the St Laurent (mid-June to September). Called 'comédies en vaudevilles', they consisted of spoken plays interspersed with well-known tunes ('vaudevilles', which circulated in great numbers both orally and in print in the seventeenth and eighteenth centuries), now outfitted with new texts. Dances, instrumental pieces, and parodies of Lully's operas supplemented the vaudeville tunes. Known collectively as the Théâtres de la Foire, they enjoyed immense popularity, and the rival institutions under government monopoly—the Opéra and the Comédie-Française—did their utmost to hinder the fair theatres, mostly by restricting their ability to employ vocal music in their offerings.

In 1715 the Théâtres de la Foire were brought under a single management, called the Théâtre de l'Opéra-Comique. That same year Louis XIV died. One of the first theatrical modifications undertaken by the regent, Philippe of Orléans, was to re-establish the Comédie-Italienne in 1716. It moved into the Foire St Laurent in 1723, and performed there until 1762, when it merged with the Opéra-Comique and moved to the Hôtel de Bourgogne. Between 1724 and 1762 the Opéra-Comique managed to persevere at the Foire St Germain despite the temporary suppressions of its activities engineered by the Comédie-Française. The witty plays supplied by Le Sage, d'Orneval, and others were to serve as a repository for later phases of French comic opera. In their own day, the vaudevilles that continued to be the musical mainstay of these comedies were arranged and orchestrated by composers (including Rameau) who also provided some music of their own.

The famous Querelle des Bouffons that erupted in Paris in 1752 and lasted for nearly two years had no direct connection with French comic opera. It had been touched off by a performance by an Italian troupe of Pergolesi's *La serva padrona*. The logical basis of comparison with the Italian manner represented by Pergolesi's intermezzi, to French minds, was the offerings of the Opéra, the only through-composed music permitted on stage in Paris. And when Jean-Jacques Rousseau (1712–78) took it into his head to produce a new French work in the spirit of Italian opera, the result was also a piece sung throughout, his 'intermède' *Le Devin du village*, first performed before the court at Fontainebleau in October 1752. But this genial and touching work has virtually nothing in common with French operatic practice (which Rousseau vilified a year later in his *Lettre sur la musique française*).

Apart from its own merits, which kept it high in public favour well into the next century, Rousseau's intermède also provided a stimulus to the Foire theatres. The next year, Antoine Dauvergne's one-act intermède *Les Troqueurs* scored a triumph at the St Laurent; it turned decisively to the Italian models Rousseau had embraced, but used spoken dialogue rather than recitative (as was obligatory at both Foire theatres). Subsequent works followed this lead and also gradually eliminated the vaudeville in favour of newly composed brief tunes called 'ariettes'. The new works came to be called 'comédies mêlées d'ariettes' and represent a new and distinctively French category of comic opera that we now refer to as 'opéra comique'. The major figure in its early cultivation was, surprisingly, not French but Italian. Egidio Duni (1709–75), who between 1735 and 1755 had made a name for himself as a composer of opera seria in Italy, felt the pull of Paris and of French comic opera while at the Frenchified court of Parma. There he composed Anseaume's *Le Peintre amoureux de son modèle* for the Opéra-Comique in 1757, one of the first and most successful of the new 'comédies', in which only a few vaudevilles are left to mingle with newly composed numbers of considerable colour and variety.

After the merger of the Opéra-Comique and the Comédie-Italienne in 1762 Duni continued to supply popular new operas. Two other important figures worked in friendly rivalry with him after 1759. Pierre-Alexandre Monsigny (1729–1817) contributed two path-breaking works to the new stage. *Le Roi et le fermier* (1762), based on a play by Robert Dodsley, enlarged the dramatic weight of Rousseau's opposition of healthy rustic innocence and corrupt courtly mores. In so doing it revealed new powers of social and political criticism. It also contains an impressive storm scene that displays Monsigny's natural flair for orchestral colour. *Le Déserteur* (1769) is Monsigny's finest work, a high point in musical and dramatic characterization in the new genre. Its serious plot, leavened by the comic eccentricities of Montauciel, maintains tension up to the closing moments of the opera, already adumbrating the dramaturgy of the rescue opéras of the Revolutionary period. Monsigny's librettist for both these works, the playwright Michel-Jean Sedaine (1719–97), was responsible for much of their novelty of plot, character, and ambience.

The composer and chess-player François-André Philidor (1726–95) equalled the innovatory contributions of Duni and Monsigny to opéra comique. Decidedly Italianate, he explored a variety of technical resources in his theatrical works (which include his impressive tragedy performed at the Opéra, *Ernelinde, princesse de Norvège* of 1767). The many imaginative numbers in his best opéra comique, *Tom Jones* (1765), include characteristic ensembles that skilfully differentiate the participants, most notably the deeply felt farewell of Tom and Sophie that leads into a richly wrought septet. The plot's dramatic momentum (somewhat stinted in Poinsinet's libretto, which Sedaine was called upon to improve) culminates in a grand obbligato recitative and dramatic aria for the heroine, a full-blooded Italian 'scena' of unprecedented sweep and intensity in the world of opéra comique.

England

A kind of popular opera similar to the turn-of-the-century French 'comédie en vaudevilles' developed in England in response to visits paid by players from the Foire theatres to London between 1718 and 1726. Taking the French plays with popular tunes as a model, in 1728 John Gay (1685–1732) created an instant sensation with the *Beggar's Opera*, the first and most memorable work in a new genre that came to be called 'ballad opera'. The more liberal cast of English life allowed for a far more direct and pungent political dimension to theatrical works than was possible in France: Gay's play draws direct parallels between its cast of thieves, fences, whores, and venal officers from the lower reaches of London life and representatives of the city's high-end institutions—the government, the professions, and Italian opera seria. The work's sixty-nine musical numbers are drawn from a wide range of sources: dances; traditional English, Irish, and Scottish airs; popular broadside ballads, such as were sold by street singers; and published French vaudevilles.

A flood of imitations and successors followed close on the heels of Gay's opera. The elements of satire and burlesque remained strong in many of these works, for example several by Henry Fielding that appeared between 1730 and 1734. But serious, naïve, historical, rustic, and patriotic themes also found in the ballad opera a congenial format. The farce, always a mainstay on the popular stage, is best represented by Charles Coffey's *The Devil to Pay* (1731), in which a magician switches the personalities of a hapless landowner's shrewish lady and the long-suffering wife of a brutal shoemaker in order to bring peace and civility to both households.

After mid-century the English ballad opera began to yield to comic operas with more and more of their music by a single composer. The transition received decisive impetus when John Beard took over Covent Garden in 1760 and began at once to set opera before spoken plays in his repertoire. Thomas Arne's and Isaac Bickerstaffe's *Thomas and Sally*, produced by Beard that November, offered an unusual but successful attempt at an Italianate brand of English-language comic opera with sung recitative. But, as in France, opera with spoken dialogue established itself as the norm. Arne and Bickerstaffe produced one of the best examples two years later with *Love in a Village*. It illustrates both the priority of dialogue over music in such works and also the English fondness for the musical pasticcio: only nineteen of its forty-three numbers are by Arne; the rest are drawn from fifteen other composers. Another talented English composer, the young Charles Dibdin, collaborated with Bickerstaffe on *Lionel and Clarissa*, produced at Covent Garden in early 1768, a work that introduced the dramatic ensemble already familiar in France and Italy into English opera. Later that year Dibdin abandoned Beard for Garrick and Drury Lane, where he and Bickerstaffe produced an even finer opera, *The Padlock*, in November.

As early as 1736 Italian intermezzi had begun to appear between the acts of opera seria productions in London. By 1748 the first full-length Italian opere buffe had made their way to England, but Italian models had little impact until Galuppi's works arrived in the early 1760s. At that time the King's Theatre decided to set up a second company to perform opera buffa in addition to its opera seria company. By the 1780s, the comic operas of Paisiello were setting the tone there, rather than the seria offerings that had so long defined operatic taste among London's élite.

Germany and Austria to 1778

For much of the eighteenth century, a troupe of itinerant actors was the characteristic form that theatrical life took in German-speaking lands. In the arena of opera, a stable institution like the Hamburg enterprise, which cultivated serious opera wholly or at least partly in German until its demise in 1738, was exceptional. Until the 1760s, a standing company at a single private or public stage, which was to be the norm during the nineteenth century, was limited to courts devoted to Italian opera. For the rest, travel was a necessity, forced on even the best companies by the relatively small size of the population centres in German-speaking lands. Travel was not only arduous and unpleasant, but also linked actors in public consciousness with disreputable bands of roving entertainers, mountebanks, and charlatans. Official disapproval of the professional actor in Germany was routinely voiced, particularly from Protestant pulpits.

A German theatrical company was normally organized by an impresario, called its *Prinzipal*, who ran the enterprise at his or her own risk and profit. The arrangements he or she struck with different courts or municipalities varied from simple permission to the concession of a theatre or opera house, together with its appurtenances, and possibly even a subvention. Events that drew large crowds of potential spectators, such as the annual fairs held at Leipzig and Frankfurt am Main, were especially attractive. Less fortunate companies found it necessary to cater to their public's often unrefined taste, which ran in the direction of rough humour, pranks, physical violence, and the improvisatory spirit familiar from the *commedia dell'arte*. These features continued throughout the eighteenth century in the popular theatres of Austria, southern Germany, and Bohemia, most notably in the person of a great actor-principal such as Josef Stranitzky, who created a local replacement for Harlequin as the Salzburg peasant Hanswurst. Music was incorporated in some modest way into many of these entertainments.

In northern Germany the traits on which Stranitzky and his successors continued to trade began to disappear towards the mid-eighteenth century, beginning with the reforms of Caroline Neuber, who collaborated with the Leipzig professor J. C. Gottsched in banishing Harlequin and his excesses from her stage. One of her actors, J. F. Schönemann, left Neuber to form his own company in 1739. Four years later at Berlin his troupe performed a translation of Coffey's *The Devil to Pay* (1731). The experiment remained an isolated one, but Schönemann along with other principals steadily built up his musical offerings in the form of ballet and pantomime. Another impresario, Heinrich Gottfried Koch, asked the poet C. F. Weisse to retranslate Coffey's ballad opera, and solicited a new setting from his music director Johann Standfuss to replace the original English tunes Schönemann had used. The success of this version at Leipzig in 1752 led to a bitter pamphlet war, initiated by Gottsched. This pale imitation of the Guerre des Bouffons succeeded only in kindling even greater public interest in the new genre.

After the disruptions of the Seven Years War (1756–63), a new and characteristic form of German comic opera established itself as a permanent part of theatrical life. The term 'Singspiel', the common designation for German opera with spoken dialogue and a comic or sentimental plot, is actually a modern application of the term, one that became stabilized only in the nineteenth century. The new genre was born at Leipzig in 1766 when Koch persuaded Weisse to revise his translation of *The Devil to Pay*, now renamed *Die verwandelten Weiber*, and enlisted Johann Adam Hiller (1728–1804) to recompose much of it. The instant and overwhelming popularity of the new version led to further collaborations. The sequel to Coffey's ballad opera, *The Merry Cobbler*, was first (*Der lustige Schuster*, 1766), but then with *Lottchen am Hofe* (1767) and *Die Liebe auf dem Lande* (1768) Weisse turned to the rustic-sentimental opéra comique as a more refined model, one he himself had experienced first-hand at Paris during the war years. His collaboration with Hiller and Koch reached its zenith with *Die Jagd* (1770), very popular well into the nineteenth century and still occasionally revived in Germany.

Essentially, these early Singspiele were spoken comedies, comprising large casts and extensive dialogue, to which modest musical numbers had been added in order to strengthen the drama's ambience and to help delineate its characters. When drawing on models from opéra comique, Weisse and others tended to choose early works that made few dramatic demands on the music. Hiller kept his music tuneful and deliberately simple, owing partly to the idealized *Volkston* of the operas but more especially to the indifferent musical skills of the actor-singers in Koch's troupe, only one of whom had a trained voice. This enforced simplicity not only made a virtue of necessity but also made it attractive for nearly every theatrical company across northern and southern Germany, no matter how modest its resources, to take up the new genre.

The typical German actor-singer was no match for the singers in the wandering Italian companies dedicated to performing both opera seria and opera buffa in Germany. Such a troupe under Pietro Mingotti had plied the same annual fairs at Leipzig in the 1740s that Koch's company worked in the 1760s and early 1770s. Really excellent singers in German companies and the kind of music that took full advantage of their talents tended to be found mostly in troupes attached to stabler court and civic stages after 1770.

In northern and central Germany the Hiller–Weisse prototype found many imitators, including especially E. W. Wolf, Anton Schweitzer, and Hiller's pupils C. G. Neefe and J. F. Reichardt, both of whom returned at least in part to the farcical spirit Weisse and Hiller had subordinated to French-derived rustic sensibility. Schweitzer marked a high point in this vein with *Die Dorfgala* (1772), as did the Gotha Kapellmeister Georg Benda with *Der Jahrmarkt* (1775). But both are better known for their contributions to serious opera in German and to the melodrama.

After Koch's death in 1775 the Singspiel experienced its most significant development as a public art-form at Berlin, especially after the arrival of Johann André as music director of the Döbbelin company in 1777. André's style, without forsaking Hiller's tuneful simplicity, strove for greater variety, seen also in his choice of librettos. He was the first to set his friend Goethe's *Erwin und Elmire* (1775, based on the Ballad of Edwin and Angelica in Goldsmith's *Vicar of Wakefield*), and later collaborated with the most popular new librettist of the era, C. F. Bretzner, who sought out new sources of inspiration in the exotic (*Belmont und Constanze, oder Die Entführung aus dem Serail*) and the supernatural (*Das wütende Heer, Das Irrlicht*). In contrast to Weisse's librettos, Bretzner's were taken up eagerly by Viennese composers, and, in exchange, by the early 1780s companies like Döbbelin's were beginning to perform new Austrian and Italian operas as their musical resources improved.

In southern and western Germany composers of Singspiele at first took their lead from the North. The new genre was taken up by travelling companies that had hitherto relied mostly on French comic operas in translation. The most important among them was the troupe first headed by Sebastiani and later brought to prominence by Theobald Marchand, which played chiefly at Mainz, Strasbourg, Frankfurt, and Mannheim. At the Stuttgart court, Christian Ludwig Dieter set several North German librettos that won abiding popularity there, including Bretzner's *Belmont und Constanze* (1784). At Munich the amateur composer Lukas Schubaur was the most significant contributor of new Singspiele to the Munich court's efforts in the 1780s to establish a creditable German opera company alongside its French and Italian establishments.

From 1728 to 1742 Vienna's Kärntnertortheater—like the Burgtheater under direct imperial control, but larger and less exclusive—was rented out to private companies that gave Italian comic operas and improvised German plays with intermixed music. Ballet and singing figured prominently in the repertoire of Felix Kurz, who at Vienna and elsewhere made his reputation as Bernardon, a less boorish version of his godfather Stranitzky's Hanswurst. Music had been an ingredient in the Viennese popular theatre since the beginning of the century, and after 1750 impresarios like Kurz began to seek out new music for works in this repertoire, including Haydn's lost *Der neue krumme Teufel* of 1758. That year, incensed by the indecency and bald social criticism in Kurz's offerings, the empress summarily banned all such spectacles.

At the Burgtheater, in addition to opera and ballet, a troupe of French actors were maintained by the court, whose offerings expanded in the 1750s to include the latest opéras comiques from Paris. At first the theatre's intendant, Count Giacomo Durazzo, wanted only vaudeville pieces from his contact at Paris, the playwright Favart, even though their popular tunes needed amending in order to please Viennese ears. But by 1759 fashion directed his attention to the newer *comédies mêlées d'ariettes*. In order to have these works performed properly at Vienna, Durazzo sought Favart's help in recruiting new singers, and Gluck was asked to arrange and, increasingly, compose new scores for them. In all he composed seven new operas and partially recomposed many others. Together his works dominated the French stage at Vienna in the early 1760s. His contributions reached their peak with his two 'Turkish' operas, *Le Cadi dupé* (1761) and *La Rencontre imprévue* (1763). Both circulated widely in translation throughout Germany and Austria.

Opera Buffa in the Age of Paisiello and Mozart

Our picture of the state of opera buffa during the last quarter of the eighteenth century is naturally dominated by the three great operas on which Mozart and Da Ponte collaborated, but both these men were somewhat unusual practitioners of the genre, writing for two cities (Vienna and Prague) far more choice and exacting in musical connoisseurship than most other European centres.

For a portrait of opera buffa at its most characteristic, one must turn to cities like Naples, Venice, Rome, Parma, Bologna, or even St Petersburg, and to composers such as Piccinni, Anfossi, Guglielmi, Cimarosa, and above all Paisiello. All five were trained at Naples and pursued international careers that were concerned as much with opera seria as with opera buffa. Each composer began by writing comic operas and intermezzi for smaller theatres at Naples and elsewhere. This served to establish a reputation that eventually led to a commission for an opera seria. Pietro Guglielmi (1728–1804) provided comic works for Naples and Rome from 1757 to 1762 before finally breaking into the San Carlo with his first serious work, Metastasio's beloved *Olimpiade*, in 1763. From then on he regularly produced three or four operas each year, both comic and serious.

The career of Giovanni Paisiello (1740–1816) is indicative of how, despite an abiding consensus over the prestige and high fees composing an opera seria ought to command, comic opera came to assume equal importance in establishing a composer's international reputation. In Paisiello's case this occurred with *La frascatana* (1774), which conquered first all of Italy and then all of Europe. Another successful comic opera, *Dal finto il vero*, produced at Naples in 1776, marked the first time that the Neapolitan court attended a performance at the Teatro Nuovo. That same year Paisiello was appointed *maestro di cappella* to the Russian court of Catherine II. Like other Italian composers who occupied this post before and after him, he was expected to supply music of all kinds, although opera came first. The court had sponsored opera seria since 1736, and the travelling company of G. B. Locatelli had brought opera buffa to St Petersburg in 1757 (presented not at the big New Court Theatre but at the Theatre by the Summer Palace). And under Catherine opéra comique had been added in 1764; not only was it popular with the aristocratic class, nearly all of whom spoke French with ease, it also had a marked impact on comic opera in Russian, which used spoken dialogue rather than recitative.

At first Paisiello's energies were channelled in the direction of his own inclinations—towards serious opera. On his way to Russia he had stopped in Vienna to pay a visit to Metastasio, and it was a libretto by the Caesarean Poet, *Nitteti*, that Paisiello set as his inaugural opera for the Russian Court Theatre. But pressure to compose comic operas eventually redirected his activities. After 1778 he wrote only one further serious opera for St Petersburg, compared with six comic operas. Among these six are several of Paisiello's best-known works, chief among them *Il barbiere di Siviglia* (1782). *Gli astrologi immaginari* (1779, later retitled *I filosofi immaginari*) became a favourite of Catherine's. She considered herself completely unmusical, but she found her indifferent ear engaged and focused at last by Paisiello's irresistible comic style, with musical gestures that were simple and transparent, yet also vivid and forceful. When Catherine renewed Paisiello's four-year contract in 1780 she granted him the right to choose his own librettos. (Her decree that an opera last no more than two hours remained in force, however.) That same year she took her entire Italian company to a conference with Joseph II, who was so impressed with Paisiello's music that he ordered copies of his operas, even though there was as yet no Italian company at Vienna to perform them. Paisiello's works from the beginning were to figure prominently in the offerings of the new Italian troupe established by Joseph in 1783 to succeed the National-Singspiel, and Paisiello himself contributed to the enterprise when he passed through Vienna on his way back to Italy in 1784. Local musicians, as usual, mounted cabals against the new work, *Il Re Teodoro a Venezia*, but these were squashed by the personal intervention of the emperor.

The comic operas of Paisiello and his contemporaries had by the early 1780s established a relatively stable set of strategies and traits. Arias no longer predominated (in the 1750s they accounted for three-quarters of a typical opera buffa's numbers), and in several cases they barely outnumber ensembles. Aria types began to change in both form and function. The two-tempo rondò was borrowed from serious opera to show the skills of the leading soprano and tenor. A special kind of writing for the comic bass evolved, alternating patter, leaps, drastic gestures, and repeated emphatic cadence figures, enlivened by melodic interplay with the orchestra. And in general arias grew simpler and shorter, a tendency that proved especially effective in sentimental comedies such as

Paisiello's *Nina, o sia La pazza per amore* (1789). As in opera seria of the time, simple recitative was reduced wherever possible. *Nina*, whose text derives from a popular opéra comique, took the unprecedented step of substituting spoken dialogue in Italian for recitative. With the reduction in recitative, important developments in the plot were incorporated into action ensembles and even into arias.

At St Petersburg Paisiello had limited all his comic operas to two acts, perhaps in response to the empress's insistence on brevity, but other composers also came to prefer two rather than three acts by the early 1780s. Ever since Goldoni had introduced the Act 2 finale into opera buffa, the third act had been inclining towards anaemia. In the new, two-act format, the finale of imbroglio migrated to the end of Act 1 and a new kind of finale incorporating the denouement took its place at the end of the second and final act. These numbers grew considerably and developed formal features that set them apart from virtually every other kind of musical pattern deployed in opera. The action unfolds in a series of well-defined sections, alternately active and reflective. Changes in musical colour and tone clearly demarcate important dramatic junctures, usually forecast by the poet with a change in verse type. Each section describes a closed tonal unit and exploits its own set of themes. So involved did some finales become in the 1780s that several run to more than a thousand bars. Balancing the sections and calculating their cumulative effect required the composer to develop a command of large-scale dramatic sensibility.

As opera buffa grew in prestige and took on greater cultural significance, composers started to take more care in choosing texts and subjects. Good comic librettists became an object of desire for court theatres as well as individual composers. Literary feuds and send-ups, previously the province of serious opera or the spoken theatre, now responded to the lively interest at all levels of society aroused by opera buffa. In the 1770s composers with limited powers of musical characterization like Pasquale Anfossi (1727–97) could still gain widespread recognition by writing limpid, mellifluous scores to well-made librettos that exploited familiar comic situations. In Anfossi's case, international acclaim came with his setting of Giuseppe Petrosellini's *L'incognita perseguitata* (1773). But his rather bland style could not meet the growing demand for sharper musical definition to situation and character. His fortunes took a turn for the worse in the 1780s, first in London during his tenure as music director of the King's Theatre from 1782 to 1786, then in Rome from 1787 to 1790, when he abandoned theatrical composition altogether.

The finest stage for the cultivation of opera buffa was created at Vienna's Burgtheater by Joseph II as a replacement for the National-Singspiel in 1783. Joseph's purpose in reinstating opera buffa—absent from the imperial stages since 1776—was not to nurture local productivity of Italian comic opera, but rather to acquiesce to what the nobles and middle class had always wanted. The emphasis was not to be on composers and new works but on singers. 'Blessed are they that hunger and thirst after Italian opera singers', ran one of the Beatitudes that a local wag published in the *Wiener Realzeitung*, 'for they shall be satisfied at the cost of high salaries'. It took the economically minded emperor a year or two to learn that by the 1780s excellent opera buffa productions were no longer to be obtained on the cheap, but learn he did, and he even initiated several negotiations himself for first-class singers on his trips abroad.

At a stroke Count Durazzo was able to engage two of the greatest singer-actors to be had, the prima donna Nancy Storace and the primo buffo Francesco Benucci, both singing at the San Samuele in Venice at the time. Two crucial male voice-types demanded and found first-class talents—a leading tenor in the person of Michael Kelly, and a basso buffo in Francesco Bussani. The initial absence of first-rate sopranos to supplement Nancy Storace's contribution was eventually redressed with the acquisition of Luisa Laschi in 1784 and Celeste Coltellini in 1785.

If many of these names sound familiar, it is because by the time Laschi arrived at the start of the second season, virtually the entire first cast of Mozart's *Le nozze di Figaro* had been assembled. During the two years leading up to the première of *Figaro*, these singers were welded into the finest buffa ensemble anywhere. Without this process of integration, the extraordinary demands made by Mozart and Da Ponte in a four-hour opera filled with action from beginning to end would have been close to unthinkable. Caroline Pichler wrote as follows about the troupe at the Burgtheater: 'Under the leadership of the monarch our stage was with respect to Italian opera perhaps the finest in existence, not even Italy excepted, and the second and third sopranos from our opera returned to Italy to appear everywhere as first sopranos.'

For the first two seasons, the repertoire at the Burgtheater was almost completely derivative. Rather than commissioning new works, the stage turned at once to a dozen of the most popular Italian comic operas from the past decade. Choice of an inaugural opera fell on Salieri's most popular opera buffa, *La scuola de'gelosi*, but decisive in this respect was not so much the composer's powerful position under Joseph's benevolent protection as the sensation Nancy Storace had created in the role of the Contessa in a production of the opera at the San Samuele in early 1783, just prior to her arrival at Vienna.

At this time there was little demand for opera seria in Vienna. The emperor, who considered it both expensive and exclusive, allowed it only on special state occasions. When he hired Lorenzo Da Ponte (1749–1838) as theatrical poet, it was not to pen celebratory *feste teatrali* but to revise and create opera buffa texts. A rivalry between Da Ponte and the librettist Giambattista Casti (1724–1803) sprang up, part of the general atmosphere of intrigue at Vienna involving composers, performers, journalists, courtiers, and theatre-goers. Casti's literary activities at Vienna began auspiciously with *Il Re Teodoro* for Paisiello in 1784, Da Ponte's inauspiciously with *Un ricco di giorno* for Salieri. So vile did Salieri consider the text that he swore he would rather hack off all of his fingers than set to music another line written by Da Ponte. The fiasco led directly to his collaboration with Casti on *La grotta di Trofonio*, one of his best texts and an attractive field for the exercise of Salieri's superior abilities in musical characterization and the application of orchestral colour. Da Ponte, forced to work with other composers, recouped his position in 1785 with a brilliant adaptation of Goldoni's *Le Bourru bienfaisant* for Martín y Soler.

It is difficult indeed to believe Da Ponte's story, first related in his memoirs in 1819, that he and Mozart offered their new opera based on Beaumarchais's *Le Mariage de Figaro* to the emperor as a *fait accompli* after Da Ponte had allayed Joseph's misgivings about its suitability as a source. Mozart, like other composers of his day, seldom undertook an operatic project without an agreement with a particular stage and knowledge of an intended cast. Whatever the circumstances of its origin, *Le nozze di Figaro* (1786) turned out to be far less pungent as a socio-political statement than many of Casti's texts. The real challenge offered by Beaumarchais's intricate plot was also its greatest attraction for the Viennese: it pushed the resources of librettist, composer, executants, and audience to unprecedented heights of sophistication. The way had been paved to an extent by the abiding popularity at Vienna of Paisiello's *Barbiere*, but even familiarity with the characters and situations of the first part of Beaumarchais's trilogy would not have been worth much without the superior aesthetic capacities of Burgtheater audiences. 'They sought intellectual pleasure', Caroline Pichler recalls, 'not a mere pastime; they wanted their feelings to be moved, and not simply to exercise their wits in finding fault. They came with fresh receptivity to the theatre.'

It is tempting to assert that with the likes of Salieri's *Grotta di Trofonio*,

Martín y Soler's *Burbero di buon cuore*, and above all Mozart's *Nozze di Figaro* the Burgtheater achieved a breakthrough in the history of opera buffa. Actually, it might be more helpful to suggest that through a fortuitous combination of circumstances and talent it moved the genre a little closer to our own very selective conception of it. All three of these operas were regarded at the time as music for 'Kenner' (connoisseurs). They made demands even on Vienna's most musically astute ears as had few if any earlier comic operas. They also placed unprecedented demands on a company of actor-singers brimming with dramatic as well as musical gifts. Both Martín y Soler's *Burbero* and Mozart's *Figaro* enjoyed revivals later in the late 1780s at the Burgtheater, and it must be regarded as a significant compliment that the theatre managers agreed to a production of *Don Giovanni* in 1787. Even a theme as dubious as the old Don Juan story could now appear on the emperor's most exclusive stage, for by virtue of Mozart's score it now shared in a Viennese conception of opera buffa as a fully-fledged category of high art.

Don Giovanni had come into being through the spectacular popularity Mozart's music to *Figaro* enjoyed at the Nostitz Theatre in Prague, where a small but skilled Italian company, organized by Pasquale Bondini, had been performing since 1783. In choosing to work with the Don Juan legend, Da Ponte and Mozart were following the lead of Giovanni Bertati and Giuseppe Gazzaniga, whose *Don Giovanni, o sia Il convitato di pietra* had been given in early 1787 at the San Moisè in Venice. Properly speaking, the tale did not belong on either stage—its roots lay deep in the popular theatre, and even the efforts of Molière and Goldoni to bring it into high art traditions had not been entirely successful. In Venice, the opera slipped in as a one-act pendant to a pasticcio by Bertati. By contrast, all of Prague expected the new opera commissioned from Mozart and Da Ponte to equal or outdo the sensation created by *Figaro*—which had gratified the rich musical palates of Bohemian connoisseurs even more fully than those of its Viennese audiences. Under these happy circumstances Mozart and Da Ponte decided to create a show that would deploy an unprecedented musical arsenal in order to subdue this most notorious and coarse portrait of unrepentant licentiousness to the strictures of the legitimate theatre.

There has been much discussion about whether *Don Giovanni* ought to be regarded as an opera buffa at all. Its inclusion of high-born personages like Don Ottavio and Donna Anna is by no means unprecedented in opera buffa, nor is that of a 'mezzo carrattere' like Donna Elvira. The real problem lies in the scenes most directly beholden to the old legend—

the 'frame' that Da Ponte took over directly from Bertati, comprising the on-stage murder of the Commendatore and Giovanni's descent to eternal punishment. For there was no way around the fact that Giovanni must be dragged off to hell in the end. He was and had to remain a phenomenon to be regarded from a distance with a mixture of fascination and horror, and—in contrast to a small-time libertine like Count Almaviva—no mirror of social comportment held up to him could possibly induce Giovanni to mend his ways.

Yet despite this essential stratum from the legend's cultivation in the popular theatre, Da Ponte labelled his libretto with the term Goldoni had routinely used for his comic operas, 'dramma giocoso per musica', and Mozart called his score exactly what he was to call Così fan tutte, an 'opera buffa'. Structurally, Don Giovanni is as much a part of buffa practice as are the other two Da Ponte operas. One notices a steady progression in the three works towards tighter control over large-scale dramatic shape. There are a number of significant parallels between the acts. Following Gazzaniga, Mozart used the 'Introduzione'—a compact counterpart to the finale—in order to give clear musical shape to the vivid opening scene of Don Giovanni. Mozart also placed unusual musical weight on the final confrontation with the Commendatore, which takes place in a ponderous and oversized central section in the Act 2 finale. These extraordinary means are justified, none the less, by the scene's powerful and overarching dramatic and musical ties with the dark hues of the slow introduction to the overture and the opening scene.

Edward Dent called Così fan tutte (1790) 'the best of all Da Ponte's librettos and the most exquisite work of art among Mozart's operas'. It is in fact one of the most 'literary' of all Da Ponte's librettos, aswim in classical allusions. It is also one of his most original; Da Ponte nearly always preferred to rework an existing theatrical piece, but no direct model has been found for Così fan tutte. Appropriately, an early rumour suggested that he had developed the story from an actual event then making the rounds among Vienna's gossips, for, despite its Neapolitan setting, the opera is the purest product to come from the intensive cultivation of opera buffa as a direct expression of Viennese musical and theatrical life.

The act as a whole now serves as the most significant constructive unit. Although he knew who was to take each role well ahead of time, Mozart composed the opera's ensembles first (which are plentiful to an unprecedented degree), then went back and tackled the arias. They remained in a state of flux right up to the première. An entrance aria for Despina was part of the plan for Act 1 until quite late. Replacing a huge, brilliant aria for Guglielmo near the end of the same act with the simple number that now stands there ('Non siate ritrosi') seems also to have been a late decision. These adjustments, which worked directly against the singers' presumed prerogatives, helped ensure an impeccable sense of musical balance in the first act that Mozart himself never equalled. For the nineteenth century, the cynical worldliness of Don Alfonso and his crony Despina was a source of endless trouble and distress. Yet the moral of the story, an object lesson in pragmatism where matters of the heart are concerned, aptly reflects the enlightened cosmopolitanism that had become a way of life in Josephine Vienna: the best way for the young men to revenge themselves on their faithless ladies is to marry them, Don Alfonso counsels, for 'happy is the man who takes up everything by its fair side, and in trials and trouble adopts reason as his guide'. No opera buffa emanating from Italy ever traded in such hard-headed realism.

Emperor Joseph II died on 20 February 1790, less than a month after the première of *Così fan tutte*. His successor, Leopold II, showed no interest in perpetuating the rich and sophisticated brand of opera buffa his brother had placed at the centre of Viennese operatic life. Eventually, opera seria and the dramatic ballet made their way back to the Burgtheater. The most memorable operatic event of Leopold's reign came when, like Paisiello, Domenico Cimarosa (1749–1801) stopped in Vienna on his way back from his years of service at the court of Catherine II. Leopold, who had met Cimarosa at Florence in the course of the composer's journey to Russia, asked him to compose an opera buffa to a text supplied by Bertati, *Il matrimonio segreto*. So greatly did it please the emperor that he not only had the entire opera repeated on the day of its première (7 February 1792) but also appointed Cimarosa as his Kapellmeister. The opera pokes fun at the efforts of a rich merchant to marry his two daughters into the aristocracy. Cimarosa treated the subject with a melodic inventiveness and sparkle that confirmed his position as the leading composer of opera buffa between Mozart and Rossini. But the fact that this spirited and utterly Neapolitan work received its première on the same stage as *Figaro* and *Così fan tutte* brings it no closer to the unique Viennese chapter in the genre's development that ended with the death of Joseph II.

French Opera from Grétry to the Revolution

During the two decades preceding the Revolution in France opéra comique continued as a stable element in Parisian theatrical life at the Comédie-Italienne. In 1780 the licence of the Comédie-Italienne was renewed, including the prior prohibition of Italian opera and restrictions on the use of choral music. While the former was fairly effective (one had to travel to Versailles or to Fontainebleau to hear the latest operas of Paisiello, done there in French translation), by the end of the 1780s the chorus and other resources formerly associated with the Opéra had become important ingredients in the new, more ambitious, and more serious look that opéra comique had come to adopt. In 1783 the enterprise opened a new and larger theatre, the Théâtre-Italien (later renamed the Salle Favart), which accommodated over 2,000 spectators and also made allowances for the larger orchestra that newer scores demanded. The stratification of Parisian operatic affairs endemic to the monopoly system that had been in force for the entire century began to break down during the 1780s, particularly with the rise of the so-called 'Boulevard theatres'—smaller institutions in the Boulevard du Temple.

The musical figure who dominated the scene during both the 1770s and 1780s was a young Belgian composer from Liège, André-Ernest-Modeste Grétry (1741–1813). Through the generosity of a local patron Grétry had received training in composition at Rome, and an Italian pre-occupation with melody remained a strong trait throughout his career. While in Geneva in 1766 he became acquainted with opéra comique and, armed with a recommendation from Voltaire, he set off for Paris in 1767. Several early successes there established him at once in public favour. Not a great harmonist, Grétry cultivated an apprehensible yet free, asymmetrical brand of melody that blended Italian suavity with the sturdy simplicity of popular French traditions.

Grétry's chief collaborator until 1777 was Jean-François Marmontel (1723–99), whose well-known *Contes moraux* (1755–9) were already a favourite source for plots (as were the tales of La Fontaine). Marmontel's texts for Grétry idealize a family-centred morality that found its byword in the famous quartet sung round the table in one of their most popular works, *Lucile* (1769), 'Où peut-on être mieux, qu'au sein de sa famille?' Marmontel introduced other features that became characteristic of the works of Grétry and his contemporaries, such as the *ingénu* from unspoilt reaches of the New World (*Le Huron*, 1768), or a new kind of heroine whose unimpeachable virtuousness now takes an active role in guiding the intrigue (*Zémire et Azor*, 1771, a comédie-ballet based on the story of Beauty and the Beast).

In 1773, with *Le Magnifique*, Grétry began his long collaboration with Sedaine, who had already supplied Philidor and especially Monsigny with some of their best texts. He proved equally effective in inciting

Grétry to musico-dramatic innovation, beginning with the very overture of their first opera—an extended pantomime scene in the streets of Florence setting the plot in motion before a word has been spoken or sung. Sedaine did not shrink from vigorous socio-political statements in his librettos, but his chief concerns were with novel settings, strong subjects, and extended dramatic tableaux that inspired the composer to a fluid combination of musical techniques, long a hallmark of the Opéra. These tendencies began with a rather daring experiment in literary and musical archaism—*Aucassin et Nicollete* of 1779, a darkling tale of passion and filial disobedience set in thirteenth-century France. In his greatest popular triumph with Grétry, *Richard Cœur-de-Lion* (1784), the royalist Sedaine established a vogue for plots involving imprisonment, battle, and rescue, which collaterally involved significantly enlarging the size of the cast and the role played by the chorus. Grétry made memorable use of his predilection for recurring melodies with the Romance played by the faithful Blondel on his violin, 'Une fièvre brûlante', written explicitly in an antique vein. Also characteristic of the coming age is the simple, triadic melodic style of Blondel's fervent aria 'O Richard! ô mon Roi!'

Sedaine's last two works with Grétry pursue similar paths. *Raoul Barbe-bleue* (1789) deals with a grisly subject scarcely thinkable a decade earlier even on the stage of the Opéra (which had in the meantime witnessed the likes of Salieri's *Les Danaïdes* in 1784). *Guillaume Tell* (1791) offered an opportunity for Sedaine to effect a prudent volte-face as a new order took shape in France, and for the melodist Grétry to turn the chorus into a central dramatic character.

During the 1770s Grétry's command of popular approval with Parisian audiences was unchallenged—the works of his closest rival, Monsigny, were performed scarcely half as often as his. In the 1780s, however, the best works of younger contemporaries began to point up the shortcomings of Grétry's manner—his lack-lustre orchestral palette, for instance, or the occasional carelessness that came from composing in haste. The mysterious Nicolas Dezède (who was not allowed to know anything of his own ancestry) took advantage of another important resource at the Comédie-Italienne, the singer Louise-Rosalie Dugazon. Her untrained soprano voice had earlier won great popularity in Grétry's rustic-sentimental comedies *Lucile* and *Silvain* (1774). The heartfelt, direct pastoral style at which she excelled matched perfectly the manner Dezède adopted in his first opera *Julie* (1772), then perfected in *Les Trois Fermiers* (1777) and more especially its sequel, *Blaise et Babet* (1783), his most successful work.

A young German named Schwarzendorf, writing under the name Jean Paul Martini, brought his extensive experience in composing military music to bear on opéra comique with his *Henri IV* (1774). As weight shifted from the solo aria to grand act-ending ensembles, such additional resources as trumpets, drums, and enlarged chorus had to be contracted for more and more routinely by the Comédie-Italienne. Examples are plentiful in the works of Grétry's chief rival from 1783 to 1790, Nicolas-Marie Dalayrac (1753–1809), especially his chilling political-patriotic *Sargines* of 1788, with a beefed-up brass section punctuating an encomiastic final scene.

German Opera from the National-Singspiel to Die Zauberflöte

In 1778 Joseph II established a company of singers to perform German opera at the Burgtheater—the National-Singspiel. The enterprise was in fact an adjunct to the distinguished National Theatre he had created in 1776 in order to promote German drama. Between its founding and its demise in 1783 the National-Singspiel by and large disappointed the emperor's hopes for a significant outpouring of new German operas from local composers. Mozart's *Die Entführung aus dem Serail* (1782) was an isolated triumph, if a spectacular one. Salieri's deputy, Ignaz Umlauf (1746–96), fared best among local composers. The one-act inaugural opera he wrote for the enterprise, *Die Bergknappen* (1778), shows the richness and variety of styles the Viennese expected, and among his later operas *Die schöne Schusterinn* (1779) and *Der Irrwisch* (1782) enjoyed considerable popularity and were revived at later dates. Salieri himself contributed a very Italianate German opera to the National-Singspiel in 1781, *Der Rauchfangkehrer*, which proved to be the season's greatest attraction. Stephanie the Younger, the poetic mainstay of the undertaking, furnished many of its new German texts; he also translated and adapted copiously from the Italians and French when the National-Singspiel turned to music from abroad to flesh out its repertoire. Vienna, its sympathies clearly in the Italian camp, showed no interest in importing anything more than the texts of North or South German operas.

After the collapse of the National-Singspiel, a second effort was made by the Viennese court to foster German opera, this time at the Kärntnertortheater. During its brief lifetime, from 1785 to 1788, Karl Ditters von Dittersdorf (1739–99) scored a series of unprecedented popular successes on this stage with *Der Apotheker und der Doctor, Der Betrug durch Aberglauben* (both 1786), *Die Liebe im Narrenhause, Hieronymus Knicker* (both 1787), and *Das rote Käppchen* (1788). Their happy blend of the opera buffa style dear to Viennese hearts and the folk-like tunefulness by now associated everywhere with the Singspiel kept these works high in public affection for decades and provided a paradigm for German comic opera outside the tradition of magic opera, for which Dittersdorf showed no interest. Especially popular examples by later Viennese composers include Wenzel Müller's *Die Schwestern von Prag* (1794), Johann Schenk's *Der Dorfbarbier* (1796), and Joseph Weigl's *Die Schweizerfamilie* (1809).

In north Germany the 1780s were arid years for indigenous operatic production as repertoires came ever more under the sway of Viennese and Italian opera. By the 1790s, most successful composers and librettists in the North were writing in imitation of opera buffa and Viennese magic opera. F. W. Gotter's *Die Geisterinsel* (1796), originally intended for Mozart, artfully combined northern and southern traditions, blending careful craftsmanship and literary polish with spectacle, the supernatural, and a mixing of high and low comic elements. It received four settings before the end of the decade, the most important being those of Reichardt (Berlin, 1798) and Johann Rudolf Zumsteeg (Stuttgart, 1798).

Austria's rich popular theatrical tradition of improvised comedy with music was by the 1780s firmly entrenched in Vienna's suburban theatres, all of them under private management. This tradition, indigenous and quite independent of German operatic developments elsewhere, contributed vitally to the character of the magic operas that dominated these theatres in the last decade of the century. Their plots were frequently derived from or inspired by the world of the German *Märchen*, or folk-tale. An early example of the enduring popular appeal at Vienna of operas mixing farce, the supernatural, and spectacle was provided by Philipp Hafner's *Zauberlustspiel* ('magic comedy') *Megära, die förchterliche Hexe* (1764).

When Emanuel Schikaneder (1751–1812) took over the Freihaustheater auf der Wieden in 1789, he initiated a series of farces around a feckless character he himself created on stage, 'der dumme Anton', in order to compete with the tremendous popularity enjoyed by the traditional 'Kasperl' of the actor Johann La Roche, whose antics made Karl Marinelli's Theater in der Leopoldstadt the most successful of the suburban theatres. The same year Schikaneder also mounted a far more substantial new musical work, Paul Wranitzky's *Oberon, König der Elfen*. Like Dittersdorf, Wranitzky here appropriated the resources of Austro-Italian opera buffa for the German stage, but now these elements were put in the service of a story at once exotic, supernatural, and medieval, with traces of Austrian farcical traditions also present in the knight Hüon's squire Scherasmin. Its setting and theme of rescue proved important for later works, including *Die Zauberflöte*. The original libretto, written by the actress Sophie Seyler for the small north German court theatre at Schleswig, had been altered by Karl Giesecke to fit the greater musical demands of Viennese traditions as well as the exciting visual effects with which the rival suburban theatres sought to outdo one another.

Far and away the greatest operatic phenomenon of the decade, *Die Zauberflöte* (1791) drew together both the popular-farcical and the literary-operatic strands already present in Schikaneder's repertoire, and in so doing decisively altered the future course of developments on Vienna's German stages, from the direct imitations supplied by the likes of Wenzel Müller and Peter Winter in the 1790s to its greatest spiritual heir, Beethoven's *Fidelio*. Mozart chose the designation 'große Oper' for his score, the term usually used at the time to translate 'opera seria'. The work's generic cross-currents indicate how vigorously Mozart embraced the new heterodoxy of the 1790s—while contemporaries like Salieri (much as he admired *Die Zauberflöte* itself) continued to write within the pure buffa tradition and inveighed against the new 'confusione dei generi'. The novel musical and visual layer of hieratic solemnity in Mozart's opera, whose roots in the world of Freemasonry cannot be doubted, redefined the operatic notion of 'serious' in a way to which German Romantic opera readily indebted itself. With Mozart's valedictory opera the eighteenth century ended in a situation at Vienna curiously similar to the one that had obtained in Italy a hundred years earlier—with comic and serious elements intermixed in colourful, visually compelling spectacles of scant literary merit but enormous popular appeal.

❦ 4 ❧

THE NINETEENTH CENTURY: FRANCE

David Charlton

The Revolution Years

'…the best of times, the worst of times…'. The extraordinary decade of the French Revolution produced extraordinary cultural change. The sheer pace of production intensified; different kinds of opera were devised to entertain and instruct royalists, Jacobins, counter-revolution-aries, and satiated cynics. However, popular opera in Paris was firmly established on business principles and remained so, for all the shocking episodes that we like to associate with the word 'revolution'. In fact, the Revolution opened up opera as a business proposition, creating far more opportunities than it did catastrophes. Most of the significant works of the decade resulted from such business-led developments, which were only reined in under central control by Napoleon Bonaparte. And yet, the supply of human genius is limited. The fascination of the 1790s lies in the fact that historians are still thinking out the degree to which revolutionary opportunities turned into creative ones.

Debate concerning the place of theatre in society was already intense: nowhere more than in Paris were opera and drama politicized by 1789. Large issues of the day were traditionally addressed in fictional forms. The beleaguered Louis XVI was allegorically visible first as the old Oedipus in Sacchini's opera *Oedipe à Colone* (1787), and then as Philip Augustus, trying to rally his people against the English, in Dalayrac's *Sargines* (1788). Stage works of all kinds expressed the need for national unity: the dream of monarch, nobility, and even perhaps clergy uniting in a new pact with the people. As early as 1785 the music-theorist and botanist Lacépède urged the modern opera composer to 'range over the various classes of society': 'Let him not disdain the hut of the poor and unfortunate', but instead 'taste the pleasures of beneficial and consoling pity'. One of the major successes of 1789 was an opéra comique doing just that:

Dalayrac's *Les Deux Petits Savoyards*. Acted, as was usual in such works, by women, the wandering southern boys are supporting their destitute mother by casual earnings at fairs and markets. They are adopted by Verseuil, a retired businessman who has bought a *seigneurie* and chateau, and who finally discovers that they are his own late brother's offspring. The final vaudeville intones: 'Name, rank, money mean nothing—Only the heart means something.'

Three years later, the traveller John Moore saw 'a great number of Savoyards of both sexes and all conditions' come to Paris for an open-air festival, 'received by the acclamations of an immense number of spectators . . . A numerous band of music then performed the hymn of the Marseillois'. This national anthem-to-be, composed by Rouget de Lisle in 1792, 'is called for every evening at every theatre in Paris, and nothing can exceed the enthusiasm with which it is heard'. Much changed after January 1791, when the Constituent Assembly demolished the system of privileges controlling French opera since its inception. The hierarchy, with the Opéra at its apex, vanished together with the annual dues payable to the Opéra by all lesser theatres. Anyone was now permitted to open a theatre and, furthermore, could stage any type of show that he or she preferred. As a result, a multitude of entertainments appeared, many of which supported orchestras. Moreover, in order to bring in audiences they had to consider all kinds of novelty. The other side of the coin was that the Paris Opéra almost died with the king and queen, who were executed in 1793.

Mythological subjects suffered a sharp eclipse for some years, being largely identified with a culture of privilege; in any case, references to kings, emperors, and princes had to be expunged for a time from all operas, such was the political need to consolidate the national position. To replace them came the cult of republican Rome; her idealized image was already defined in great paintings by J.-L. David: *The Oath of the Horatii* (1784–5), and the *Brutus* (1789). David's neo-classical influence on popular fashion, and on the design of revolutionary festivals, promoted the taste for simplicity and naturalness of line and colour. Musicians responded with festival music that forged its own classicism: dignified melodies and hymn-like chordal progressions. Many composers were Freemasons, and there is obvious kinship between Republican neo-classicism in music and the kind of solemnity we hear in Mozart's *Die Zauberflöte* (1791). Paris did not quite produce a parallel opera to this, but its equivalents were the democratic fables put on at the Paris Opéra in 1793–4 and using Greek or Roman material: *Fabius* by Le Froid de

Méreaux; *Miltiade à Marathon* by Lemoyne; *Horatius Coclès* (the story of
Horatius defending the bridge) by Méhul; and the story of the fugitive
tyrant Dionysius the younger at Corinth, disguising himself as a school-
master: *Denys le tyran*, by the veteran Grétry.

Even more obviously designed as propaganda-operas were those
interesting but elusive works which the Revolution intended for its own
mythology: the staging of recent events deemed worthy to enter the
annals of the nation. While clearly the counterpart of such paintings as
David's *Marat Assassinated*, propaganda-opera required a little fictional
framing to retain dramatic plausibility. They were often subtitled '*fait his-
torique*'—'historical deed' or 'feat'—and were staged as early as October
1790, when the composer Henri-Montan Berton (later to be an enemy of
Berlioz and all dangerous innovation) put on *Le Nouveau d'Assas*. This
one-acter dramatized the heroism of a young soldier who had tried to
mediate between mutineering troops and government forces at
Châteauvieux near Nancy the previous 31 August: his strategy had been
to clasp the mouth of a cannon. In 1792 Rodolphe Kreutzer composed *Le
Siège de Lille*, following the lifting of that siege on 7 October 1792. In 1794
three operas were written about two young 'martyrs' of the Revolution,
Joseph Bara and Agricol Viala (both d. 1793), the composers being Grétry
and Louis Jadin.

Even the Paris Opéra adopted the trend. The death of Colonel Beau-
repaire, as he defended Verdun against Prussian troops in September
1792, was apotheosized in an 'opéra héroïque' by Pierre Candeille five
months later. Candeille's orchestra included two serpents, quoted the
'Marseillaise', and used a 'Bell for the dead' during a Mahlerian funeral
march in C minor, complete with black-draped drums on stage.

Didactic opera was never the most popular sort, however. Comedy
aside, what the public most enjoyed was a type with spoken dialogue
already known before 1789: adventure-plots, often using castles or dun-
geons as their setting, and shortly to be enhanced by *frissons* of the supernatural, derived from the fashionable Gothic novel. Ample opportunity
was taken to portray unjust confinement—the image of the Bastille was
never far from people's minds—and to show humane acts of deliverance.
Such things echoed the general sense of a people 'freeing themselves',
relishing an optimism later recalled by Wordsworth (twice a visitor to
the French capital at this time): 'Happy is he, who, caring not for Pope, |
Consul, or King, can sound himself to know | The destiny of Man, and
live in hope' (5th Sonnet to Liberty).

The need for new audiences led to the heightening of informal realism on stage and a quickening of dramatic tension that composers developed through their music. Viscount Palmerston's diary recorded a visit to the Opéra-Comique to see *Adélaïde et Mirval*, by Armand Trial *fils*, on 28 July 1791:

It is interesting and well acted. The latter part resembles the deserter [i.e. of Monsigny's opera] and the distress is carried farther to a degree highly disgusting, as the hero of the piece is actually placed on his knees with his eyes covered and his hands tied, & the party who are to shoot him are just levelling their musquets when the reprieve arrives.

On the other hand Palmerston, together with all Paris, was thrilled at a different realism at the Opéra-Comique and the Théâtre Feydeau, where 'Two new operas of the same name [by Cherubini and Kreutzer] are performing... They are called *Lodoïska*. The scenery in both is extremely fine with a great deal of old castle and towers which in the last act are burned and blown up upon the stage with an effect of fire beyond any representation I ever saw.' As an *habitué* of the London stage, Palmerston was well qualified to deliver such a verdict.

The rivalry between these two theatres lasted for ten years, by which time they were economically exhausted: thus they merged. But in their heyday they nurtured an operatic avant-garde that affected the whole history of the art-form. At the Opéra-Comique theatre were the composers Dalayrac, Kreutzer, Berton, and Méhul; at the Feydeau were Gaveaux, Le Sueur, Devienne, and Cherubini. Between them they created works that became a touchstone of French achievement for decades to come. Dalayrac was already established in comedy, and yet versatile enough to go on developing. In the Gothic *Castle of Monténéro* and the political-historical *Léhéman*, he made impressive advances in the use of reminiscence motives, influencing Carl Maria von Weber in the rising generation.

The name of Étienne-Nicolas Méhul (1763–1817) was to become synonymous with dedication and pre-Romantic high endeavour. Méhul's method, discussed by Berlioz in *Evenings in the Orchestra*, was never to hesitate in favour of 'a series of accents that are true but do not yield any surface pleasure'. For Méhul, musical expressiveness 'does not dwell in melody alone'; 'everything concurs either to create or destroy it—melody, harmony, modulation, rhythm, instrumentation, the choice of deep or high registers... a quick or slow tempo'. Such willingness to experiment with ends and means gave Méhul's operas distinctiveness and colour, appropriate to their subject; in this alone we may identify the

Romantic spirit. His finest works of the 1790s were *Euphrosine, Stratonice, Mélidore et Phrosine*, and *Ariodant*: all four are inspired more by psychology than visual sensation, still less explosions and conflagrations. Méhul's operatic characters would have been created in the same mould had the Revolution never existed. Gone is the old security of an imagined social structure that will finally absolve the passions portrayed. Méhul's characters inhabit isolated worlds, where anger, jealousy, and frustration seem to wreak intolerable damage and throw the future into doubt, whatever convention be used to round off the work. The operas have the maximum of character-development possible within a concise, three-act format. In so doing they reopen an aesthetic question asked by Sedaine in his librettos of the 1760s, a question that would be asked by Georges Bizet (a great admirer of Méhul) a century later: what should be the proper subject-matter for a French opera with spoken dialogue?

It would have been possible to follow the aesthetic principles of the librettist La Chabeaussière, writing in 1787 to justify a picaresque opera set on a desert island (*Azémia*, with music by Dalayrac):

I wanted to write a dramatic novella after the style of Shakespeare's *The Tempest*, that of Dryden, the story of *Robinson Crusoe*, and the various histories of voyages... I left the supernatural, enchanting and festive to the [Paris] Opéra; character-development and portrayal of manners to the Comédie-Française; and kept for [opéra comique] variety, picturesque effect, surprise, everything that seemed likely to diversify a musical score.

This clearly opened the way for *faits historiques* and suchlike; but in the meantime it was Méhul and his librettists F.-B. Hoffman and A. V. Arnault who maintained the conscience of the imagination in a unique decade.

The rival Théâtre Feydeau was a child of 1789: not of the proletariat, but of the nobility and well-to-do who were determined to establish a home for native Italian opera in Paris. Neither the imported Italian singers nor their operas long survived the fall of the monarchy in August 1792. What did survive was something special: a company dedicated to working as a team, knowing they had the best orchestra in Paris and were led by the indisputable genius of Cherubini. Luigi Cherubini (1760–1842) had worked in Italy and London before settling in Paris, but he was still very young. The Feydeau management head-hunted the finest set designers they could get from Italy, as well as the machinist (the 'stage manager') of the Paris Opéra itself.

The operatic result of this potent mixture was a series of Cherubini operas whose fame has never been forgotten: *Lodoïska* (1791), *Eliza* (1794), *Médée* (1797), and *Les Deux Journées* ('The Water-Carrier') of 1800. The first three of these embraced the implications of revolutionary stagecraft in order to create a totality of music, drama, design, and action that was prodigious. If *Lodoïska* had its escape from the burning castle of the tyrant Dourlinski, *Eliza* anticipated Romanticism by filling the stage with three-dimensional scenery representing the snow and ice of the St Bernard Pass. The climax of *Eliza* showed the attempted suicide of the 'hero' Florindo, who then became near-victim to an avalanche, realistically portrayed on stage. All this, witnessed by other characters on the mountain, was set to music in a specially conceived ensemble. Opera stepped decisively out of the conventions that had governed it hitherto, and it was only a question of time before the Paris Opéra, and a new generation of writers, would take up the mantle of this kind of operatic experience. When they did, it was in a work that stands as no less than the prototype of French grand opera: Auber's *La Muette de Portici* (1828), which ends with a suicide within sight of a volcanic eruption.

Cherubini's genius lay not least in expressing argument, coercion, or action between two people. The basis—as for Méhul—was the inherited method of declamatory word-setting that Grétry especially had perfected, in moulding a voice-line to the ebb and flow of verbal rhythms and meanings. Yet Méhul and Cherubini also updated purely orchestral writing in opera, giving it a feeling of symphonic growth that acted as metaphor for the developing thoughts of the actors, and seemed to make them clash. There can be a nervous insistence about these orchestral figures which is not immediately attractive—probably what Berlioz meant in referring to truth without 'surface pleasure'. Once gripped, however, the hearer experiences that elusive drama-in-music to which French opera consistently aspired, and which is so intimately linked with the French language itself.

1800–1850

The debate on French singing, so vividly stoked up by Charles Burney in *The Present State of Music*, continued into the nineteenth century. If anything, matters became yet more pressing owing to the ascent of Bonaparte. When the Peace of Amiens in 1802 brought English visitors back to Paris, one of their guidebooks cast its eye favourably over society, manners, and of course theatre. At the Opéra, 'The splendid decorations, the dancing, which appears to exceed human powers, the spacious stage, the rapidity and exactitude of the scene shifting, are no where to be equalled. Picturesque in the highest degree are the attitudes of the actors and actresses.' But different observations pertained to what was heard: 'It is, nevertheless, to be lamented, that in their ardour for the advancement of the arts, the Parisians should have neglected to purify their taste, by an importation of the Italian school of music. Nothing can be worse than the stile of singing which characterizes the French School.' The story of French opera from 1800 to 1830 is vitally concerned with its international acceptance: in fact, its transformation into an exportable commodity. This, in turn, required the infusion both of Italian singing style and of many elements of Italian vocal writing.

The battle was already joined by 1800; enthusiasm for the Italian style of singing of Pierre Garat was such that he could command a thousand francs a performance. However, Garat always refused to sing on the operatic stage. Yet at the Opéra the favourite singers were François Lays, totally identified with the French style, and Caroline Branchu, a dramatic soprano who excelled in the operas of Spontini and Gluck. The latter were regularly revived, so purely Italian taste flourished at a new theatre opened with Napoleon's support in 1801. This was eventually to become the celebrated Théâtre-Italien, the most fashionable house under the July Monarchy. Parisians under Napoleon applauded Josephina Grassini and the great castrato Girolamo Crescentini, and were exposed to a wide range of Italian works. The first of many Rossini operas heard was *L'italiana in Algeri* in 1817. Rossini was formally contracted as the theatre's musical director from 1824 to 1826, whereafter the French government named him 'Inspector-general of singing in France'.

It was precisely during the 1820s that the other main managements—the Opéra and Opéra-Comique—were finally forced to come to terms with the Italian vogue. In 1826 Rossini's *Le Siège de Corinthe* (recreated from *Maometto II*, 1820) triumphed at the Opéra; in 1827 it was the turn of *Moïse et Pharaon* (recreated from *Mosè in Egitto*, 1818). Fresh from his successful *Il crociato* (1824), Meyerbeer—an almost equally young lion—arrived in Paris from Italy in 1825; his *Marguérite d'Anjou* (1820) was revived for the Odéon (1826). By 1827 the Opéra-Comique was waiting for him to complete *Robert le diable* for their stage. (Its fate turned out to be yet more spectacular.)

This inexorable process helped create a sense of disorientation among the musical veterans of the Revolution, which was complicated by the power of Bonaparte himself. Native opéra comique was not discouraged, but felt obliged to go on mining the same vein of clean-cut jollity, with witty spoken dialogue playing a crucial part. Even in Boïeldieu, the youngest of the group, the Frenchness of the music recalled the Grétry tradition constantly: orchestral restraint, word-dominated vocal lines, frothy ensembles. What changed most was the implantation of melodic material emulating Mozart, whose own music was extremely highly regarded in Paris from the late 1790s.

Disorientation was certainly also caused by the great Italian stalking-horse himself, Gaspare Spontini (1774–1851): but in his case the French were confronting a talent of European stature. He came direct from success in Italy, found a natural ally in the empress Joséphine, and a ready-made Théâtre-Italien to show off his *La finta filosofa* in February 1804. By May 1804 his *La Petite Maison* appeared at the Opéra-Comique, followed by *Milton* in November and *Julie* the following March. All were single acts, but they showed his colours well enough in their spacious vocal lines, imaginative harmony, and highly wrought orchestration. Not for nothing was Spontini to become an idol of Berlioz: already in *Milton* he subdivided violins so that half were playing with mutes while the other half were playing normally. Of *Julie* a music journalist complained 'the whole melody is in the orchestra—that's Spontini's method. ... he seems to regard voices merely as orchestral instruments'. (The writer was probably affronted by the divided violas and cellos in one of Verseuil's arias.) Statements such as this show how far some had turned against the storm and stress works of the 1790s. Now Paris wanted to be part of Europe again, and opéra comique rang endless changes on stories of politely expressed love. *Milton* is typical of this: the blind poet, his reciting part of *Paradise Lost*, his problems with the monarchy: these are decorative elements adorning the love story of his daughter Emma. A foreign critic such as E. T. A. Hoffmann could be excused for thinking, apropos of Boïeldieu's *Le Nouveau Seigneur de village*, 'the French have no genuine opera buffa, but only comedies with an incidental admixture of vocal music'. Spontini's influence was chauvinistically resisted, when possible. The director of music at the Opéra privately congratulated Boïeldieu on his *Jean de Paris* (1812) with the opinion that it would 'lead back opéra comique to its true genre' with 'simple, natural' melodies, 'grace without mannerism', and 'fine workmanship without pedantry'. It was a counsel of stagnation.

The conspicuous avoidance of politics on the stage was itself a political fiction. In reality Napoleon was gradually turning opera management back to the hierarchical centralism of the old days. By 1807 he had handed back the Opéra its role as a state show-piece, and was vetting, when not actually suggesting, the subjects proposed for musical treatment. The Opéra-Comique repertory was also controlled; and in the same year the emperor cut the number of Paris theatres from about thirty down to eight. Essentially, French opera up to 1864 had to cope with a *dirigiste* legacy that was rarely relaxed in principle, in spite of the changes caused by the revolutions of 1830 and 1848. Not until the licensing of the Théâtre-Lyrique (1851) and Offenbach's Bouffes-Parisiens (1855) was there a permanent sense of change, though temporary ventures came and went (e.g. operas at the Odéon from 1823 to 1828). Not until 1864 did Napoleon III, emperor since the 1852 *coup d'état*, ordain that 'Any person may build and run a theatre' and that 'Dramatic works in all genres, including those in the public domain, may be given in all theatres'. Even this was rather a pyrrhic victory for theatrical freedom since, as the historian Nicole Wild points out, Napoleon III had already 'suppressed the little, popular community theatres, less controllable than the larger ones; had started redistributing theatres within Paris; and continued to exercise surveillance through the device of censorship'.

Two works of the First Empire, however, stand out as prophetic: both were derived from Ossian. Like Brahms in the Second Serenade, Méhul boldly eliminated all the violins from his orchestra in *Uthal* (1806), thereby hoping to evoke the Scottish landscape. The violinists were to play violas, giving a veiled quality to the orchestration; a harp featured prominently. It is helpful to think of *Uthal* in terms of contemporary literature or painting. 'Ossian', the supposed Homer of third-century Caledonia, was devoured by French readers as by German ones before them; Goethe had made his Charlotte and Werther read Ossian's *Berrathon* on their last evening together. Méhul's opera derived from the very same poem, and well captured its high-toned melancholy:

The winds begin to rise. The dark wave of the lake resounds. Bends there not a tree from Mora with its branches bare? My harp hangs on a blasted branch. The sound of its strings is mournful. Does the wind touch thee, O harp, or is it some passing guest? It is the hand of Malvina!

The successors of *Uthal* in France were to be the 'literary' operas of the Second Empire: for example Gounod's *Le Médecin malgré lui* (Molière), his *Roméo et Juliette*, Thomas's *Mignon* (Goethe), Berlioz's *Béatrice et Bénédict* (Shakespeare), Bizet's *Djamileh* (de Musset), *La Jolie Fille de Perth* (Scott), and *Carmen* (Mérimée).

Partly through Napoleon's predilection for Ossian, French painters created important images that sometimes distorted the poetic sources for patriotic ends. Girodet's *Apotheosis of French Heroes* is one of them, prefiguring Germanic Walhallas taken from genuine Nordic mythology. A much larger French opera than *Uthal* forms an exact parallel to Girodet's painting: *Ossian, ou Les bardes* (1804) by Jean-François Le Sueur (1760–1837). The importance of this relatively successful work is multifold. Le Sueur was later to be Berlioz's most important teacher and friend. (As a maverick figure himself, Le Sueur had lost his chair at the Paris Conservatoire in 1802.) *Ossian* is of epic proportions and dramatizes religious conflict; it returned to the five-act format of the baroque period; and it required new, costly effects to realize a semi-symbolic dream vision, a choreographed ritual showing the warriors' afterlife. As did Girodet's painting, so this scene contained a shimmering light caused by celestial meteors. Sixteen harps created bardic local colour, as did 'folk' themes to characterize the opposing parties (Scandinavians and Caledonians). Finally, Le Sueur made a brief allusion to Napoleonic policy concerning the Concordat with Rome. None of these features has anything in common with the formal laws laid down in Gluck's Enlightenment operas; all of them have much in common with the Romantic *grands opéras* of the 1830s and after.

Born in Hamburg, the 22-year-old Sophie Leo came to Paris in 1817. Her impression was that 'Though at the time of my arrival all three opera houses were deteriorating, a very few years sufficed for their rehabilitation... the singing, the personnel, the costumes and the buildings themselves were improved.' In fact, the Opéra was rebuilt by François Debret in 1821 on the rue Le Peletier; this was its home during the Romantic period. (It burned in 1873, to be replaced by the enormous Salle Garnier in 1875.) But even more important to the development of French opera was the availability of good librettos. This point was forcibly made in a letter by Meyerbeer in 1823, waiting in the wings in Milan:

Where but Paris can one find the huge resources that French opera gives an artist wishing to compose truly dramatic music? Here, we desperately lack librettos, and the public likes only one type of music. At Paris there are excellent librettos, and I know your [French] public welcomes all types of music without distinction, provided it is handled with genius.

This assessment remained true for the whole nineteenth century. Perhaps Meyerbeer was already half-thinking of Eugène Scribe (1791–1861), his exact contemporary. Scribe was to become Meyerbeer's most important French collaborator and was already developing new ideas in opéra comique, working with established musicians.

Prolific, almost virtuosic in conceiving stage situations derived from literary sources, Scribe did more than any other writer to put French opera in the forefront of exportable commodities. To read the average composer's letter to Scribe is to witness a courtier soliciting a regal favour. In the spoken theatre Scribe cut his dramatic teeth writing comédie-vaudeville and evolving the dextrous plot style for which he remains noted. Contact with the popular stage was to be crucial when he turned to *grand opéra* and history. 'Romanticism' as a fashion was always somewhat suspected as bad taste by the French. Scribe wrote for that great majority who wanted something more civilized, while still partaking of fashionable motifs: the exotic, the ghostly, the risqué, the ball-scene, the villain, the castle, the coincidence, the spectacular. As a writer who genuinely understood musical theatre, Scribe provided opéra comique with a modern sense of dynamism and relevance. Set-piece solos were rationed: often a solo establishes a main character in Act 1; there may well be a song, ballad, romance, or equivalently 'local' solo. This typically sets a work's geographical or historical compass, and also gives the necessary background information as a 'tale within a tale'. (All this had originated in Grétry and Dalayrac.) The new opéra comique normally had a chorus, firmly establishing itself in one or more characterful roles. Where Scribe excelled was in using musical ensembles as vehicles for stage action. This could involve just principals, or it could involve the chorus, acting and singing on a different narrative level.

The year 1825 was a turning-point: Scribe gave Boïeldieu his finest hour in *La Dame blanche*, and sealed his partnership with Auber in *Le Maçon*. The former made use of Walter Scott's *The Monastery* and *Guy Mannering*. Recently enriched by contact with Rossini and Weber, Boïeldieu's music rose to the challenge of haunted castles and Scottish landscape. *Le Maçon* was the sixth of thirty-six joint ventures that set a standard, and indeed were to develop in style over the thirty-eight years of their authors' collaboration.

Daniel Auber (1782–1871) enjoyed international popularity, especially for opéra comique, and he benefited from modern publication methods: his joyful, dance-like tunes were arranged and disseminated in huge quantities, presumably reaching a new mass public that had no immediate access to live theatre. The titles of his best works were long fixed in mainstream culture: *Fra Diavolo* (1830), *Le Cheval de bronze* (1835), *Le Domino noir* (1837), *Les Diamants de la couronne* (1841), *Haydée, ou Le secret* (1847). Part of Auber's appeal today lies in the knowledge that his considerable gifts (freely admired by Wagner in an obituary) might at any time produce surprises. He went through a Rossini phase, absorbed Weber, made history—as will be seen—in a grand opéra, *La Muette de Portici*, and yet lacked the urge to attend the first nights of his own works. In him, or in Hérold, Halévy, Thomas, or Adam, we recognize the likeable, urbane persona of the July Monarchy: the voice of the bourgeois moderately interested in the arts, and journeying to the leafy suburbs of a Sunday. These composers were the cream of a sizeable class, most of whom were musically highly educated and of broad sympathies. The early death of Ferdinand Hérold (1791–1833), after *Zampa* (1831) and *Le Pré aux clercs* (1832), is considered a major loss. Fromental Halévy (1799–1862) seems to have preferred the ironic wit of the librettists F. B. Hoffman and V. de Saint-Georges in opéra comique. *Le Dilettante d'Avignon* (1829) was a successful burlesque of current musical Italomania. *L'Éclair* (1835)—staged up to 1879—is a serious comedy with only four characters. This last would repay revival, as indeed might *Les Mousquetaires de la reine* of 1846. Ambroise Thomas (1811–96), the most intellectual of the group, made a slower start, beginning with the subtle *La Double Échelle* (1837), its text by Planard. Thomas's *Le Panier fleuri* (1839) had as fast a text and as memorable melodies as one could want in light comedy. The *petits-maîtres* of the genre were Monpou, Grisar, Bazin, and Clapisson (1808–66).

The name of Adolphe Adam (1803–56) is perennially linked with his masterpiece *Le Postillon de Lonjumeau* (1836); but his *Le Chalet* (1834) was no less popular, and Adam produced at least one averagely successful comedy a year. Their names often bear the same lack of pretentiousness as their scores (*The Brewer of Preston*; *If I Were King*), and Adam's career began on the secondary stages of the Gymnase and Vaudeville theatres. But that cannot explain the contempt Berlioz seems to show for Adam in his private letters. Berlioz, the élitist of feeling, could only regard the average opéra comique as a cheap betrayal of music itself. He let fly sublimely in a mock-review in his book *Evenings in the Orchestra*:

Diletta [i.e. Adam's *Giralda*] .... but................ very................ the
music.................... always........................ colourless.................... platitude.

Sincerity of endeavour, however humble the results, always earned Berlioz's respect. What angered him about mid-century opera in Paris was its naked commercialism. The following attack was on grand opéra but it applied equally, for this reason, to opéra comique:

[Librettists and composers] are like a meadow mown and mown again down to the roots, with no time allowed for the seedlings to come up. With or without ideas, one must write—write fast and often; one must pile up acts, so as to pile up premiums, so as to pile up royalties, then capital, then interest... One knows that by putting together notes and words in this or that way, combinations result that will be accepted by the public of all Europe. Why then try to put them together differently? These combinations are merely the packaging round the ideas; to change the colour of the label is enough, since it will take the public a long time to discover that the packaging contains nothing. (Epilogue to *Evenings in the Orchestra*)

Money loomed especially large in grand opéra: it was after all a state monopoly. It is undeniable that most of its audience was socially privileged, if not also aristocratic: the smug protestations of its business-manager Louis Véron (appointed in 1831 in a gesture of revolutionary reform) must not be misunderstood: 'I said to myself, "The July Revolution is the triumph of the bourgeoisie: this victorious bourgeoisie will be fond of lording it, of having a good time; the Opéra will become its Versailles..."' (*Mémoires*). Memorable scenes in French Romantic novels, set in various opera houses, amply testify to the social meaning of 'going to the opera'. Such literary set-pieces became ubiquitous. Balzac's Rastignac in *Père Goriot*—set in 1819, though published in 1834–5—'felt as though someone had waved a magic wand when he entered a box facing the stage, and found himself the target for all the lorgnettes...'; Balzac's narrative pointedly bypasses the identity of the Italian opera being performed or indeed any mention of it, as such, whatsoever. As perspicacious and musical an observer as the painter Delacroix could not but have qualms, writing in his Journal as a frequent opera-goer:

... the great and the rich are blasé... They enter good boxes furnished with good carpets... They do not arrive before the exact moment when the piece is beginning and... generally miss the best part of it through their lateness. The habits of society people cause them to converse on the most frivolous subjects... It is a very imperfect pleasure to hear even the most beautiful music in a box with people of fashion. The poor artist seated in the parterre and alone in his corner, or beside a friend as attentive as himself, is the only one who completely enjoys the beauty of a work. (1849)

Today we can concentrate on the minority of grands opéras that were deeply meditated and have stood the test of time. They show opera developing on all levels, from the smallest element of historical detailing to the largest concatenation of musico-dramatic effects. It was opera for an age of industrialization. (In fact the development of public railways from the 1840s encouraged people to travel in to the city for opera performances.) The best composers, however, were immune from mass production. The pioneer Spontini composed only three full-scale works

for Paris: *La Vestale, Fernand Cortez,* and *Olimpie.* Meyerbeer's grands
opéras number but four: *Robert le diable, Les Huguenots, Le Prophète,* and
L'Africaine. To these we should add Halévy's best offerings—which still
caused Berlioz profound unease, not least because as chorus-master at
the Opéra Halévy had automatic privilege in getting his work put on—
La Juive, Guido et Ginevra, La Reine de Chypre, and *Charles VI.* The stakes
were steep enough to discourage Rossini from writing anything to follow *Guillaume Tell* (1829) and Auber from attempting the high style after
La Muette de Portici and *Gustave III.*

Spontini's orchestral richness, which we mentioned earlier, was balanced by a strong element of Italian spaciousness in the vocal lines: a sort
of musical counterpart to Empire art and architecture which, as Hugh
Honour points out, quitted Greece for 'the florid opulence of Imperial
Rome. The abstemious severity of Doric was replaced by Corinthian
richness and splendour.' Decadent neo-classicism, seen in a painting
such as Gérard's *Cupid and Psyche* (1798), relates to *La Vestale* (1807) in so
far as the opera is a tale of forbidden love (the main character, Julia, is a
temple virgin) in which concerns of state or even religion appear to pose
material more than moral threats. The huge impact of Spontini's opera
also stemmed from its scaling-up of forces: its use of modern chromatic
harmony and dissonance, lending violence to the voices of authority, and
of stage rituals, whether in the temple or in the enormous procession
that introduces Licinius (Julia's lover) as a military hero. The setting is
deliberately historicized: the librettist Étienne de Jouy (1764–1846) speci-
fies its sources and the year of the action, AD 269.

History, military might, religious conflict, and (happily resolved) love-
interest were ingredients equally central to Spontini's *Fernand Cortez*
(1809); now, however, the greater spectacle and greater political interference conspired to create problems. There is no doubt that Napoleon contrived to angle the work, even during composition, to make Cortez's
bloodless conquest of Mexico 'legitimize' his own policy towards Spain,
namely in replacing the Bourbon king and subordinating the Inquisition
(represented in the opera by fanatical Aztec priests). Though the opera
was a success, and the score published, obscure difficulties caused a hesi-
tant stage history, and it was revised in 1817. Part of its success lay in the
sort of trappings that were, and sometimes still are, seen as proper for a
'grand opera': seventeen horses (justified by Jouy on strictly historical
grounds); a dive by the heroine into a lake; and the destruction of the
lurid Aztec temple.

The orchestra became a Napoleonic juggernaut, rolling with unique and repellent power to the sound of trombones, military clarinets, tremolando strings and woodwind, and a battery of percussion including triangle, tam-tam, cymbals, and (originally) an *ajacaxtili*. Mexico city seen in flames was echoed by fortissimo tam-tam strokes, two in every bar. It was also Spontini's adventurous harmony that upset the critics, even as it reached out to the Romantics. One French critic, perhaps mindful of the work's official support, ventured: 'We would only desire that [Spontini] were a little less prodigal of those over-frequent modulations, which cut up the melodic regularity and cause a disagreeable sensation'. E. T. A. Hoffmann's feelings were somewhat differently expressed: 'an almost desperate straining after the most striking effect... a sudden lunge into the remotest key possible... the ears are deafened... This drunken sobriety, this cold ardour, this unsonorous noise'. With *Olimpie* (1819), Spontini retreated into a no less brutal, but rather more restrained world, its fable derived from Voltaire's tragedy. By then Hoffmann had come to admire Spontini, and collaborated with him when *Olimpie* was revised for Berlin in 1821.

In an essay published in 1826 Jouy expressed a clear-headed idea of what serious opera was: 'the epic muse should preside at the invention of the subject, and the tragic muse should determine its plan'. His retrograde sensibility demanded that the ending must be happy because in opera 'all speaks to the senses and the heart, not the reason'. Sources, Jouy thought, should come from legend, even the supernatural, but also from history. In fact history, and the tragic ending, were to be the effective conduits, and within this reformulation the novels of Walter Scott were the catalyst. When Scott came to popularity, mere period settings—historical local colour and detail—were already regular aspects of operatic experience. For example, the Gothic revival, for which France hardly lagged behind England in enthusiasm, and which dwells so strongly in the atmosphere of Meyerbeer's *Robert le diable* (1831), was visually familiar before 1789. Interest in the past, though, implied analysis of the present. As we saw, the Revolution created operatic dramas of 'modern history', however simplistic, and also its Graeco-Roman propaganda operas. All these explorations make the case of Cherubini's masterly *Les Deux Journées* (1800) more than usually interesting. The unproven point is often made that its librettist, Bouilly, used a true escape story (a water-carrier conceals Count Armand in his barrel, allowing him to flee Paris). More important is that the action is set in the historical seventeenth century, the repressive rule of Cardinal Mazarin having caused Armand to run for his life not as an individual, but as a parliamentarian. In other words, this universally admired opera was actually a pocket historical drama that interfused the personal and the political in the dynamic manner that would be widely adopted after the vogue for Scott had come in, though typically on a much greater scale.

Armand and his wife represent political power. In any historical drama, Herbert Lindenberger points out, a people asserts the continuity between its past and its present, in order to examine power:

Most of the great historical dramas are centrally concerned either with the transfer of power from one force to another [e.g. *Richard II*, but also *Les Deux Journées* or *Fernand Cortez*] or with the means by which a force already in power manages to stabilize itself against the onslaught of contending forces [as in the grands opéras *La Muette de Portici* and *Les Huguenots*]. Conspiracy can best be dramatized in situations where both the ruling authority and its opponents are visible to the audience.

It would be left to the age of Scribe to develop historical opera on a five-act scale, enabling such conspiracies to take convincing dramatic shape.

Jouy, in his essay, saw the possibility of a five-act opera where the 'nature and majesty of the subject' might demand 'splendid civil and religious ceremonies'—clearly he envisaged expansions of what he had created in the three-act *La Vestale*, for instance. Such 'ceremonies' necessarily implied the opera's chorus: it was arguably in historical opera that this found its ideal role, namely in representing a politically coherent group of people.

French opera had cherished its choral contingent from the days of Lully, but in the nineteenth century it added a turbulent, even epic, resource to drama itself. Through the chorus a people could express its will with an oath, a dance, a protest, a march, or a prayer. As mentioned earlier, choral music readily found itself in combination, dialogue, or opposition with solo singers. The chorus now sometimes entered the narrative level of the principals, and on such occasions the power of opera to involve its audience emotionally could be overwhelming. If grand opéra was art for an industrial age, it was also born of a democratic one: 1848, after all, saw the effective start of male universal suffrage in France. (It was a moment that made many shudder, including Berlioz. His three operas were certainly more inspired by the literary than the historical muse: *Benvenuto Cellini*, *Les Troyens*, *Béatrice et Bénédict*.)

The revolution of 1830 turned out to have two curtain-raisers in which the 'voice of the people' was in fact the main theme: *La Muette de Portici* (also known as *Masaniello*) of 1828 by Scribe and Auber, and *Guillaume Tell* of 1829 by Jouy, Bis, *et al.*, set by Rossini. The latter ends optimistically: following legend, the Austrians are routed from Switzerland. Rossini's dignified style unifies a large canvas naturally suited to operatic contrast, particularly choral statements juxtaposed with individual drama. Structurally the opera differs starkly from those of the Romantic school, and could be compared to a far smaller *Guillaume Tell* with forceful music by Grétry, seen throughout the 1790s. The structural difference lies in the absence of ironic narrative technique, or of a sense of historical 'process' being created or enacted. In the *grand opéra* developed by Scribe, we feel drawn into the story because of some intimate involvement of the agent currently in power with the protagonist set up to challenge that power. The *Tell* operas admit of no such involvement, although each uses the blinding of Melcthal as an equivalent dramatic trigger. Scribe's grand opéra structure can, typically, maintain its five-act length through an internal management of tension that will propel interest forward over a span of three to four hours of music. And if an opera based on history is not capable of articulating the detail of conspiracy, betrayal, and coincidence typical of spoken historical drama, it at least provides an analogous degree of involvement between the two conflicting parties, and compensates for necessary losses by other kinds of gain. In Lindenberger's formulation, the 'epic quality' is provided by the chorus as character; the 'national feelings' are evoked by music's immediacy; local and historical colour are elements that music can suggest well; and the feeling of 'something larger' which music gives us reveals 'more the essence than the particularities of conspiracy'.

La Muette de Portici tells the story of the failed Neapolitan revolt against the Spanish in 1647, led by Thomas Aniello. Indeed, the fable had been dramatized several times before, on the English stage in D'Urfey's *Rise and Fall of Masaniello* (1699) and the Hamburg stage in Reinhard Keiser's opera *Masagniello furioso* (1706). It is an object lesson in identifying Scribe's ingenuity to compare his libretto for Auber with a London play by George Soane with incidental music by Bishop (1825), or the opéra comique composed by Carafa in Paris (1827), both entitled *Masaniello*. Soane and Carafa cover the same basic ground as Scribe: Masaniello's successful, even justifiable leading of 'his' people's protest against higher taxes, and his downfall either through overwork and madness (Soane) or betrayal and poisoning (Carafa). Scribe is alone in creating an effective drama connecting the rulers and the ruled, and again he used Scott: borrowing the dumb role of Fenella (in *Peveril of the Peak*) he gave Masaniello a sister who has been abducted and seduced by the ruling Spanish duke d'Arcos, whose wedding ceremony occurs in Act 1 of the opera. At once the personal is entwined with the political, and Scribe can build a sequence of coincidences that gives a continuing illusion of the revolutionary process in action; additionally, it involves the audience on the side of the working people. Fenella's mute state, as though the result of a trauma, only increases her stature, perhaps even coming to personify the inarticulate will of the Neapolitans, one that is finally destroyed as Fenella leaps from the palace walls. Such metaphysical feeling is made more explicit as, simultaneously, the eruption of Vesuvius is interpreted by the chorus as an act of divine judgement. But on whom? Spaniards or revolutionaries? *Chacun à soi*: when the opera was given in 1830 in Brussels, 'students left the theatre shouting "Down with the Dutch!" and "Down with the Ministry!" The student riot turned into a revolt, and the revolt spread... By October a provisional government had been established' and independence won for Belgium (Charles Breunig, *The Age of Revolution and Reaction*).

How forcefully Auber's music deals with the realistic atmosphere of the libretto can best be seen in Richard Wagner's account, 'Reminiscences of Auber':

Each of the five acts presented a dramatic picture of the most extraordinary animation, where arias and duets in the wonted operatic sense were scarcely to be detected any more, and certainly, with the exception of a single prima-donna aria in the first act, did not strike one at all as such; in each instance it was the ensemble of the whole act that riveted attention and carried one away.... Auber made his music reproduce each contrast, every blend, in contours and colours of so drastic, so vivid a distinctness as we cannot recall seeing before.

Another aspect of the Scribe approach was to hold in mind the visual structure of the action. This meant more than the use of the great procession (found of course already in Spontini, and in Soane's *Masaniello* too) for the triumphant entry of Masaniello on horseback in Act 4. In 1827 the Paris Opéra had decided to face head-on the need for scenic and theatrical co-ordination that it had so far ignored, while in the meantime popular theatres had moved ahead with elaborate lighting, scenery and effects, and historically accurate costumes. The Opéra created a committee to take advantage of such ideas, which has recently been analysed by the historian Karin Pendle. She has shown a remarkable number of features that found their way rapidly into grand opéra: copious changes of scenery; detailed local or historical chorus costuming; mute characters; use of mime and special music to interpret it (not unlike silent film music, of course); characteristic national dances (Auber's *Muette* contains a guaracha, a bolero, and a tarantella as well as an important vocal bar-carolle); practicable scenery; and extraordinary lighting effects. The use of gas for some stage and front-of-house lighting had first occurred at the Opéra in 1822 for the fairy-tale opera *Aladin*, music by Isouard and Ben-incori. The same period saw Daguerre's invention of double-painting a scenic canvas so that it appeared to transform itself when illuminated from different sides. This effect was used in both *La Muette* and *Guillaume Tell* as a climactic ingredient.

Wagner is usually thought of when the 'total work of art' (*Gesamtkunstwerk*) is mentioned; yet the apparent fusion of all possible elements of theatrical art was an overwhelming impression provoked by Giacomo Meyerbeer's *Robert le diable* at the Opéra in 1831. The subject had been worked up from opéra comique material into a full-scale response to elements of *Der Freischütz*, *Faust*, ancient chapbooks, boule-vard melodramas, the English Gothic novel, Daguerre's scenography, and the latest ideas in musical invention. Meyerbeer (1791–1864) had pre-pared his career gradually, training alongside Weber in Germany, then proceeding to Italy to master vocal writing and singer's opera. In Paris Meyerbeer achieved the synthesis of styles that helped to lend his works an unparalleled influence. He used the French system of constant response to word; but he also used prominent devices from Italianate singing style. Like the French generally, he was interested in orchestral colour and novelty—*Robert le diable* has a cor anglais solo and one for a new type of keyed trumpet, for whose execution two musicians were recruited from Italy. But Meyerbeer's orchestra often recalls the 'sym-phonic' development style of Cherubini, underpinning a dialogue or an ensemble with varied use of a short motif. Two further qualities mark out Meyerbeer's mature musical style: harmonic and rhythmic restless-ness. His harmony is constantly shifting through chromatic progres-sions, which must have seemed much more innovative 150 years ago than today. On the other hand, his metrical ingenuity is still easy to appreciate. It surfaces on many levels: relation of a melodic rhythm to its accompa-niment; abrupt shifts of metre to match new utterance; surprise and a feeling of instability when certain of these shifts occur; and—as his career progressed—increasingly bold experiments with new time signatures. There is even evidence to suggest that Meyerbeer planned the long-range tensions of an operatic act through graduated employment of diff-erent metres.

Each of Meyerbeer's French operas inhabits a distinct musical and dramatic world. (The same thing is true, to a greater extent, of Berlioz's and Wagner's operas.) In part this comes through conscious unifying of materials, or recurring themes; in part it comes through thinking of an appropriate general local colour that can pervade the mood. When Meyerbeer was at a dinner one evening in 1853 his thoughts on local colour were heard and noted afterwards by Eugène Delacroix:

They were talking at table about *local colour*. Meyerbeer was saying, rightly, that it depends on an indefinable thing, which is not at all the exact observation of usages and customs. 'Who is there who has more of it', he said, 'than Schiller in his *William Tell*? And yet he had never seen anything of Switzerland.'

Exactly the same sentiment occurs in Victor Hugo's famous 1827 preface to the play *Cromwell*: 'Local colour ought not to be on the surface of the drama, but deep down, in the very heart of the work, from where it spreads outwards' so that 'one only notices when going in and coming out that the century and the atmosphere have changed'. *Robert le diable* partakes of both the medieval and the supernatural modes: contemporary audiences had the incomparable advantage of seeing the ghosts of nuns dancing in a moonlit cloister designed and painted by the great Cicéri, which has become celebrated as a *locus classicus* of Romantic scenography (The nuns appeared through trapdoors.) Only with their associated details of staging, in fact, can Meyerbeer's operatic works be fully appreciated.

In fact the exact details of original productions—though unfortunately not with associated set designs—were habitually published for all important French operas, starting with *La Muette de Portici* in 1828, inviting producers to respect the intentions of the group of artists who had conceived these complex works. Meyerbeer, for one, took an active part in the final stages of a work's production. Though the texture of his rehearsal method is lost, striking evidence of his scenic, or simply theatrical, imagination at work occurs in a letter written to Scribe about the replanning of their final enterprise, *L'Africaine*:

I think I have an idea for a good and clear opening scene which would also provide a wonderful musical introduction. It would be a festive council scene of the Portuguese admiralty before which Vasco [da Gama] presents his plans for the discovery of India . . . The head of the council would be Vasco's rival . . . the members of the council are not in agreement. Each supports his own views, but finally the cabal against Vasco prevails . . . Vasco has an outburst of rage, issues threats, is relieved of his office and banished. He leaves in a rage, exclaiming that he shall take it upon himself to secure and equip a ship in order to prove he was not mistaken....I am presenting you with this idea just as it occurred to me, my dear friend.

This letter duly became the matrix for *L'Africaine*'s exposition.

Probably the most memorable example of functional local colour in Meyerbeer is the character of the gruff retainer Marcel in *Les Huguenots* (1836), whose recitatives are accompanied by cello chords (sounding like a viola da gamba). Marcel is musically associated with the Lutheran chorale 'Ein' feste Burg', 'weaving a thread throughout the entire opera', as Meyerbeer wrote in 1837: '[Marcel], with his simple but unshakable faith, could even be considered as a martyr.' *Le Prophète* (1849) is yet more ambitious. This time the historical central character, John of Leyden (1509–36), is possessed of messianic impulses. The opera traces his ascent from obscurity to deification by anabaptist revolutionaries in Münster cathedral. During this most famous of grand opéra coronation scenes, he is recognized by his long-abandoned mother, but silences her in a 'miracle'. Eventually the revolution is crushed and the main characters destroyed in flames. The sweep of the work enabled Meyerbeer to incorporate even brief buffo episodes in Act 3, so that perhaps this opera is ultimately the one that aimed most closely at a Shakespearian conception of romantic music-drama, using history. Meyerbeer's formation took place during the period of early Romanticism, the time when in *Cromwell* Hugo laid down Shakespeare as *the* model for drama, expressed through 'the sublime and grotesque, which intersect in the drama as they intersect in life and in creation. For true poetry, complete poetry, is in the harmony of contraries.' It is tempting to go further and connect Hugo's theory of beauty and ugliness with Romantic music: the 'sublime' is the exceptional element, the 'grotesque' his picture of humanity at large; similarly, music's concords, like Hugo's beautiful, are 'of only one type', whereas its discords, like the 'thousand forms of the ugly', can in Romantic music come to seem the orthodox state, not least when pursued by Meyerbeer's restlessness.

Les Huguenots was to remain Meyerbeer's most perfect work: the one in which history and tragedy, politics and doomed love, are acted out through a supremely inventive and economical musical score. Its achievement, musically, perforce casts a shadow over the grands opéras of Halévy, which in other respects can be very similar to Meyerbeer's. *La Juive* (1835) forms an obvious parallel with *Les Huguenots*, and the sweep of *La Reine de Chypre* (1841) could be compared to that of *Le Prophète*. Halévy's music lacks his rival's complexity; but it was more up to date as concerns orchestral 'gesture': the creation of instantly emotive sound-images. In fact some of them were taken up and developed by Wagner, who heard these works during his Parisian years, 1839–42, and who arranged the piano score of *La Reine de Chypre* for the publisher Schlesinger. The other influential 'Wagnerian' aspect in Halévy was his invention of flexible solo declamation—a pregnant style of recitative with memorable solo instrumental participation. Halévy's brother Léon recalled, 'He also had the eminent power of fusing recitative within the melodic tissue of the work, while totally preserving its character.'

Léon Halévy also bore witness to his brother's constant demand for rhythmic variety in the verses of librettos: ' "Rhythmical, inflected lines", he repeated endlessly, "No regular caesuras!" ' This interventionist manner was wholly typical for French composers, though the intimate traces of such dealings are not widely recorded. In the exceptional case of candid memoirs such as Grétry's (1797), we have evidence for it; normally the evidence is haphazardly left in letters. A fascinating one exists from Meyerbeer to Alexandre Dumas *père*, with whom the composer was planning an opera in the early 1830s:

Dear colleague,
I am enclosing several examples of good musical rhythms which are suitable for various genres, and I have indicated them—. I would like you to use one particular rhythm frequently, since it can be employed on all occasions. This rhythm is as follows:

> O Seigneur | ta clémence
> a calmé | ma souffrance
> ta grandeur | ta puissance
> égale ta bonté.

Since French librettists traditionally published their operas in a final form that did not necessarily include alterations made by or for composers, we can often see the considerable differences that arose in making a music-dramatic work out of its constituent elements. In the evolution of nineteenth-century opera, the name of Charles Gounod (1818–93) is widely recognized for the brilliance of certain arias and choruses. Less well appreciated is his once-controversial system of word-setting. Whereas composers of Meyerbeer's generation, influenced partly by the setting of Italian poetry, valued regular rhythmic patterns and periodic musical phrases, Gounod and those who followed chose to exploit a freedom inherent in French verse that makes its 'spoken rhythm' frequently override its strictly prosodic rhythm. Gounod himself talked of this 'expression of truth' to which was opposed 'the exactitude of language', and he formulated a new principle. According to this, melodies flow unpredictably with the poetic reading, while at the same time retaining the convention of the regular (periodic) musical phrase-length. It was an elegant form of liberation, but none the less vital.

Similar concerns had Emmanuel Chabrier cajoling the poet Catulle Mendès in 1891, when collaborating on the unfinished opera *Briséis*.

> It's not much. After these lines:
> No. 1 { Jésus, j'ai reçu le baptême
>   { J'adore les clous et la croix
>   '*Je t'aime*
>   *Et je te crois*' are *too brief* and
>   would flag after the rhythm of the two preceding...
>   a line of 8 feet
> | | | | | | *je t'aime*
>   *Et je te crois!* would suit me very well.

'Send them over tomorrow or the next day', concludes Chabrier, after several more points, 'you can do them in a quarter of an hour...'.

1850–1890

Some French composers, even in the later eighteenth century, had written their own librettos: Rousseau, Framery, Dezède, and Berton. Thus it should not have been seen as an act of hubris when Hector Berlioz (1803–69) chose to compose words as well as music for *Les Troyens* ('The Trojans') in 1856–8. But he and his genius were feared and mistrusted, not least owing to his devastating tongue: 'The most eminent artists, his equals, experienced in his presence a kind of awkwardness. Gounod has often spoken to me of this', recalled Berlioz's friend and patron Ernest Legouvé. For his part, Berlioz had suffered grievously in 1838 over *Benvenuto Cellini*. This is now understood as a quintessentially Romantic opera, but part of that essence lay in its very nonconformity: its swaggering text (by Barbier and Wailly); its parable of a great artist thumbing his nose at convention; its tremendous musical audacity. *Cellini* was scuppered when the leading tenor, Duprez, walked out after three performances. But such was the temperamental nature of the Opéra. It was a hive of individualists, from the director down. Véron's *Mémoires* tell more than one story of artists holding *him* to ransom. Duprez's great predecessor, Adolphe Nourrit, once refused to sing the part of a robber in an opera by the Spanish composer Gomis. Since the score had been commissioned, Véron had to indemnify Gomis and his librettist to the tune of 6,000 francs. Even the Italian trumpet players in *Robert le diable* extorted extra money from Véron.

Berlioz's masterpiece *Les Troyens* stood little chance of performance in such an ambience, and in any case 'The two conductors on [the Opéra] staff are my enemies', as Berlioz said in a petition to Napoleon III on the subject. In 1863 the composer acquiesced in the desire to see at least some of his opera, which was divided in two for the purpose. *Les Troyens à Carthage*, itself mutilated and further cut down, lasted for twenty-one performances at the new Second Empire theatre, the Théâtre-Lyrique. The composer had to pay for some of the musicians himself. His own account near the end of his *Mémoires* plumbs the abyss separating the noble Virgilian epic in his mind from what was realized in 1863. Berlioz's approach to the text had been 'Virgil Shakespeareanized', as he put it; but fidelity to Virgil demanded a dramaturgy totally unlike Scribe's. Cassandra is the narrative's central character in Acts 1 and 2; after the sack of Troy, Aeneas and Dido are the focus of the remainder. Berlioz's art is 'classical' in defining its events through the resources (and spirit) of Gluck: separate musical numbers; primacy of vocal melody; passion conveyed through objectively felt control. One can posit a similar development in Delacroix's career (especially the *Triumph of Apollo* (1850–1) for the Louvre ceiling), and it is noteworthy that Berlioz's Act 4 tableau of the removing of Dido's wedding-ring was inspired by a neo-classical painting by Pierre-Narcisse Guérin, *Aeneas Recounting the Misfortunes of Troy*.

Les Troyens embodies truly formidable stage demands. But they were calculated for a company whose resources the composer knew. Some idea of the awesome extent of those resources is captured in an English review of Gounod's five-act *Polyeucte* (after Corneille), given its première nine years after Berlioz's death, in the new Salle Garnier. The *Musical Times* of 1 November 1878 writes:

Let us look at the manner in which the opera itself was got ready, and draw, as we inevitably must, an unpleasant, though perhaps wholesome, contrast with what takes place in the same way nearer home...

First of all it was necessary to determine the principal artists, both of 'creation' and *partage*. This task, in virtue of right and custom, fell to M. Gounod...

Then came the copying of the parts, which alone cost between 6,000 and 7,000 francs; and next the important matter of the scenic arrangements.... While M. Daran [the stage designer] and his colleagues were thus busy [creating *maquettes*], the designer of the costumes, M. Lacoste, had an equally important and responsible task ... no fewer than 123 different costumes, all as correct as research could make them, were provided ... and altogether over 1,000 complete dresses entered the wardrobe of the theatre for use in *Polyeucte* alone. The pains taken with the costumes were immense ...

The hundred chorus-singers were first exercised in reading their music, the time adopted being as slow again as that indicated by the composer. Then the serious studies commenced, taking place twice a week ... Even more care was bestowed upon the orchestra. Beginning by simply reading their music without attention to anything but the mere notes, the instrumentalists passed to a methodical study of each number. This done, a grand rehearsal was given ... Then, every person being perfect in his or her work, came the *répétitions générales*, with scenery, dresses, etc. Of these there were eight, the last taking place on 3 October, when the arduous labours of a year ended, and *Polyeucte* was pronounced ready for the public.

Polyeucte ran for twenty-nine performances.

It was against the gigantism and corruption sensed at the Opéra that the tide turned after the revolution of 1848, whose subsequent years of unrest abutted in Napoleon III's *coup d'état*. An air of plurality and purpose gave rise to new comedy (Offenbach's career in particular), and new theatres (Offenbach's Bouffes-Parisiens; the Théâtre-Lyrique; the re-siting of smaller theatres following Haussmann's destruction of the Boulevard du Temple). Offenbach's aim was to counteract with operetta the over-seriousness, as he saw it, of contemporary 'opéra comique'. He even instigated a competition to encourage new light works: the young Bizet was a joint winner with *Le Docteur Miracle* in 1857. Comedy had never ceased to exist, of course, but the same stalwarts were producing— as Berlioz put it—'those pleasant and useful commodities which are daily manufactured in the manner of meat-pies, and which go by the name of opéras-comiques'. Offenbach's own revolution was, ironically, consummated in *Orphée aux enfers* (1858): debunking classicism and Gluck as well, it was received with fascinated horror, but grew as universally popular as *Les Troyens* remained universally unknown.

The 1850s was in fact a vintage decade for light opera: Massé's *Les Noces de Jeanette* (given 1,393 times up to 1942); Bazin's *Maître Pathelin*; Adam's *Si j'étais roi* and *Le Bijou perdu*; and many more perennial favourites by Berlioz's despised pie-merchants. Gounod successfully tackled comedy in *Le Médecin malgré lui* (in repertory up to 1945), and the same trend probably lay behind Berlioz's own *Béatrice et Bénédict* (1862) written for Baden-Baden.

Yet Offenbach had correctly identified a trend towards a more pretentious attitude to literary sources in opéra comique, and a new-found impulse towards what might be called the 'semi-serious' genre at the Opéra-Comique and Théâtre-Lyrique. It was prone to incorporate substantial acting-singing roles within an ambitious or exotic framework. Recitative could replace spoken dialogue. Meyerbeer's *L'Étoile du nord* (1854) and *Le Pardon de Ploërmel* (1859) represent an extreme of this trend, the former set in Peter the Great's Russia, the latter in a timeless Brittany. Women play the dominating dramatic parts in each. The same centrality is given to women in analogous contemporary operas: Auber's *Manon Lescaut* (1856), Halévy's *Jaguarita L'Indienne* (1855), and Félicien David's *La Perle du Brésil* (1851, rev. 1859). Offenbach called them 'little grand operas', because of their historical and geographical explorations, their mixture of dramatic tone, and their more challenging treatment of love and relationships. Halévy's Jaguarita and David's Zora were portrayed as shrewd and decisive, while at the same time retaining the fascination of exotic origins, in Brazil and Dutch Guyana respectively. Auber's Manon Lescaut retains the spirit of Prévost's heroine, if not the detail, and Scribe broke with convention by imposing a tragic ending (in New Orleans, following the literary source).

Set against this background, the advent of Gounod's *Faust* in 1859 represents something of a culmination. It was carefully constructed, using both a popular play (*Faust et Marguerite*, 1850, by Michel Carré) and Goethe's *Faust*, Part One. The librettist, Jules Barbier, was becoming an outstanding force in French opera, chiefly in partnership with Carré, with whom he wrote over thirty librettos. They include Gounod's *Roméo et Juliette* (1867), Ambroise Thomas's *Mignon* (1866) and *Hamlet* (1868), and Meyerbeer's *Le Pardon de Ploërmel*. Carré, alone, wrote *Mireille* (1864) for Gounod; for *Les Pêcheurs de perles* (1863) by Bizet, he wrote with E. Cormon. *Faust* is a representative example of this new generation of 'literary' opera: sophisticated, addressing a public that was probably much better-read than that of the late twentieth century, and willing to develop the implications of a dramatic theme. In the hands of the best composers, music's contribution fleshed out a new gallery of characters who were neither trivial nor solemn, and were given the responsibility of emotional growth. Gounod, and *Faust* in particular, played a pivotal role in the modernization of French opera. The musical score opened the way for a 'music of the future', in the Wagnerian sense—Gounod was well aware of international currents. In pacing, expressive range, chromatic harmony, and melodic confidence, *Faust* defined the path that Bizet, Thomas, Lalo, and Massenet followed, to say nothing of the more overtly Wagnerian Saint-Saëns. For Gounod it was axiomatic that the orchestra should play an enhanced role in the narrative. This is a complex area, since the orchestra's identity became both varied and pervasive, able to suggest a range of aspects of inner psychology and outer orientation. Control over tone colours became as vital as the usual French sensitivity to word-setting. As the baroque distinction between 'speaking in song' (prosaic recitative) and 'singing' (heightened utterance) began the last stages of its dissolution, so the orchestra was brought in to provide narrative continuity. And on a more obvious level, it became the norm to have recourse to recurring motifs in the orchestra, conveying an opera character's thought and feeling directly, without their having to utter. Such motifs readily took on idealistic or symbolic meaning. For example, Faust's vision of Marguerite has an orchestral theme in Act 1 which clearly corresponds to the rose-tinted effect that Méphistophélès deliberately designs. Meyerbeer's Catherine believes in a star of destiny, whose theme recurs throughout *L'Étoile du nord*. The celebrated duet theme in Bizet's *Les Pêcheurs de perles* is used repeatedly to recall the spellbinding impact of the priestess Léila upon the two friends Zurga and Nadir. Thus a distant time, a place, or a dramatic recollection could be effectively—and emotively—conveyed to the audience.

Gounod's modern use of Wagnerian harmony threw open a wide range of possibilities in exploring operatic character. But, simultaneously, the free handling of the orchestra allowed more vivid possibilities for musical scene-painting to come to the fore. This potential conflict in the balance between the fictional inner and outer life was a problem attaching to other arts too. In the novel, the current debate concerned the issue of excessive description and detail, for example in Flaubert's *Salammbô* (1862). In poetry, a shocking subjectivity entered the poems of Baudelaire, Verlaine, and Rimbaud; Baudelaire was prosecuted for *Les Fleurs du mal* (1857). Tristan Corbière's 1873 poem *Matelots* employs an ironic view of comic-opera representation, diametrically opposed to the real thing:

> Vos marins de quinquets à l'Opéra...comique,
> Sous un frac en bleu-ciel jurent 'Mille sabords!'

> Your footlight sailors at the Opéra...comique swear
> 'Shiver me timbers!', wearing sky-blue tail-coats.

Nevertheless, most operas with any sense of progress in the French tradition now attempted some conscious exploration of both 'inner' and 'outer' worlds. Gounod had but limited success in using the Provençal epic *Mirèio* ('Mireille'), issued by Frédéric Mistral in 1859, and so in *Roméo et Juliette* (1867) he wisely settled for a simpler concentration on the inner life of Shakespeare's doomed couple. Their love music helped confirm the Wagnerian tendency of French opera, which—it must be stressed— faced the strongest opposition from professional critics. Wagner's name and music had been objects of hatred in this quarter from the 1850s, and when Wagner brought his *Tannhäuser* to the Paris Opéra in 1861, with its new Bacchanale and Venusberg scene, the Jockey Club wrecked it for political reasons. (It had cost 164 rehearsals and a quarter of a million francs to put on.) After the Franco-Prussian war of 1870, rioting became common in Paris when Wagner's music was advertised at Pasdeloup's 'Concerts populaires'. But an essay such as Baudelaire's 1861 'Richard Wagner and *Tannhäuser* in Paris' shows that the magic of the new style appealed forcefully to a section of hearers. After quoting from his own celebrated poem 'Correspondances', Baudelaire explained his sensa- tions of 'rare joy', 'vast horizons', 'diffused light', and ecstasy that the music provoked, continuing, 'No musician excels as Wagner does in *depicting* space and depth, material and spiritual.' Outer and inner worlds were explored with equally 'passionate energy of expression'.

It was in such an atmosphere of conflict that Georges Bizet produced those few works he completed before his early death in 1875. But as well as drinking from the Wagnerian fountain, Bizet much admired Verdi, whose music had found widespread approval in Paris in the 1860s. Bizet's early-maturing genius gradually absorbed from these two what was needed, and his route to *Carmen* (1875) conceals a hard-won synthesis, steered by his own, French view of music theatre, and characterized by his superb rhythmic and melodic gifts. Strong evidence of these two last traits occurs in *Les Pêcheurs de perles* (1863); its first act has unforgettable beauty, though only to evoke a world of picturesque ritual and romance in the setting of Ceylon. *La Jolie Fille de Perth* (1867), after Scott's *The Fair Maid of Perth*, produced problems of consistency not surprising in an adaptation from this lengthy novel. After that Bizet used literary sources of both distinction and greater brevity.

For Bizet's *Djamileh* (1872) Louis Gallet's libretto was based on the fine philosophical poem *Namouna* by Alfred de Musset, published forty years earlier. Here, the outer casing of fantasy—the sybaritic Cairo of a hun- dred paintings, or of Gérard de Nerval's *Voyage en Orient* (1851)—is dis- solved into an ironic questioning analysis of emotion itself. Bizet's music responded with subtle transparency and emotional understatement, and is exquisitely challenging. Condemned by the newspapers as bizarre and confused, it disappeared after eleven performances. In *Carmen* (1875) Bizet again chose a source that treated passion in an objectified way. Mérimée's short story of the Spanish Gypsy is set in a double literary frame and carefully highlights local colour. In the opera the equivalent power derives partly from a dramaturgy that is like a Greek tragedy, and partly from the pervasive musical local colour. The recurring idea of fate—objectified in Carmen's fortune-telling scene and also given a musical motif—is at one both with the outer material (the known traits of Gypsy culture) and the obsessional psychology of the 'European' Don José, a simple soldier who finally commits murder. Bizet's score provoked both controversy and indifference in France to start with; but it has created an archetype that now seems as fixed as the tale of Oedipus or Don Juan. Its blazing unsentimentality inspired Nietzsche to hymn its praises on several occasions, even as he condemned the Wagnerian world of pessimism: 'I could imagine a music whose rarest magic would consist in this, that it no longer knew anything of good and evil...' (R. J. Hollingdale's translation from *Beyond Good and Evil*).

After Bizet's death a vacuum was caused which could only be filled by degrees of emulation on one hand, and a growth of Wagnerism on the other. Most notable in the first category were Delibes's *Lakmé* (1883) and Lalo's *Le Roi d'Ys* (1888). *Lakmé* tells of the tragic collision between a British officer in India and the daughter of a Brahmin priest; it is an operatic equivalent of Kipling (who was actually in India up to 1889), distinguished by evocative dances, as might have been expected from the composer of the ballets *Coppélia* and *Sylvia*.

In *Le Roi d'Ys* opera also responded to a vogue for Breton culture begun by the poet Auguste Brizeux in the 1830s; regional societies had published Breton folk-songs, and indeed Lalo's opera takes care to include one of them. But its legendary subject-matter itself indicates Wagnerian influence, since it was widely assumed that (as Saint-Saëns put it in 1892) 'the new art differs *fundamentally* from the old, musical drama must be drawn from legend, the old and the new are separated by an unbridgeable gulf'. Wagner's spell produced a whole cluster of allied works, including César Franck's *Hulda* (written 1881–5), Chabrier's *Gwendoline* (1886), d'Indy's *Fervaal* (1897), and Chausson's *Le Roi Arthus* (1903). In none of them was a satisfactory balance attained between outer form and inner content, and they are rarely staged today.

By the 1870s the Wagner style was admired privately more than professionally: Katharine Ellis has shown that the *Revue et gazette musicale de Paris* had four committed Wagnerians on its staff, none of whom seems to have published a word on Wagner. Its most pro-Wagner language occurred in an 1878 review of *La Statue* (1861), a highly wrought opéra comique by Ernest Reyer. In the meantime Reyer was working on France's own version of the nordic sagas and the death of Brunehild. This large conception does not deserve its current neglect and was to prove a success: the five-act *Sigurd* (1884). At around the same time, the precociously Wagnerian Saint-Saëns was compelled to withhold *Samson et Dalila* (first seen at Weimar in 1877). As did the best of Bizet, so Saint-Saëns's work achieved its successful 'French' synthesis of outer and inner truth by the way it objectified passion. That is, the 'Wagnerian' love music in Act 2 portrays, on Dalila's side, a calculated intention that will bring Samson's ruin. The obverse is the oriental/antique music representing the Israelites and Philistines in Gaza: not the least modern aspect of *Samson et Dalila* is its almost self-analytical mix of styles. Unfortunately, Saint-Saëns's ten later operas never achieved this overall level: *Henry VIII* (1883) and *Ascanio* (1890) had the most success.

Modern critics have been disturbed by the issues of racism, sexism, and anti-Semitism provoked by reading *Samson et Dalila*; indeed the great number of 'oriental' *femmes fatales* in late-nineteenth-century opera will continue to provide solid food for thought. Writers will probably arrive at the conclusion that, if any composer was unwilling to separate the seductiveness of a voice from that of the actress providing it, that composer was Jules Massenet (1842–1912). Havelock Ellis's *Psychology of Sex* even mentions the supposed aphrodisiac qualities of his music. Massenet's case makes Herbert Lindenberger's claim seem a laughable overstatement: 'there is no reason to think that the great 19th-century composers or their librettists ever thought seriously about what the Victorians called the "woman question" '. Massenet's extreme eclecticism of subject-matter was revealed in a stage career extending between 1867 and the posthumous *Cléopâtre* (1914), and stretching between operetta and tragedy, taking in an 'opéra légendaire' (*Amadis*, c.1895, first seen 1922), an 'opéra romanesque' (*Esclarmonde*, 1889), and a 'miracle' (*Le Jongleur de Notre-Dame*, 1902) on the way. Larger-than-life seductive heroines perform in the 'Indian' *Le Roi de Lahore* (1877), the 'Louis XV' *Manon* (1884), the 'Byzantine' *Esclarmonde*, the 'Early Christian' *Thaïs* (1894), and *Hérodiade* (1881). They seem tailored for a Paris public characterized by Lalo in 1883 as having 'remained ignorant, not having heard more than the same ten or fifteen operas for the last 30 years, hardly knowing Beethoven, and gnashing its teeth at the names of Wagner and Berlioz'. Occasionally, however, Massenet's lyrical voice strikes through and allies with the orchestra in a convincing Wagnerian continuous texture. More-over, *Werther* (1892) is a lasting testimony to the potency of the 'literary' movement of the 1850s.

It may be that French opera's best legacy to the twentieth century came from the world of fantasy. The fantastic in drama and music was a strong thread, stretching back to collaborations between Lully and Molière, to the fairgrounds of the eighteenth century, and to surreal bur-lesques under the Revolution. The establishment of the operetta idiom enabled serious fantasy to take root beneath the disguise of the popular and ephemeral, staking out a path that broadened after 1918. It is thus appropriate that *The Tales of Hoffmann* (1881), Offenbach's last, unfinished work, should have been an influential masterpiece. Hoffmannesque lit-erary fantasy was known to the French from 1830, and surfaced regularly on the stage; but nearer the end of the century its own surreal legacy was developed anew, often with the addition of social satire. Chabrier was particularly involved, most notably in *L'Étoile* (1877) and *Le Roi malgré lui* (1887). Like so many twentieth-century pieces, these employ satirical quotation from earlier music by other hands, distancing the spectator. Together with cabaret-influenced works, they helped create the condi-tions that would lead to the early modernism of Erik Satie.

❦ 5 ❦

THE NINETEENTH CENTURY: ITALY

William Ashbrook

Some Background

THE battle of Marengo (14 June 1800) can be taken in rather a crude way to establish one set of parameters for viewing Italian opera in the nineteenth century. Napoleon's victory, less than two weeks after his capture of Milan, would unsettle, temporarily at least, the established dynasties of the courts throughout the peninsula. In those court theatres Metastasian opera seria had long held sway as it so often reinforced the ruling status quo. Napoleon's intervention led to the creation, temporarily again, of some improvised governments up and down Italy, creating a sort of paradigm for the improvisations and intrigues central to opera buffa plots. And by 1900, the battle of Marengo has itself become an incident in an operatic libretto, when in the second act of Puccini's *Tosca* Sciarrone bursts into Scarpia's apartment to inform his master that, contrary to initial reports, Melas has been defeated and Napoleon is victorious, news that heightens the stakes in this melodramatic plot.

The course of history, even the history of a form as illogical and elusive as opera, is rarely neat, chronologically speaking. It is true, however, that as the eighteenth century drew to a close Metastasian opera seria did not immediately become extinct, nor did the castrati automatically retire from the stage, but these developments, the latter coming more swiftly than the former, were clearly imminent.

One consequence that can be partially attributed to the changes brought about by the French-inspired switch of governments throughout the peninsula was a surprising increase in the number of theatres, many of which would perform operas during some portion of the year. For instance, in 1800 Milan had two theatres, La Scala and the Canobbiana, but by 1815 there were nearly two dozen, at least half of which for some part of the year would host performances of opera. This increase in theatrical activity was more generally manifest in the centres of the North, but it was imitated to some degree in the South: Naples, for instance, had by the 1840s some half-dozen stages that put on operas. The increase was in part an aspect of urban growth, resulting from the movement of people from less prosperous rural surroundings to towns, a pattern repeated throughout Europe during the latter half of the eighteenth century.

More theatres meant an increasing demand for material. At the beginning of the nineteenth century, Italian audiences rarely encountered music more than twenty-five years old. There was no sense of an accrued repertory of masterpieces. What the public wanted was novelty: either a new work or one which had recently been favourably premièred elsewhere, particularly one in which favourite singers appeared to advantage. Instead of being primarily a diversion for court circles, opera would become for Italians in the nineteenth century an art belonging to a much larger segment of the population.

Further, it should be remembered that in Italy at the beginning of the nineteenth century there scarcely existed the concept of an opera as a discrete work containing a fixed corpus of material; rather an opera was regarded as a loose concatenation of interchangeable numbers, capable of hosting insertions from other works by the same or different composers. Singers travelled to their engagements carrying with them what used to be known as *arie di baule* (literally, arias from the trunk), solos in which they might appear to particular effect; these then could be grafted into whatever opera was scheduled. The generic character of many early nineteenth-century librettos, especially the arias of joyous relief common to the *lieto fine* of most operas, made such substitutions of material potentially less incongruous than they might at first appear.

Another consideration: at the beginning of the nineteenth century what we think of generically as Italian opera was not confined geographically to the peninsula. In Paris there was a full-time, state-supported theatre that gave its repertory in Italian, the so-called Théâtre-Italien, which hired the most famous singers of the day and would from time to time commission new works, among them Valentino Fioravanti's *I virtuosi ambulanti*, Bellini's *I puritani*, and Mercadante's *I briganti*. There were important Italian performances, as well as performances of operas of non-Italian provenance in Italian, annually in London during 'the season' (April–June) at a number of different theatres right down the century: among them the King's (later Her Majesty's) Theatre, from time to time at the Haymarket, but chiefly at Covent Garden. St Petersburg, and at the opposite end of Europe such centres as Madrid and Lisbon, for most of the century featured an Italian season almost every year, while many German-language theatres, such as the Kärntnertor in Vienna (most years until 1848), and those in Dresden and Prague gave an appreciable part of their time and repertory to Italian works, and in the first half of the century more often than not hired Italians to supervise them and compose for them. Beyond this, occasionally there would be important tours of Italian companies, such as when Verdi took his new *Aida* to a number of cities beyond the Alps.

The Transitional Years

Ferdinando Paer (1771–1839) was perhaps the most historically significant composer of Italian opera in the interregnum following the period dominated by Paisiello and Cimarosa and ending with the triumph of Rossini's *Tancredi* (1813), although much of his career was centred first in Vienna and Dresden and later in Paris. Most frequently mentioned as the composer who wrote *Leonora* (1804) on the same subject as Beethoven's *Fidelio* of the following year, Paer is more important for his part in the development of opera semiseria, a genre well adapted to the vogue for melodramatic plots with happy endings, works similar to the 'rescue' plots popular in Paris and elsewhere in the wake of the French Revolution. Besides *Leonora*, the most significant of his semiserie was *Agnese di Fitz-Henry* (1809), derived from Mrs Opie's *The Father and the Daughter* of 1801. Very frequently performed throughout Italy for the next twenty-five years, *Agnese* (as it was usually called) was a domestic drama with a strong emotional content, proving that the semiseria with its mixture of the comic and the (dominant) serious was a vehicle that could attempt to address moral and social issues in a period of strict censorship. An effective composer rather than a strikingly original one, Paer made a contribution whose significance should not be ignored.

Another noteworthy composer of this transitional generation was the Bavarian Johann Simon Mayr (1763–1845), who came to Italy in 1787 and was active first in Venice and later in Bergamo, where he established an influential music school, while continuing to write for Italian stages up to 1825. Mayr wrote operas in all the genres then popular, developing a more flexible orchestration than was then common in Italy, an aspect that spoke of his familiarity with the music of Haydn and Gluck. Further, with his bent towards musical education he became a channel that introduced ultramontane influences into Italy. He was responsible, for instance, for the first Italian performance of Mozart's *Don Giovanni* (Bergamo, 1811). Two of Mayr's most influential operas date from 1813: *La rosa bianca e la rosa rossa* (to Felice Romani's first libretto) and *Medea in Corinto*. In both of these are musical numbers combining solo passages with choral interjections, and they involve changes of tempo and include alternations of arioso and accompanied recitative. These varied structures created dramatic entities more complex than the self-contained arias usual in operas of that time. In the long view, however, Mayr's greatest contribution to Italian opera lay in his being the teacher of and example to Donizetti.

Gioachino Rossini (1792–1868)

Born on Leap Year Day 1792, Rossini initiated his career, following study with Padre Mattei in Bologna, with *Il cambiale di matrimonio* (1810). Seven operas later, all but one of them comedies, he emerged as a dominant influence of his age with his 'melodramma eroico', *Tancredi* (1813). Although his earlier operas had demonstrated a knack for effective orchestration, rhythmic acuity, and skill as a witty concocter of overtures, *Tancredi* contained undeniable evidence of his ripening talent with a richer font of melody, a broader emotional range, and, most of all, a readily identifiable musical personality. With this work his international reputation was launched.

More a codifier of practice than an inventor of forms, Rossini helped establish structural conventions; and he then used them with such clarity (and subtle variety) so that they would dominate the syntax of Italian opera through the middle of the century and beyond. These involve compound patterns, usually quadripartite. A solo *scena* was mostly apt to consist of an introductory passage, an elaborate aria in slow tempo, followed by a transitional passage resulting in change of mood, and concluding with a two-statement aria (called a 'cabaletta') usually in faster tempo and in a major key and in duple rhythm. In the second statement of a cabaletta, although on the page a repetition of the first, a singer was supposed to introduce some ornamentation of the vocal line, as Rossini himself told the English soprano Clara Novello. In duets, the pattern would customarily begin with dialogue, leading into an allegro with separate but balanced solo passages, followed by a slower, more lyrical episode with the voices harmonizing *a due*, and ending with a three-statement cabaletta (one for each soloist and a final one either in unison or parallel intervals). In duets of confrontation, the lyrical middle section was apt to be omitted, though it is almost always found in duets of *rapprochement*. The concertato finale often begins with musical dialogue over an orchestral melody, followed by some unexpected arrival or event which precipitates a slow ensemble of reaction (an expanded moment); the musical dialogue is then resumed, sometimes carried on over the orchestral melody of the first section and working up to some crisis which launches an allegro conclusion (called a 'stretta'), featuring contrasting thematic ideas, often involving a ground-swell crescendo, to fill out its basic two-statement structure.

Some three months after *Tancredi*, the first of Rossini's three opera buffa masterpieces *L'italiana in Algeri* ('The Italian Girl in Algiers') was brought out in Venice. The incisive wit and madcap inventiveness of the music underscore those qualities in the plot, epitomized by the hilarious midpoint finale, and stand witness to the composer's mastery of comedy. *Il barbiere di Siviglia* and *La Cenerentola* (a clever adaptation of the Cinderella story) were produced in Rome in 1816 and 1817, respectively. The former, with its famous patter song, 'Largo al factotum' (one that Rossini himself would frequently sing in salons during the 1820s), soon came to be regarded as the greatest opera buffa of the early nineteenth century. The apt use of the crescendo in Don Basilio's 'calumny' aria, for instance, or the cross-purposes at play in the 'Buona sera' ensemble in Act 2, the general high level of the music, made the opera enjoyable to an international audience, even to those with insufficient Italian to follow all the intricacies of the plot. The more romantic, even sentimental, *Cenerentola*, on the other hand, disappeared from the stage during the latter half of the nineteenth century because lyric mezzo-sopranos with a mastery of coloratura—the vocal type for which Rossini had tailored the leading part—were in short supply. It is only in the last fifty years or so that singers capable of meeting the taxing demands of this score have helped to re-establish *Cenerentola* in the affections of the public.

The recent revival of many of Rossini's serious operas has corrected the misleading impression that he was at his best as a composer of comedies. It used to be thought that his notorious self-borrowings from serious to comic contexts implied that his serious works were somehow trivial. For instance, what we tend to think of as the overture to *Il barbiere* had earlier been attached to his *Aureliano in Palmira* (1813) and also (in modified form) to *Elisabetta, regina d'Inghilterra* (1815). Rossini adapted part of Elisabetta's entrance aria to use some three months later as the cabaletta of Rosina's 'Una voce poco fa' (*Il barbiere*). Self-borrowings were regarded as perfectly permissible as long as the reused material was introduced in a town different from that which had heard it in its original context, and, in all fairness, it should be pointed out that Rossini, like Donizetti a little later, rarely borrowed from himself without reworking the material.

After *Tancredi*, Rossini's next considerable success with a serious subject was the opera that introduced him to Naples, *Elisabetta*. There he found a constellation of greatly gifted singers and for them he developed the vocally elaborate style that reached a climax in *Semiramide* (1823), his last opera written for Italy. It used to be repeated that he wrote out his ornamentation to avoid the hazards of having singers supply their own embellishments, but this is not true. In his earliest works his melodic lines were more simple and straightforward, but as he developed his idiosyncratic style the increasing vocal elaborations, instead of being intended as something purely decorative, become expressive of a wide range of moods: from flirtatiousness to intensity of purpose and imperiousness.

It was in his Neapolitan opere serie that Rossini's powers of invention found a remarkable outlet. He gave up writing *recitativo secco* for these works, replacing it with expressive, string-accompanied recitatives. In the last act of his *Otello* (1816) he achieved an atmosphere of foreboding and brooding intensity: the off-stage song of the Gondolier who quotes Dante's lines about the pain of remembering past happiness when one is miserable; the varied strophes of Desdemona's Willow Song; the surging duet; all these create a feeling of musical cohesiveness unusual for that time. The Prayer for solo voices and chorus, 'Dal tuo stellato soglio', from *Mosé in Egitto* (1818) is a persuasive example of solemn, unadorned eloquence, which in the drama is answered by the parting of the Red Sea. His most intense prefigurement of Romanticism, *La donna del lago* (1819), freely adapted from Scott's *The Lady of the Lake*, anticipates the nature tone-painting that would animate the sunrise episode at the close of *Guillaume Tell*.

After *Semiramide*, Rossini left Italy to pursue his fortune elsewhere, going first to London, and then settling in Paris, where he adapted two of his Neapolitan operas for the special requirements of the Opéra. These works were *Le Siège de Corinthe* (1826; deriving from *Maometto II*, 1820) and *Moïse* (1827; from *Mosé in Egitto*). In adapting them he increased the choral participation, often simplifying the solo vocal lines, and replaced some arias with ensembles. In *Le Siège de Corinthe*, he substituted a tenor for what had been the contralto *musico* character of Calbo, as these male hero roles played by female contraltos were in Italy a transitional phase from the period when such parts were assigned to alto castrati, but as the latter had never been popular in France there was no tradition of such heroes *en travesti* on the stage of the Opéra. The total effect of Rossini's French adaptations of these scores is a greater sense of formality. He also wrote one Italian *pièce d'occasion* for the Théâtre-Italien, *Il viaggio a Reims* (1825), a cantata for the coronation of Charles X, much of which he later inserted into his French opéra comique *Le Comte Ory* (1828). His chief new opera for Paris was *Guillaume Tell* (1829), with its great patriotic choruses, its noble arias, effective ballet music, and programmatic overture. The most imposing success of his career, this work is generally regarded as his finest achievement.

After *Tell*, Rossini retired from writing for the opera stage. Various reasons are advanced for this: his poor health, his finding the political and cultural climate after 1830 less congenial, and, perhaps chiefly, because he had sufficient investments to give him an independent living. Rossini lived until 1868, half his lifetime after retirement. His later compositions included a few religious works, among them the *Stabat mater*, besides a quixotic collection of vocal and instrumental amusements.

Gaetano Donizetti (1797–1848)

Five years younger than Rossini, Donizetti came from impoverished parents (his father was night porter at a pawnshop). He received a musical education only because Mayr had opened a free school to train choristers and musicians for church services. The boy revealed such a marked talent for improvisation and the rapid development of musical ideas that Mayr arranged to have him sent to Bologna for two years' study in counterpoint with Padre Mattei, who had taught Rossini. After several of Donizetti's inconclusive early attempts at writing operas, put on by a travelling company in Venice and Mantua, Mayr turned over to his pupil a commission to write for the Teatro Argentina in Rome. This work, *Zoraide di Granata* (1822), won sufficient favour with the public that Donizetti was offered a contract to go to Naples, arriving there just as Rossini was terminating his seven-year engagement.

Unlike Rossini, who had established his dominance by the age of 21, Donizetti was 33, and his operatic output almost equalled the number of his years, before he produced a true international success, with *Anna Bolena* (1830). During the 1820s a number of composers like Nicola Vaccai (1790–1848), whose *Giulietta e Romeo* (1825) earned a temporary *réclame*, and some like Saverio Mercadante (1795–1870) and Giovanni Pacini

(1796–1867), who made rather more durable splashes in the pool of Italian opera, then seemed more likely candidates than Donizetti for lasting eminence. His long apprenticeship would bear more lasting fruit, but for nearly eight years he worked to master the gamut of genres then current in Italy: Neapolitan farce, opera buffa, semiseria, the *azioni sacri* that were intended for performance during Lent, and the sort of serious opera with its happy ending then obligatory in conservative Naples. At that time death scenes, with the signal exceptions of those in Rossini's *Otello* and Carafa's *Gabriella di Vergy*, were not encouraged by the local censors. Indeed, when in 1826 Donizetti wanted to write one for his own practice and without a contract for its production, he made a setting of the text of Carafa's *Gabriella*. His first on-stage death scene occurs in *Imelda de' Lambertazzi* (1830), where the heroine succumbs confessing her guilt and begging forgiveness of her father.

Musically, Donizetti's early operas offer a surprising variety of experiments. *L'ajo nell'imbarazzo* ('The Tutor in Difficulties', 1824) is the first of his stage works to attain some lasting success; there have been a number of revivals of it in this century. Benefiting from a superior libretto by Ferretti, *L'ajo* is a fluent treatment of comic formulae in Rossini's vein, while Donizetti's future comic style is anticipated in the deft lyricism of the ensembles and in the tincture of pathos that humanizes the plot. Among the one-act farces, *Le convenienze teatrali* ('Theatrical Habits', 1827; sometimes given today as *Viva la Mamma!*) is a spoof on the pretensions of a second-rate opera troupe. Musically undistinguished for all its stageworthiness, but containing some pointed parodies of banal serious operas, this work can boast the unusual feature of a baritone *en travesti* as the termagant Mamm'Agata, the mother of the *seconda donna*. Among the serious operas, *L'esule di Roma* (1827) is a work of greater scope than any Donizetti had undertaken heretofore: it has elaborate choruses, a once-celebrated trio, to say nothing of his first mad scene (the baritone's 'Entra nel circo'), a funeral march, and a brilliant aria-finale for the soprano. *Elisabetta al castello di Kenilworth* (1829) presents the first of Donizetti's operatic portraits of Queen Elizabeth; further, it is his first stage work to contain two major female roles. Besides much efficient music, it has several elaborate arias and employs a quartet (instead of a full-scale concertato) for the first finale.

Anna Bolena, which has the benefit of a fine libretto by Felice Romani, contains more psychological penetration and complex interaction of character than was common in those days. Donizetti came to insist on the dramatic qualities of the texts he set, even to the extent of participating in their composition, and as far as he could he frequently pressed at the limits of what was possible in so far as the censors were concerned. Notable in *Anna* is the increased proportion of duets and ensembles to arias, although it concludes with a brace of *arie-finali*: the first is for the tenor and then comes an elaborate *scena* for Anna, which contains three lyric sections, the middle one being a chamber-setting of the tune of 'Home, Sweet Home', a rare example in operas of this period of an attempt at local colour. Another uncommon practice occurs in the Act 1 Giovanna [Jane] Seymour–Enrico duet, where phrases from the first section are repeated in the cabaletta, an effect he would revert to in the Norina–Malatesta duet in the second scene of *Don Pasquale*.

It used to be stated as fact that *Anna Bolena* was much more advanced than Donizetti's earlier operas: that it demonstrated how he had worked his way through the Rossini-isms of his formative years to find his own style, and also that it showed how Donizetti had been influenced by Bellinian *melos*. The chief point about *Anna Bolena* is that it marks a significant phase in Donizetti's own development. As he was composing for Milan, a city where relatively few of his twenty-nine earlier operas had then been performed, he felt free to reuse in revised form music from six of those scores in *Anna*. To claim that he had freed himself from Rossinian imitation depends on what aspect of Rossini's practice is being stressed. If by that is meant the compound structures that Rossini had employed, these had become a kind of *struttura franca* (as opposed to *lingua franca*) used extensively by everyone composing Italian operas in the 1820s and 1830s. But if by Rossini's style one means the declamatory vocal flourishes that many of his arias begin with, Donizetti had come to use this device sparingly, and hardly at all in *Anna Bolena*. As to the influence of Bellini, it is usually argued that Anna's beautiful larghetto in the Tower Scene, 'Al dolce guidami' with its plangent cor anglais obbligato, reflects the example of Bellini, but the melodic germ of this aria is a distillation and elaboration of a melody from Donizetti's very first staged opera, *Enrico di Borgogna* (1817), further evidence that *Anna Bolena* springs from Donizetti's personal musical experience.

After the success of *Anna Bolena*, the first of his operas to reach the stages of Paris and London, Donizetti began to compose for theatres throughout Italy, and even more so after 1832 when he won a release from the contract that had bound him almost exclusively to the Neapolitan houses. The general direction of his interest at this time was towards operatic tragedy and his desire to increase the dramatic temperature of *melodramma*. Typical of this interest is *Lucrezia Borgia* (1833), the first major opera to be based on one of Victor Hugo's plays, with its intrigue and multiple poisonings, a subject regarded as so explosive that two years passed before anyone dared to give the opera, so successful at its pre-mière, a second production. Musically, *Lucrezia* shows Donizetti's skill at modifying structural convention: in the Prologue, the ensemble-finale has a very brief allegro conclusion rather than a full stretta, and in the finale to Act I the trio that serves as its lyric slow section is capped with a cabaletta in the form of a duet. An unusual episode in which two subor-dinate characters plot while the orchestra sounds a sinister melody was recollected by Verdi when he wrote the dialogue for Rigoletto and Spara-fucile that opens the second scene of *Rigoletto*. Verdi had just come to Milan to study when *Lucrezia* had its opening run of thirty-three perfor-mances at La Scala, and Donizetti's score played a significant part in the formation of the younger man's musical imagination.

Lucia di Lammermoor (1835), based on Scott's novel, was the greatest single success of Donizetti's career. As was usual for composers in that decade, the work was designed to fit the strengths of the original cast: in this case Fanny Tacchinardi-Persiani, a great vocal technician, as Lucia, and Gilbert-Louis Duprez, the prototype of the Romantic tenor, as Edgardo. With its famous Mad Scene followed by the Tomb Scene (with Edgardo's suicide), both lovers kept apart by fate but anticipating their permanent reunion in heaven, *Lucia* became a touchstone of Romantic sensibility. The concision of the opera, its distinctive horn *tinta*, and the deeply felt elegance of its melodies are qualities that ensured the work a permanent place in the repertory.

One of the most interesting features of Donizetti's output is his fond-ness for subjects derived (often at several removes) from English history. *Elisabetta al castello di Kenilworth* and *Anna Bolena* have already been men-tioned, but the list includes not only the youthful, inexpert *Alfredo il grande* (1823) and the underrated *Rosmonda d'Inghilterra* (1834; dealing with Rosamund Clifford, Henry II, and Eleanor of Aquitaine), but also two works that only comparatively recently have assumed their rightful importance: *Maria Stuarda* (1835) and *Roberto Devereux* (1837). The former is derived from Schiller's play and contains the powerful (and fictional) confrontation of Elizabeth and Mary Stuart, an episode that brought Donizetti into difficulties with the censors; the power of the final scene, which includes an impressive Prayer and a touching aria-finale for Maria, is among his major achievements. Containing the most grandiose of his various portraits of Elizabeth, *Roberto Devereux* has a second act of great dramatic intensity, powerfully realized in musical terms, while the third act gives eloquent, compound arias to both Essex and Elizabeth. Oddly enough, the queen's last line is an offer to abdicate and permit James I to succeed her!

Nor was Romantic tragedy the only genre that Donizetti made his own. With *Il furioso all'isola di San Domingo* (1833) and, particularly, *Linda di Chamounix* (1842), he demonstrated his mastery of the difficult opera semiseria genre, which presents an essentially serious plot, has one buffo character, and comes to a happy conclusion. The first of these works boasts a sextet in the midpoint finale that is as moving as the much more famous one in *Lucia*, and the latter has a one-movement finale to Act 1 (an eloquent Prayer), a dramatic father-daughter duet in Act 2, and a touching pantomime scene near the beginning of Act 3. *Linda* contains, further, some of Donizetti's most felicitous use of reminiscence motives.

Although comedies are less frequent in Donizetti's output after *Anna Bolena*, some of his most enduring work belongs to this vein. The pastoral *L'elisir d'amore* (1832), the opéra comique *La Fille du régiment* (1840), and *Don Pasquale* (1843) are three works that have largely resisted the dimming of Time's hands, so fresh are the melodies, so infectious the humour that animates them, each of them containing that saving touch of pathos that adds sincerity to what might otherwise seem heartless. The innate good taste that lay at the heart of Donizetti's art is nowhere more accessible than in his mature comic works.

The final phase of Donizetti's career was an international one, for he moved to Paris in 1838 and after 1841 divided his year between the French capital and Vienna. He produced three works for the prestigious Opéra: *Les Martyrs* (1840; an expansion and modification of his 1838 score *Poliuto*, which had been banned in Naples), *La Favorite* (1840), and *Dom Sébastien* (1843). All of these have interesting features. The best parts of *Les Martyrs* are all contained in the tautly impressive pages of *Poliuto*, particularly the powerful Temple Scene, which anticipates in a number of ways the Triumphal Scene from *Aida*. *Dom Sébastien* imposes great demands of spectacle, as in the great Funeral March with catafalque in Act 3, which was staged with some 500 supernumeraries. Musically, it contains passages of interrelated reminiscence that show Donizetti moving towards a more flexible concept of musical drama. The most important of these works is *La Favorite*, which maintained itself as a French classic until World War I, and in Italian translation has proven even hardier. Spare and restrained, the music, often relying on severe scalar patterns, has sweep and passion, as in the arias of King Alphonse or the final duet for Léonor and Fernand. Indeed, the whole last act, which also contains Balthazar's

Mozartean evening prayer and the tenor's 'Ange si pur' (or 'Spirto gentil'), has long been recognized as masterly.

The beautifully crafted *Linda* and the tensely melodramatic *Maria di Rohan* (1843), his two operas for Vienna, reveal other aspects of Donizetti's maturity. It is only recently that his true measure has come to be generally appreciated. For too long he was regarded as the weakest member of a tripartite composer named 'Rossini-Bellini-Donizetti', a man who wrote too much too rapidly. Now, however, there is a more realistic understanding of the unfavourable conditions under which a composer of his time in Italian opera houses was forced to work. Brand new operas today rarely enter the permanent repertory and there have been numerous revivals of operas from the first half of the nineteenth century to replenish opera-house fare; the healthy result is that our judgements are based on a good deal more actual exposure to these works than was possible until recently, both in the theatre and through recordings; the old prejudice has pretty well disappeared. First of all, it is clear that one may admire all three composers—Rossini, Bellini, and Donizetti—for their particular merits without pointing out one's virtues at another's expense. Comparisons, as people used to say, are invidious. There is no denying that Donizetti's total of sixty-five operas contains much more of value than had hitherto been imagined and that his influence on the *melodramma* and on the so-called 'international' style that becomes prominent in the 1870s is difficult to overestimate.

Vincenzo Bellini (1801–1835)

Bellini was four years younger than Donizetti, but he succeeded in establishing himself earlier as a leading composer of Italian operas, with *Il pirata* (1827), only his third work. His first, a semiseria *Adelson e Salvini*, had been written in 1825, while he was still studying composition at the Naples Conservatory, and it was sufficiently well received to win him a contract to write a *Bianca e Gernando* for the San Carlo, Naples, in 1826. This opera was later revised as *Bianca e Fernando*, the use of 'Gernando' having arisen originally from censorial objections to the stage use of the name of King Ferdinando of Naples.

With his next work, *Il pirata*, Bellini gave a powerful impetus to what would become a Romantic revolution in Italian opera, not one of musical structure, as the conventional framework proved still viable, but of subject-matter, with increased emphasis on powerful emotions and acute suffering. Bellini's great gift for conceiving long-limbed melodies, as in Imogene's aria-finale, 'Col sorriso suo', introduced by a lengthy instrumental statement, made him stand out as a composer with a potent personal style. The contributions to its success by the librettist Felice Romani (1788–1865), hereafter Bellini's favoured collaborator, and by the tenor Giovanni Battista Rubini, who helped acquaint the composer with his particular brand of vocal filigree, were of great importance. This impression of Bellini's originality was reinforced by the relatively unconventional *La straniera* (1829), with its more straight-forward word-setting and the relative scarcity of coloratura passages. At its introduction the Milanese critics were somewhat put off by what they regarded as its excessive novelty.

The one setback of Bellini's career was the failure of *Zaira*, which was written for the opening of Parma's famed Teatro Regio in 1829. A good half of the score was salvaged and worked into his next attempt, *I Capuleti e i Montecchi* (1830), a setting of the Romeo and Juliet story (but drawn from several Italian sources rather than from Shakespeare), which was successful at Venice the following March. Bellini and Romani were next drawn to Victor Hugo's *Hernani*, but not wishing to run foul of the censors (the plot involved a conspiracy) they turned instead to the pastoral vein of *La sonnambula* (1831). Here Bellini's melodic gift, as in the evolving (non-repetitive) phrases of 'Ah, non credea mirarti' (Act 2), conveys tenderness and pathos through the music's reflection of natural verbal accent. The participation of Giuditta Pasta as Amina and Rubini as Elvino did much to ensure the work's initial success. Even greater was Pasta's effect in *Norma* (1831), when that classic tragedy, after a contested première, went on to become recognized as Bellini's masterpiece. Norma's famous incantation 'Casta diva' was rewritten a number of times, tradition has it, before Pasta was perfectly satisfied with it. The score boasts a number of vocally grateful duets, an impassioned trio-finale to Act 1, and a chromatically rising ensemble at the work's close that is supposed to have been in the back of Wagner's unconscious when he conceived the Liebestod. Although Wagner was contemptuous of most Italian opera, he had a marked tolerance for Bellini's music.

The next opera, *Beatrice di Tenda* (1833), is best known as a work that caused a rupture in the relationship of Bellini and Romani, the composer wanting his poet to devote his talents exclusively to him and not write for Donizetti and others. *Beatrice* has never shared the success of Bellini's better-known works, but the eloquent quintet (Act 2) deserves closer acquaintance.

At the behest of Rossini, Bellini was invited to Paris to compose for the Théâtre-Italien, and this provided the occasion for his last major success. *I puritani* (1835) contains a sensational role tailored to Rubini, asking the tenor to sing an F above high C, and a grateful role for the heroine with a brilliant *polacca* and a full-scale Mad Scene. Oddly enough, the beautiful larghetto to that scene, 'Qui la voce sua soave', seems to have originally been conceived as a song, 'La ricordanza', and then adapted for *I puritani*. The famous baritone–bass duet, 'Suoni la tromba', served as the basis for the set of variations, *Hexamoron*, by Liszt and other leading pianists of the 1830s.

Later that year, a few months before his 34th birthday, Bellini died betimes of what was diagnosed as a liver infection. All the leading singers then in Paris sang at his funeral.

Two Representative Lesser Figures

Saverio Mercadante (1795–1870) studied in Naples, with Zingarelli among others, and started out as one of the more competent *rossiniani* of the 1820s, making his mark with *Elisa e Claudio* (1821). He is best remembered today for the reforms that he introduced first in *Il giuramento* (1837) (probably his most consistent achievement), hoping to break the stranglehold of the traditional structural conventions of the time and to increase the dramatic propulsiveness of the action; but after pursuing this path through his three next operas he dropped back into his former habits. There are eloquent pages in Mercadante's best works, but a tendency to over-complication in accompanying figures and harmonic twists too frequently robs his music of spontaneity. Undoubtedly a figure of considerable reputation in 1840, Mercadante had some influence on the youthful Verdi, but it is now clear that Donizetti, whose example can be detected in Verdi's work even of his middle period, made a deeper impression. Blind in his old age, Mercadante dictated the last three of his total of fifty-eight operas to an amanuensis. Even more prolific was Giovanni Pacini (1796–1867), who composed eighty-nine stage works. His fame was confined to Italy, but he represents the plight of a composer enmeshed in the then insatiable demands of the Italian opera houses for new material. Rossini ironically observed of him: 'If Pacini ever learns to understand music, look out!' Of all his works, only *Saffo* (1840) keeps a tenuous grip on life. Pacini was primarily a melodist, but all too apt to prove inept in his accompaniments and concerted writing, and was notorious in his day as *il maestro delle cabalette*.

Giuseppe Verdi (1813–1901)

Born the same year as Wagner, Verdi came to dominate the field of Italian opera in the latter half of the nineteenth century just as surely as his coeval would eclipse German rivals. Verdi had the good fortune to live on into a time when the place of the composer in the hierarchy of the Italian opera house rose significantly, and with it the financial rewards. This happy circumstance would in time release him from the necessity of writing an opera directly on the heels of its predecessor, as Donizetti had been forced to do. Such a relaxing state of affairs, however, did not obtain during the 1840s, the decade that Verdi later grimly referred to as his years as a 'galley-slave'.

Verdi's earliest compositions were chiefly for the band in his native Busseto, but they demonstrated enough potential for his local backers to underwrite his going to Milan to study in 1832. Seven years would elapse before his first opera, *Oberto*, was produced at La Scala, earning a modest success. Its immediate successor, a comic opera called *Un giorno di regno* (1840), was withdrawn after a single performance.

With *Nabucco* (1842), his third opera, Verdi scored a decisive victory. The score has its blatant moments, but a restless energy animates much of it and there are many intimations of Verdi's future. Although the aria for chorus 'Va, pensiero' has since become by far the most celebrated piece, early reviews do not mention it in particular, perhaps a reflection of the extent to which Verdi's reputation as a 'patriotic' influence in nineteenth-century Italy was a creation of later generations. The chamber orchestration of Zaccaria's prayer gives the lie to the charge that all early Verdi is noisy and obstreperous. The great soprano–baritone duet in Act 3 reveals Verdi's sensitivity to the interaction of characters. There are clear allusions to Rossini, Bellini, and Donizetti in the score, but they are on the way to being integrated into the expression of a distinctive musical personality.

Ernani (1844) marks an appreciable advance over *Nabucco*. There is a tightness of focus in the three men, the dashing outlaw (tenor), the predatory king (baritone), and the ruthless old noble (bass), each of whom wants Elvira (soprano) for himself, and their musical characterizations are sharp. Elvira's taxing entrance aria, 'Ernani, Ernani involami' (Act 1), requires a range of over two octaves and rhythmic energy to produce its effect. The king's aria and the finale to Act 3, which dispenses entirely with its allegro pendant, shows Verdi's successful exploitation of the baritone *persona*. The climax of the score is the fine trio in Act 4, where the tug-of-war between the tenor and bass, with Elvira in the middle, is underlined harmonically as each tries to impose dominance, and ends with sixteen bars of poignant adagio as Ernani dies. This terse but expressive final act of *Ernani* demonstrates Verdi's keen sense of musical theatre. Here he reached a level that he did not always maintain in his next scores, although each minor work contains some signs of his unusual talent.

Verdi's capacity for development is shown most markedly in *Macbeth* (1847; revised for Paris, 1865). Some of the most strikingly original pages, the hushed duet for Macbeth and his wife 'Fatal mia donna!' and Lady Macbeth's Sleepwalking Scene, date from the first version and create a substantial musical equivalent to Shakespeare's poetic imagery. The score is undeniably uneven, however: the gibbering witches in the opening scene and later the assassins waiting to ambush Banquo are laughably unfrightening; nor is the Hecate ballet added for Paris exactly out of the top drawer. However, these lapses are not serious enough to detract from the greater amount of highly expressive and original music the score contains.

Luisa Miller (1849), derived from Schiller's *Kabale und Liebe*, finds Verdi turning towards the more intimate arena of domestic tragedy. The opening scene with its tone of rustic simplicity admirably establishes the vulnerability of the heroine, and here Verdi's experiments include an allegro aria for Luisa, cabaletta-like in feeling but in ternary form, and giving it as a pendant 'T'amo che d'amor esprimere', which, although described in the score as 'terzetto e stretta dell' introduzione', functions in fact as an ensemble-cabaletta to Luisa's aria and ends unconventionally with a musical 'dissolve' as the stage empties. There are many further signs of Verdi's reaching towards greater flexibility of expression in *Luisa*, as in the challenging unaccompanied quartet (Act 2), and particularly in the tenor's strophic 'Quando le sere al placido' (Act 2), which has with reason been described as 'Schubertian'. The closing act contains a wonderfully melancholy father–daughter (soprano–baritone) duet, and caps it with a trio surprisingly direct in its passionate intensity.

His next opera, *Stiffelio* (1850), deals with a Protestant pastor and his unfaithful wife, a social problem almost incomprehensible to most Italians of that time. Later revised, with a new last act, rechristened *Aroldo* (1857) and with the setting moved to medieval Britain, the work continued to resist public acceptance. After this singular divergence, Verdi's next three operas promptly became part of the core of the standard repertory. The first, *Rigoletto* (1851), which derived from Hugo's drama *Le*

Roi s'amuse (1832), is in some important respects the most unconventional of the three. During this period, Verdi expressed the wish to write an opera made solely from 'a series of duets', and that phrase has considerable resonance when applied to *Rigoletto*: most of the solo numbers are in a single movement, the duke's Act 2 aria being the only one with a typical cabaletta, 'Possente amor' (often cut in performance). He supplied foreshortened cabalettas to two duets, 'Addio, addio' for Gilda and the duke, and 'Sì, vendetta!' at the close of Act 2. There is some simple use of reminiscence motives: the thudding phrase associated with Rigoletto's response to Monterone's curse (first heard in the prelude), and the tune of the duke's 'La donna è mobile', by which Rigoletto learns that his intended victim has escaped. The most forward-looking aspect of *Rigoletto*, however, is the musical integrity of the last act, with the famous quartet that contrasts the seductive duke, the flirtatious Maddalena, the grieving Gilda, and the vengeful Rigoletto. Later, the climax of the tragedy is reinforced by the depiction of a musical storm, the effect of the wind rising and falling imitated by the chorus humming backstage.

Il trovatore (1853) is structurally more traditional than *Rigoletto*, but it contains new elements. No other score of Verdi's exploits sheer tunefulness so abundantly as this work, as in the famous 'Anvil Chorus', but there are finely crafted melodies, too, such as Di Luna's 'Il balen' and Leonora's 'D'amor sull'ali rosee'. The mezzo-soprano role of Azucena, the obsessed old gypsy, is a new kind of vocal persona in Italian opera, and a reflection of Verdi's having seen Meyerbeer's *Le Prophète* in Paris, that work containing the powerful mezzo-soprano figure of Fidès. *Il trovatore*, with each of its four acts divided into two compact scenes, possesses an admirable balance and pace that some of his later works did not achieve.

La traviata (1853) is derived from Dumas's recent *La Dame aux camélias* (1852), a tragic view of the contemporary *demi-monde*. At first, the opera was regarded as morally suspect, and for the first half-century of its existence its action was 'distanced' by seventeenth-century sets and costumes. In contrast to the melodrama of *Il trovatore*, *La traviata* contains much psychological sensitivity in depicting Violetta's response to Alfredo's declaration in the musings of 'Ah, fors'è lui', or in her scene with his father, in which she allows herself to be persuaded to renounce Alfredo, or in her coming to terms with her illness in 'Addio del passato'. This sensitivity is achieved in some measure through Verdi's greater restraint in orchestration and his keener sense of the possibilities of instrumental colour, as in the divided strings in the preludes to the first and last acts, or in the clarinet solo that accompanies Violetta as she writes her letter of farewell, or the oboe figures in her 'Addio del passato'. Other signs of Verdi's increasing expressive range show up in the vocal writing for his heroine: the coloratura effects are confined to Act 1, appearing in her badinage with Alfredo and, chiefly, in her cabaletta 'Sempre libera', which celebrates her madcap life as a courtesan; but in the rest of the opera her cantilenas are subtly inflected, as in the 'Dite alla giovine' passage in her duet with Germont, or her 'Alfredo, Alfredo' solo in the concertato that ends Act 2.

As the self-acknowledged opera capital of the world in the nineteenth century, Paris possessed an irresistible magnetic pull upon Verdi. He first came there to prepare not a new work, but a French version for the famous Opéra of his 1843 score *I Lombardi*, rechristened *Jérusalem* (1847). Although this patchwork was not particularly successful, Verdi remained for several years in Paris, then the refuge of a sizeable number of Italian political exiles, and he absorbed much of the activity of the French stage, both lyric and spoken. His next offer to compose for the Opéra would result in the sprawling *Les Vêpres siciliennes* (1855), composed to a recobbled libretto that in 1839 Scribe had supplied to Donizetti as *Le Duc d'Albe* (a work left incomplete at Donizetti's death). Although *Vêpres* possesses some eloquent pages and occasional phrases of a distinctly French contour, the overall musico-dramatic impression lacks the vividness to be found in each of his later operas.

On his return to Italy, Verdi composed *Simon Boccanegra* (1857), a gloomy work that had to wait until 1881, when it was extensively revised by Verdi with changes to the libretto by Arrigo Boito, to make its way into the fringes of the repertory. More general acceptance greeted *Un ballo in maschera* (1859), although problems with the censors involved changing the locale from Sweden to colonial Boston and demoting the tenor from the rank of king to the less exalted one of colonial governor. *Ballo* is the first of Verdi's works successfully to mix comic elements with predominantly tragic ones, and possesses a compactness and balance of structure that the composer would not recapture until *Aida*. Musically, it is wonderfully varied and shows how thoroughly he had absorbed certain French techniques into his own idiom: in the songs of Oscar the page; or the love duet in Act 2, where the expansive phrases Italianize a famous effect from the Valentine–Raoul duet in *Les Huguenots*; or in the last act, where a surreptitious dialogue is set against the rhythms of a courtly dance. *La forza del destino* (St Petersburg, 1862) presents a gamut of social types in a variety of milieux: its genre is a bold mixture of the ecclesiastical and the military. Verdi has developed a type of single-movement aria, as in Leonora's 'Madre, pietosa vergine', that is no longer capped by a florid cabaletta, but now moves from a more declamatory beginning towards a series of broadly expansive phrases. This was a device that Leoncavallo (in 'Vesti la giubba') and Puccini (in 'Vissi d'arte') would later adapt to more modest proportions. Among the subordinate characters Verdi manages to make a neat obeisance to two of his predecessors: the pedlar Trabuco is a linear decendant of Isacco in Rossini's *La gazza ladra*, as the *vivandière* Preziosilla is of Donizetti's daughter of the regiment. For the introduction of *Forza* to La Scala in 1869, Verdi revised his score extensively, without making it any more cohesive, but most significantly by ending it with a noble trio that resolves the conflict with something approaching Manzonian resignation.

For *Don Carlos*, written for Paris in 1867, Verdi turned once again to Schiller, finding there the inspiration for a musical portrait gallery of troubled souls as revealed in the searching soliloquys of Philippe II, the remorseful Eboli, and in Elisabeth's 'Toi qui sous le néant'. Although Verdi's ability to find musical expression for subtle inflections of character reaches one of its peaks, the work's lack of compactness was not remedied by a number of later revisions. *Aida* (1871), written for the opening of the Cairo Opera House, shows Verdi's masterly assimilation of the international style, a human action highlighted against a massively realized background, here tinted with exoticism suggestive of Pharaonic Egypt and incorporating balletic elements. The lyricism of the contrasting episodes in the Nile Scene (Act 3) reveals his adroit modification of traditional forms coupled with a shrewd sense of theatrical timing.

Except for the *Requiem* (1874), Verdi put aside composition permanently, so he believed, until his publisher Giulio Ricordi launched a campaign that, through suggested revisions of earlier works that had not proven their lasting viability and by turning up a literary figure of distinction, Arrigo Boito (1842–1918), as a potential collaborator, succeeded in stimulating Verdi at the age of 74 to return to the stage with *Otello* (1887). Boito's libretto does not quite deserve the praise usually accorded it. Although it succeeds in simplifying Shakespeare's plot into four unit-acts, at the same time it distorts it both by oversimplifying Iago's motivation and by substituting his own rhetorical idiosyncracies for Shakespeare's potent imagery and lofty verse. However, Verdi's keenly developed sense of orchestral colour, his modally enriched harmonies, and his fully mature ability to conceive whole acts as continuous musical compounds, all combine to set *Otello* head and shoulders above his previous accomplishments.

The triumph of *Otello* persuaded Verdi to write his final opera, *Falstaff* (1893), again with Boito's collaboration in adapting Shakespeare. Boito succeeds brilliantly here because his wit and his love for strange words are applied to a lesser play and give it new lustre. Verdi's quicksilver music belies his nearly eighty years in this, his nearest approach to a true ensemble opera, climaxed by the biting irony of its final fugue.

After Verdi

Verdi so overwhelmingly dominated Italian opera houses up to 1890 that composers a generation younger than he managed to produce at best ephemeral impressions. The two chief exceptions are Amilcare Ponchielli (1834–86) and Boito. With *La gioconda* (1876) Ponchielli showed his aptitude for the international style, making musical capital of the Venetian setting, including a big ballet ('The Dance of the Hours'), and providing supercharged melodies for a cast that requires six major singers. Using the sobriquet Tobia Gorrio, Boito produced the libretto for *La gioconda*, and under his own name wrote both text and music for *Mefistofele* (1868). This was a resounding fiasco in its original 'reform' guise, owing to Boito's deficiencies in conceiving and developing musical ideas, yet he managed to salvage the work by revising it extensively for a revival at Bologna in 1875, ironically enough removing most of its 'reform' features in the process. Much of the work seems a pageant; only the Prison Scene (Act 3) generates real dramatic tension. Today *Mefistofele* survives to the extent that star basses find the kitschy title role a congenial vehicle.

In 1890 Pietro Mascagni's *Cavalleria rusticana* burst upon the operatic world like a bombshell; its impact was felt around the world in record time. Derived from a naturalistic short story by Verga, this one-act opera with its drama of infidelity and revenge among Sicilian peasants launched a vogue for what is known as 'verismo'—the approximate operatic equivalent of literary naturalism. For a work that was regarded as revolutionary in its day, *Cavalleria* contains much that is conventional. A novel touch was the insertion of a tenor serenade into the prelude, but it leads to a traditional opening chorus, then Alfio's description of his self-evident occupation as carterer, followed by an Easter hymn for the villagers. It is not until one-third of the way into the score, at Santuzza's brief, intense arioso 'Voi lo sapete', followed by two impassioned duets, that the score attains emotional immediacy. The denouement—a village woman screams and shouts that Turridu has been killed in a duel—makes for a melodramatic final curtain.

The great success of *Cavalleria* spawned a sickly swarm of imitations, and not just in Italy. The only work to demonstrate anything approaching its staying power is Ruggero Leoncavallo's *Pagliacci* (1892). Finding difficulty in obtaining a hearing for his more pretentious operatic projects, Leoncavallo decided that verismo was the way to catch the public's attention, and he deliberately set out to match the effectiveness of *Cavalleria*. The blatant contrast between the celebration of Easter and the sordid tragedy in Mascagni's work finds a counterpart in the opposition between the artificiality of the *commedia dell'arte* playlet and the 'real-life' emotional conflicts of the actors taking part in it. Leoncavallo's prelude is interrupted not by a serenade but by a Prologue; Tonio's clever exposition of literary theory has become a favoured moment for baritones, as has the tenor's 'Vesti la giubba', in which Canio the clown must laugh although his heart is breaking.

Neither Leoncavallo (1857–1919) nor Mascagni (1863–1945), turn out operas as they would, succeeded in writing another that manifested anything like the durability of *Pagliacci* or *Cavalleria*, which speedily became the Castor and Pollux of the repertory. In that generation the pattern of being a 'one-opera' composer was to some degree contagious; there are four others principally remembered for a single work: Francesco Cilea (1866–1950) for *Adriana Lecouvreur* (1902), Umberto Giordano (1867–1948) for *Andrea Chénier* (1896), Italo Montemezzi (1875–1952) for *L'amore dei tre re* (1913), and Riccardo Zandonai (1883–1944) for *Francesca da Rimini* (1914).

Puccini

Although their elder by several years, Giacomo Puccini (1858–1924), unlike Mascagni and Leoncavallo, found success elusive until his third opera, *Manon Lescaut* (1893), caught public attention with its effective compound of frank sensuality and pathos floated on arresting melodies, the score confectioned with a glint of fashionable Wagnerianism. It seems more than fortuitous that Puccini, who most nearly succeeded to Verdi's hold upon the general public's affections, should first make his mark a little more than a week before the première of Verdi's last opera, *Falstaff*.

La bohème (1896), Puccini's next opera, significantly added to his popularity. It demonstrates his sensitive grasp of theatrical effect, particularly in the finely judged mixture of humorous and pathetic scenes, nowhere more succinctly presented than in the quartet at the conclusion of Act 3 that sets off two sentimental lovers against a squabbling pair. This opera, with its subject of down-at-heel artists and their girl-friends set in the Latin Quarter in the days of Louis-Philippe, appealed to a new segment of the audience, working people who could identify with the bourgeois emotional atmosphere of the plot. Puccini's mastery of depicting stage atmosphere that prefigures dramatic situations comes to the fore in such an episode as the opening of Act 3 at the Barrière d'Enfer in the snow.

One could say that Puccini humanized verismo practice. Instead of the overwrought passions of a *Cavalleria*, the pathetic plight of Mimì as intensified by the poignant recall of music associated with happier times was intended to move rather than shock an audience. From the time of *La bohème* onwards, Puccini understood the importance of having a libretto tailored to his finely calibrated sense of drama, and his exigence with collaborators became notorious. With this opera another of his traits as a composer came to the fore. Following the première of one of his operas and experiencing it repeatedly in the theatre, he would adjust his score repeatedly: adding an episode here, eliminating a few bars there, or transposing a passage down a half-step to make it less taxing for the singer.

With *Tosca* (1900) Puccini achieved another success, this time with a much more overtly melodramatic plot (derived from Sardou's *La Tosca*). More than either *Manon Lescaut* or *Bohème*, *Tosca* raises emotions to prime verismo levels, even though the plot is peopled by artists and public officials rather than by peasants. The sense of geographical and historical realism is aided by the settings (a specific Roman church, palace, and prison) and by the imitation of period music in the gavotte and later the cantata heard through Scarpia's window in Act 2. In the prelude to Act 3 Puccini achieves a memorable sense of time and place by using an off-stage shepherd boy's ditty in the local dialect and by imitating the overlapping clanging of Roman church bells as they sound matins.

Puccini's tendencies as a local colourist took a more exotic turn in his next opera, *Madama Butterfly* (1904), for with it he established the cultural contrast of the conflict by citing both 'The Star-Spangled Banner' and some authentic Japanese tunes. He also demonstrated his skill at fashioning his own pseudo-Japanese motifs and at imitating the sound of native instruments. Indeed, Puccini's subtlety as an orchestrator emerges in high relief in this work. A fiasco at its première, this owing as much to organized opposition by Puccini's rivals as to certain mis-calculations in the score, *Butterfly* was revised for a successful relaunch-ing at Brescia some three months after its unhappy introduction at La Scala, and Puccini continued to fine-tune his adjustments over several years.

For a setting that had been little exploited on the Italian opera stage, Puccini next turned to the United States, specifically California in the days of the Gold Rush, drawing his plot from Belasco's play *The Girl of the Golden West*. At the time of its world première at the Metropolitan in New York (1910) and the succeeding series of local *prime* both in the United States and Europe, Puccini's *La fanciulla del West* provoked initial curios-ity and subsequent disillusionment. It lacked the judiciously placed short arias with their opportunities for applause that had endeared Puccini to his public; for all its moments of high-gear melodrama, this new opera produced no pathetic catharsis—not a single character dies; the spectacle of Italian *comprimario* 'miners' shouting 'Allo' and ordering 'wheesky' struck many of the earlier viewers as disaffecting, if not downright grotesque. With the passage of time, however, the considerable merits of *Fanciulla* are easier to discern. Puccini was moving away from his former style, of building up a score out of brief episodes as one might a mosaic; rather he was coming to conceive a work in much larger units, such as the extended episode for Minnie and Johnson at the close of Act 1 or her exciting poker game with the sheriff in Act 2, which achieves the dra-matic immediacy of Belasco's play. The notion that this plot is in the nature of a redemption myth and that the happy ending is legitimately optimistic is confirmed by the rearrangements of material Puccini had his librettists impose on the American play and by his stress upon the-matic and tonal interrelationships in the score.

In his restless search for novelty (and for profits), Puccini was tempted next to invade the world of Viennese operetta. His innate sense of his own capabilities, and the intervention of World War I, which found Italy and Austria on opposite sides of the conflict, made the original scheme more than impractical, indeed unpatriotic. The work that emerged out of these untimely antecedents turned out to be a through-composed opera, *La rondine* (1917). Slender dramatically, it contains music of much charm and sophistication, attaining its climax in the Act 2 quartet (for two sopranos and two tenors); but of all Puccini's mature works it has the most tenuous hold on a place in the repertory.

His next effort was a series of three one-act operas, designed to be per-formed together as *Il trittico* (1918). These form contrasting views of love and death. *Il tabarro* with its grim triangle among bargees on the Seine is Puccini's most completely veristic work, but his score subtlely combines Debussian harmony with his own surging melos. *Suor Angelica*, concerned with a mother's grief and suicide in a convent setting, is perhaps Puccini's most musically understated score (except for the hysteria and 'miracle' at the end). *Gianni Schicchi* is a true miracle of sardonic Italian humour, a tale derived from a hint in Dante's *Divine Comedy* about a father impersonating one Buoso Donati in order to make a new will, which he is shrewd enough to arrange in such a way that his daughter will have a dowry and be able to marry a relative of Buoso. This medieval jape is clothed in music of much wit and irony, happily leavened with lyrical moments, as in the well-known 'O mio babbino caro' or the miniature love-duet for Lauretta and Rinuccio (just fifteen bars in length) near the end of the opera.

Puccini did not live to complete *Turandot* (first performed 1926), for which he had turned to a play by the eighteenth-century Venetian dramatist Carlo Gozzi, set in China's legendary past. Once again, the composer availed himself of some genuine native melodies as well as devising some pentatonic tunes of his own to create an exotic atmosphere. Furthermore, as one who strove to remain *au courant* with musical trends, his score contains passages reminiscent of both Musorgsky and Ravel. For richness of musical texture and thematic coherence this work stands as Puccini's masterpiece, even though he left it unfinished. Puccini found it difficult to complete his opera, it seems clear today, because the emotional impact of his music for Liù's death and cortège created a problem of shifting sympathies to the Unknown Prince's determination to thaw the heart of Turandot. The final crucial fifteen minutes of music were supplied, partly on the basis of Puccini's sketches, by the young Italian composer Franco Alfano (1876–1954).

Italian operas did not stop being written after *Turandot*. Yet that work stands as a worthy milestone to mark the end of the vitality of the tradition that had animated nineteenth-century Italian opera. That the human voice in more recent works no longer dominates as the most immediately communicative and affecting of musical instruments is a sad fact separating the time covered in this survey from the days that followed.

❦ 6 ❦

THE NINETEENTH CENTURY: GERMANY

Barry Millington

W HEN revolution broke out in Dresden in March 1848, Kapellmeister Richard Wagner threw himself energetically into the fray. He assumed a prominent role on the streets and barricades, allowed at least two political gatherings to take place in his garden at which the arming of the populace was discussed, and appears to have been involved in the manufacture of hand-grenades. A warrant was issued for his arrest and, although Wagner made his way to a haven in Switzerland, he only narrowly avoided capture and a possible death sentence.

Had such a sentence been carried out, Wagner would be remembered today not as the man who changed the course of operatic history, but as the composer of three fine Romantic operas and three rather more derivative works worthy of occasional revival.

To ponder on the course German opera would have followed had Wagner not lived to complete the *Ring*, *Tristan*, *Die Meistersinger*, and *Parsifal* is to embark on speculation as intriguing as it is pointless. Doubtless operatic form would have continued to evolve, as it had begun to do about the time of Wagner's birth in 1813, but the precise nature of that reform can only be surmised. Inevitably, Wagner occupies a pivotal role in any account of the history of German opera—indeed, of opera generally. The present chapter aims to demonstrate just how fundamental Wagner's reform programme was, and how imposingly his shadow falls across the entire century, while endeavouring to do justice to the individual contributions of the other major composers of the era.

Nineteenth-Century German Opera before Wagner

The traditional German form of the Singspiel—in which self-contained musical numbers were interspersed with spoken dialogue—reached its zenith in the last decade of the eighteenth century with Mozart's *Die Zauberflöte*. The genre did not suddenly wither and die, however. Beethoven's *Fidelio*, composed in 1804–5 but reaching its final form only in 1814, is essentially a Singspiel, though it also draws heavily on the tradition of French opéra comique, especially 'rescue opera', of the Revolutionary period. Of the eleven dramatic works completed by Schubert, more than half, including *Der vierjährige Posten* (1815), *Claudine von Villa Bella* (1815), and *Die Verschworenen* (1822–3), were designated 'Singspiele'.

But now there was a new spirit abroad. German Romanticism was on the verge of giving birth to its most characteristic genre: through-composed opera on serious, weighty themes. Before that process got fully under way—and even for some time after—a transitional genre of German Romantic Singspiel was essayed by several composers. To this genre belong, most notably, Spohr's *Faust* (1816), Hoffmann's *Undine* (1816), and Weber's *Der Freischütz* (1821), the last generally regarded as a landmark in operatic history, but anticipated in several respects by the two earlier works.

Faust, by Louis Spohr (1784–1859) with a libretto by Joseph Carl Bernard, was based on various versions of the legend (but not that of Goethe) and is of considerable historical importance for two reasons. In the first place, it marks a significant shift away from construction by self-contained numbers towards what might be called 'scene complexes': in other words, numbers begin to be grouped—the first step on the road towards through-composed opera. (In the 1850s Spohr even agreed to set the dialogue to music so that the work could be performed as a grand opera.) In the second place, Spohr's use of recurring (or 'reminiscence') motifs, identified with hell, love, a magic potion, and Faust himself, represented an advance towards thematic unification—a process epitomized by the Wagnerian system of leitmotif.

Undine, music by E. T. A. Hoffmann (1776–1822) to a libretto by Friedrich de la Motte Fouqué after Fouqué's own story, treats that archetypal Romantic theme of the confrontation of the spirit and mortal worlds. Undine is a water spirit who acquires a mortal soul on her marriage with the knight Huldbrand. The knight fails to heed her warning that she must return to her element, and even kill her husband, if he is unfaithful to her. Huldbrand abandons Undine, who finally reappears to draw him down to a watery grave. The same story was later to form the basis of an opera by Albert Lortzing (1845), but its central theme—the tragic consequences of the incompatibility of the mortal and spirit worlds—was to resurface in numerous operas throughout the century, most notably Marschner's *Hans Heiling* and Wagner's *Lohengrin*. Hoff-mann's *chef d'œuvre* is historically important in musical terms, too, for its use of reminiscence motifs and for its structural continuity (notwith-standing its spoken dialogue), achieved partly by its greater emphasis on the role of the chorus and of ensembles generally.

Der Freischütz, by Carl Maria von Weber (1786–1826), may have fol-lowed in the wake of *Faust* and *Undine*, but it far outstripped them in terms of both influence and popularity. *Freischütz*, with its interspersed spoken dialogue, folk-song-inspired melodic style and popular choruses, still harked back to the Singspiel tradition, but in its evocation of the dark, mysterious forest of German Romanticism—that world already familiar from the elemental, supernatural themes treated by the painters Caspar David Friedrich and Moritz von Schwind—it struck a chord that resounded in the hearts and minds of German composers and audiences well after Weber's premature death in 1826. The supernaturalism is at its most intense in the Wolf's Glen Scene, in which Caspar invokes the evil spirit Samiel to help cast the magic bullets which will put Max in his power. The weird apparitions and revelling in supernatural horror find their counterpart in the stock musical elements of tremolo strings, diminished sevenths, and tritones.

With *Euryanthe*, designated a 'grand heroic-Romantic opera', Weber a few years later (1823) advanced the development of German Romantic opera still further. The inadequacies of the libretto, by Helmine von Chezy after a medieval French romance, have generally been held responsible for the opera's inability to find a place in the repertory. Yet again this is a work whose resonances are felt in more than one work by Wagner (*Lohengrin* and *Siegfried*, in particular) and which blazed a trail for indigenous German opera with its eschewal of spoken dialogue, and the dramatic conviction of its music.

Weber was not quite the first to write a through-composed opera: two of his friends, Johann Nepomuk Poissl and Ignaz von Mosel, had already done so, as had Schubert in *Alfonso und Estrella* (1822). (Schubert reverted to spoken dialogue in *Fierrabras*, 1823, which in spite of a good deal of inspired music, fails to convince on dramaturgical grounds.) And Weber was further just pipped to the post with his première of *Euryanthe* on 25 October 1823 by that of Spohr's *Jessonda*, which reached the boards in July of that year. Spohr and Weber were friendly rivals, a fact which sharpens the irony that *Euryanthe*, though deemed from the start to be flawed by its impracticable libretto, has always been admired for its purely musical qualities, whereas *Jessonda* was enthusiastically acclaimed as a masterpiece in its time, but has since been virtually consigned to oblivion.

The contemporary popularity of *Jessonda* is undoubtedly explained, in part, by the oriental flavour of its story: this was, after all, a period of intense fascination with the East. Jessonda is the widow of a rajah, called upon to perform the ritual of suttee, or self-immolation, out of respect for her dead husband. The opera is the story of her deliverance from the 'barbaric', oriental ritual by the forces of Western civilization, in the shape of the Portuguese general Tristan d'Acunha. Ideological polarization of this sort appealed strongly to audiences of the time—several versions of the play on which it was based (Antoine Lemierre's *La Veuve du Malabar*), some with music, were current in German theatres until the middle of the nineteenth century—even if the benefits for operatic treatment were questionable. Spectacular visual effects were supplied in the form of big choral and ballet scenes, solemn ritual ceremonies, and exotic local colour.

In an article published in the *Allgemeine musikalische Zeitung* shortly before the première of *Jessonda*, Spohr issued a manifesto for the future of German opera—an indication of the extent to which the matter was exercising the minds of composers. *Jessonda*, with its substitution of recitative for spoken dialogue, and its tightening of the musical and dramatic structure into an almost continuous flow, was clearly intended to be the practical realization of that theoretical model: in effect, a German grand opera. Surprisingly, however, the role of reminiscence motifs is less decisive than in Spohr's earlier *Faust*.

Another modest innovator of the period was Heinrich Marschner (1795–1861) whose three best-known operas—*Der Vampyr* (1828), *Der Templer und die Jüdin* (1829), and *Hans Heiling* (1833)—all played a part in the evolution of German Romantic opera. The element of the supernatural was a prominent feature, the Gothic horror of the literary *Schauerromantik* exercising its lurid hold over the imagination of composers and librettists alike. The eponymous vampire of the first of Marschner's trio—actually his eighth completed opera—has to deliver to Satan three virgin brides if he is to extend his leave of absence from hell. The task proves none too easy and in fact his third intended victim eludes him. Notwithstanding the improbable story and the passages of comic relief, the tone of *Der Vampyr* is sombre, and the atmosphere of diablerie is heightened by the use of melodrama, i.e. speaking or acting against an orchestral accompaniment.

Der Vampyr received its first performance in March 1828 at Leipzig, where the 15-year-old Wagner lived. In December of the following year Marschner's next opera, *Der Templer und die Jüdin*, based on Scott's novel *Ivanhoe*, was also introduced to the public via the stage of the Leipzig Stadttheater. These works were part of the musical culture absorbed by the young Wagner, though it was not until he became a chorus master at Würzburg, in 1833, that he had direct practical experience of them. Marschner's *Hans Heiling* was actually given at Wagner's theatre in Würzburg, only a few months after its Berlin première. Beyond admitting its influence on his early opera *Die Feen*, Wagner made little of the impact of *Hans Heiling*. But its imprint is unmistakable in *Der fliegende Holländer*, *Tannhäuser*, and *Lohengrin*, in the preoccupation with the tragic interaction of the mortal and supernatural worlds. If the *mise-en-scène* of the prologue to *Hans Heiling* seems to foreshadow that to the *Ring* (i.e. *Das Rheingold*) with its subterranean cave of the Earth Spirits and its busy dwarfs, there is a distinct pre-echo of *Tannhäuser* in the struggle of Heiling to leave the underground world and return to the upper world, and in the queen's repeated urging him to stay. Marschner advanced his action largely in discrete numbers, but a modest use of scene complexes provided a stepping-stone to the through-composed music drama, while his colourfully dramatic orchestration—and even specific melodic and harmonic ideas—clearly left their mark on Wagner's developing style.

If the theme of mortal / spirit contact was hugely popular at this time, it was because it satisfied the post-Enlightenment Romantic notion of humankind's reunion with nature. The *Undine* settings of Hoffmann and Lortzing have already been mentioned. Other treatments of the legend include *Melusine* (1833) by Conradin Kreutzer (1780–1849), better known for his Romantic opera *Das Nachtlager in Granada* (1834) and his 'magic fairy-tale' *Der Verschwender* (1834), and *Der Bergkönig* (1825) by Peter Joseph von Lindpaintner (1791–1856). The latter composer, who also succumbed to the rage for vampire stories with his *Der Vampyr* of 1828, was a hard-working musician—one of the finest German conductors of his era—whose many operas were well received at the time, though their lack of originality and slight texts have caused them to disappear from the repertory.

Albert Lortzing (1801–51), who even in his own time scarcely made his reputation on the basis of originality, has nevertheless survived rather better. It is a curious fact that in the third quarter of the twentieth century his operas received more performances than those of any other German-speaking composer with the exception of Mozart. Yet so rooted in their native tradition are they that they are rarely performed outside the German-speaking countries. Lortzing's characteristic vein is not so much the serious Romantic one of *Undine*—something of a departure in his *œuvre*—but that of comic opera. In a steady stream of such operas, with skilfully crafted comic ensembles and unequivocally self-contained solo songs, often narrative in function, Lortzing achieved an unrivalled reputation in this field in the Germany of the 1830s and 1840s. Being 'not driven by the power of genius', as one contemporary observer noted, 'he aims for the easily graspable'. But in Biedermeier Germany it was a recipe for commercial success, as Lortzing's sustained popularity demonstrates. Nor should his compositional skills be underrated. In the three-act *Zar und Zimmermann* (1837), the czar of whose title is the young Peter the Great, there is considerable sophistication in the handling of dramatic structure, while Lortzing's comic masterpiece *Der Wildschütz* ('The Poacher', 1842) realizes the comic potential of the somewhat absurd story with such spontaneity and lack of pretension as to disarm criticism.

Tapping a similar vein, but under a more explicit Italian influence, was Otto Nicolai (1810–49), whose *Die lustigen Weiber von Windsor* (1849), based on Shakespeare's *Merry Wives*, has also remained in the repertory, largely on account of its attractive melodies and skilfully contrived comic situations.

Successful as Lortzing and Nicolai were, their achievements did little to advance the evolution of a characteristically national German opera in the nineteenth century. Their works thus stand at a tangent to the broad curve, with Wagner at its apex, traced by this chapter. Before that climactic point is reached, the efforts of two major composers, who nevertheless made only a minor contribution to that evolutionary process, need to be considered: Felix Mendelssohn (1809–47) and Robert Schumann (1810–56). Both illustrate, if only by default, the high premium placed by nineteenth-century German composers on a successful opera. It is no surprise that Mendelssohn, whose prodigious talents were apparent almost, it seems, from the cradle, should have attempted a dramatic work at an early stage of his career. What is astonishing is that he should have completed no fewer than six substantial dramatic works before the age of 21. These include the one-act Singspiele *Die beiden Pädogogen* (1821) and *Die wandernden Komödianten* (1822), a three-act comic opera, *Der Onkel aus Boston* (1824), and the single-act Liederspiel *Die Heimkehr aus der Fremde* (1829). But his most important opera, and the only one to receive a fully public performance in his lifetime, was *Die Hochzeit des Camacho*

(1827). All Mendelssohn's dramatic works, with their interspersed spoken dialogue, belong firmly to the Singspiel tradition. In *Camacho*, however, there is clear evidence of the adolescent Mendelssohn's awareness of contemporary trends. He knew Weber's *Der Freischütz* and Spohr's *Jessonda*, and in *Camacho's* advanced use of scene complexes, recurring motifs, and orchestral sonority, there are echoes of both works. The Berlin première of *Camacho* was only a qualified success and Mendelssohn himself was not sufficiently proud of his achievement to seek further performances. Yet the imperative to score a real success with an opera, and hence the struggle to find a suitable libretto, never diminished. In 1831 he commented to a friend, with a touch of poetic licence: 'Put a real opera [libretto] into my hands and in a few moments it will be composed, for every day I long anew to write an opera.' But although he was to consider and even embark on several operatic projects, he never completed another.

Schumann, in spite of his achievements in most of the established forms, likewise found that success on the dramatic stage eluded him. His only completed opera, *Genoveva* (1850), based on the medieval legend of Geneviève of Brabant, was conducted at its 1850 première by the composer himself and five years later by Liszt, whose comment to Anton Rubinstein acknowledges both the merits and demerits of the score: 'Of the operas that have been produced over the last 50 years it is certainly the one I prefer (Wagner excepted—that is understood)—in spite of its lack of dramatic vitality.' *Genoveva* intersperses melodically inspired arias and simple folk-like songs with a form of recitative that borders on lyrical arioso. But it undeniably lacks the sharpness of characterization and the dramatic momentum that are essential ingredients for any operatic work, irrespective of style or period.

Richard Wagner (1813–1883)

By the time Wagner secured his first professional appointment in 1833, the genre of German Romantic opera, nurtured by Weber, Spohr, and Marschner, had already begun to decline. *Hans Heiling*, first performed in that year, was to produce after-echoes in the works of Wagner at least as late as *Die Walküre* in the 1850s, yet it signally failed to breathe new life into the form. How it became the personal mission of Wagner to 'rescue' German Romantic opera and transform it into the 'artwork of the future', or music drama, is the subject of this section. But first we can get a vivid idea of the crisis facing German composers of the period by look-

ing at Wagner's first three operatic attempts: *Die Feen, Das Liebesverbot,*
and *Rienzi.*

Each drawing on a different set of influences, these three works illustrate not only the range of options available to an operatic composer of
the time, but also the political considerations inherent in the choice of
genre. For *Die Feen* (1833–4; first performed 1888) Wagner turned naturally to the tradition with which he had grown up—that of German
Romantic opera. Weber and Marschner are the acknowledged influences, and their brand of tonal colouring is evident too in Wagner's
score, likewise dealing with supernatural subject-matter.

Die Feen is yet another treatment of the theme of the tragic conjunction of the human and spirit worlds, but there are two particular topoi in
this work that were to recur later in Wagner's career. The first is redemption, though interestingly it is a man—the faithful Arindal—rather than
a woman, who is the agent: following his petrified, beloved Ada into the
underworld, he restores her to life, Orpheus-style, by singing and playing the lyre. The second topos is that of the forbidden question. Arindal
is permitted to marry the half-fairy, half-mortal Ada only on condition
that he refrain for eight years from asking who she is. As with Elsa in
Lohengrin, desire fully to apprehend the loved one finally overpowers
Arindal: he pops the forbidden question and Ada's magic realm disap-
pears. The conventional forms of aria, recitative, romanza, cavatina, as
well as various ensembles (trio, quartet, and septet), are all deployed in
Die Feen, and with a good deal of skill. Characteristically, Wagner also
picks up the most advanced element of his models—the shift towards
scene complexes—and offers a notable example in both Act 2 and Act 3.

For his second opera, *Das Liebesverbot* ('The Ban on Love', 1836), Wagner turned away from German Romantic opera and towards Italian and
French models, in particular Bellini and Auber. The thinking behind this
temporary reorientation was ideological: under the influence of the radical literary movement Young Germany, Wagner had, in his essay *Die
deutsche Oper* ('German Opera') of 1834, rejected Teutonic 'erudition' and
'pedantry' in favour of Italianate lyricism. The resulting effervescence of
the score of *Das Liebesverbot* reflects the nature of the subject-matter: a
celebration of sensuality in a Sicilian reworking of Shakespeare's *Measure
for Measure*. If the lightness of touch and the melodic flow are the most
obvious Italian features, others are the composite structure of the two
lengthy finales and the use of the *banda*—a military-type band playing on
or behind the stage.

The nationality of the composer of *Das Liebesverbot* is nevertheless evident in many of the opera's most prominent ideas, from the appoggiatura-laden melodies to the echoes of the 'Dresden Amen' in the nuns' Salve Regina in Act 1. We also find the first sustained use in Wagner's works of what was later to be called the 'leitmotif'. The leitmotif (which will be discussed more fully later in this chapter) developed out of the so-called 'reminiscence motif', a technique dating back to the latter part of the eighteenth century, whereby a motif (even just a chord or timbre), complete melody, or even an entire number would be recalled for associative purposes. The technique was employed by Méhul and Cherubini, among others, and developed, in Germany, by Weber, Spohr, and Marschner. In *Das Liebesverbot* the most prominent of the recurring motifs is that associated with the regent Friedrich's ban on love. Since the plot revolves around the salacious Friedrich's hypocrisy, much ironic humour is extracted from the various reappearances of this motif—an indication of the comic potential that Wagner might have drawn from the technique in later works had he so chosen.

The motivation that underlay the adoption of the style of French grand opera for *Rienzi* (1842) was different. With his attention focused on Paris, the young Wagner hoped to launch his career with a popular success at the Opéra. Monumental historical drama, spectacular stage tableaux, and brilliant vocal numbers were what the Parisian audiences craved—a desire satisfied unstintingly by Meyerbeer, as well as Spontini, Auber, and Halévy, all of whom Wagner admired at this stage. Wagner's avowed aim, in *Rienzi*, was to 'outdo all previous examples' of the genre with the 'sumptuous extravagance' of his own effort. Hence the marches, processions, and ballets, not to mention the massive crowd scenes, clamorous excommunications, and collapsing buildings. Acts 1 and 2 come closest to the models of French and Italian grand opera. The composition of Acts 3–5, coinciding with Wagner's move from Riga to Paris and with his growing dissatisfaction with the self-contained numbers of conventional opera, indicates a palpable stylistic advance: recitative and aria begin to be fused, and the orchestra acquires something of a more interpretative function.

With *Der fliegende Holländer* (1843), Wagner returned to his Germanic roots, and with that opera and its two successors, *Tannhäuser* and *Lohengrin*, the zenith of German Romantic opera was reached. That is not to say that other influences did not obtrude: vestiges of the traditional, Italianate finale are perceptible in *Tannhäuser* (Act 2), while elements of Parisian grand opera can be found in both that work and *Lohengrin*.

All three operas are transitional within Wagner's *œuvre*, forming a kind of rainbow bridge to the Valhalla of the fully through-composed music drama. In the *Holländer*, Wagner continued the process begun by Weber and Spohr of combining numbers in scene complexes: over half of Act 1, for example (from Daland's sighting of the ghost ship to the end), is designated 'Scene, Duet and Chorus'. Senta's Ballad is an interpolated narrative song in the German Romantic tradition—indeed it bears a close resemblance to the song sung by Emmy in Marschner's *Der Vampyr*—and there are still jarringly conventional passages, such as the cadenza to Daland's Act 2 aria 'Mögst du, mein Kind' or Erik's third-act cavatina.

What disquieted the first audience in Dresden, however, was not the formal incongruities but the overall conception of the piece and its sonic realization. By this time, many were beginning to weary of supernatural themes, and the unremittingly doom-laden atmosphere of the story—a recasting of the legend of the sea captain condemned to roam the oceans until Judgement Day unless saved by a woman's devotion—drew from Wagner a score of unprecedentedly portentous character. Yet one has only to compare *Holländer* with, say, Spohr's *Faust*, on a similar demonic theme, to see the vastly increased potency that Wagner could secure from his more consistent application of dramatic colour.

Less sombre and more obviously melodious, Wagner's next opera, *Tannhäuser* (1845), aroused more enthusiasm in its first audiences. Based on a combination of the legends (previously separate) of the crusading knight Tannhäuser and the song-contest at the Wartburg, Wagner's opera sets up a polarity of two kinds of love, sensual and spiritual, represented by the Venusberg on the one hand and by Elisabeth and the Wartburg on the other. That polarity is reflected directly in the music, for the key of E major is identified with the Venusberg, while E flat major is associated with the pilgrims, holy love, and salvation.

A more fundamental polarity can also be discerned in the association of the reactionary Wartburg court with more traditional, old-fashioned operatic features, while the sphere of the Venusberg, symbolizing liberation from bourgeois sexual hypocrisy, is characterized by the more progressive style of music drama towards which Wagner was steadily moving. Thus the song-contest itself in Act 2 is essentially a series of more or less self-contained arias, while Wolfram's well-known hymn to the evening star in Act 3 is also highly conservative in its regular, eight-bar phrases and tonal scheme. Venus's music, on the other hand, especially in the extended version made for performances in Paris in 1861, constantly breaks free from the constraints of traditional word-setting.

The most progressive passage in the opera from a stylistic point of view is the Rome Narration of Act 3, in which Tannhäuser tells how he went as a penitent pilgrim to Rome and was rebuffed by the Pope. Here the vocal line reflects the dramatic narrative with a fidelity that anticipates the mature music dramas to come. The orchestra too acquires a decisive role in this passage, illustrating and underlining the dramatic argument with unprecedented expressive effect.

With *Lohengrin* (1845–8; first performed 1850) Wagner advanced a stage further. Elements of grand opera are still present in the use of diablerie, spectacle, and crowd scenes, with minster, organ, fanfares, and bridal processions. Indeed, the interrupted wedding procession at the end of Act 2 is a trope of grand opera. Nor have the traces of old-fashioned recitatives, arias, and choruses quite been obliterated. On the other hand, even those numbers which have acquired celebrity as set-pieces, such as Elsa's Dream or Lohengrin's Narration, are carefully integrated into the structure.

The technique of the leitmotif is neither prominent nor pervasive in these three Romantic operas. But there is one particular example in *Lohengrin* that does look forward to the *Ring*. It is the motif of the Forbidden Question, which recurs as a constant reminder of Lohengrin's stern injunction to Elsa not to enquire after his name or origin. Such leitmotifs as do exist in *Lohengrin*, however (including that of the Forbidden Question), are in general fully rounded themes with complementary phrases, whereas those of the *Ring* tend to be both more succinct and more malleable. Motifs in *Lohengrin* also serve a different structural function, in that they have only an illustrative purpose, whereas the transformation of motifs in the *Ring* is a major determinant of the cycle's structure.

Der fliegende Holländer, *Tannhäuser*, and *Lohengrin* each pushed back the boundaries of operatic form a little further. But by the end of the 1840s Wagner was formulating more radical solutions to what he, and others, regarded as the crisis of opera. Nor is it coincidence that this reappraisal was taking place at precisely the time that social revolution was breaking out all over Europe. For Wagner, the issues of art and society were inextricably intertwined: true art could flourish only in a society free from oppression and exploitation. But works of art could also have a liberating function and play a part in the advancement of the utopia.

In *Die Kunst und die Revolution* ('Art and Revolution'), the first of the series of polemical essays he wrote in the wake of the Dresden uprising of 1848–9, Wagner insisted that art be taken out of the realm of capitalist speculation and profit-making. The 'artwork of the future' would restore the integrity of classical Greek drama by reuniting all the media within the framework of a drama. In two further essays, *Das Kunstwerk der Zukunft* ('The Artwork of the Future') and *Oper und Drama* ('Opera and Drama'), these ideas were elaborated. The new genre was to be a *Gesamtkunstwerk* ('total work of art'), combining music, poetry, and dance on a basis of equality, and simultaneously allowing architecture, sculpture, and painting to regain their authentic classical status. The central preoccupation of *Oper und Drama* was the relationship of poetry to music. Wagner proposed a new kind of declamation, called *Versmelodie* ('verse melody'), in which the musical setting of a line was responsive to all the nuances of the verse. Since clear projection of the text was the primary purpose, there would no longer be any place for duets, trios, and choral ensembles. The old German alliterative verse form of *Stabreim* would be restored, and a system of presentiments and reminiscences (i.e. leitmotifs, though the term was not used by Wagner) would enable key ideas to resonate through the score like 'emotional signposts'.

The 'artwork of the future', then, was Wagner's radical solution to the malaise affecting art and society alike. Its principles were embodied in the music-drama—a term used, then renounced, by Wagner, though it has generally been retained to distinguish the *Ring*, *Tristan*, *Die Meistersinger*, and *Parsifal* from the earlier, more conventional operas. The theoretical prescriptions of *Oper und Drama* were not observed to the last detail. For one thing, as in any manifesto, there was a strongly utopian element that served a polemical as much as a practical purpose. For another, Wagner was a sufficiently pragmatic musician to adapt his compositional procedure in the light of experience.

For a suitable subject for his world-redeeming music drama, Wagner turned to the medieval epic poem the *Nibelungenlied*, a work whose stock had risen dramatically in the 1840s with the surge of German nationalism. In addition to the *Nibelungenlied*, he drew on various Scandinavian sources, notably the Poetic (or Elder) Edda, the *Völsunga Saga*, and the Prose Edda by Snorri Sturluson—all compiled in Iceland probably in the first half of the thirteenth century—as well as *Thidreks Saga af Bern*, a prose narrative written *c*.1260–70 in Old Norse.

In conjuring up the remote mythological world of the *Ring*—a world inhabited by gods, heroes, giants, and dragons—Wagner was by no means renouncing the revolutionary impulse behind the 'artwork of the future'. On the contrary, the tetralogy is patently to be understood as an allegory, more specifically a critique of contemporary social relations. Wagner's condemnation of capitalist exploitation and oppression is particularly evident in *Das Rheingold*, the first opera of the cycle, but the remaining parts—*Die Walküre*, *Siegfried*, and *Götterdämmerung*—also reflect his disdain for social structures based on contractualism, property rights, and hierarchies of power.

The composition of the *Ring* occupied Wagner for some twenty-six years (1848–74), during which period his style inevitably underwent changes. At the outset, with *Das Rheingold*, he endeavoured to enshrine his theoretical principles faithfully, though not literally, in his work. Thus individual numbers and ensemble singing (apart from the Rhinemaidens, who are treated as a single entity) were completely eschewed and the entire text projected in a free arioso responsive to the poetic meaning of the verse and its natural accentuations. With *Die Walküre*, Wagner managed to balance that fidelity to the poetry with rather more consistent musical interest. The *Versmelodie*, or musico-poetic synthesis, as it is sometimes called, is seen at its most ingenious in *Die Walküre*. By Act 3 of *Siegfried* and *Götterdämmerung*, a palpable shift towards musical predominance has taken place, and the grand operatic origins of the latter work are evident in the chorus of Hagen's vassals and the conspiratorial trio for Brünnhilde, Gunther, and Hagen (both Act 2).

Wagner's technique of leitmotif underwent a comparable evolution over the course of the *Ring*. In *Das Rheingold*, the association of motifs with particular characters (e.g. the giants or Freia) or objects (e.g. the spear or sword) is generally unambiguous. In *Die Walküre* and the first two acts of *Siegfried*, the motivic representations are not always so literal, while in *Siegfried* Act 3 and *Götterdämmerung* motifs pour forth in such riotous profusion that any attempt to pin restrictive labels on them is doomed to failure. Throughout the *Ring*, leitmotifs have also, as mentioned above, a structural function. That is to say their transformation serves the purposes of musical development as much as 'emotional signposting' or identification with props. Often, too, the tonal scheme of whole passages, even scenes, may be dictated by the keys with which particular motifs are associated.

Each of Wagner's three great final music dramas—*Tristan, Die Meistersinger*, and *Parsifal*—in its different way exploits the genre to offer a world-redeeming meditation on a timeless subject. *Tristan und Isolde* (1859; first performed 1865) is not simply the greatest love story ever told, but a metaphysical disquisition on the nature of existence itself. Under the influence of the philosopher Arthur Schopenhauer, Wagner presented the relationship of the lovers in terms of the shedding of their separate phenomenal forms (that is, themselves as they appear to the outer world) and the merging of their identities in the realm of the single, undifferentiated noumenon. The noumenon, symbolized in the opera by night, is the ultimate 'reality', the inner consciousness; the outer material world of phenomena is symbolized by day.

Die Meistersinger von Nürnberg (1865; first performed 1868) is, alone among the mature music dramas, set in a precise historical period and location: mid-sixteenth-century Nuremberg. Nevertheless, the themes treated by the work are, on one level, as timeless as those of *Tristan*: the old must give way to the new, yet even youthful creativity in art has to be subject to the rules of form. On another level, though, *Die Meistersinger* can be seen as the artistic counterpart of Wagner's ideological crusade of the 1860s—a crusade to restore national pride, to reawaken the 'German spirit', and to purge it of alien elements. The anti-Semitic undertow of *Die Meistersinger* focuses on the character of the town clerk, Beckmesser, and his pathetic attempts to demonstrate that he is endowed with true creativity; in fact, he can do no more than mimic the genuine artist, Walther, and is ritually humiliated for his hubris.

In *Parsifal* (1882), on the other hand, purity of blood is a central theme. Only by cleansing the corrupted community of knights with the pure blood of Christ could the degeneration of the human race be reversed and the necessary regeneration be effected. Again, *Parsifal* should be seen as the artistic counterpart of Wagner's ideological obsessions— which in this case found their expression in the racist 'regeneration essays' of 1878–82. This is the underlying message of *Parsifal* and its enigmatic religious symbolism, though the issues are sufficiently broad, and their representation sufficiently resonant, to offer a wealth of enlightenment—not to say intoxicating self-indulgence—to those with the inclination to respond.

With the music drama in its most developed form—as seen in the *Ring*, *Tristan*, *Die Meistersinger*, and *Parsifal*—Wagner fulfilled the promise of his theoretical essays from the Zurich period in the broadest sense. The new *Versmelodie* may not have conformed to the theory in precise detail, nor was the utopian ideal of the *Gesamtkunstwerk* literally realized. But in its rejection of the trivial and meretricious, and its pursuit of profound spiritual truths, the music drama did indeed become the testimony of a would-be social reformer. The promulgation of that message necessarily entailed a revolution in operatic procedure. Not only would opera never be the same again, but it became impossible for composers of the late nineteenth and early twentieth centuries to approach the form without confronting the legacy of Wagner in one way or another.

Wagnerians

No one was more aware of the danger of being suffocated by Wagnerism than Peter Cornelius (1824–74). Related to the celebrated artist of the same name, Cornelius came under the spell of Wagner's operas during the course of his musical training. In 1852, at the age of 27, he presented himself at Weimar, where Liszt, as one of the leaders of the New German School, became his mentor. Recognizing that he risked appearing as a pale shadow of Wagner, Cornelius originally intended to make his mark in different territory: that of comic opera. To that end, he prepared a libretto, in 1855–6, for a light opera on a story from *The Thousand and One Nights*. The resulting *Der Barbier von Bagdad* (1858), an oriental-flavoured love story, was to remain his most famous work, though its appearances in histories of opera are rather more regular than those on stage. Its influences included the Turkish music of Mozart and Rossini, as well as Berlioz's *Benvenuto Cellini*, but it was nevertheless perceived as a product of the New German School and consequently fell victim to the anti-Liszt cabal at Weimar: the première there was marred by a demonstration against Liszt, who was conducting, and who relinquished his post in the town as a result.

Notwithstanding his original intentions, Cornelius could not long resist the pull of Wagnerian subject-matter. In his other two operas, *Der Cid* and *Gunlöd*, he turned respectively to historical drama and Nordic legend. Indeed, it was shortly after beginning work on *Der Cid* in 1860 that Cornelius first came into direct contact with Wagner in Vienna. Wagner exerted much pressure on Cornelius to set up house with him: first he suggested Wiesbaden in 1862, then in 1864 he returned to the onslaught from Munich. Cornelius, fearing the loss of his artistic and probably emotional independence—he knew Wagner's tendency to swamp those to whom he was close—withstood all blandishments until the end of 1864, when he became Wagner's musical assistant and subsequently a teacher at the music school re-established by Wagner and Hans von Bülow.

Der Cid (1865), on the subject of the eleventh-century Christian hero, combined historical realism—the battles between the Spanish crusaders and the Moors—with a personal conflict of love and duty: Chimene, though desiring revenge on the Cid, the murderer of her father, falls in love with him. If a dramatic parallel with Wagner's avenging Isolde suggests itself, the music is more reminiscent of *Lohengrin*, which Wagner had been producing in Vienna at the time of Cornelius's first encounter with him. Despite Cornelius's sustained effort on the composition between 1860 and 1865, *Der Cid* is, in comparison with *Lohengrin*, dramatically inert. Wagner himself offered to conduct the opera in Weimar in 1864, but nothing came of the suggestion. The work was given only twice in Cornelius's lifetime, the Weimar première being overshadowed, ironically and appropriately enough, by that of Wagner's *Tristan* in Munich three weeks later.

Cornelius's third and final operatic venture was even less successful. *Gunlöd*, begun in 1866, was left unfinished at his death in 1874, and not performed until 1891. Most of the first act was written and a substantial part of the second, but none of its intended three acts was orchestrated. Its debt, once again, to *Lohengrin* suggests that the individuality of *Gunlöd* would have been unlikely to outstrip that of *Der Barbier* in another genre.

Comic opera, then, was perceived as a genre in which composers might express themselves without too direct a comparison with Wagner. Another who chose to continue the tradition of *Die lustigen Weiber von Windsor* and *Der Barbier von Bagdad* was Hermann Goetz (1840–76), in his *Der Widerspenstigen Zähmung* (1874), a reworking of Shakespeare's *Taming of the Shrew*. Goetz began work on it in 1868, significantly after rejecting his librettist's suggestion of a drama on the Parzival legend. The most striking thing about the opera is its abundant tunefulness: extended passages of arioso/recitative advancing the plot represent progress over those of *Lohengrin* only in their melodiousness. The arioso constantly blossoms into fully-fledged lyrical aria, the forms all but closed, linked only by the most tenuous of threads. Following hard on the heels of *Die Meistersinger*, Goetz's opera was bound to be viewed in its light. In fact, it owes virtually nothing to that work: formally it is closer to *Tannhäuser* and *Lohengrin*, while in its unadventurous harmonic language it is even more conservative. Yet the dramatic pacing and handling of the humour are adroit. A second large-scale opera, *Francesca da Rimini* (1877), was left incomplete at Goetz's death in 1876, but he would surely be content to be remembered, on the strength of *Der Widerspenstigen Zähmung*, as the composer of one of the finest German comic operas of the nineteenth century.

An equally independent spirit was Karl Goldmark (1830–1915), a Hungarian-born composer who spent most of his working life in Vienna. Of Goldmark's six operas, it was his first, *Die Königin von Saba* ('The Queen of Sheba'), begun in 1865 but not staged until ten years later, that made his reputation. The plot, centring on a historico-biblical love story, together with the large crowd scenes, ballet, and local (in this case oriental) colour, give notice of the work's indebtedness to the grand opera tradition. In fact, despite the tendency of Goldmark's score towards closed, song-like forms, the influence of Wagnerian music drama is also evident in the chromatic harmonies and a certain flexibility of approach in the handling of large-scale structure.

The shadow of Wagner's achievement hovered even more intimidatingly over the young Austrian composer Hugo Wolf (1860–1903). Already in his teens—to his parents' horror—Wolf was a dedicated Wagnerian. But the genre in which he attained mastery was not music-drama but the Lied, the significance of which extends beyond Wolf himself to the atmosphere in Vienna in the 1880s and 1890s. Viennese Wagnerites were anxious to promote composers who could be seen to have embraced Wagnerian ideals; on the other hand, they could not be allowed to challenge the Wagner legacy by attempting to imitate the inimitable. Wolf's Lieder were eagerly welcomed by such Wagnerites as a possible solution to the problem: in their text-setting they were clearly imbued with the Wagnerian spirit, while their inhabiting a different, 'lesser' form—the solo song—ensured that they posed no ultimate threat.

Having established his reputation as a Lieder composer by the end of the 1880s, Wolf himself longed to tackle the more ambitious form of opera. For temperamental reasons, however, he was reluctant to pursue the kinds of themes treated by Wagner. When it was suggested to him that Buddha might make a suitable subject, he replied: '. . . but not in the wilderness with locusts and wild honey; I'd prefer him in a happy, unconventional social setting, with the twanging of guitars, lovers' sighs, moonlit nights, champagne banquets, etc.—in a word, in a comic opera without the gloomy shade of a world-redeeming philosopher of the Schopenhauer sort lurking in the background.'

Thus it was that Wolf came, at the end of 1894, to set Rosa Mayreder's light-hearted libretto on the subject of 'The Three-cornered Hat', *Der Corregidor* (1896). The libretto, by an inexperienced dramatist, is flawed—Act 4 has an excessive amount of recapitulation of preceding events, for example—but it drew from Wolf a wealth of good-humoured, imaginatively scored music. The orchestra required is a large one, larger even than that for *Die Meistersinger*, and it is used by Wolf with great skill to generate warm, glowing textures appropriate for a sunny Andalusian story. The opera is through-composed, but with two self-contained songs woven into the fabric. The attentive ear of the Lieder composer is evident in the subtle depiction of details of character and incident, for example the ostinato figure that represents the monotonously turning mill-wheel in the opening scene. All of the characters have their own leit-motif, and the themes are developed in a quasi-Wagnerian manner.

For all its dramaturgical flaws, *Der Corregidor* succeeded as a post-Wagnerian opera that refused to be crushed by the weight of the legacy. This chapter comes full circle with two composers, Siegfried Wagner and Engelbert Humperdinck, who were particularly vulnerable to the dangers of that legacy—the former as Wagner's son, the latter as his acolyte—and whose struggles to free themselves from its burden bear eloquent testimony to the plight of opera in *fin-de-siècle* Germany.

Siegfried Wagner (1869–1930) was not groomed unquestioningly for the succession: his father had no wish to impose it on him and in fact Siegfried began by studying architecture. But by his twenties he was acting as assistant at Bayreuth, and in 1896 he conducted the second production of the *Ring* there, subsequently undertaking productions of his own and eventually, from 1906, taking control of the festival itself.

In his compositions, as in his productions, Siegfried was a competent craftsman rather than an innovator. His operas, of which a dozen were completed, belonged to the genre known as *Märchenoper* ('fairy-tale opera'), a form traceable to the eighteenth century but which came into its own at the end of the nineteenth. The plots of such operas may or may not feature fairies, but elements of the supernatural or magical are invariably found. The treatment of the stories is often simple, even naïve, yet they are not intended necessarily for children. Indeed, these operas were often richly symbolic or allegorical, articulating a world-view or bearing a moral message.

The supernatural had, as described earlier, always been a staple ingredient of Romantic opera. Works such as *Oberon* and *Hans Heiling* were in effect *Märchenopern*, even if not so designated by their composers, while Wagner's *Siegfried* is not far removed from the genre either. The disillusionment of many German artists and intellectuals at the end of the century, however, with the world they saw about them—a world corrupted by the unfettered pursuit of materialism and technological progress—provoked a resurgence of interest in the realm of the irrational. Escapist stories recounted in what often appears to modern-day audiences to be sentimental terms expressed the perceived malaise of contemporary society under the impact of 'civilization'.

Engelbert Humperdinck (1854–1921), who wrote nine operas, also tended towards the genre of *Märchenoper*. The enduringly popular *Hänsel und Gretel* (1893) ends happily with a hymn-like ensemble, as the neglected children are delivered from the wicked witch and her gingerbread cottage. *Königskinder*, given in Munich in its original version in 1897 and in New York in revised form in 1910, offers no such comforting ending. This time the fairy-tale elements—another wicked witch, a prince, a goose-girl, and a loaf of poisoned bread—are deployed with passion and pathos: the royal children of the title meet their end starving and penniless, victims of an uncaring society. The operas of Humperdinck, as of Siegfried Wagner, are charged with Wagnerian resonances, both musical and dramatic. Like the Goose-girl in *Königskinder*, Humperdinck's progress may have been checked by the casting of a spell—in his case by the Sorcerer of Bayreuth—but his predicament is as eloquent and affecting as the death of the royal children that brings the curtain tragically down on a century of German opera.

RUSSIAN, CZECH, POLISH, AND
HUNGARIAN OPERA TO 1900

John Tyrrell

FOR two centuries Italian opera dominated all of musical Europe except France. Even an area as culturally vigorous as Germany was unable to sustain a continuous tradition of vernacular opera until the early nineteenth century. When German opera finally began to flourish, it inhibited the development of opera in other Germanic-language regions: Scandinavia and the Netherlands suffered from having to compete against German opera just as opera in the Iberian peninsula suffered by having to compete against Italian. Slavonic and Hungarian opera had at least the advantage of sounding very different from anything else around them. Not all the nations of east-central Europe or the Balkans established their own vernacular operatic traditions in the nineteenth century. Independent nations such as Russia or Poland (up to its final partition), regarded opera in the national language as a matter of pride, and began to foster it at much the same time as the various German Singspiel traditions emerged. The subject nations of the Habsburg empire, such as the Hungarians, the Czechs, the Croats, and the Slovenes, were closely linked to Vienna and thus to one of the leading musical centres of the period; they too had little trouble grafting vernacular opera on to existing musical traditions. The situation was more difficult in the nations emerging from the gradual disintegration of the Ottoman Empire, such as Greece, Romania, Bulgaria, and Albania. Here contact with the musical centres of Europe was more tenuous, musical and dramatic traditions less established. Regions with Italian connections such as the Ionian islands got off to an earlier start (the first opera in Greek was given in Corfu in 1857); similarly the linguistic links between Romanian and Italian meant that opera was given in the 1830s in Bucharest, though regular opera seasons with opera in Romanian had to wait until 1885. The first

Bulgarian, Albanian, and Macedonian operas were written only in the twentieth century.

As the new nationalisms emerged, stronger ones suppressed weaker ones. When in the *Ausgleich* ('Compromise') of 1867 the Habsburgs were forced to divide their empire into Austrian and Hungarian territories, the minor nationalities of the Austrian half (such as the Czechs or the Slovenians) flourished as never before under a regime that saw tolerance as a way of keeping the ramshackle empire together. Those nationalities controlled by the newly dominant Hungarians (such as the Slovaks, the Croats, or the Romanians of Transylvania) had a thin time keeping afloat amidst aggressive Magyarization. The Croats, with the first Croatian opera written as early as 1845, had a head start, and the prolific Ivan Zajc (1832–1914) was able to maintain and develop national opera in Zagreb on his return there in 1870. But the history of Slovak opera runs behind that of Czech opera by more than a century, with the first opera in Slovak performed as late as 1928. The history of Slovak opera and other 'late' nationalities belongs to the twentieth century. This chapter will focus on the four earliest and best-established operatic traditions in Europe outside the main streams: Russian, Polish, Czech, and Hungarian.

Beginnings

The dates of the first operas in Czech (1747), Russian (1755), Polish (1778), and Hungarian (1793) are misleading as a guide to the state of operatic culture in these regions or to their future development. The first Polish and Hungarian operas were written by composers born in what is now Slovakia, the first Russian opera by one of the long line of Italians working at the imperial court in St Petersburg. Only the first Czech opera *Pargomotéka* (1747) was written by a native (probably a monk) and this fact, together with the humble circumstances of its performance—at a monastery near the Moravian ecclesiastical capital of Olomouc—is evidence more of the rich musical culture of everyday Czechs in the eighteenth century than of the presence of an established metropolitan operatic tradition; the first Czech opera by a professional composer (though still performed by an amateur company), František Škroup's *Dráteník* ('The Tinker', 1826), came eighty years later and between these two dates stretches a whole sequence of small-scale, 'amateur' operas in Czech, many of them in rural dialects.

The Czechs have more in common with the late-comers, the Hungarians, than with their Slavonic sister nations. The Czech lands

(Bohemia and Moravia, both originally Czech-speaking but much Germanized by the late eighteenth century) and Hungary were part of the Habsburg Empire from 1526, though the Czechs preserved some autonomy until the failure of the rebellion of the Czech nobility in 1620. While links with Vienna and its musical traditions led to a fruitful interchange of music and musicians, it also meant that the Czech and Hungarian capitals were in effect provincial backwaters in which there was no imperial court to foster opera as a regular part of dynastic assertion, as it did in the sovereign states of Poland and Russia. Opera was thus the responsibility and hobby of rich aristocrats or the church. In the eighteenth century there were important operatic centres on aristocratic estates—in small provincial outposts such as Kuks in Bohemia, Jaroměřice nad Rokytnou in Moravia, Nagyvárad and Eszterháza in Hungary (where the bishop of Nagyvárad and Prince Esterhazy enjoyed the services respectively of Dittersdorf and Haydn). It is symptomatic that provincial capitals such as Prague, Brno, Buda/Pest, or Poszony (Pressburg; Bratislava) had nothing comparable until much later. The first purpose-built stone theatre in Prague opened only in 1783 (this is the famous Estates Theatre which saw the première of *Don Giovanni*, and is still in use); the even later date for a proper theatre in Pest (1812) also reflects the retarding effect of the long Turkish occupation (1541–1686).

The kingdom of Poland had the oldest operatic tradition of east-central Europe, with important Italian connections which go back to the early seventeenth century. As a prince, Władysław IV (reigned 1632–48) had encountered opera in 1625 at the Tuscan court and when he ascended the Polish throne he had a theatre erected in his palace where Florentine-type operas were given, many with music by the master of the Royal Chapel Marco Scacchi. Any further developments, however, were hindered by successive invasions by the Swedes, the Russians, and the Turks and by the fact that from 1697 the Polish throne was occupied by the Elector of Saxony, whose excellent Court Opera occasionally visited Warsaw and Cracow, but naturally performed mostly in Dresden. Nevertheless the first public theatre in Poland opened in Warsaw in 1725, to be supplanted by a bigger one in 1748 built by the opera-loving Augustus III (reigned 1734–63), who, expelled from Saxony during the Seven Years War, cultivated opera in Warsaw on a lavish scale.

Russia, in contrast, had been ignorant of opera in the seventeenth century, but after the Westernization which Peter the Great encouraged, the first Italian opera companies began to visit from the 1730s and German Singspiel was given from 1740. The empresses Anna (reigned

1730–40) and Elizabeth (reigned 1741–62) encouraged the establishment of a permanent opera in Russia and attracted a succession of Italian composers to work at the imperial court, beginning with Francesco Araia, the composer of the first opera in Russian (1755). Elizabeth's successor Catherine the Great was no less forward in promoting opera, writing several librettos herself, and by the end of the 1770s native Russian composers had begun to write operas in Russian. By the end of the century more than a hundred had been composed. The influence of French opéra comique and German Singspiel was important for a young tradition in which performances were mostly in the hands of actors rather than singers, at least until the early nineteenth century. (Glinka's first opera in 1836 was the first continously sung opera in Russian.) Although Russian composers of increasing stature—Yevstigney Ipatyevich Fomin, Alexey Nikolayevich Verstovsky, and the church-music composer Dmitry Stepanovich Bortnyansky—wrote operas, foreign composers continued to flourish. Giovanni Paisiello (in St Petersburg 1776–84, where his *Il barbiere di Siviglia* was premièred in 1782) and Mozart's Spanish rival Vicente Martín y Soler (in St Petersburg 1788–94, 1798–1806) were only two of the better known. The most durable was Catterino Cavos (1775–1840), whose long career in Russia stretched from 1798 until his death.

Poland's earlier start was jeopardized by the decline in its political fortunes. Its last king, the highly cultured (and, above all, Polish) Stanisław August Poniatowski (reigned 1764–95) presided over a cultural flowering which saw the opening of a National Theatre (1779) and the composition of the first operas in Polish, but, with the final partition of Poland in 1795, royal opera and royal munificence ceased. Several of the talented amateur composers who had written operas in Polish went into exile; the director of the National Theatre, the actor, singer, and prolific librettist Wojciech Bogusławski (1757–1829), regarded as the 'father of Polish opera', himself left Warsaw for Lemberg (Lwów) in Austrian Poland. The dismemberment of the country, and the halting of its political processes, had at least the advantage that Polish culture, and Polish opera, became even more important in maintaining national morale and cohesion. While in Lemberg, Bogusławski met the German Silesian composer Józef Elsner (1769–1854). Elsner is best remembered as Chopin's teacher, but he was also Kapellmeister at Lemberg's theatre, where he had written two German operas. Under Bogusławski's influence he now wrote Polish ones, and, with Bogusławski's return to Warsaw in 1799 as director of the National Theatre, Elsner joined him as its

principal conductor. Another of Bogusľawski's appointments was Karol
Kurpiński (1785–1857) as second conductor (1810) and, at Elsner's retirement, first conductor (1824–40). Each wrote some thirty Polish stage
works (ranging from plays with music to full-blown operas) and
together they constitute the most substantial period of Polish opera
before its major talent, Moniuszko.

The establishment of opera in all four countries or regions was
affected not only by imperial presence and interest, but by the national
status of the vernacular language and the strength of its competition.
Bohemia's early linguistic start, was no help. Under the medieval
Bohemian monarchy, Czech had established itself as a literary language,
its orthography was regularized by the religious reformer Jan Hus (d.
1415) and later by the Kralice Bible (1579–94). But this was of little avail in
the light of the Germanization which the Habsburgs forced upon the
local populace after 1620. When in 1807 the Italian opera company which
had sung at the Estates Theatre was disbanded, it was a German company, not a Czech one, that replaced it. German was overwhelmingly the
language of the cultured middle classes, and it was only in the second half
of the nineteenth century that the linguistic balance changed in Prague
in favour of the Czechs. Subsequently the real history of opera in Czech
is one that begins not with the occasional opera by Škroup or his predecessors, but with the opening in 1862 of the first theatre exclusively for
Czechs, the 'Provisional Theatre', so called because it was expected to be
replaced shortly by a larger, permanent theatre financed by public subscription. Since fund-raising took longer than expected, and the opulent
National Theatre opened only in 1881 (it was burnt down almost immediately and reopened in 1883), the majority of the operas by Smetana and
his contemporaries were written expressly for a very small theatre, a factor that had considerable impact on the character and even the conventions of early Czech operas.

Although more recent than Czech in terms of written records and
cultural use, the status of Hungarian as a national language was much
aided by the survival of a Hungarian aristocracy. The Czechs lost their
native aristocracy in 1620 and thus the national revival was headed by
middle-class patriots whose artistic achievements for many years
suffered the stigma of being seen as culturally inferior. In contrast, the
Hungarian landowners, especially after the Napoleonic upheavals,
increasingly put their wealth and influence into the cause of Hungarian
autonomy. As in Prague, German opera in Pest took over from Italian in
the early years of the nineteenth century, but while a permanent Czech

'national' opera was established only in 1862, a Hungarian national opera opened in Buda in 1837.

Things were different in Poland, where by 1795 (the date of the final dismemberment of the kingdom) a national language and promising operatic tradition were well established. Although the nation was now dispersed among three different countries, two of them German-speaking, Polish language and musical culture continued to flourish. The largest part of Poland was allotted to Russia, which until the 1830 Revolution allowed autonomy in cultural matters. By 1830, over 140 Polish operas had been performed.

Early vernacular operas are usually little more than foreign opera traditions transplanted to new soils, often with poor word-setting and scant individuality. The early history of vernacular opera tends to centre not on quality but on claims for primacy and the occasional flash of 'national spirit'. Much more important than the 'first' opera in a language is the first opera which by popular consent achieved the status of a national opera. The fact that it was such operas which appealed to and captivated a wide audience is evidence of an altogether new dimension. It is significant that there were operas written on the same topics before Glinka's *Zhizn' za tsarya* ('A Life for the Tsar', 1836) or Smetana's *Libuše* (1881) but which achieved none of the nationalist impact of these later works. Catterino Cavos had composed his opera *Ivan Susanin* (the same story as in Glinka's *A Life for the Tsar*) in 1815 (performed 1822); Škroup had written his *Libušin sňatek* ('Libuše's Marriage') in 1835 (the Libuše story was in fact a popular one for early Italian operas, and inspired German plays and operas—even Beethoven considered a Libuše opera). But neither Cavos's nor Škroup's versions established themselves. National consciousness needed first to be fostered, sometimes by stirring external events, more often by the diligent repetition and accumulation of patriotic literary and musical motifs. A trivial example is the concept of the 'Czechness' of the lime tree (as opposed to the 'German' oak). This notion was first promoted through the second edition of Kollár's influential poem *Slávy dcera* ('Daughter of Glory', 1832). Lime trees do not feature in Škroup's opera, written only three years later, but a generation later, in Smetana's opera, the legendary Czech Princess is discovered sitting in judgement under a lime tree, and her consort-to-be communes with his lime trees when he is seen alone in the next act. In terms of nationalist input, Smetana's opera *Libuše* had the added advantage of half a century's national myth-making. As for the musical stature of the two Libuše operas, there can be no comparison.

Unlike the pre-*Freischütz* history of German opera, which includes composers of the calibre of Mozart and Beethoven, there are no early composers of vernacular opera in east-central Europe to match the musical qualities of Mikhail Ivanovich Glinka (1804–57), Ferenc Erkel (1810–93), Stanisław Moniuszko (1819–72), and Bedřich Smetana (1824–84). The result is that these figures loom particularly large within their respective operatic traditions. In some cases, too, nationalist propagandists such as the Czech Zdeněk Nejedlý, or the Russian Vladimir Vasilyevich Stasov deliberately played down the contribution of other, lesser contemporaries or predecessors so that the 'founding' composers can be seen in a more dramatic and heroic light.

The National Operas of the Russians, Poles, Czechs, and Hungarians

Glinka's *A Life for the Tsar* (1836), Moniuszko's *Halka* (1848, final version 1858), Smetana's *Prodaná nevěsta* ('The Bartered Bride', 1866, final version 1870), are all incontestably the respective 'national' operas of the Russians, the Poles, and the Czechs. The choice is less clear-cut in Hungarian opera, with some proposing Erkel's popular *Hunyadi László* (1844) and others his later *Bánk bán* (1861), which represents a further stage of the absorption of Hungarian elements. Both works will form part of the following comparison.

Taken as a whole, these four (or five) works encapsulate many of the differences that distinguish their four operatic traditions. Whereas Moniuszko and Erkel dominate Polish and Hungarian opera respectively, with no composers of comparable stature following them in the nineteenth century, the operas of both Glinka and Smetana represent a fruitful starting-point. Smetana was followed by Dvořák, Fibich, and, at the end of the century, Janáček; the history of Russian nineteenth-century opera is taken further by Dargomïzhsky, Musorgsky, Serov, Tchaikovsky, Rimsky-Korsakov, and Borodin.

Local elements: subject-matter and folk music   The Hungarian operas *Hunyadi László* and *Bánk bán* and the Russian *A Life for the Tsar* are historical operas. *A Life for the Tsar* describes an incident in 1612 at the start of the Romanov dynasty where a loyal peasant (Ivan Susanin) deliberately sacrifices his life—hence the title—by leading the attacking Poles to their deaths in the snowbound wastes of Russia. The young Mikhail Romanov does not appear; imperial censorship forbade the depiction on stage of members of the ruling dynasty. Glinka's choice of subject-matter was shrewd. The dynasty for which Ivan Susanin gave his life was still on the throne when Glinka wrote his opera, and would be throughout the period discussed. (It was Tsar Nicholas I who suggested its final title during rehearsals.) Quite apart from the intrinsic merits of the opera, it conveniently exemplified the concept of 'official nationality', the dominant ideology of the period, formulated in Nikolay Karamzin's *History of the Russian State* (begun in 1818). This link with the regime also meant that it would cause problems when the regime changed. The Soviet administration could hardly ban such a centre-piece of Russian opera, so instead, under its original title of *Ivan Susanin*, it was duly adapted to stress Susanin's loyalty to his fatherland, rather than to the tsar.

Hungarians, Czechs, and Poles—unlike the Russians—were not independent nations in the nineteenth century and historical operas inevitably created problems with the censor unless the subject appeared so remote as to present no threat to the present occupying force. *Bánk bán* and *Hunyadi László* are thus set well before 1526 (when continuous Habsburg rule started): *Bánk bán* in 1213 and *Hunyadi László* in 1456–7. Kings appear in both, but as subsidiary figures. In *Hunyadi László* the 17-year-old László V (Ladislav V, 'Posthumous') is depicted as weak, manipulated, and insincere (he is cast as a somewhat oily tenor), to put into sharp focus the heroic Hunyadi family, three members of which appear in the opera. The head of the family, János Hunyadi, has already died, leaving a fearful widow Erzsébet Szilágyi and two sons. Erzsébet appears only in Acts 2 and 3, but by virtue of her demanding and dominating music is the most memorable character of the opera. At her entrance, she reveals her fearful vision of the death of her older son. At the end of the opera, set over some of the storm music of the overture, László's death takes place according to her vision: a gruesome affair since the (off-stage) executioner succeeds in beheading László only on his fourth attempt—all vividly described in Erzsébet's (literally) blow-by-blow commentary. Although a minor and dramatically dispensable figure in comparison with his mother or with his elder brother (who gives his name to the opera), Matyás Hunyadi is historically the most important member of the cast. As Matyás I (Matthias I, 'Corvinus') he became one of the most successful native Hungarian kings. He enlarged the realm (he was briefly Czech king as well, and as such was 'Matěj' the King in Dvořák's opera *Král a uhlíř* ('King and Charcoal Burner', 1874)) and presided over the Renaissance flowering of the Hungarian kingdom. At the time of the opera, however, he was only 16 and was cast as a breeches part for soprano.

While *Hunyadi László* prefigures one of Hungary's greatest rulers, *Bánk bán* presents a historical scenario of more relevance to nineteenth-century Hungary: the power struggle between powerful, patriotic aristocracy and central authority. The king of the opera (Endre (Andrew) II, reigned 1205–35) is away on his wars for the first two acts and returns to restore order in the last. Unlike László V in *Hunyadi László* he is depicted sympathetically, or at least neutrally: a baritone who sings with calm authority (usually slow, against brass) but is no match in charisma for his unpopular termagant German wife Gertrudis or the rock-like Bánk bán (a 'bán' was the governor of a banat, or region). Based on a remarkable play, published in 1820, by the young law student József Katona (1791–1830), the opera deals with the provocation that Bánk suffers as the queen encourages one of her relatives to seduce Bánk's wife. The combination of this outrage with the sad state of the country during the queen's regency eventually forces Bánk to confront the queen and, in self-defence, to kill her. The plot is thus emblematic of the part played by Hungarian aristocracy throughout the country's history, and especially in the nineteenth century, when they led the national rebellion against unpopular foreign rule—by this time, that of the Habsburgs.

In Poland such a libretto was not politically possible or sensible. Censorship in all three sectors of the partitioned country was understandably alert, and Moniuszko's operas attempt nothing as overtly political as these Hungarian operas. But although the Polish monarchy had been swept away, the Polish aristocracy had survived and provides the subject-matter for most of Moniuszko's operas (he himself came from minor gentry). The love intrigue set in aristocratic circles that provides the plot of *Straszny dwór* ('The Haunted Manor', 1865) is typical and, to the outside observer, harmless enough, though even this unassertive piece fell foul of the censor, who clearly believed that anything popular was undoubtedly seditious. Moniuszko's *Halka*, however, has a more obvious political dimension. Halka is a peasant girl; rejected by her aristocratic lover (the father of her child), she goes mad and commits suicide. The passionate and pathetic nature of her music is a reflection of the strong emotions prompted by the story, but perhaps even more if one sees, as contemporary audiences seemed to, the rejected Halka as a proxy for the rejected Polish nation.

Unlike the Poles and the Hungarians, the Czechs did not retain their native aristocracy: most fell at the Battle of the White Mountain in 1620, and were replaced by Habsburg appointees. Czech opera accordingly has no character comparable to Bánk bán, and aristocrats play a comparatively small part. Those few operas which, like Moniuszko's *The Haunted Manor*, depict mostly aristocratic society found little favour with the public. Of the major Czech opera composers, Antonín Dvořák (1841–1904) was the most ready to set librettos with aristocrats in the cast, as in the early *King and Charcoal Burner*, but also the later *Jakobín* ('The Jacobin', 1889); these librettos are generally of a conservative and idyllic nature, in which all sectors of society know their place and are happy with it. This, too, is the surprising conclusion of Janáček's first staged opera, *Počátek románu* ('The Beginning of a Romance', 1894), in which all elements of irony have been lost in the adaptation of Gabriela Preissová's short story for the operatic stage.

The depiction of Czech kings and queens was as thorny a subject as in Hungary—generally the earlier the better, with the mythical Libuše the best of all. When, at the end of Smetana's opera *Libuše*, the heroine embarks on a visionary survey of Czech history (to a series of *tableaux vivants*, a fashionable genre of the period), the 'mists' helpfully prevent her seeing in the future any ruler later than the fifteenth-century Hussite king Jiříz Poděbrad.

Czech society in the nineteenth century, and most especially that which attended theatre and opera, was overwhelmingly middle class. The Czech middle classes preserved a sentimentally affectionate attitude towards rural life. They were aware, too, that they were unlikely to find many allies for their political agenda among the German aristocracy, and needed to look instead to the rapidly growing Czech proletariat. Such attitudes find their reflection in Czech operas of the period. Smetana's first opera, *Braniboři v Čechách* ('The Brandenburgers in Bohemia', 1862–3; first performed 1866), depicts the interregnum in the country during the regency of Otto of Brandenburg in 1278 and the successful expulsion of the Brandenburgers from the country (for Brandenburgers of course read German-speaking Austrians). At the end of the opera the burghers of Prague symbolically extend the hand of friendship to Jíra, the leader of the rioting mob in Act 1; they do not bother uniting with the aristocracy. This opera, to a libretto by Karel Sabina (a writer recently released from prison for his part in the 1848 revolution), was politically the most radical that Smetana wrote. It was popular with its first audiences, but never became the model for future Czech operas. Instead it was Sabina's idealized portrait of the Czech village which Smetana set as his next work, *The Bartered Bride*, that served as the quintessential Czech national opera, and a model that almost every Czech composer of Smetana's generation attempted to emulate.

The popularity of the opera, which was not immediate and achieved only slowly as it went through a series of revisions, depended on a number of factors. Musically it was Smetana's lightest opera, its simplicity accounted for partly by its origins as an operetta with spoken dialogue. The numbers themselves are mostly simple structures with few tempo changes. Though beautifully crafted (the overture begins with an energetic fugato), they present few problems for the unsophisticated listener. Many of these numbers, moreover, reflect the rhythm, metre, and character of the two most popular Czech dances: the fast, duple-time polka and the slower waltz-time *sousedská*. Smetana, essentially a townsman, was against the introduction of Czech folk-song to establish a Czech character—those few instances in his works, such as the pastorella lullaby in *Hubička* ('The Kiss', 1876), are for specific purposes. Folk dances were a different matter. Though many Czech dances had their origin in the countryside, they had been enthusiastically taken up by Czech townsfolk, for instance in the *beseda* (a quadrille-type medley made up of Czech dances). The polka, by far the most popular of all, was a recent invention. Its name (which in Czech also means a 'Polish woman') suggests a Polish origin, a gesture of solidarity with the Poles after their failed 1830 Revolution. The polka achieved a quite extraordinary resonance among the Czechs. The young Smetana wrote stylized polkas for piano as readily as Chopin wrote waltzes and mazurkas, and they became something of a trademark for him. Significantly, many of the later additions to *The Bartered Bride* were dances: a *furiant* (a fast dance with changing metre), a *skočná* (a fast, polka-like dance in duple time), and, most significantly of all, a polka.

In Czech opera the depiction of a peasant society carried with it a specific message: it was here in the country that Czech had survived, while in the towns the middle class had enthusiastically Germanized itself. By the last third of the nineteenth century this Germanization was so entrenched that many Czech nationalist opera composers (Dvořák and Fibich, for instance) had written their first operas in German, while Smetana, the most nationally aware of them all, was never able completely to overcome his German education—it was only in his fourth opera *Libuše* that he learnt how to set the Czech language with correct stressing. The depiction of a peasant society that had kept Czech going through the darkest years was thus an eloquent image. Such emphatic use of a peasant setting found little reflection in the mainstream operatic traditions until the Turiddus of the verismo generation.

Folk dances, and music based on their distinctive rhythms and metres, helped not only to depict the Czech village in *The Bartered Bride*; used in later works, such as the ubiquitous polkas in the bourgeois setting of Smetana's *Dvě vdovy* ('The Two Widows', 1874), they helped generally to establish a Czech character, and the dance-based chorus is a feature of Smetana's operas right up to his last, *Čertova stěna* ('The Devil's Wall', 1882), with its extensive double chorus in Act 3: a polka for the women, and a gentle *sousedská* for their menfolk.

Stylized Polish folk dances, on the other hand, have a different pedigree and associative world. While the polka did indeed become an international salon dance, it was the only Czech dance that achieved this sort of status, and in comparison with the Polish dances it was a mere youngster, having achieved world-wide popularity only in the 1840s. The Polish triple-time dances, the mazurka and the polonaise, were known outside Poland from the eighteenth century or earlier, the polonaise in particular acquiring international names (French *polonaise*, Italian *polacca*), and a high-class status evident from its use in stylized dance suites and collections from Bach to Beethoven. With the international sympathy that the unlucky Poles had achieved, Polish dances remained topical and were furthermore being popularized in fine stylizations from the 1830s by Poland's most famous composer, Chopin. By the time Moniuszko included them in his operas they had become associated more with the gentry that had patriotically espoused them than with their peasant roots. For example, Act 1 of *Halka*, mostly given over to the depiction of aristocratic society, opens with a polonaise and ends with a mazurka. *The Haunted Manor*, set even more exclusively in aristocratic society, ends with a *krakowiak* (a duple-time dance from Cracow) followed by a mazurka. There are polonaise- and mazurka-based arias in most of Moniuszko's 'gentry' operas—*Halka*, *The Haunted Manor*, *Hrabina* ('The Countess', 1860), and *Verbum nobile* (1861).

Such usage did not preclude the use of dance to depict peasant genre scenes, such as the Highlanders' dances which form the centre-piece of Act 3 of *Halka*. These (simply called 'tańce') make their claims to evoke a folk scene, not through the stylized rhythms of the polonaise and mazurka, but through the modal colour of their melodies and harmony. Their models were probably Rossini's ballet *divertissements* for his Swiss peasants in *Guillaume Tell*, or Auber's 'Neapolitan' dances in *La Muette de Portici*.

Halka is much more emotionally charged than *The Haunted Manor*, its tragic power coming from the collision of these two worlds—the aristocratic and the peasant. Act 1, an 'aristocratic' act, achieves a disturbing *frisson* when Halka intrudes with her simple 'song' upon the exalted company. A fragment of this song, heard off-stage virtually unaccompanied, makes a vivid contrast to the showy, polonaise-based male-voice choral ensemble that opens the act and the conventional trio that follows. This technique is mirrored in Act 4, where Halka's faithful peasant lover Jontek laments Halka's sad fate in a *dumka*, which is followed immediately by the perfunctory chorus drummed up by the Steward to welcome the newly-married aristocratic couple.

Although the folk associations of Jontek's *dumka* are reinforced by the preceding scene with the bagpiper (musically suggested by a perky oboe tune with a sharpened fourth over a drone), the thrust of the piece is more towards pathos than *paysanterie*; any folk suggestion from the dotted rhythms and regular phraseology of the opening section is undermined by its chromatic harmony, and even more by the more conventional melodic and rhythmic character of the middle section. In fact the *dumka* has no particular peasant association (its origins are in Ukrainian hero songs), and as a regular feature of Moniuszko's operas it is just as likely to be given to an aristocratic singer, such as Jadwiga in *The Haunted Manor* or Zuzia in *Verbum nobile*.

Like Smetana, Moniuszko was not well placed by background and upbringing to make use of much genuine folk-song in his operas. Glinka, though also from a privileged background, had more connections with the folk-song traditions around him. His use of identifiable Russian folk-song is not particularly extensive (there are a few scraps that he apparently took down himself), but early contact with folk-song traditions on his family's estate seems to have resulted in his absorption of Russian folk-song at a deeper level than is suggested by merely including them in his works. A contemporaneous review by Y. N. Neverov made a comparison with Verstovsky's use of folk-song in *Askol'dova mogila* ('Askold's Tomb', 1835)—'essentially nothing more than a collection of, for the most part, delightful Russian tunes joined together by German choruses, quartets and Italian recitatives'. Glinka, in contrast,

set about it differently; he has looked deeply into the character of our folk music, has observed all its characteristics, has studied and assimilated it—and then has given full freedom to his own fantasy...Many who heard his opera noticed something familiar in it, tried to recall from which Russian song this or that motif was taken, and could not discover the original. (Neverov (1836) quoted in Brown (1974), pp. 112–13)

There are of course strikingly folk-like numbers in *A Life for the Tsar*, such as the unaccompanied responsorial opening for soloist and male chorus, the celebratory 'Slavsya' chorus at the end (almost a second national anthem), or, the jewel of the whole opera, the 5/4 women's bridal chorus, distinctive not only for its early use of such a metre, but for its imitation of peasant part-singing. These examples are remarkable because of their folk suggestions, all the more so since Glinka had been able to integrate the folk idiom further into the work. Thus at the end of Act 1 during the pre-wedding celebrations of Susanin's daughter with the soldier Sobinin, the dramatic news of the approach of the Poles generates an Italianate largo concertato-plus-stretta finale. But the minor-mode slow round of the concertato has a mournful Russian air to it that sets it apart from its Italian models. Similarly Antonida's solo and rondò in Act 1, again Italianate in structure, has the orchestral coloratura of the opening inflected with 'Russian' intervals—in fact, as David Brown (1974, pp. 115–16) demonstrates, an artful variation of the opening peasant chorus.

Although there are occasional suggestions of peasant instruments—a balalaika imitation of plucked strings in a chorus accompaniment in Act 1, or the suggestion of the Russian folk zither, the *gusli*, in the harp accompaniment of Susanin's final aria—Glinka characterized his Russian peasants overwhelmingly through vocal means. The enemy Poles, on the other hand, are represented by dance music: here the long-established international status of the polonaise and mazurka was somewhat relentlessly exploited. The contrast is acute, for instance between the end of Act 1, with Russian peasants pouring out their anxiety in a full-blooded vocal ensemble, and the Polish Act 2, made up mostly of brilliantly orchestrated dances. When the two worlds clash in Act 3 they do so with simple oppositions: Poles ask questions or give orders to their jaunty three-in-a-bar dance rhythms; Susanin replies solemnly in slow duple metre. In one highly experimental passage, the two metres are imposed one upon the other. The resulting characterization is clear, if oversimplified: the Poles come across as worldly, flashy, and superficial; Susanin (and by implication all Russians) as serious and utterly reliable.

The case of Erkel is again different. His chief musical localizing device was not an attempt to incorporate into his operas Hungarian folk-song (whose genuine roots were discovered only at the end of the century by Kodály and Bartók). Instead he made use of a style of music that had been associated with Hungary since at least the seventeenth century. The title by which it became known, *verbunkos*, occurs however for the first time only at the end of the eighteenth century as a Hungarian corruption of the German *Werbung* ('recruitment'). Today the traditional explanation of the *verbunkos* as glamorous military dances (often played by virtuosic gypsy musicians) to drum up recruitment has been largely discounted; nevertheless a number of *verbunkos* elements have military associations. The metre is always a march-like duple or quadruple, never triple. The melody is characterized by dotted figures (a familiar musical topos of the nineteenth century to depict military men), often with repeated notes (anticipating the next main beat), and standardized cadential flourishes. Speeds are either fast or slow, and usually alternate one with the other. Melodically, the use of augmented seconds is a reminder of the oriental origin of the Magyars. Like the Polish mazurka and polonaise, *verbunkos* style became international and is familiar, for instance, from some of Liszt's consciously 'Hungarian' pieces such as the Hungarian Rhapsodies, or from the 'csárdás' that Strauss gives to Rosalinde, disguised as a 'Hungarian countess' in Act 2 of *Die Fledermaus*.

As a conventionally trained musician, Erkel made only fitful use of the style in his first opera, *Bátori Mária* (1840). This is appropriate, given the romanticized treatment of Hungarian history that constitutes the plot of this opera. But, as Gyula Weber (1976) demonstrates, *verbunkos* style thereafter became a distinguishing feature of Erkel's musical language. In his next opera—and greatest success—*Hunyadi László* (1844), the hero László is naturally enough characterized by *verbunkos* style right from the overture's opening with a theme associated with him: *verbunkos* style is generally thought of as being heroic and ostentatiously masculine. What is more surprising is that *verbunkos* style is used also for women, and for villains or bad patriots (such as the king). For example László's mother Erzsébet, even in the so-called 'La Grange aria' (written later for a French interpreter of the role), has a cantabile–cabaletta aria where *verbunkos* traits mingle with vocal virtuosity to create the most demanding soprano aria in the Hungarian repertory. Gara, otherwise a conventional baritone villain, has a rather jaunty *verbunkos* aria to celebrate his contemplated triumph in Act 1 (reprised at its fulfilment in Act 3); the king enters and departs to a dignified *verbunkos* slow march whose laid-back character cleverly suggests his complacency and inaction. The only members of the cast not allowed *verbunkos* style are the male chorus representing the foreign mercenaries, contrasted—naturally—with patriotic Hungarian soldiers in clear *verbunkos* style. In instrumental music, slow, doom-laden *verbunkos* passages suggest tragedy and sorrow; fast *verbunkos* sections, celebration and joy. The fine overture to *Hunyadi Lás-*

zló, composed some years after the opera was first performed and almost a miniature tone poem in itself, is an impressive compendium of *verbunkos* styles and devices.

Foreign elements   It is noteworthy that Erkel, of the four nationalist composers the most reliant on foreign models, was able to forge a consistent style with such a distinctive local content. All four nations, however—Russia, Hungary, Poland, and Bohemia—were heavily indebted to international models for their structures, styles, and approach to voice types. The chief influence was naturally Italian, followed by French. German opera was less developed and had less to offer at the time. (It was only towards the end of the century that Wagnerian influence began to be felt.) In the case of the Czechs, Hungarians, and half of the Poles, German opera had the added disadvantage of being in the language of their political masters.

For a century up to the death of Catterino Cavos in 1840 Russia had had a succession of Italian opera composers living and working in the capital. The world première of Verdi's *La forza del destino* in St Petersburg in 1862 gives some idea of the persistence of this trend, and Italian opera continued to be lavishly subsidized there until the 1880s. Glinka himself, the father of Russian opera, completed an unsystematic musical apprenticeship in Italy (1830–3), in which he heard much Rossini, Bellini, and Donizetti, and explored his impressions in nothing more ambitious than instrumental operatic transcriptions and fantasies. It was in the midst of this Italian world that he conceived the idea of *A Life for the Tsar*, and it is not surprising that, for all its Russian colour, it is heavily indebted to Italian models. The Italian double-aria structure (cantabile–cabaletta) lies behind several numbers, most obviously in Vanya's final *scena* in which he arrives to warn the Russians of the dangerous proximity of the Poles. His opening recitative (compassion for his exhausted horse) is followed by a lyrical cantabile (exploring his own feelings) and, after exchanges with the chorus, a triumphant cabaletta with choral backing by the now aroused Russians. The Act 1 finale is, as mentioned previously, essentially a Rossinian largo concertato plus stretta. Susanin and his adopted son Vanya (a breeches part for mezzo) are simply Russian transplantations of the patriot William Tell and his son Jemmy. Even Glinka's orchestration, often taken to represent the finest and most original part of his technique, is in many ways a development of late Rossini, with its clear, unblended colours and its penchant for climatic trombone tunes which cut through the orchestral texture. Glinka's trombones take up where Rossini leaves off; the daring, whole-tone descent of the trombone in the overture to *Ruslan and Lyudmila* became a Russian trademark that infected even the symphonies of Borodin.

Italian opera was no less in Erkel's blood. In the two years (1838–40) between his appointment as chief conductor at the Hungarian National Theatre and the première of his first opera *Bátori Mária*, Erkel conducted twenty operatic premières, ten of which were of Italian operas (Spontini, Bellini, but chiefly Donizetti). An analysis of the repertory by performances of the Hungarian National Theatre from its opening in 1837 up to *Bátori Mária*, reveals an even more evident Italian bias. Altogether there were 180 operatic performances, of which 125 were Italian, 43 French, and 12 German. The most performed opera was Bellini's *Norma* (25 performances) followed by Auber's *Gustave III* (18 performances). These statistics make an interesting comparison with repertory at the Czech Provisional Theatre in the four years before the première of Smetana's first opera, *The Brandenburgers in Bohemia*. Here French operas were somewhat ahead of Italian in terms of numbers of different productions (in actual performances they were almost equal). It was with French Revolutionary opera that Weber, in his term as music director of the Prague Estates Opera House (1812–16), had sought to turn away from the Italian bias that had remained even after the disbanding of the Italian company in 1807 and to encourage German opera. Fifty years later, Smetana and his contemporaries did the same, though now it was the grand operas of Rossini, Auber, Meyerbeer, and Halévy rather than the operas of Cherubini and Méhul that became the approved models.

In his theatre reviews Smetana railed against old-fashioned Italian operas such as Bellini's *Norma*, and when in 1866 he became chief conductor he sought to steer the repertory in other directions. He nevertheless came up against the Italianate training of his singers, and the tiny dimensions of the theatre, its chorus, and orchestra. All this meant that Italian opera was often the most practical foreign repertory to perform. In his own works he was unable to escape entirely some of the trends that he so deplored. Sopranos such as the prima donna Eleonora z Ehrenbergů, were given coloratura passages on occasions, and even in his third opera, *Dalibor* (1868), there are vestiges of a cabaletta duet to bring Act 1 to a close. Such traits are even more pronounced in Smetana's, *The Brandenburgers in Bohemia*, but here, especially in its libretto, the influence of French grand opera is also prominent. In his next, comic opera, *The Bartered Bride* (1866), French opéra comique, with its spoken dialogue, is the model rather than Italian opera buffa. Although its spoken dialogue was later upgraded to recitative, spoken dialogue was used once again (and once again subsequently upgraded) in Smetana's fifth opera, *The Two Widows* (1874), this time actually based on a French play. Even where Smetana appears to be striking out on his own, by avoiding the voice-type of the baritone villain that dominated mainstream opera of the period, it is not necessarily a personal preference. Rather it is a reflection of the small team of soloists at the Provisional Theatre: the principal baritone Josef Lev, for whom Smetana wrote most of his baritone parts, was essentially a passive, non-dramatic singer suited best to lyrical parts.

With Erkel, however, the models are unashamedly Italianate. Act 2 of *Hunyadi László* is typical. Apart from an aria for the villain Gara (written originally as an ABA form, but truncated to BA in the post-Erkel revision in which the piece is usually heard), all the solos and solo ensembles are based on the double-aria principle: two arias for the widow Erzsébet, a duet for her son László and his bride-to-be, and a trio for Erzsébet and her two sons. The final chorus celebrating the betrothal of László and Maria invokes, with its 'religioso' organ, the church-music gestures tapped by Meyerbeer a few years earlier in *Le Prophète*. What is abundantly obvious is the Italianate approach to voice types, from the active baritone villain Gara, the breeches mezzo part for the young Matyás (another Jemmy), to the *tenore spinto* for László. In particular the elaborate coloratura for Erzsébet indicates the availability of Italian-trained singers able to cope with such daunting demands.

The emphasis on vocal agility is one factor that particularly unites the operas of Erkel and Moniuszko. *The Haunted Manor* has a similarly taxing soprano part for Hanna (her Act 4 aria shows it at its most extreme). Coloratura may be thought appropriate for the high-class ladies that inhabit most of Moniuszko's operas, but even the humble Halka goes (like Bánk's wife Melinda) to her suicide, her mind wandering, with Lucia-like gestures. As a whole though, Moniuszko, with a solid musical education in Berlin, is less Italianate than Erkel. Polish sympathy for France as an antidote to Russia also left its trace in the extensive ensemble element that can be found for instance in *The Haunted Manor*.

Later Developments

The strong musical personalities of Glinka and Smetana meant that their musical styles in *A Life for the Tsar* and *The Bartered Bride* became synonomous respectively with Russian and Czech music. When in his next opera, *Dalibor*, Smetana strove to advance Czech opera from its opéra comique limitations to something more ambitious, the work flopped, and Smetana found favour again only when he wrote a more overtly folklike piece in *The Kiss*. The peasant milieu and *The Bartered Bride* style were imitated by most of Smetana's contemporaries, such as Vilém Blodek (1834–74) in his charming one-act opera *V studni* ('In the Well', 1867), and even the early operas of Dvořák. It was rather later that the full range of Smetana's achievement became appreciated.

Glinka's second opera, *Ruslan i Lyudmila* ('Ruslan and Lyudmila', 1842) at first suffered much the same fate as Smetana's later operas; for instance Dargomïzhsky in his *Rusalka* (1856) took Glinka's first opera, not *Ruslan*, as a model, and it was only the next generation of Russian composers who built on the musical potential and implications of Glinka's second opera. Even a composer as progressive and individual as Musorgsky, when he later added the Polish act to his *Boris Godunov*, found himself reverting to the 'Polish' formulas and even the lyrical style of *A Life for the Tsar*.

But while the founding fathers of Russian and Czech opera had, in the end, established several types of national opera for future exploitation, Erkel and Moniuszko had more limited successes in providing workable models for Hungarian and Polish opera. Moreover, neither was succeeded by composers of comparable stature. The further political history of Poland (with another tragically failed uprising in 1863) acted as a dampener on creativity; composers and audiences played safe. Even *The Haunted Manor* was performed only in three productions and then banned and not heard again until 1914. Another 132 Polish operas were premièred between 1866 and 1914, but Poland had to wait until its revived independence in 1918 for an opera of real stature such as Szymanowski's masterpiece *Król Roger* ('King Roger', 1926) to emerge. Rather more surprisingly, in view of the relative political autonomy achieved by the 1867 *Ausgleich* with Habsburg Austria, it was a similar story in Hungary. Erkel's operatic career continued longer than Moniuszko's, with works written in collaboration with his sons: another historical tragedy, *Brankovics György* (1874), and his final opera *István király* ('King Stephan', 1885) showing a steering away from the earlier Italianate bias towards Wagnerian music drama. But it was several decades before the reinvigoration of Hungarian opera by Bartók and Kodály. Of the four regions examined only in Russia and Bohemia (and latterly in Moravia) were interesting operatic developments still being pursued by the end of the century.

Ruslan *and its Progeny*

Of Glinka's artistic legacy to Russian opera composers it was his second opera, *Ruslan and Lyudmila* (1842), that was ultimately to prove the more fruitful. It is based on a fantastical poem (1820) by Pushkin (1799–1837), whose works were to be quarried for librettos by almost every Russian opera composer: Dargomïzhsky, Musorgsky, Rimsky-Korsakov, Tchaikovsky, and Cui in the nineteenth century and many more in the twentieth all wrote operas after Pushkin. *Ruslan*'s strain of fairy-tale fantasy was one that became important to Russian opera and in a way that distinguished it from other operatic repertories. German operas based on tales or legends, whether in Wagner's myth-heavy music dramas or in the less assuming Humperdinck strain, suggest significance quite beyond their humble beginnings. In contrast, Russian fairy-tale operas generally are based on a colourful, neutral story, with few morals and few conclusions, but plenty of opportunity for musical and scenic display. In essence, *Ruslan and Lyudmila* is a quest or rescue opera. At the feast for Lyudmila's three suitors, the bride suddenly vanishes. Her father promises her to the suitor who finds her and it is naturally Ruslan, after many adventures, who does so.

The story is slight, the dramaturgy universally condemned as inept, but the subject provided many occasions to stimulate Glinka's harmonic and orchestral imagination. Just as the Poles and the Russians were sharply differentiated in *A Life for the Tsar*, there are clear stylistic contrasts between the opening and closing Russian scenes, the exotic locales explored by the suitors on their travels, and the supernatural world against which Ruslan contends. Russia is evoked with broad, lyrical melodies, sometimes modally inflected, sometimes ballad-like (the *gusli* with which Bayan accompanies himself in the opening number is imaginatively represented by a harp and a piano—a very early use for colouristic purposes of a piano in the orchestra). Faraway places are depicted in the exotic dances, especially the extraordinary Georgian *lezginka* in Act 4, or in the haunting Persian chorus of Act 2, with constantly repeated tune and constantly varied orchestral background (a technique perfected in Glinka's orchestral variations *Kamarinskaya* (composed 1848) and thereafter employed by many later Russian composers). Most famous of all is the pioneering use of the descending whole-tone scale to represent the supernatural forces of evil and the grotesquerie of the strange harmonic juxtapositions and weird orchestrations in the March of the dwarf Chernomor.

The Polovtsian Dances and stumbling dramaturgy of *Knyaz' Igor'* ('Prince Igor', 1890), the only (almost) complete opera of Alexander Porfir'yevich Borodin (1833–87), were obviously descended from Glinka's *Ruslan*, but the greatest beneficiary of this exotic side of Glinka was Nikolay Andreyevich Rimsky-Korsakov (1844–1908). His large operatic output (fifteen operas) is uneven, mostly unknown in the West and curiously distributed, with three early operas, a long gap, and then the bulk of his output concentrated in his final eighteen years of life. Although he experimented with several types, the genre he felt most comfortable with was the exotic fairy-tale, for instance *Skazka o Tsare Saltane* ('The Tale of Tsar Saltan', 1900) or *Zolotoy petushok* ('The Golden Cockerel', 1909), operas both based on Pushkin 'folk tales' (though suitably Russified, their provenance is western European, as characters' names such as Guidon and Dodon suggest). *Tsar Saltan* is another tale of a quest, here brought about by the wicked plot of the jealous sisters of the Tsar's young bride—their come-uppance occurs memorably when they are stung by the young Tsarevich Guidon, temporarily turned into a bumble-bee (whose 'flight' provided the most famous number in the opera). *The Golden Cockerel* is a darker tale. From a mysterious astrologer the old King Dodon acquires a magic cockerel that, when the realm is threatened, crows in the direction of the danger, even when the 'danger' turns out to be the mysterious queen of Shemakha, whom Dodon brings back to his court as his bride. When the astrologer demands the queen as his payment, Dodon refuses and kills the astrologer, whereupon the cockerel swoops down and pecks Dodon to death. The astrologer explains in an epilogue that all is invented. Only he and the queen are 'real'.

Here the emphasis on the piece's lack of 'significance' suggests in fact that there was more to the tale than meets the eye, as the censor certainly concluded, holding up the performance of the opera until 1909, after the composer's death. It was not difficult to see analogies between the way King Dodon and his two foolish sons wage war (despite the timely warnings of the cockerel) and Russian incompetence in the conduct of the Russo-Japanese war of 1905. However this political topicality was unusual for Rimsky-Korsakov. After his first, historical opera, *Pskovityanka* ('The Maid of Pskov', 1873; final version 1901) with its depiction of Ivan the Terrible and the 'republican' council of medieval Pskov (both aspects that needed intervention at a higher level to appease the censor), Rimsky-Korsakov concentrated on a line of operas whose range was limited to exotic fairy-tales (*Tsar Saltan, Golden Cockerel,* and *Sadko,* 1898), earthy village comedies after Gogol (*Mayskaya noch',* 'May Night',

1880; *Noch' pered rozhdestvom*, 'Christmas Eve', 1895), and folk tales with either a pantheistic slant (*Snegurochka*, 'The Snowmaiden', 1882) or, less usually, a Christian one (*Skazaniye o nevidimom grade Kitezhe i deve Fevronii*, 'The Legend of the Invisible City of Kitezh and the Maiden Fevronyia', 1907). One reason why this last opera is sometimes described as Rimsky-Korsakov's masterpiece is its greater emotional engagement. On the whole, Rimsky-Korsakov was most at ease with highly coloured, decorative music—illustrative rather than dramatic or emotionally committed—and where his skill as one of the finest orchestrators of the nineteenth century could be employed. It is hardly surprising that the most durable residues of *Tsar Saltan* or *The Golden Cockerel* were the orchestral suites extracted from them, or that *Sadko* began life as an orchestral suite, with a libretto constructed to accommodate existing instrumental leitmotifs.

Fairy-Tale Operas in Bohemia

Although Vienna-inspired fairy-tale plays (*báchorky*), often with quite a strong musical element, were an important part of Czech drama in the 1840s, they left no trace on Smetana's output except perhaps in the 'quest' element of some of his later operas. Thus Kalina, burrowing in the earth for his 'treasure' (in Smetana's *Tajemství*, 'The Secret', 1878), or the lovers Vendulka and Lukáš, at odds throughout Act 1 of *Hubička* ('The Kiss', 1876) and coming to their senses in the literal and metaphorical 'forest' of Act 2, are only a few degrees away from Tamino and Pamina undergoing the rituals of fire and water in *Die Zauberflöte*. But here the quest, unlike the Tsarevich Guidon's efforts to put matters right in Rimsky-Korsakov's *Tsar Saltan*, is moral—a personal exploration, not a colourful story.

Towards the end of his life Dvořák wrote a couple of Czech fairy-tale operas, *Čert a Káča* ('Kate and the Devil', 1899, based on a Czech folk-tale) and *Rusalka* (1901). *Rusalka* shares its title with Dargomïzhsky's opera (1856, another Pushkin-based fairy-tale opera, though this time set mostly in rural Russia), but for all Dvořák's pan-Slavonic sympathies and the fact that Dargomïzhsky's opera had been staged in Prague (in 1889), Dvořák's opera is nearer the German than the Russian world. The chief source of the libretto, like that of the 'Undine' operas by Hoffmann (1816), Lortzing (1845), and for that matter Tchaikovsky (composed 1869; destroyed and partly recycled), is the novella by Dietrich de la Motte Fouqué in which a water-sprite becomes 'human' but her relationship with a mortal (the reason for her wanting to become human) ends tragically. Pushkin's and Dargomïzhsky's *Rusalka*, on the other hand, is the tale of a poor girl betrayed by her princely lover. She drowns herself, becomes a watersprite, and revenges herself upon her lover. In its text Dvořák's opera differs from the German 'Undine' operas because of the 'Czech' supernatural periphery added by his librettist Jaroslav Kvapil from the folk-like ballads of K. J. Erben, and in the interpretation of the central character—a suffering Slav heroine rather than the skittish young girl of the German operas.

The opera was written at the height of Dvořák's career, with a distinguished series of instrumental works and eight, somewhat uneven, operas behind him, ranging from comic works in peasant settings to grand opera such as the splendid *Dimitrij* of 1882. While the rich Wagnerian language of *The Devil and Kate* seems ill at ease with the slight and would-be humorous plot, Kvapil's tragic *Rusalka* gave Dvořák, for once, a libretto tailor-made to his lyrical and illustrative strengths; the result was his most popular and most successful opera. The reason for its appeal lies not only in the music. Dvořák's and Kvapil's Rusalka, unlike her German counterpart Undine, has to make a sacrifice to gain a human soul: she gives up her voice, and throughout the second act, set in the palace of her prince (who soon loses interest in her), she is silent. Just as the peasant heroine of *Halka* (revived in Prague a second time in 1898, shortly before Dvořák began work on *Rusalka*) could stand proxy for the rejected Polish nation, Rusalka too could symbolize the Czechs, who had almost lost their language to the politically dominant Germans.

Westernizing Opera

Because of the more westerly location of Bohemia and the contact with current mainstream developments provided by nearby Vienna and by the German opera house in Prague (which continued to flourish, under very distinguished direction, right up to the end of the Second World War), Czech opera inevitably took up a more Western stance than did Russian. A keen Lisztian, Smetana believed that his duty was not so much to develop Czech opera from its own roots (let alone from Czech folk-song), but to follow the most progressive trends in mainstream opera, the Czech contribution being limited to the libretto and the idiomatic setting of the Czech language. This tendency is seen at its clearest in the Lisztian thematic metamorphoses that run through *Dalibor*

(1868), an almost monothematic opera. Zdeněk Fibich (1850–1900), the composer assiduously promoted as Smetana's successor, was even more extreme in this respect, for instance in the dense leitmotivic web from which his fine, though unloved *Nevěsta messinská* ('Bride of Messina', 1884) is constructed. Apart from the choruses and choral-based ensembles, there is an avoidance of simultaneous singing—*Dalibor* luxuriated at least in impressive love duets. Furthermore, while all of Smetana's operas are set in Bohemia and most are based on Czech sources, Fibich's operas are based mainly on European sources (Shakespeare, Byron, Schiller). After the Wagnerian postulates of *The Bride of Messina* seemed to have been abandoned in a mid-life and mid-career crisis, Fibich sought out librettos principally for their dramatic opportunities and their tales of passion, at the end of which their protagonists were mostly dead, rather than edified or educated as in Smetana's last operas. Fibich was a major operatic talent with a real interest in drama and the psychological life of his characters, and had the most rigorous musical training and widest cultural background of any Czech composer of his time. Nevertheless he suffered for his pro-European stance, and apart from his most nationalist opera, *Šárka* (1897), one of only two that he based on Czech material, his operas have fallen out of the repertory.

Much the same fate struck the more European wing of Russian opera. The operas of Alexander Nikolayevich Serov (1820–71) inhabit history books, not opera houses today, though two of his three completed operas, *Yudif'* ('Judith', 1863) and *Rogneda* (1865), were popular in their day. He admired Liszt and wrote enthusiastically about Wagner, helping to organize the first Russian performance of a Wagner opera, *Lohengrin*, in 1868, but the foreign models behind his operas were mostly French, Meyerbeer in particular. Musorgsky, whose incomplete *Salammbô* (1863–6, after Flaubert) is more Meyerbeerian than one might expect from the Realist of his later years, admired him, as did the most distinguished Westerner among Russian opera composers, Pyotr Il'yich Tchaikovsky (1840–93). But while Serov's connections with a local style were limited, Tchaikovsky made extensive and conscious use of Russian folk music and was able on occasions to turn out imitations indistinguishable from Rimsky-Korsakov.

Tchaikovsky may have earned his reputation as a 'Westerner' from his close association with the Rubinstein brothers (Russia's first professionally trained composer, he studied with Anton in St Petersburg, and was a member of Nicholay's staff at the Moscow Conservatory), and from his open enthusiasm for Western music. He adored Mozart, his favourite foreign opera was *Carmen* (both enthusiasms are evident in his penultimate opera *Pikovaya dama*, 'The Queen of Spades', 1890). Like Serov (e.g. in his biblical *Judith*) he had no inhibitions about setting librettos based on non-Russian subjects, though these are not his most successful works: after the destroyed *Undina*, *Orleanskaya deva* ('The Maid of Orleans', 1881, after Schiller) and his final opera, *Iolanta* (1892, after a Danish play).

But for all the Meyerbeerian orientation of his first surviving opera, *Oprichnik* ('The Oprichnik', 1874) or the affectionate rococo pastiches in the *Queen of Spades*, Tchaikovsky nevertheless had ties with the Establishment Russianists—the *kuchka*, and especially their guru Mily Balakirev (one of the few Russian composers of the time who did not write operas). Despite his large symphonic, chamber, and concerto output—all suspicious signs of Western orientation—Tchaikovsky's stage works are no less extensive and are exceeded in number only by those of the prolific Rimsky-Korsakov. There are attractive Russian and Ukrainian genre scenes in his early *Kuznets Vakula* ('Vakula the Smith', 1876, based on the Gogol story which later spawned Rimsky-Korsakov's *Christmas Eve*), in *Charodeyka* ('The Enchantress', 1887), and in his masterpiece *Evgeny Onegin* ('Eugene Onegin', 1879). In the latter two operas the Russian element penetrates no further than Act 1, but where *The Enchantress*, like so many of Tchiakovsky's operas, fails, and where *Onegin* triumphantly succeeds, is in the level of personal engagement. When the focus of attention moves from scene-setting to the individual, Tchaikovsky was on less certain ground, and needed strongly to identify with his protagonists.

Tchaikovsky began composing *Onegin* with the letter-scene in which the naïve Tatyana pours out her love to the Byronic man of the world Onegin. His sympathy for Tatyana sustains the work and provides a focus, whether she is seen against her rural background of the first two acts or the grand society of St Petersburg; whether she is the gauche lovesick girl of Act 1 or the self-possessed and loyal wife of Prince Gremin in Act 3. Without such a focus Tchaikovsky falls back on formulas. The foreign operas, *The Maid of Orleans* and *Iolanta*, seem to have engaged him even less (there is a letter to his brother Modest in the middle of composing *Iolanta* regretting the commission). Personal engagement, however, is what keeps his least lyrical opera, *The Queen of Spades*, alive and stageworthy. Again a revealing letter to Modest makes quite clear Tchaikovsky's self-identification with the protagonist Hermann. The fact that the loss of Pushkin's layer of irony turns *The Queen of Spades* into a melodramatic ghost story counts for little in view of the strong dramatic presence and committed characterization.

Realism

Russian opera flourished from the late 1860s with composers such as Tchaikovsky, Musorgsky, Borodin, and Rimsky-Korsakov all hard at work. There is, however, a surprising gap between Glinka's *Ruslan and Lyudmila* in 1842 and Tchaikovsky's first opera *Voyevoda* ('The Voyevoda', 1869; later destroyed). The gap is filled only partly by the operas of Serov, the early Russian operas of Anton Rubinstein (1830–94), who thereafter concentrated his efforts on German operas mostly to biblical subjects, or a couple of pieces by César Antonovich Cui (1835–1918). But the most influential figure in these two decades was Alexander Sergeyevich Dargomïzhsky (1813–69). Like Glinka he had little formal musical training and, having abandoned a career in the civil service, spent most of his life teaching singing. His grand opera *Esmeralda* (1847, based on Victor Hugo's novel) was not a success; his *Rusalka* (1856), however, has stayed in the repertory, chiefly perhaps because of the effective 'Russian' choruses *à la* Glinka and the prototypes of characters that were to recur in later Russian opera: the suffering Slavonic heroine and the figure of her father, the Miller, maddened with grief at his daughter's death.

Dargomïzhsky's chief claim to fame, however, is his word-for-word setting of one of Pushkin's 'Little Tragedies', *Kamennïy gost* ('The Stone Guest', 1872), a variant of the Don Juan story. The setting was done virtually publicly at the piano amidst an admiring coterie who took over and completed the piece at Dargomïzhsky's death in 1869 (Cui dealt with the unfinished scenes; Rimsky-Korsakov, naturally, did the orchestration). What was so remarkable about the work, and the aspect which captured the imagination of his younger contemporaries, was that it was composed to an otherwise unchanged play text.

Conceived essentially as an experiment, it is not really a piece intended for theatre. Apart from the Glinka-derived whole-tone harmony for the arrival of the supernatural, contrasts and characterization are muted. Commentators not attuned to its delicate scale have found it monotonous. The dissimilarity from Dargomïzhsky's *Rusalka*, with its acceptance of chorus and ensemble conventions, the combination of voices, and fully-fledged lyricism in the Glinka tradition, could not be greater, except perhaps in the earlier opera's realistic treatment of dialogue. Nevertheless the influence of *The Stone Guest* was profound.

Thirty years later, Rimsky-Korsakov made an uncharacteristic experiment by setting another of Pushkin's 'Little Tragedies' in the same way
(*Motsart i Sal'yeri*, 'Mozart and Salieri', 1898), though here his introduction of Mozart pastiches and the opening of the Requiem does at least
provide more variety.

The composer most taken with the experiment, however, was Modest Petrovich Musorgsky (1839–81). Dargomïzhsky's example, and
Musorgsky's strong interest in 'realistic' setting of speech—derived,
Richard Taruskin has suggested (1993, p. 79), from the German literary
historian Georg Gottfried Gervinus—helped to deflect him from his previous Meyerbeerian orientation to become the best-known exponent of
Russian musical realism. The first operatic evidence of his conversion
was his setting of Gogol's satirical play *Zhenit'ba* ('The Marriage'). But
whereas Dargomïzhsky responded to the iambic pentameters of *The
Stone Guest* with small-scale, if non-repetitive, lyricism, Musorgsky
avoided even that in his relentlessly anti-lyrical setting of Gogol's
unchanged prose text. Musorgsky worked at the piece in a concentrated
burst during the summer of 1868, completed one act, and then abandoned it. Thereafter he modified his approach so that sung prose became
only one of the levels of musical discourse in his later operas (employed,
for instance, in the Inn scene in *Boris Godunov*, which is otherwise mostly
in iambic pentameters). In its original, seven-scene version (1868–9) *Boris
Godunov* is little more than a dialogue opera with choruses and arioso
solos. But in the subsequent revision (1871–2; performed 1874) songs and
even duets were added. Perhaps the most valuable lesson Musorgsky
learnt from his prose experiments was the greater attention he now
focused on word-setting, leading to a more subtle type of realism that did
not aim to present merely a sung stylization of speech, but rather the
character that lies behind the words. This is the reason why Musorgsky's
Boris is capable of eliciting tragic sympathy in a way that the equally brutal Mazeppa of Tchaikovsky's opera (*Mazeppa*, 1884) never does. With its
impressive crowd scenes, its historical pageant, and its riveting central
character, *Boris* is indisputably the masterpiece of Russian nineteeth-
century opera. Sadly its successor in the same historical vein *Khovanshchina* (composed 1872–80; performed 1886), despite its many powerful
moments, lacks focus. It was left unfinished at Musorgsky's death and
subsequent realizations have proved problematic.

Only in Russia, where talented composers were able to experiment
without the constraints of too much formal musical education, could an
opera such as *Boris Godunov* have come about, seemingly decades ahead

of its time (Rimsky-Korsakov, the self-trained professor at the St Petersburg Conservatory, spent years taming its apparent crudities). The work was unknown outside Russia for many years so that, although parallels are frequently drawn between Musorgsky and the Czech composer Leoš Janáček (1854–1928), there is little to connect the two except a preoccupation with similar matters and the later ministrations of would-be helpful 'improvers'. Some of Musorgsky's comments about the revelation of the 'soul' through a person's speech could have come straight out of one of Janáček's essays on his 'speech-melody' theory. The route, however, was completely different.

Janáček had started as a conventional Czech nationalist composer, writing as his first opera *Šárka* (composed 1887–8), a work whose plot was based on Czech mythic history, the continuation, in fact, of Smetana's *Libuše*. Janáček, and the Czech public, did not hear the piece until 1925 and instead Janáček's career took a different turn. For his second opera *The Beginning of a Romance* (1894) Janáček espoused Moravian folk music so enthusiastically that much of the opera was little more than Moravian folk songs and dances with new words fitted across existing music. By this stage, however, European Realism had made its impact and invigorated Czech theatre. Marrying an interest in folk culture and the new theatrical trends, the young Gabriela Preissová (1862–1946) wrote two plays, produced in Prague in 1889 and 1890, which attempted to paint a more realistic picture of the petty rivalries and squalid cruelties of village life. How even this unsentimental subject-matter could nevertheless be transformed into conventional operatic language was evident from the way that Josef Bohuslav Foerster (1859–1951) set the first play, *Gazdina roba* ('The Farm Mistress'), as his *Eva* (1899). But while Foerster first turned the play into verse, and omitted most of the realistic periphery, Janáček left the play he set, *Její pastorkyňa* ('Her Stepdaughter'), in prose.

Jenůfa (1904), as the opera is known in the West, was not easy to write. There is evidence, especially in Act 1, of a number opera carved out of the prose text (modified into a sort of quasi-verse), with discernible arias for the main characters, choruses, simultaneous singing, and even a largo concertato ensemble. After completing Act 1, Janáček seems to have put the opera aside in a thoughtful pause lasting several years. But unlike Musorgsky with his *The Marriage*, Janáček took up the opera again, and, four years later, much of the character of his later style was in place. Moravian folk music became absorbed at a subconscious level (there was no direct folk music quotation in the opera). Instead a preoccupation with realistic and penetrative word-setting grew in this opera and remained with Janáček all his life.

Like the later Musorgsky, Janáček was happy to include songs and choruses, the songs chiefly for genre purposes, the choruses often given a symbolic role that Janáček learnt from his encounter with another prose opera, Charpentier's *Louise*. In this work (given with huge success in Prague in 1903), Janáček saw a fashionable justification for procedures he had stumbled upon on his own, and he continued to pay homage to *Louise* by imitating aspects of it in his next works. Even if Janáček saw it necessary in practical terms to acquire some of its modish trappings in order, unsuccessfully as it happened, to gain a Prague hearing for his next opera, *Osud* ('Fate', never performed in his lifetime), Janáček as a composer had done well enough on his own: he had, like Musorgsky, found his own, individual route to trends which were then dominating mainstream European opera. That he was able to compete with them artistically is another way of saying that with Janáček Moravia and later Czechoslovakia had a composer whose contribution, unlike that of many of the figures discussed in this chapter, was not only to a nationalist culture, but to operatic culture world-wide.

❧ 8 ❧

THE TWENTIETH CENTURY:
TO 1945

Paul Griffiths

Opera in the Twentieth Century

THE very nature of this book testifies to how much opera has become grounded in its history, and though conservation is necessarily a part of any culture, it is arguably more so of opera than of any other area of western civilization, and more so now than at any time in the past. To give an illustration, the average age of works chosen for the 1991–2 English National Opera season was 142 years, the repertory including two seventeenth-century pieces, three from the eighteenth century, nine from the nineteenth century, and five from the twentieth century, of which only three post-dated 1910 (Weill's *Street Scene*, Britten's *Billy Budd*, and a new opera, John Buller's *The Bacchae*). Any history of twentieth-century operas, i.e. of works written in the twentieth century, is therefore only very partially a history of twentieth-century opera, i.e. of the genre's life during the century. It takes no account of, for example, the closing of the international repertory around a core of thirty or forty works, or the contrary vast extension of the operatic literature available in recorded form, or the influence that recording has had on how opera is presented and experienced, or the growing importance of the stage director, or the reawakening of opera before Mozart (three such, two by Monteverdi and one by Handel, were in the 1991–2 ENO schedule, so that in this case post-1910 musicology has been precisely as important as post-1910 composition).

This chapter and the next will, nevertheless, concentrate on twentieth-century operas. However, perhaps because new works have become increasingly marginal to operatic activity during the century, their history has a certain weightlessness, in that no appeal can be made to generally recognized standards: those standards have been drawn around a repertory of classics from which twentieth-century works are largely excluded. *Moses und Aron* would be an example of an opera which has all the qualities of greatness except frequency of performance. And among more recent works criteria of judgement seem to be in constant suspension: *The Rake's Progress* (1951) is perhaps the latest work to have gained a regular place in the international repertory, to have been recorded several times, and to have stimulated a large body of critical commentary. The revival in the 1970s and 1980s of interest in the operas of Zemlinsky and Schreker, and at the same time the irruption of Broadway musicals into opera houses and scholarly libraries, emphasizes how much the history of twentieth-century operatic composition, even where the early part of the century is concerned, remains unstable.

Revolutions and Rebirths, 1901–1918

As in so many other areas of artistic, scientific, technical, and philosophical endeavour, the period up to the end of the First World War was one of crucial and rapid change in opera: within a decade of Verdi's death (in 1901) Strauss's *Elektra* and Schoenberg's *Erwartung* had been written, and by 1917 Berg was at work on *Wozzeck* and Stravinsky on *Histoire du soldat*. The reasons for such a ferment, without parallel before or since, were obviously complex, and it is correspondingly hazardous to separate cause from effect. However, the coincidence of the operatic revolution with a revolution in harmony—and both *Elektra* and *Erwartung* have long been recognized as landmarks in the history of harmony—is strongly suggestive. Opera, which had originated at the time when major-minor tonality began to be determinative, had gained its drive from harmonic forces: for instance, resolution in opera, whether in Mozart or in Wagner, is at once harmonic and dramatic resolution. Harmony provides narrative with an engine; narrative provides harmony with an explanation. But the increasing complexity of harmony in the early twentieth-century was beginning to rob it of its onward urge, and hence to deprive opera of its motive power. One response was to revel in the complexity, and often, in opera, to find exotic or fantastic subjects that might justify an ornate musical world and offer dramatic reasons for compensatory lashings of orchestral and rhythmic energy: the operas of Puccini, Mascagni, and Rimsky-Korsakov provide examples. Another, Schoenberg's, was to abandon tonality altogether, and to discover a kind of drama in which a striving for resolution would be the constant condition. Yet another, Debussy's, was to accept the current indecisiveness of tonal harmony and to create an opera of uncertainty. Or again there was the recourse of irony, the creation of flagrantly artificial worlds in which the characters are stylized (as in Ravel, Stravinsky, or again Rimsky-Korsakov), or in which the setting makes possible an allusion to earlier conventions, with Mozart a favourite point of reference (as in works by Busoni, Wolf-Ferrari, Nielsen, and Strauss). Still another reaction to the problems of the period might be creative silence, in which light one could see Puccini's later career: his difficulties in finding a suitable libretto after *Madama Butterfly* (1904), the relative weakness of his next three ventures, *La fanciulla del West*, *La rondine*, and *Il trittico* (except for the ironic *Gianni Schicchi*), and his failure to complete *Turandot*. Of course, these responses—elaboration, unhooking, ambiguity, irony, silence—will overlap in the most complex works, such as Schreker's *Der ferne Klang*, Pfitzner's *Palestrina*, or Strauss's *Der Rosenkavalier*.

The awareness shown by Claude Debussy (1862–1918)—that the new state of music, or at least the new state of his music, necessitated a quite new kind of opera—is evident from before he began *Pelléas et Mélisande*. His letters and reported conversations make it clear that he did not want to 'tell lurid anecdotes' in music, that he wanted 'things only half-said'. These he found in abundance in Maurice Maeterlinck's play, which he read in 1893 and began to set the same year, completing the composition draft in 1895, though the orchestration was not done until shortly before the first performance, in 1902. Maeterlinck's text answered to his theatrical ideals; at the same time, the experience of writing the opera seems to have enabled him to achieve his musical ideals, for it was while working on the draft that he finished the *Prélude à 'L'Après-midi d'un faune'*, while several later works, particularly *La Mer*, are almost glosses on the opera.

If the Maeterlinck was able to act as Debussy's midwife, that was perhaps because of how much it resembled, and also how much it differed from, the texts of Wagner's music dramas, for Debussy's writings indicate the powerful, ambivalent, son–father relationship he felt to Wagner. Like Wagner's chivalric works, Maeterlinck's play takes place in a vaguely medieval world, and like those of *Tristan* in particular, the characters have no obligations other than to their own feelings. The essential difference is that they so rarely know what those feelings are. Almost all the characters' utterances are short, and a great many of them are inconclusive, consisting of unanswered questions, unmotivated remarks, and unfinished sentences. The importance of this to Debussy was not so much that it offered him something he could complete with his music— in general the music is expressively explicit only where the text is—but rather that the incompleteness could be maintained, and even justified, by the nature of the music.

Since he appears to have decided at once to accept the play as it stood, making cuts but not going through the intermediary stage of a libretto (itself a revolutionary way of working at the time but common in the twentieth century), the absence of long speeches removed any temptation to compose arias. The opera has only two substantial solo passages, one of them the recitation of a letter, the other a song, Mélisande's from the tower, which would probably have to be sung in any spoken production of the play (both Fauré and Sibelius provided songs for this scene in their incidental scores). Otherwise the text is delivered for the most part in syllabic arioso which transmits the words but usually remains neutral or ambiguous as to their affect.

This is less true of Golaud's part than of the others. His jealousy is vividly underlined as he taunts his wife Mélisande, and even more so as he presses his son Yniold (the first important treble role in opera) to spy on Mélisande and his half-brother Pelléas. It is also musically useful that his lines consist so often of questions, which the others generally fail to answer, whereas whenever he is asked a question his response is immediate and direct. He is like a character from an earlier age of opera, who insists that the others—those who occupy the centre of Debussy's opera: Pelléas and Mélisande—give some account of themselves. Without him they would perhaps continue forever in silence (in the early days of working on the opera Debussy wrote to Chausson that he had 'discovered something...I found myself using, quite spontaneously too, a means of expression which I think is quite unusual, namely silence'). Without him, too, there would be no actions (marriage, homecoming, violence, persuasion, murder, birth, death) to provide a dramatic shape. Golaud is the candle that lights up the mist, and in doing so shows how different the mist is from itself.

In his apartness and his inquisitiveness Golaud is also like a member of the audience appearing on stage. He asks the questions which the audience at a Verdi or Wagner opera would expect to hear answered: where has Mélisande come from? What happened to her before the opera began? What are Pelléas and Mélisande doing between the scenes in which they appear? Have they been lovers? If Debussy's opera fails to answer those questions, that is only partly, and perhaps least importantly, because of a teasing, playful avoidance on the composer's part. In a striking phrase Debussy once wrote of music's power to reveal 'the naked flesh of emotion'; *Pelléas et Mélisande* asks us to understand that this 'naked flesh' is not necessarily what we might think it to be from an experience of Puccini. That sort of emphatic statement does exist in the opera, not only in Golaud's part but also, for example, in the awareness of love that Pelléas at last attains in his final scene. Much more characteristic of this work, though, are modes of suggestion, hesitancy, and doubt which are essential to the nature of the figures on stage. The characters reveal themselves only indirectly because they know themselves only indirectly, and though the text may be suspected of cheating in its concealment, of pretending to hide what it simply does not know, Debussy's score gives extraordinarily full, wide-ranging, and direct access to indirection.

There is nothing self-concealing or ill defined about the music. A few leitmotifs are employed, but Debussy's deepest debt to Wagner is the continuous invention within the orchestra. He wrote of 'that orchestral colour which seems to be lit from behind, of which there are such wonderful examples in *Parsifal*' and of 'orchestral *certainties* such as I have encountered only in *Parsifal*', and though both these quotations come from the period of *Jeux*, the luminosity and the definition are qualities also of *Pelléas*, as is the kinship to Wagner's last opera, which Debussy had seen on visits to Bayreuth shortly beforehand, in 1888 and 1889. However, Wagner's paternity is no more manifest here than Musorgsky's: the old king Arkel, for example, owes as much to Pimen as to Gurnemanz in his confident but questionable narrative authority, and the repeating two-bar phrase structures are a direct inheritance from *Boris*. Despite all that, *Pelléas* conveys something quite new in the fluidity and allusiveness of its harmonic language. Chords, thanks to Debussy's insinuation of church modes and artificial scales, come to be as ambiguous in their meanings and intimations as statements or feelings, and out of this arrives an opera in which a 'lurid anecdote', an elementary triangle of love, is the least important part of what is told.

The most perspicacious comment after the first performance of *Pelléas* at the Opéra-Comique was Erik Satie's: 'One must look elsewhere'. Debussy himself contemplated various operatic projects during the remaining sixteen years of his life, and got some way with a double bill after stories by Poe; but nothing was completed. *Pelléas* had been necessitated by a musical style whose emergence it itself facilitated: a new opera would have required, and been required by, a new style, which Debussy went only part way towards achieving in his music for Gabriele d'Annunzio's spectacle of drama, dance, and choral paean *Le Martyre de Saint Sébastien* (1911). Like *Fidelio*, *Pelléas* is thus the unique dramatic expression of a whole musical world, and just one of its legacies to twentieth-century opera has been the view that each new work should reconsider the whole nature of the genre. In that respect its progeny includes not so much the minor French operas of the next two decades as *Der Rosenkavalier, Wozzeck, Lulu, Moses und Aron, The Rake's Progress, Punch and Judy, Donnerstag,* and *Saint François d'Assise.*

More immediately it was followed by another Maeterlinck setting which goes so far as to include Mélisande as a character and even to quote from Debussy's score, being able to do so because its own quality is so different: *Ariane et Barbe-Bleue* (1907) by Paul Dukas (1865–1935). The difference belongs partly to the libretto. Instead of the short-phrased dialogues of *Pelléas,* Maeterlinck here provides a long central role for Ariane, and the only other important part, that of her nurse, is essentially a device enabling her to express herself. Barbe-Bleue is a transitory and powerless presence: indeed the opera, so much dominated by female voices, has been seen as supporting women's emancipation, though its undeluded view of the difficulties of freedom has wider implications. Ariane arrives in the castle of Barbe-Bleue (this is another important difference from *Pelléas:* Debussy's opera swings between outdoor scenes—forest, coast, garden, sea cave—and interiors, whereas Dukas's takes place entirely inside a lightless hall and its crypt) and finds five of his former wives held captive. She wants to free them, but they all refuse to go; her only victory can be that of freeing herself. Musically the opera affirms the exertion necessary for freedom and independence, in that its sumptuous language is constantly threatening to lapse into that of Debussy or Wagner, Musorgsky or Strauss. Other composers who ventured into this area, such as Ernest Bloch (1880–1959) in his *Macbeth* (1910), were less successful in maintaining an individual course.

The line from *Pelléas* through *Ariane* continues to Béla Bartók (1881–1945) and his *Duke Bluebeard's Castle,* composed in 1911 and first performed seven years later by the Budapest Opera. Béla Balázs's libretto radically simplifies and alters Maeterlinck's play to produce a single act with only two characters of equal importance: Bluebeard and his new wife, now called Judith. Led into his castle, she finds seven locked doors and demands to know what lies behind them. Reluctantly he gives her the keys, and progressively she discovers not only the evidences of his power—armoury, treasury, domains—but also proof of his cruelty and distress. The successive openings offer cues for lavish orchestral depiction in a manner Bartók inherited from Strauss's tone poems and perhaps also from Dukas's opera, while the syllabic word-setting relates to the Debussy work (in her distanced provocativeness, too, Judith is close to Mélisande, while the bass-baritone Bluebeard has elements of Arkel and Golaud) and also to Hungarian folk music. There is a further connection with *Pelléas* in that this was its composer's only opera, besides being a work which, in its economy of cast, setting, and action, again offers a new vision of what opera could be.

Another composer to profit from the illustrative range and precision of the Straussian tone poem was Richard Strauss (1864–1949) himself. His first opera, *Guntram* (1894), though by no means immature in date, is so indebted to Wagner as to be a parody; the full power and resource of the tone poems emerged only later, and hugely, in *Salome* (1905) and *Elektra* (1909), which have several features in common. Both are settings of plays, by Oscar Wilde (in German translation) and Hugo von Hofmannsthal. Both play continuously—perhaps necessarily so when the dramatic and musical atmosphere is in both cases extraordinarily fevered and focused on a single character, whose death provides the only possible close. Both are scored for large orchestral ensembles, and both demand a protagonist of great vocal and histrionic force, continuing Wagner's fearless use of the dramatic soprano voice in Isolde, Brünnhilde, and Kundry. Both, too, have climactic moments of solo dance—Salome's Dance of the Seven Veils and Elektra's final dancing of herself to death—in which the orchestra can assert its paramountcy. But there are also differences, provoked partly by the difference of setting. *Salome* is the culmination of operatic orientalism, picturing the decadent Herodian court against which the severity of Jokanaan (John the Baptist) and the amoral purity of Salome stand in relief: both are radiant extremists in a context of decadence. Elektra is an extremist too, waiting only for vengeance of her father, but though Aegisth and Klytämnestra have some of the unsavoury qualities of Herod and Herodias, their repugnance stems from a single act (the murder of Agamemnon) rather than a condition of corruption. The later opera is driven by the consequences of that act; its music is correspondingly more massive and compelled.

Elektra also presses further the expressionist equation between dissonance and intensities of emotion experienced in waking life (Elektra's lust for revenge) or in dreams (Klytämnestra's nightmare monologue). There is the same match in Arnold Schoenberg (1874–1951), whose almost exactly contemporary *Erwartung*, composed in 1909 but not performed until 1924, is a short, again continuous piece in which the sole unnamed character is a woman who may be searching a forest for a lover who may be dead, though equally her feelings of terror, dread, exhaustion, and nostalgia may be those of a nightmare. The indefiniteness is crucial. Schoenberg's tone painting—both in the ricochets of the vocal line and in the darkly brilliant, constantly changing orchestral landscape—can be as descriptive as Strauss's, with the added resources of a musical language that is now completely atonal and unbounded by metrical consistency. But where in *Elektra* the extravagant music seems to be demanded by the extravagant action, in *Erwartung* the text seems an attempt to name feelings and events which are fundamentally musical. *Elektra* obliged Strauss to move deeper into dissonance; *Erwartung* provided Schoenberg with a dramatic armature to use in a musical world he had already discovered, in his first atonal works a year before. Schoenberg's artistic purposes were thus engaged in this new world in a way that Strauss's were not: Strauss's position was more objective.

So the pursuit of *Elektra* by *Der Rosenkavalier* (1911) need not be interpreted as a volte-face. Strauss had never said he was interested in atonality *per se*: he was interested in Elektra, and perhaps even more so in *Elektra*. He could now move, without self-contradiction, to an interest in the pastiche Mozartian world Hofmannsthal created for him. Moreover, the harmonic severities of *Elektra* are not entirely abandoned, and the most signal feature of *Der Rosenkavalier*—its rampant and unashamedly anachronistic waltzing—had been prepared by the climactic dance sequences of *Salome* and *Elektra*, where, of course, the Viennese waltz is hardly less anachronistic. *Der Rosenkavalier* also shares with its predecessors a conviction that the soprano voice is essentially a sensuous instrument. All the female characters in the earlier operas had been given an erotic charge, whether corrupted in the case of Herodias and Klytämnestra, naked in Salome, latent in Chrysothemis, or diverted into murderousness in Elektra; similarly the three women central to *Der Rosenkavalier* are erotic beings, and their culminative trio is a piece of carnal opulence. What is new in *Der Rosenkavalier* is the extension of musical illustration into all the vocal parts to bring striking individuality to a great number of minor characters, however brief their appearances: such scenes as the levée would seem to have been written in order to exploit this incisive portraiture. What is also new in the work is the reappraisal of the characters, though not the music, of another composer, with Oktavian and the Marschallin being light disguises for Cherubino and the Countess. This was the first hint that Strauss's objectivity would lead on to the self-reflexiveness of his later operas about opera, from *Ariadne auf Naxos* to *Capriccio*.

Ariadne, originally presented as a one-act piece in which the story of

Bacchus's claiming of the abandoned Ariadne is interrupted by down-to-earth advice and interruption from a troupe of *commedia dell'arte* players (1912), was in its second version (1916) given a prologue involving preparations for the opera. Once again the setting is a glowingly fantasized eighteenth century, with the Composer, a soprano *en travesti*, a cousin of Oktavian. Of course, the work he produces is not the 'opera seria' he declares it to be in the text, but rather a rhapsodic setting of Hofmannsthal's psychological drama, in which Strauss, as the real composer, seems to suggest his music is more on the side of immediacy and succumbing, as represented by the *commedia* star Zerbinetta (a new type of Straussian soprano: the vivacious coloratura), than on that of the argument of the main drama, which he uses as a means of projecting delayed gratification. Strauss's single nod to the real eighteenth century in *Ariadne* is a reduction of the orchestra to thirty-seven players, though still with two harps and a celesta. His next opera, *Die Frau ohne Schatten* (1919), is again on the scale of *Elektra*, using its immense and variegated resources to follow the iridescent scenes and characters of Hofmannsthal's fairy-tale of quest and self-discovery.

Fairy-tales were frequent in the operas of this period, often carrying with them the subtext of an innocent world in collision with hard reality: Zemlinsky's *Der Traumgörge*, written in 1904–6, is quite explicit on this point, and it is the incompatibility of dream and reality that creates the tragedy too of Delius's *A Village Romeo and Juliet* (1907). The theme of the search for an illusory ideal is also the subject of *Der ferne Klang* (1912) by Franz Schreker (1878–1934), in which the hero Fritz is a young artist who goes off to seek the 'distant sound' of the title, leaving his beloved Grete, who, in the middle act, is discovered ten years later in a house of pleasures on the Venetian lagoon. Fritz goes on to write a play, which intimations suggest may be *Der ferne Klang* itself, but this fails, and he finds his goal only when he dies in Grete's arms. The infinite regress of the opera which explains its own composition is to be found also in Janáček's *Fate*, which Schreker cannot have known, since, though composed in 1903–5, it was not performed until after its composer's death in 1928. Another remarkable feature of *Der ferne Klang* is its diversity of means: it incorporates a good deal of speech over music, and, particularly in the second act, places where the musical-dramatic continuity is split between different, separate scenes. In both these respects Alban Berg, who made the vocal score, may have learned something from Schreker, and the dislocation of simple tunes in a rich, static harmonic style (as in the Count's fairy-tale song) surprisingly presages Weill, though the more typical

Schreker sound is one of plangent ostinatos, usually featuring harp and celesta, playing over rapturous but stationary textures beneath the lyrical arioso of his vocal writing.

In *Die Gezeichneten* (1918) Schreker's style is more conventional, restoring aspects of Wagner (specifically *Tristan*) and Puccini, but there is still the same free-floating, illusory quality to the music. Such aural hedonism might seem merely self-indulgent—especially when it entwines, as it does still more here, sensual hedonism in the action—but Schreker's position is fascinatingly and disturbingly ambivalent. Fritz's creation in *Der ferne Klang* is a failure, and Alviano's brothel island in *Die Gezeichneten* is manifestly a paradise of pretences: in both cases Schreker criticizes the pleasure-seeking abandonment from responsibility on which his own theatrical world is founded.

In that respect his works join sides with Hans Pfitzner's *Palestrina* (1917), in which the debate about artistic responsibility is conducted very differently, from within a bulwark of tradition where the musical foundations are supplied by *Die Meistersinger* and Brahms. Like Schreker, Pfitzner (1869–1949) wrote his own text; like Schreker too, he wrote his own artistic concerns into his central character (this Romantic conceit of the artist hero, going back to Berlioz's *Benvenuto Cellini*, was to be taken up again by Hindemith in *Mathis der Maler*, by Davies in *Taverner*, by Britten in *Death in Venice*, and by Stockhausen in *Licht*). Palestrina, like Pfitzner, feels himself to be the guardian of an endangered heritage. He composes his Pope Marcellus mass and thereby wins a victory for polyphony (the second act vigorously shows the clash of ecclesiastical principle, political allegiance, and personal animus among the bishops at the Council of Trent), but he is aware that he is working in the twilight, and that the future belongs to Florentine monody. It is this awareness that makes Pfitzner's opera a work of tragic grandeur and not a piece of embattled traditionalism.

If Pfitzner and Schreker both stared out with some concern at the new breadth of the musical landscape—the freedom which could so easily become licence—other composers reacted by erecting manifestly artificial domains, with an irony more intense than Strauss's in *Der Rosenkavalier* and *Ariadne*. Often, as with Strauss, artifice was justified by an eighteenth-century setting, sometimes with direct reference, which Strauss dextrously evaded, to eighteenth-century musical style: examples include Nielsen's *Maskarade* (1906), Busoni's *Die Brautwahl* (1912), and Wolf-Ferrari's *I quattro rusteghi* (1906) and *Il segreto di Susanna* (1909). Strauss's introduction of the *commedia dell'arte* into *Ariadne* also had its counterparts in a wilder fascination with masks and marionettes in Busoni's *Arlecchino* and *Turandot* (1917). These works resemble *Ariadne* too in their light scoring, an economy encouraged by war and to be found also in such dissimilar works as Holst's Buddhist fable *Sāvitri* (1916) and Stravinsky's small-scale morality play *Histoire du soldat* (1918), where opera is split into its rudimentary constituents of speech, music, and movement.

Stravinsky (1882–1971) had earlier written a work belonging much more within the operatic tradition, and specifically within the tradition of Rimsky-Korsakov's fairy-tales: *The Nightingale* (1914), based on Andersen's story. But the clear formality, the stylizing of the characters, and the compacting of three acts into the space of one all exaggerate the irony, as if the piece were a miniature, toy version of a real opera. Maurice Ravel's *L'Heure espagnole* (1911) is unashamedly an operatic mechanism. Set in a clock shop, and introduced by an extraordinary prelude of atmospheric orchestral tickings, the piece concerns characters whose behaviour is precisely governed by time. This is a comedy, and a sharp one, concerning the erotic arrangements of the clock-maker's wife, who can receive lovers only during the hour when her husband is attending to the municipal clocks. There is, too, an exuberance that comes, as in *Der Rosenkavalier*, from a strong undercurrent of dance, the style here being Parisian-Spanish. But in exposing the workings of opera to view—in taking the back off the clock by making the orchestra, through dance, an agent of the drama, and by presenting characters who are in the same situation as the singers who portray them, coerced by time—Ravel's piece belongs with those of Strauss, Schreker, and Pfitzner as an example of the creative self-consciousness of the period. It also succeeds in finding what Satie had required: something different after *Pelléas*.

Germany, 1918–1933

The Weimar Republic brought with it one of the golden ages of opera, or at least of opera history: no other period is so rich in works which, though almost never performed, ineluctably find their way into guides such as this—works like Paul Hindemith's *Neues vom Tage* (1929), representing the opera with a modern setting, or Ernst Krenek's *Jonny spielt auf* (1927), whose whirlwind success seems to have been due to jazz elements that now seem rather demure, or Darius Milhaud's elaborate, multistaged *Christophe Colomb* (1930). Possibly these and other works had a short life in the theatre because they were expressly made to be topical:

composers thought they were making history, and in a melancholy sense so they were. As part of that effort there was the post-war determination to cut loose from the psychological, opulent, Romantic operatic past, and to create new models of social and political reality with a new orderliness of musical and dramatic means that went under the banner of 'Neue Sachlichkeit' ('new objectivity'). There was a new generation at work, led by Hindemith, Weill, and Krenek, and many older composers, like Schreker and Zemlinsky, were touched by the new spirit.

It even marked Strauss. The first opera he wrote after the war, *Intermezzo* (1924), has a contemporary setting, being a domestic comedy based on an episode in his own private life (for the first and only time since *Guntram* he wrote his own libretto), and bringing back dry recitative (though typically in his own harmonic style). Moreover, its structure, in short scenes, may reflect an influence from the cinema, as in the case of many younger composers, most notably Berg in *Wozzeck*. It was followed by two more collaborations with Hofmannsthal, *Die ägyptische Helena* (1928) and *Arabella* (1933), repeating the partnership's pre-war styles of psychological mythology and characterful Viennese charm.

Strauss's last three Hofmannsthal operas have been criticized for excessive dramatic complication, though they seem algebraically logical beside Schreker's *Der Schatzgräber* (1920), where elements of magic, role-playing, and deception dissolve any certainty in the characters' motivations, or indeed the composer's. For instance, the third act is an extended love scene for the Wagnerian tenor–soprano couple Elis and Els, but Elis is perhaps being manipulated by the Fool at the behest of the King, and Els is in the habit of having her lovers murdered by another man. The work is more consistent in musical style than Schreker's previous operas, but no less slippery, opaline, seizing on opportunities for luxuriation and gorgeousness. Its total of fifty productions during this period bears witness to the thirst for new operas in Weimar Germany.

Alexander von Zemlinsky (1872–1942) used the harmonic and instrumental richness of the Schreker style, but to a very different effect of Ravelian precision in his one-act piece *Der Zwerg* (1922), which was one of the last of the fairy-tale operas, being based on Wilde's story 'The Birthday of the Infanta'. The artificiality of the Infanta and her entourage is shown in brilliant, often almost pentatonic music featuring high soprano voices, in complete contrast with the characterful and expressive part for the Dwarf, who completes a line of tenor grotesques, some more sympathetic than others, going back through the Fools of *Der Schatzgräber* and Schoenberg's *Gurrelieder* to Mime. The poignancy of Zemlinsky's Dwarf may have an autobiographical edge to it, not only because the composer was himself physically ill-favoured, but also because the Dwarf's estrangement from the court of beauty is so easily seen as that of the Romantic artist in a post-Romantic age. As opera conductor at the German theatre in Prague, Zemlinsky was responsible for the first performance of his brother-in-law Schoenberg's *Erwartung*, but his creative inclinations lay elsewhere.

Ferruccio Busoni (1866–1924) was another who saw the future but felt the past. His *Doktor Faust* (1925) belongs to the remarkable twentieth-century repertory of unfinished and perhaps unfinishable operas, a repertory which also includes *Turandot*, *Lulu*, and *Moses und Aron*. But that is not the only reason why it is a dark, mysterious work. The Faustian urge to know everything is taken on by the score, which ranges from Wagner (the magician Faust is a descendant of Klingsor) forward to Schoenberg and back to Bach, but without stylistic discord: the opera creates its own world of miasma. Indeed, the absence of irony makes Busoni's association of his *Faust* with the old German puppet plays slightly misleading: the characters are fully formed, not at all things of wood and string, even if the drama is presented in self-contained panels (as scenes from a *Faust*, much of which is assumed) and the choral-orchestral environment is often awry, pursuing a course of musical invention and discovery independent of the action.

Busoni's use of abstract forms (variations, dance suite) has parallels in Alban Berg (1885–1935), whose *Wozzeck* (1925) is in three acts patterned as a set of character pieces, a symphony, and a sequence of 'inventions'. But of course the musical language is very different. As Schoenberg's pupil, Berg profited from the fast-moving orchestral imagery of *Erwartung* and developed the speech-song of *Pierrot lunaire*, while incorporating also such Mahlerian elements as parodic military and dance music and a passionate orchestral slow movement in D minor. Abrupt changes of tone and texture are built into the work, and dramatically justified by the violence, speed, and fragmentation of what happens, for Berg's music fulfils Georg Büchner's play as completely as Debussy's does Maeterlinck's. Moreover, it does so in a similar way, by creating a world in which separate scenes—emotionally intensified and often bizarre in *Wozzeck*, evasive in *Pelléas*—can be gathered into a continuity, with orchestral interludes and transitions playing an important part in both works.

The first act of *Wozzeck* consists essentially of duologues which introduce the main characters, and which, from the dramatic point of view, could have been assembled in other orders (Büchner's draft consists of

1. Uffizi Theatre, Florence, interior, with the first intermedio of Marco da Gagliano's *La liberazione di Tirreno e d'Arnea, autori del sangue toscano*, 6 February 1617, engraving by Jacques Callot after the design by Giulio Parigi

2. Senesino and Faustina in Geminiano Giacomelli's *Gianguir*, Venice, San Cassiano, 1729, caricature drawing by Marco Ricci

3. Antonio Bernacchi (1685–1756), an alto castrato in a caricature by Pier Leone Ghezzi

4. The noble tenant of a box at the Paris Opéra on the eve of the French Revolution of 1789

5. Bolshoy Theatre, Moscow, an engraving by Jules Caildran from *L'Illustration* (16 February 1861)

6. 1864, the Garden Scene of Gounod's *Faust*: Adelina Patti (1843–1919) leans on the breast of Giovanni Mario (1810–83); Jean-Baptiste Faure (1830–1914) regards them as Méphistophélès.

(i) Verdi

(ii) Rossini

(iii) Wagner

(iv) Weber

7. The two greatest opera composers of the nineteenth century, Giuseppe Verdi (1813–1901) and Richard Wagner (1813–1883), are accompanied by two of their most important predecessors, Gioachino Rossini (1792–1867) and Carl Maria von Weber (1786–1826).

8. Poster for *Tosca*, designed by Hohenstein (*c.*1900).

9. Boris Godunov, portrayed by the role's most famous interpreter, Fyodor Shalyapin (1873–1938).

10. Kirsten Flagstad (1895–1962) as Isolde

11. Birtwistle's *Gawain*, a scene from the original production at Covent Garden in 1991, designed by Alison Chitty.

independent scenes without a final shape). Wozzeck, a barely articulate soldier, is seen with the Captain who mocks him, with his friend Andres, with his mistress Marie, and with the Doctor who uses him as an experimental animal in the pursuit of his crazed medical obsessions. Finally, in the only scene in this act where Wozzeck does not appear, Marie is seduced by the Drum Major, a figure of rampant male sexuality (a heroic tenor, if unhinged in the nightmare manner of the work, whereas Wozzeck is a baritone). The second act, the symphony, has a more inevitable dramatic progress (the musical progress is inevitable right through the opera, since in Berg atonality by no means annihilates powerful forward movement). Wozzeck's jealousy is aroused by the sight of the Drum Major's gift of earrings to Marie, further provoked by taunts from the Captain and the Doctor, and then, after a manic tavern scene, proudly and noisomely confirmed by the Drum Major himself. In the last act Wozzeck kills Marie, unleashing a double savage blast on a single note from the orchestra in the ensuing transition, and dies himself in searching the lake for the knife he threw there. The final scene features the child of Marie and Wozzeck. Again as in *Pelléas*, there is no resolution: the tragedy passes to a new, orphaned generation.

Berg's music seems, in its emotional force, to be speaking on behalf of people whose ability to express themselves is attenuated by deprivation, particularly in the case of Marie, whose vitality and warmth come from what she sings, and then abundantly in the case of Wozzeck, when the D minor interlude arrives as his requiem, intoning with massive resolution the motif associated with his phrase 'We poor people' (the work is as rich as the *Ring* in motivic correspondences). But at the same time the music is capable of creating complete caricatures in the Doctor and the Captain. The coexistence of human beings and puppets, without either seeming to know the difference (though the music knows), is one of the extraordinary achievements of this opera, and a source of its perturbing fascination.

If not the runaway success that *Der Schatzgräber* was, *Wozzeck* did well enough to assure Berg an income for several years; it may also have helped stimulate the operatic efforts of younger composers, even if most still preferred a more tonally rooted style. Indeed, neo-classicism—whether stemming from Busoni, from Stravinsky, or from political or social-critical programmes—was the essential musical method of Neue Sachlichkeit, and Hindemith's strenuously neo-classical opera *Cardillac* (1926) gave a lead in the new direction. Like Busoni in *Die Brautwahl*, Hindemith (1895–1963) chose an E. T. A. Hoffmann story and set it to music evoking genres and textures of the eighteenth century, but *Cardillac* is a stark drama and not a fantastical comedy, and its parade of self-generating musical form is more severe and imposing: the music is vigorously polyphonic, and continues for long stretches without a change of tempo, like some monster machine. The characters and action may seem rather incidental to this driving musical energy: two crucial scenes are played largely in dumb show; most of the solo parts, with the exception of the title role, are examples of vocal types instead of being musically characterized; and the word-setting can appear arbitrary, as if the voices were merely other instruments. The effect is to present the story, concerning a goldsmith who murders his clients so that he can recover his creations, as a parable. On one level it is a political parable, with Cardillac as the representative of capitalist rapacity. However, the background presence of Bach's Passions emphasizes the view of the goldsmith as sacrificial victim, and makes the opera a contribution to the continuing debate about the artist's role in society.

The manner of *Cardillac*, showing itself as a case-study, exemplifies the theatrical alienation associated particularly with Bertolt Brecht (1898–1956), and Hindemith went on to work briefly with Brecht in 1929. However, the much more fruitful collaboration at this time was Brecht's with Kurt Weill (1900–50), giving rise especially to *Die Dreigroschenoper* (1928) and *Aufstieg und Fall der Stadt Mahagonny* (1930). By taking the popular song style of the time, and distorting it through neo-classicism and an expanded tonal harmony, Weill created the music for Brecht's images of oppression and moral collapse in bourgeois society. Where every human feeling, especially sexual desire, is devalued by the balance sheet, music has to become sordid and parodic. The irony is that these two works, meant and heard as savage condemnations of contemporary society, have come to be the chief representatives of that society in the living repertory.

Schoenberg's one-acter *Von heute auf morgen* (1930) is a social satire in a double sense, a comedy of manners aimed at people eager to be up to date, and simultaneously a dig at composers doing the same thing. Schoenberg resisted, though not entirely, the fashionable avenues of neo-classicism and hit-song imitation, creating the first twelve-note opera, and thereby perhaps opening the way for a far more important work, *Moses und Aron*. What Schoenberg achieved of this was largely composed in 1930–2, and so belongs to the Weimar period, but the last of the three acts of Schoenberg's own libretto remained unset, and the first (concert) performance took place only after his death, in Hamburg in 1954.

With its biblical subject, its big choral set-pieces, and its generally static action, the work has something of the character of an oratorio, and indeed the dialectic between oratorio (presentation, argument) and opera (enactment, illusion) is central to it. Moses, whose part is in authoritative but musically inchoate speech-song, is able to perceive God, but unable to articulate his vision to the Jewish people. Aron, a voluble tenor, finds no difficulty in communicating, but in relaying Moses' message he distorts it. Moses demands allegiance to an invisible, unimaginable deity; Aron responds to the people's need for signs and representations, for miracles and an icon. The climactic scene is an orgy of dance and sacrifice around the Golden Calf while Moses is on the mountain receiving the tables of the law. On his return the image vanishes at a signal from him, but he cannot surmount Aron in debate, and the opera ends with him despairing his inability to give voice to his thought. That the work should finish at this point is thoroughly appropriate. In that it exists at all, the opera is an expression of Schoenberg-Aron, the teacher and composer. In that it is broken off, it is an expression also of Schoenberg-Moses, the rigorous thinker. And though Schoenberg resisted interpretation of the work in terms of his own personality, the subject does seem to answer to his creative character and to the nature of his music, the twelve-note series being itself an idea, like the Mosaic God, which cannot be grasped but only partially revealed, as here in an astonishingly rich variousness of invention.

Contemporary with *Moses und Aron* was another never-completed twelve-note opera, Berg's *Lulu*, of which a two-act version (1937) held the stage until Friedrich Cerha's completion of the score was presented at the Paris Opéra in 1979. As with *Wozzeck*, Berg assembled his own libretto from an existing dramatic work, in this case Wedekind's pair of plays on the rise and fall of a woman who is not so much a character as a male dream of female sensuality, a dream that evades possession and is thereupon destroyed. But where *Wozzeck* follows a classical pattern of preparation, culmination, and catharsis (even if the catharsis is profoundly pessimistic), *Lulu* has a tightly symmetrical structure, with strong correlations of action and music on each side of the pinnacle represented by Lulu's defiant song of self-determination. It is this position of independence that she has reached through her career hitherto, upwardly mobile through a succession of lovers and husbands, and that thereafter cannot be tolerated by men or by society. For the drama of *Lulu* springs not only out of the war between the sexes but also from the difficulty any society finds in coping with the erotic appetite.

Musically the range is vast, encompassing everything in German opera of the period. There is the languorous glitter of Schreker's metaphors of sexual enslavement, as well as the complex simultaneity (in the third act) of the second act of *Der ferne Klang*. There is the popular song style of Weill, and the jazz flavour of saxophone and vibraphone. There are the closed forms of neo-classicism, though often disguised or interwoven in longer continuities. There is the full spectrum of kinds of vocal delivery, from speech through intermediate forms to song. There is also an exuberant variety of characters, rivalled only by the cast of *Der Rosenkavalier*. And yet there is very definitely a *Lulu* style, controlled perhaps not so much by the twelve-note principle (Berg's technique is very free) as by other features: harmonic character, melodic shape, instrumentation.

As in *Wozzeck*, some characters are sharply sketched as caricatures (the athlete Rodrigo, the Schoolboy) while others are more roundly modelled, particularly that of the composer Alwa, patently a self-projection: when he suggests making an opera out of Lulu's story, the orchestra quotes from *Wozzeck*. Lulu herself, however, is deliberately enigmatic. In one respect she is not a person but a mirror for the designs of others: the Romantic ardour of Alwa, the cynicism of his father Dr Schön, the life-rejection of Jack the Ripper, by whom, in squalor, she is finally murdered. In another way she is a pre-person, a human animal that has escaped moral and social conditioning. But the only real escape she can have, within the world as it is, is the escape into death. Her death is accompanied, as Wozzeck's is, by an orchestral threnody, but the tone is different: where in *Wozzeck* protest is mixed with lament, in *Lulu* the near-final adagio is an acceptance, and even a homecoming. Lulu's only possible erotic partner is the man who will kill her.

If Lulu can also be seen as a personification of opera—a persistent, unattainable ideal for composers—then the work is an elegy for the genre within which it was conceived. The period of its composition, 1929–35, saw the crisis and extinction of German democracy, and the liquidation of a thriving operatic culture that had drawn in new works from outside German-speaking Europe: from Milhaud; from Stravinsky, whose *Oedipus Rex* had a notable production at the adventurous Kroll Opera in Berlin in 1928; from Gian Francesco Malipiero (1882–1973), composer-librettist of *L'Orfeide* (1925), *Tre commedie goldoniane* (1926), and *Il mistero di Venezia* (1932); and from Janáček. All that was now over. But the finality of *Lulu* seems to have wider implications, and to be sounding the end of opera as a bourgeois art form.

Eastern Europe, 1919–1945

Born four years before Puccini, Leoš Janáček (1854–1928) was in his sixties and seventies when he wrote most of the works by which he is remembered, including the operas *Katya Kabanova* (1921), *The Cunning Little Vixen* (1924), *The Makropulos Case* (1926), and—yet another work posthumously completed—*From the House of the Dead* (1930). The reasons for this late flowering were partly personal (Janáček discovered his muse in a young woman he met during the war), partly patriotic (Czechoslovakia had become a nation in 1918), and partly professional (he at last had a performance outside his own region when *Jenůfa* was given in Prague in 1916), but he may also have needed to wait for the state of the musical language to catch up with him. For though his style is totally individual— marked by a splitting intensity of expression and colour forced into small motifs, and of energetic ostinatos under broad lyrical lines—his mature music belongs in the age of Stravinsky and Bartók rather than in that of Elgar and Mahler.

Jenůfa (1904) shows the emergence of the new style from within a Smetana-like celebration of peasant vitality, and does so partly because the music was ten years in the making. After it came the ill-fated *Fate*, concerning a composer who, by the third act, has turned his lively experiences of the first two into an opera, and the comic fantasy *The Excursions of Mr Brouček* (1920), about a modern Czech everyman transported to the moon and to the fifteenth century. These two works display Janáček's boldness in tackling unusual subjects and dramatic forms—a feature also of his last three operas. In *Katya*, however, he took up the more traditional operatic theme of *Jenůfa*, that of the female protagonist whose love goes beyond the bounds of convention.

Janáček found his material in Ostrovsky's play *The Storm*. Katya is effectively imprisoned by a weak husband and a termagant of a mother-in-law. While her husband is away on business she yields passionately to another man, but her consciousness of sin forces her to confess before committing suicide. It was a story that perfectly fitted both the emotional fervour and the propulsive energy of Janáček's music, since the overpowering, forbidden feelings of the heroine cannot but lead to tragedy. At the same time, the creation of Katya provided a focus for his own feelings of love, while the other characters are drawn with the vividness of one who made a study of the rhythms and melodies of natural speech.

In *The Cunning Little Vixen* Janáček turned this gift for mimicry towards the animal kingdom, creating a quite unsentimental world of foxes, birds, and insects in which the human beings lag behind in wit and size of heart, and in which the evocative sounds and ostinato patterns of the characteristically brilliant, tangy orchestration now convey the colours and cyclicity of nature. Nevertheless, the work is anthropomorphic in that the central role of the Vixen expresses and compels sympathy for her as a conscious being. She is, therefore, as much the emotional focus of her opera as Katya is of hers, and again the root conflict is between human society and natural life. So it is also in *The Makropulos Case*, though with the difference that here the heroine is not the embodiment of nature but herself a perversion of it: a woman who has taken an elixir to extend her mean existence.

Both these last operas were Czech in origin, being based on a newspaper cartoon serial and a Čapek play, but in *From the House of the Dead* Janáček returned to Russian literature, specifically to Dostoyevsky's prison novel, and in doing so took on the challenge of making an opera without a heroine, indeed without any female characters at all (though he was able to introduce one soprano to sing the role of a boy). The greater challenge, though, was to put on to the stage a work which has no commanding plot: the libretto (Janáček's own, as in the two preceding operas) is a succession of dialogues and narrations in which nothing really happens. In spending so much time telling stories to one another, the inmates suggest that life is elsewhere. The music, however, vehemently insists that it is there too in the prison.

Janáček's realism was not the only way for eastern European opera between the wars: this was also the period of Martinů's French surrealist dreamscape *Julietta* (1938) and Szymanowski's bejewelled rewriting of *The Bacchae* in the exotic context of medieval Sicily as *King Roger* (1926). It was in the Soviet Union, however, that the case for documentary realism was debated most heatedly. Some repertory works were adapted to the needs of the revolutionary moment: the rebaptism of *Tosca* as *The Battle for the Commune* (1924) is an irresistible example. But the production of new works appears to have been hampered by a tension between modernists and popularizers, a tension resolved in 1932 by the promulgation of the doctrine of socialist realism, even though the nature of realism in opera remained disputable. The official example was Ivan Dzerzhinsky's bland *Quiet Flows the Don* (1935), contrasting completely with the critical course through irony, caricature, and violent incongruity taken by Dmitry Shostakovich (1906–75) in *The Nose* (1930) and *Lady Macbeth of the Mtsensk District* (1934).

The fantastical but sharp-edged satire of these works has deep roots in Russian culture—in Musorgsky, for instance, and in Gogol, the author of the story on which *The Nose* was based—which may explain a similar quality in the operas of exile composers, as in Stravinsky's *Mavra* or Sergey Prokofiev's *The Love for Three Oranges* (1921). Prokofiev (1891–1953) had used a whirling rhythmic energy to underline the hero's obsession in his Dostoyevsky opera *The Gambler*, composed in Russia in 1915–17 but not staged until more than a decade later, and then only in the West. *The Love for Three Oranges* unlooses the ostinatos from any psychological purpose, and instead has them spinning the wheels of a comic fantasy based on a Gozzi play (like Busoni's *Turandot*, and, at a greater distance, Puccini's) combining aspects of fairy-tale and *commedia dell'arte*, and mocking the hallowed certainties of stagecraft. Prokofiev's next opera was a return to the pathology of obsession in *The Fiery Angel*, a story of religious hysteria and madness, but this was not produced until after his death, and could hardly have found a place in the Soviet repertory.

Nor were Shostakovich's operas favoured for long. *The Nose*, in which the title character parts company with its owner to lead a colourful existence of its own, could justify its modernism and playfulness as tools of fantastical comedy, but *Lady Macbeth* was recognized as digging deeper in using similar techniques to satirize the authority not only of the bourgeois family but of the police, and to give heated expression to the erotic life of the multiple murderess who is the heroine. The work was officially denounced in 1936, when it became clear how circumscribed the world of Soviet opera would have to be: only in 1963 did it reappear, in a revised version as *Katerina Izmaylova*. Even Prokofiev's Soviet operas, though unimpeachably patriotic, ran into difficulties. *Semyon Kotko* (1940), a tale of peasant heroism during the immediately post-revolutionary civil war, was soon dropped from the repertory, and has rarely been revived, whether in Russia or beyond. *The Duenna*, a bright neo-classical comedy after the Sheridan play, was composed in 1940–1 but not produced until after the war. And *War and Peace*, interleaving lyric scenes and epic tableaux from Tolstoy's novel, suffered repeated hold-ups: the work was essentially complete by 1943, but its first performance in anything like complete form came only in 1957, some four years after the deaths (on the same day) of both Prokofiev and Stalin.

France, 1919–1945

Stravinsky's *Mavra* (1922) belongs in the preceding section by virtue of its Russian text, but was written in and for a non-Russian society: its destined audience, therefore, was one which would not understand the words. The piece would seem foreign; Stravinsky could exploit that in making its foreignness deliberate, in creating it as an example of a non-existent, synthetic foreign culture, where Bach, Tchaikovsky, and jazz bands are all contemporary, and all collaborating on an opera buffa. Not inappropriately, outrageous disguise is essential to the plot, in which a hussar cross-dresses to take the place of cook in his sweetheart's house, only to be found out when he is discovered shaving. This story, based on Pushkin, is set as an overture and thirteen short numbers lasting altogether under half an hour.

However unpretentious in scale (and therefore difficult to programme), *Mavra* may well have influenced composers from Hindemith to Shostakovich with its parodies and its fundamentally wind-band scoring. It also provided Stravinsky with a blueprint for the neo-classical future, soon to include the 'opera-oratorio' *Oedipus rex* (1927), though neo-classicism was very much in the air, and Arthur Honegger (1892–1955) had already followed a more innocently Bachian oratorio style in his 'dramatic psalm' *Le Roi David* (1921). Honegger's next stage work, *Antigone* (1927), was even closer to Stravinsky, in that its text was an adaptation of Sophocles by Jean Cocteau (1889–1963). In asking Cocteau to perform the same service for *Oedipus rex*, however, Stravinsky added the demand that the libretto be delivered in Latin, for he wanted 'a medium not dead but turned to stone'. Latin was thus to be in the new work what Russian had been in *Mavra*: a means of defamiliarizing. If opera was becoming a museum culture, Stravinsky's response was to create a museum piece, with a curator—the Speaker, addressing the audience in their own language—to introduce the various musical items as they appear. The work thus becomes a documentary on itself, and attains an alienation more austere than that of Hindemith's and Weill's operas.

This way of presenting the story, as an object to be observed from an irreconcilable distance, is intensified by Stravinsky's preferred manner of staging the work, with the singers appearing in masks and behind fixed cut-out 'costumes'. 'They should', according to the score's preface, 'give the impression of living statues'. But of course it is the music that contributes most to the opera's archaeological character. As a sequence of arias and choral numbers, with only one short passage where two soloists (Oedipus and Jocasta) sing together, the work looks back to eighteenth-century precedents, to Bach's Passions and opera seria; but there are many other forces at work here. The rude, harsh sound of the male chorus is at once modern and primitive, while the soloists are stuck in the tracks of the operatic repertory: Jocasta's big aria 'Nonne erubeskite, reges', in particular, is pure Verdi, occupying a curious middle ground characteristic of the work between respectful imitation and the sort of send-up Shostakovich or Prokofiev would have produced. The expressive weight of the nineteenth century is carried over into the new context, but, like the verbal language by which it is conveyed, it is 'turned to stone'.

Since attention is concentrated on how the story is told, not on what happens (which the Speaker generally announces beforehand, as if uncertain of his audience's classical education), almost any myth might have served. Stravinsky may possibly have picked the Oedipus story for its Christian echoes: the Latin, even though the score demands ancient rather than Italian-style ecclesiastical pronunciation, introduces a liturgical feeling, and Oedipus becomes increasingly through the piece a suffering victim. But equally, the refusal of psychological understanding, in this of all stories, makes the work something of an anti-Freudian manifesto.

It is only the story, and therefore the most arbitrary element, that Stravinsky's work shares with Enescu's *Oedipe* (1936), a grand and richly conceived tragic opera in which the stylistic disparities of *Oedipus rex* are necessarily eschewed in favour of a Romantic language loosened (and also given an antique colouring) by aspects of Balkan folk music. Enescu's central character, taken by a bass-baritone rather than Stravinsky's ringing tenor, is a doomed, doubting seeker after truth, and the opera smoothly unfolds his whole story, from birth to death. It is a work of great variety, including choral ceremonials, anguished monologues, and an extraordinary vocal character in the screeching mezzo-soprano Sphinx, but one that maintains a unique atmosphere.

Altogether opera in France during this period gives an impression of single, special achievements rather than of currents of development: other examples would have to include Roussel's *Padmâvatî* (1923), a spectacular opera-ballet in an ancient Indian setting, and Ravel's *L'Enfant et les sortilèges* (1925), with a Colette text in which a misbehaving child is punished by having the things he has abused—objects, animals, trees, a fairy-tale princess, even a rattling row of numbers—torment him with songs and dances. The result is a sequence of lustrous and acute musical mini-atures, including a ragtime dance for a teapot and a Chinese cup, a col-oratura aria sung by Fire, a cats' duet, a magical veil of garden music with croaking frogs' ensemble, and the lament of a wounded tree, all of them, though they terrify the child, made to delight. In that respect, and in the sophistication of its craftsmanship and allusions, the work is designed for an adult audience, as much as *L'Heure espagnole*, with which it belongs in its amused irony and orchestral brilliance.

An adult's response to *L'Enfant et les sortilèges* must have the sadness of looking at a world which cannot be re-entered, so in that respect Ravel's work is as removed from its audience as *Oedipus rex*. In another episode from childhood, Manuel de Falla's *El retablo de Maese Pedro* (1923), this frontier of the footlights is comically ignored by Don Quixote, who fails to understand that he belongs on a level different from that of the puppet show he is watching, and who tries to join in the courtly romance on behalf of the hero and heroine. The puppet show itself, adumbrating Stravinsky's opera-oratorio however unpretentiously, is acted out after explanations from a singing boy narrator, and the whole piece has the swift economy of a travelling entertainment. Like other short quasi-operatic pieces for small forces, Stravinsky's *Renard* (1922) and Milhaud's *Les Malheurs d'Orphée* (1925), Falla's work was commissioned by Princesse Edmond de Polignac for her salon. However, there was also a wider wish for brevity and restraint as part of the anti-Romantic move-ment of the time: other examples include Milhaud's *Trois Opéras minutes* on Greek myths (1928), Hindemith's twelve-minute *Hin und zurück* (1927) and the centre-piece of Malipiero's *L'Orfeide* trilogy, *Sette canzoni*, in which seven different operas are done in a single act.

As far as French composers were concerned, the interest in small-scale opera and mixed genres may have been encouraged by the stagna-tion of the official institutions. Only under the German occupation was operatic life from across the Rhine reflected in Paris, and then of course it was *Palestrina* that was presented, not *Wozzeck*. But France was not alone in its quiescence and insularity. Except for Puccini's *Turandot*, this was an extraordinarily barren period in Italy, with Malipiero finding most of his important opportunities in Germany. In England the most impor-tant opera was probably Ralph Vaughan Williams's setting of the Synge play *Riders to the Sea* (1937).

The United States and Germany, 1933–1945

After 1933 composers in Germany were subject to official control as intensive as that exercised at the same time in the Soviet Union, and many during the following few years took the path of exile, most usually to the United States, which had been seen longingly as a paradise of freedom and artistic rejuvenation in *Jonny spielt auf*, or at least in *Mahagonny*, as the place where life was being lived most crucially. Krenek (in 1939) and Weill (in 1935) duly emigrated to America, as did Schoenberg in 1934, Stravinsky in 1939, and Hindemith in 1940. What they found, though, was an operatic life that had virtually no use for new works. The Metropolitan Opera had been active in presenting premières earlier in the century, productions there including, in the remarkable year of 1910 alone, *La fanciulla del West*, Humperdinck's *Königskinder*, and Converse's *The Pipe of Desire*, but this openness was soon over, and the American operas that did get staged soon lapsed from the repertory, at least until Douglas Moore's *The Devil and Daniel Webster* (1939).

By contrast, the commercial theatre was clamouring for new musicals, and it was in this area that Weill determined to continue his career, notably with *Knickerbocker Holiday* (1938), *Lady in the Dark* (1941), and, after the war, *Street Scene* (1947), *Love Life* (1948), and *Lost in the Stars* (1949). *Lady in the Dark* used music in three dream sequences developing out of the heroine's psychoanalytic treatment, but in the other works Weill kept up his commitment to social criticism, *Street Scene* being set among the poor of New York and *Lost in the Stars* taking up the theme of racial conflict in South Africa. Nor was this political engagement unique to Weill. Marc Blitzstein (1905–64) dealt with the organization of a trade union in *The Cradle will Rock* (1937) and the victimization of immigrants in *No for an Answer* (1941). And George Gershwin (1898–1937) in his all-sung *Porgy and Bess* (1935) placed the old operatic themes of love and jealousy among a community of poor blacks, whom he insisted be portrayed by black singers.

Where Weill in *Mahagonny* had used American popular music in a critical sense, as a degraded language, there is no suggestion that the characters of *Porgy and Bess* are to be understood as constricted by what they sing: on the contrary, it is in this language that they live and express themselves, with seemingly unfettered ease and fullness. The situation is exceedingly ambiguous. A commercial language is being used to idealist ends; a medium devised for consumption and entertainment is being turned, without any conscious irony, to criticize the society that created it. And on the level of aesthetic categories, the distinction between high and low culture is being undermined: Gershwin called *Porgy* an 'American folk opera', a formula which suggests that for him Broadway music was folk music, and could be used as Smetana had used his country's folk music. There remains the difference, though, that the Broadway style was a synthetic product created for theatrical and commercial success, and having foundations there makes *Porgy* a puzzling achievement, however immediate its musical appeal and unquestionable its dramatic sentiments. At the very least it reopens the question of what opera is, and asks why, in a book such as the present one, there should be room for this piece and not for the works of Jerome Kern, Cole Porter, and Richard Rodgers.

Meanwhile in Germany there was no possibility of any kind of opera by Krenek or Hindemith being produced. Krenek's large-scale twelve-note opera *Karl V* was withdrawn even in Vienna when it went into rehearsal in 1934, and was eventually staged in Prague in 1938. Hindemith's *Mathis der Maler* similarly went abroad for its première, to Zurich the same year. Both works are set in the early sixteenth century, but both are concerned with a contemporary situation that was inescapable, Krenek projecting a utopian vision of a peaceable Catholic Europe and Hindemith finding metaphors in the life of the painter Matthias Grünewald for his own anxieties as an artist in a world where art might seem a luxury. His response, within the musical nature of the opera as well as its stage action (for the first time he wrote his own libretto), was to fight the demons within his art and to overcome the harmonic and formal angularities of *Cardillac* in a more fluent, consonant style, manifesting a far deeper sense of history than the Nazis' in its use of old German chorales and folk-songs.

Inside Germany the opera houses were left to minor figures such as Wagner-Régeny, Egk, and Orff, with only Strauss among composers of international reputation. His operas of these years continue to exhibit variety, from the opera buffa Ben Jonson adaptation *Die schweigsame Frau* (1935) to the grim, fortress-bound *Friedenstag* (1938), the effulgent *Daphne* (1938), and the rich *Die Liebe der Danae*, written in 1940–1 but delayed in production until 1952, when it was performed at the Salzburg Festival. These last two operas are again on mythological subjects, and *Danae* was an expansion of an idea originating with Hofmannsthal. However, the crown of this period is Strauss's last opera, *Capriccio* (1942), which surveys old themes through a radiant gauze of nostalgia. The central figure, the countess, is, like the Marschallin in *Der Rosenkavalier*, a woman at an emotional crossroads, having to decide not between abandonment and dignity but between rival suitors, a poet and a composer. The setting is, as in *Ariadne*, a grand house in the eighteenth century (though both works have frequently been updated to the twentieth in production), and the debate about the relative importances of composer, librettist, and performer is continued from that work. On that level the countess is metaphorically the soul of opera, having to choose between words and music. Of course the question remains open.

THE TWENTIETH CENTURY: 1945 TO THE PRESENT DAY

Paul Griffiths

Opera in English, 1945–1960

On both sides of the Atlantic the immediate post-war years found a lively operatic renewal. In 1945 England saw the first performance of *Peter Grimes* by Benjamin Britten (1913–76), a work soon regarded as a landmark, for unlike the operas of Vaughan Williams and Holst, it gained a place on the edge of the regular international repertory and initiated a flourishing tradition: Britten himself had produced nine more operatic works by 1960, and his example had been followed, at first chiefly by older composers (Tippett, Walton, Bliss, Benjamin). In the United States the stimuli were more complex. They included the continuing buoyancy of the musical, and the continuing urge to find hybrids between musical and opera: Britten and Auden had collaborated on a musical of sorts, *Paul Bunyan* (1941), during Britten's brief American exile, but Weill's place was taken more permanently and prominently by Bernstein. At the same time other composers looked towards the European Romantic tradition: most conspicuously the Italian Gian Carlo Menotti (b. 1911) but also such native composers as Douglas Moore (*The Ballad of Baby Doe*, 1958) and Carlisle Floyd (*Susannah*, 1955). What is remarkable about all these ventures is their rootedness, in local subjects and locations (for Britten, Moore, and Floyd) and in venerable musical traditions.

But Stravinsky's *The Rake's Progress* (1951) once more lays the presence of the past quite open, and does so without the jarring stylistic disparities of *Mavra* and *Oedipus rex*. The world is self-consciously Mozartian, with its eighteenth-century setting (Stravinsky asked Auden for a libretto based on Hogarth's cycle of paintings) and its use of dry recitative (with a harpsichord: not the piano Strauss had used in *Intermezzo* and Britten in *The Rape of Lucretia*). There are, in particular, close references to *Don Giovanni*, which crowd in upon the opera as it proceeds. Tom Rakewell, like the hero of Mozart's opera, rides roughshod over morality until he is called to account in a graveyard; like Don Giovanni, too, he has a servant with whom he can discuss his thoughts; and Stravinsky's opera ends like Mozart's with a sudden change of mood, an epilogue, and a moral.

But the nearness to Mozart is illusory. The work knows about a great deal of other music, both later (Rossini, Donizetti, Verdi, Tchaikovsky, and of course Stravinsky) and earlier (Monteverdi, whose *Orfeo* is semi-quoted in the opening fanfare and in the progressive identification of the hero with Orpheus). Moreover, the relationship with *Don Giovanni* has more of reversal about it than imitation. In *The Rake's Progress* it is the master, Tom, who is the simpleton, and the servant, Nick Shadow, who is the demonic character finally drawn down to hell. Shadow's initial appearance is cued by Tom's giving himself into the hands of materialism ('I wish I had money'): it is then possible for him to guide the rake's progress through an exhaustion of sensory pleasure into a world of counterfeits represented first by a bearded lady, the stupendous Baba the Turk, whom he persuades Tom to marry, and then by a machine to create bread from stones. Poor Tom is taken in by the phoney, and only wakes up at the critical moment when—in the graveyard, playing cards with Shadow to decide the future of his soul—he hears the voice of his original sweetheart, Anne Trulove, and remembers what genuine feeling is. Love keeps open the perpetual possibility of return: love does not change. The devil insists, however, that there is no going back, and Shadow—though love forces him to return, to hell—still has the power to prevent Tom from short-circuiting his progress. He makes him mad, and so substitutes for one sort of escape from time (love) another (insanity).

The opera can speak for both love and the devil by virtue of the duplicity in Stravinsky's own music of return. On one level *The Rake's Progress* is an affectionate homage to Mozart and to its other models, but on another it is a piece of satire and sabotage. For example, the moral of the epilogue ('For idle hands | And hearts and minds | The Devil finds | A work to do') is not only an unusually awkward piece of phrasing for this artful libretto but also misleading in its substance, since this is barely at all the message of the opera. The more the work draws close to Mozart, the more it deceives. There is no solid ground here, no comprehensive illusion, and the absence of that is what derails the hero's progress. Where Shadow is perfectly happy in a world of appearances, and where Anne in her innocence does not notice that she is in such a world, Tom finally attains the only kind of authentic existence possible in a world lacking rules and certainties: madness.

Stravinsky apparently had wanted to write an opera in English from the time of his arrival in the United States, in 1939, and had been encouraged, or stung, by the runaway success of Menotti, whose double bill of *The Telephone* (1947) and *The Medium* (1946), a light comedy and a melodrama, ran for several months on Broadway. Menotti continued his career with a full-length 'musical drama', *The Consul* (1950), and a Christmas opera for television, *Amahl and the Night Visitors* (1951). He also wrote the libretto for Samuel Barber's Romantic tragedy *Vanessa* (1958), which treats the theme of preserving the past in a very different manner from Stravinsky's: the heroine's world, fittingly presented in the music, is one entirely of nostalgia. It opened only a few months after *West Side Story* (1957), an apotheosis of the Broadway musical coming after its composer Leonard Bernstein (1918–91) had brought a popular song style to bear on more sophisticated dramatic forms in his one-act opera of modern marital manners *Trouble in Tahiti* (1952) and his operetta *Candide* (1956).

Vanessa was the only American work introduced at the Metropolitan Opera during this period, and although opportunities existed among smaller companies and in colleges, even there the predominant taste seems to have been for works which, though distinctively American, would be as like repertory operas as possible. In England there was the same feeling. Britten had two commissions from Covent Garden, for *Billy Budd* (1951) and *Gloriana* (1953), but he preferred working for and with a small touring ensemble, the English Opera Group, which was formed around *The Rape of Lucretia* (1946) and *Albert Herring* (1947), and for which he wrote a version of the *Beggar's Opera* (1948), the children's opera *The Little Sweep* (1949), *The Turn of the Screw* (1954), and *A Midsummer Night's Dream* (1960). With this ensemble—consisting of sympathetic singers, including Britten's life-companion Peter Pears, and an orchestra of a dozen or so—it was possible to explore an ambiguous, consciously marginal relationship with traditional opera and its artistic-economic machinery. In plot, character, and dramaturgy, Britten's operas have much in common with the Romantic naturalism of Verdi or Tchaikovsky, but the intimacy of the vocal writing, especially in the parts written for Pears, is that of a Schubert song, given an injection of coloratura and characterful shaping that came from Purcell. There is, moreover, a sense of disaffiliation in Britten's music—of not quite belonging, or of withholding complete commitment (complete commitment, in musical terms, to a key)—that suited it to a species of opera conventional in every respect but size. Britten may not have invented chamber opera (Boris Blacher's *Romeo und Julia*, written in 1943, has some claim to priority, though of course the seeds were there in Stravinsky's *Renard* and *Histoire du soldat*, or Schoenberg's *Pierrot lunaire*, or indeed Monteverdi's *Combattimento*), but he made the genre his own.

When he was called upon to write for full-scale resources, those resources came to embody a mechanism for destroying the central character: the self-righteous small-town community that makes a victim of Grimes; the naval discipline, beyond the scope even of the captain to budge, that catches Billy Budd in its grip; the court that does not see the woman behind the icon in the opera based on the last years of Queen Elizabeth I. At the same time Britten could use large resources to create the sort of rich musical and dramatic environment that was not available to him in chamber opera. *Peter Grimes* is punctuated by orchestral seascapes which prolong or prepare the mood of the action; it is also a powerful opera for the chorus. *Billy Budd*—set entirely on board a ship during the Napoleonic wars, and therefore restricted to male singers—is again charged with the sounds of the sea and of massed voices. *Gloriana* incorporates the pageantry of celebrations and choral dancing, and the colour of period music, while finding its heart elsewhere.

Among Britten's chamber operas, *Albert Herring* once more concerns a small community, but a much more benign one than that of *Peter Grimes*. This is a sunny comic idyll of Englishness, using satire only to deflate customary targets (the bombastic lady, the vicar), but creating one quite unusual character in Albert, a simple young man who thoroughly enjoys dirtying, however tamely, his lily-white reputation. This theme of innocence defiled then returns in a quite different mode in *The Turn of the Screw*, where a 'twelve-note row' of keys is used to reinforce the inevitability of the action, and the inevitability also, indeed, of tonality in Britten's musical-dramatic world. In this adaptation of a story by Henry James, the boy Miles is the prize in a psychological war between the governess and the ghost Peter Quint, a war represented musically by a tension between A and A flat, and also by a conflict of different ideals: order, purpose, and rationality in what the governess sings, against the lingering harmonies, rapturous tone colours, and vocal roulades (this is another Pears role) of Quint's music. Psychologically and musically it is a battle between social responsibility and individual desire, a battle which almost always in Britten's operas leads to the destruction of the protagonist.

A Midsummer Night's Dream is of course an exception. Nevertheless, here too the separate levels of the action allow the projection of a world of sensuality and strangeness, the fairy world, quite distinct from the everyday operatic reality of the Athenian court and the human lovers, while the rude mechanicals allow further scope to the parody manner of *Albert Herring*, which extends to the guying of Italian operatic melodrama in the play of Pyramus and Thisbe. The ethereal unreality of the fairy music is enhanced by the use of boys' voices (employed too in *The Little Sweep*, *Billy Budd*, and *The Turn of the Screw*) and also by casting Oberon as a countertenor—perhaps the first high adult male voice in opera since the castrati. Also important here is the variety of colour and texture Britten was able to create with a chamber orchestra. He never returned to the full-scale resources of *Peter Grimes*, *Billy Budd*, and *Gloriana*.

But his reluctance was not universal. In addition to the last two of these operas, Covent Garden staged the first performances of Arthur Bliss's *The Olympians* (1949), Vaughan Williams's *The Pilgrim's Progress* (1951), William Walton's *Troilus and Cressida* (1954), and Michael Tippett's *The Midsummer Marriage* (1955), a record to be explained not only by Britten's example but also by post-war patriotic idealism (at this point Covent Garden was a national rather than an international house) and also perhaps by the kinship that could be felt between opera and the new verse drama in the spoken theatre. Yeats and Eliot were important to Tippett (b. 1905) in particular, and *The Midsummer Marriage* combines their influences with those of Jungian psychology and *Die Zauberflöte*, in a rhapsodic, rhythmically sprung musical world resting on recent Stravinsky and Hindemith and on English music from the madrigalists to Purcell.

These were foundations for Britten too, but where Britten maintains a distance between reality and dream, Tippett's characters rush headlong into the supernatural. *The Midsummer Marriage* concerns a pair of lovers, each of whom has to achieve a psychical completeness before their union is possible: she has to learn earthliness, he spirituality, in a process that is guided by repositories of ancient wisdom and represented largely in a sequence of ritual dances. As in *Die Zauberflöte*, the main action is shadowed on a more mundane level by another couple; as in Mozart, too, it is the music that has to justify oddities and incongruities in the libretto (Tippett's own, and typically a commonplace book of literary quotations, contemporary slang, and unlikely turns of phrase).

Opera in Mainland Europe, 1945–1960

One thing held in common by the outstanding British and American opera composers of this period was an adherence to tonality, which made possible a traditional kind of operatic form, whether straight, as in Britten, or deeply ironized, as in Stravinsky. In much of mainland Europe, however, the pressure for change was irresistible. The composers who had been banned by the Nazis, notably including Schoenberg and Berg, were restored to performance and respect, and the twelve-note technique, which had barely been accepted outside Schoenberg's circle before the war, became almost universal. For opera composers this meant that the essential models were *Wozzeck* and *Lulu* (*Moses und Aron* was not staged until 1954), and so Bergian expressionism, justifying dissonances of harmony and style by extremes of emotion and violent changes of mood, became the dominant manner for musicians who had come of age during the Hitler years, such as Klebe and Henze. The new freedom also marked their elders, including Wolfgang Fortner in his Lorca setting *Die Bluthochzeit* (1957) and Luigi Dallapiccola (1904–75), who had developed personal and creative contacts with Schoenberg's school before the war, but who moved fully into the twelve-note field only afterwards, notably in his powerful one-act opera on a *Fidelio*-like theme of oppressive tyranny, though without the realization of hope: *Il prigioniero* (1949). Frank Martin's career was broadly similar, and led to his Shakespeare opera *Der Sturm* (1956). In eastern Europe, however, this path remained closed. In the Soviet Union the outstanding opera of the period was Shaporin's *The Decembrists* (1953), a Borodinesque epic on an abortive Russian uprising of the early nineteenth century; in East Germany ideological opposition prevented Hanns Eisler from realizing his *Johann Faustus*, intended as a Marxist rejoinder to *Mathis der Maler*, a critical examination of the intellectual who stands apart from class conflict.

But the contrast between an open West and a constrained East was qualified. The exhaustive re-examination of music that was being carried out by, for example, Boulez, Stockhausen, Nono, and Xenakis, was reflected not at all in the opera houses, and the influence of Berg remained on the level of expressive amplification rather than form, most operas of this period being content to follow the outline of a literary classic rather than remake it through music as Berg had done. The operas of Hans Werner Henze (b. 1926) even show a deepening move into tradition. His first, *Boulevard Solitude* (1952), is a retelling of the Manon Lescaut story; his second, *König Hirsch* (1956), a Gozzi fable endowed with great musical richness. Then in *Der Prinz von Homburg* (1960), an adaptation of Kleist, he returned, as he wrote, to 'Bellini's serene melancholy, Rossini's sparkle and brio, Donizetti's heavy passion, all united and condensed in Verdi's robust rhythms, his hard orchestral colours and melodic lines that set one's ears tingling', albeit from a still Bergian standpoint.

Opera and Music Theatre, 1961–1975

Two phenomena at the beginning of the 1960s broke open the conservative cast of post-war opera. One was the arrival at last of the international avant-garde, led by Luigi Nono (1924–90) with his *Intolleranza* (1961). The other was the innovation of music theatre, which also owed much to composers who had come to maturity since the war, though Stravinsky provided one of the first examples in *The Flood* (1962). *Intolleranza* was not the first opera to use electronic music on tape: that distinction belongs to Karl-Birger Blomdahl's science-fiction opera *Aniara* (1959). Nono's achievement was rather to create a new, aesthetically and politically challenging kind of opera by means of a rugged, cluster-based orchestral style and a highly charged interchange of musical-dramatic images, ranging from lyrical immediacy to oratorical detachment. These are still connected to a plot, concerning an immigrant at the mercy of the police and of capitalist society, but in Nono's second opera, *Al gran sole carico d'amore* (1975), this is no longer the case. Instead the text is a patchwork of quotations providing materials for varied musical treatments of the class struggle.

This tendency towards the disintegration of the stage illusion, and towards the politicization of opera, was by no means restricted to Nono. It can be seen in Henze's move from the luxurious worlds of *Elegy for Young Lovers* (1961), *Der junge Lord* (1965), and *The Bassarids* (1966) to the strident revolutionary engagement of *We Come to the River* (1976). It can be seen in the whole nature of music theatre, which disassembled the pretence of opera by presenting singers and instrumentalists on the same platform, usually in a concert hall and without scenery. And it can be seen also in Bernd-Alois Zimmermann's *Die Soldaten* (1965), where, although the subject and the style are close to *Wozzeck*, the combination of separate musical-dramatic streams, sometimes with three scenes playing simultaneously, discloses the artifice of the proscenium arch as a window into a coherent world.

Stravinsky's *The Flood* was not in the first place intended for the stage, and its numerous short episodes might seem to presuppose television performance, as also its diversity of means: much of the piece is narrated or enacted in speech over music, but there are also sung sections and movements devised for dancing. Moreover, the use of a large orchestra, with chorus and soloists, for a piece under half an hour in length does not fit the economy of the theatre. Britten's 'church parables' are in that respect more practical, being scored for small ensembles of singers and instrumentalists. The model here—anticipating the direction in which many younger composers were to look during the next few years—was the Japanese Noh theatre, and in particular the play *Sumidagawa*, of which the first parable, *Curlew River* (1964), was a near translation, though into a Western history of religious drama: the piece is presented as if by a community of monks, and gives a distinctly Christian slant to the story. A madwoman, searching for her lost son, eventually hears his voice as 'a sign of God's grace'. The later two parables are also concerned with the theme of the miraculously returning child, but now take subjects from within the Jewish-Christian tradition: they are *The Burning Fiery Furnace* (1966) and *The Prodigal Son* (1968).

Two days before this last work, and also at the Aldeburgh Festival, had come the first performance of Harrison Birtwistle's *Punch and Judy*, which strikes out from the example of Stravinsky in a different way. Like Stravinsky in *Renard*, Birtwistle (b. 1934) here takes up a form of popular theatre having more to do with ritual than with psychological drama. The work is intensively formalized, proceeding through short, highly distinct numbers arranged in cycles of repetition. At the same time the vocal styles—a different one for each character—are all precisely defined, and in most cases fiercely extravagant, accentuating the garish, violent way in which these beings (they are not people, but embodiments rather of the puppets from the original plays) behave. The work brings opera's most traditional themes of sex and murder to an extreme of intensity and artificiality; it represents an extreme, too, in the twentieth-century history of opera as puppet play. At the same time, its projection of instrumental soloists (particularly on wind and percussion) as independent characters, with parts as individualized and theatrical as those of the singers, opened new paths both for music theatre and for pure musical drama in instrumental forms. *Punch and Judy* was both an end and a beginning: a work which could not have been imagined before Stravinsky, but which seems to catch familiar operatic characters—the lover, the love object, the barrier between the two—at a primitive, pre-socialized level, as if it were a crude prototype for the whole history of opera.

The work equally seems to exist prior to any distinction between opera and music theatre. Composed for the English Opera Group, it is scored for forces similar to those of Britten's chamber operas (six singers and fifteen instrumentalists), but the dramatization of the instrumental parts—which becomes unmistakable if, as the score requires, the wind quintet play on stage—brings singers and players together in the manner of music theatre. Birtwistle then went further from opera towards the *Histoire du soldat* ideal in *Down by the Greenwood Side* (1969), in which another English vernacular entertainment, the Christmas mummers' play, is performed by actors with instrumental music and the interleaving of a song. This was part of a brief flowering of English music theatre, which produced also Britten's church parables and Peter Maxwell Davies's *Eight Songs for a Mad King* (1969), where a lone soloist sings the part of the demented King George III, accompanied by a percussionist, a keyboard player, and four other instrumentalists performing from within bird cages, one of the central images of the piece being that of the king trying to teach finches to sing.

The ferocious virtuosity Davies (b. 1934) demands of his soloist is entirely within the tradition of expressionist opera, extending from Strauss, Schoenberg, and Berg to, within this period, Henze, Penderecki, and Alberto Ginastera (1916–83). Penderecki's *The Devils of Loudun* (1969), with its scenes of religious and sexual hysteria, exemplifies a melodramatic exuberance to be found also in Alberto Ginastera's *Don Rodrigo* (1964), *Bomarzo* (1967), and *Beatrix Cenci* (1971). It is perhaps in the light of such works that one needs to read Pierre Boulez's polemic against the operatic world, published in an interview with *Der Spiegel* in 1967. Boulez's essential point was that there had been no regeneration of opera since Berg, and that the fixed routines and repertories of opera houses positively worked against innovation: all that was wanted of composers was the occasional new piece following traditional, even Verdian patterns of musical dramaturgy, and packing in the shocks.

The violence of Penderecki's and Ginastera's operas, or the luxurious sophistication of Henze's two collaborations with the team of W. H. Auden and Chester Kallman that had written *The Rake's Progress* for Stravinsky (*Elegy for Young Lovers* and *The Bassarids*), or the time-defying Romanticism of Samuel Barber's *Antony and Cleopatra* (1966) all support Boulez's view of opera as lost in past dreams, but the position was not irretrievable, as *Punch and Judy* showed in making a finely tuned brutality the essence of a wholly new musical and dramatic world, rethought down to each jagged fragment. And there were other new departures, including some made possible by the collapse, notably in Boulez's own music, of the notion of the work as a fixed ideal. Bruno Maderna's *Hyperion* (1964), for example, provides various components which can be assembled and staged in many different ways, the narrative element being abstract, with the principal role taken by a flautist. Henri Pousseur's *Votre Faust* (1969) has a stronger story line, concerning a composer whose pact with the devil is a commission to write a Faust opera, but the materials are variable in many different ways, including at one point an opportunity for the audience to vote on the dramatic outcome. The work also takes up the new resources of music theatre, requiring actors, singers, and instrumentalists in the same space: the image of a fairground is crucial, as also in the nature of *Punch and Judy* (or indeed *Renard*), the fair providing an ideal more socially and aesthetically permissive than the theatre or, still more so, the opera house.

In addition to Stravinsky, Birtwistle, and Pousseur, there was also György Ligeti (b. 1923) offering a startling alternative to conventional opera in his *Aventures* (1963) and its sequel *Nouvelles Aventures* (1966). Ligeti put these pieces together within a complex scenario of wild theatrical activity owing something to Dada, something to silent-film comedy, and something to the new performance art of the time (this was the age of the 'happening'). However, the fundamental jokes are intrinsically musical, depending usually on the absurdity and excess of the three soloists' vocal behaviour. Since they have no words, there is no explanation for their crazed contours and freakish effects, nor for the rapidity with which moods of fright, joviality, adoration, and jealousy flash past. In that respect these works are not only humorous sketches but critiques of so much contemporary opera.

The humour and the criticism are there too in a work by another composer who, like Ligeti, stood observantly on the edge of the international avant-garde of the 1960s: Maurice Kagel's *Staatstheater* (1971). Written for a house which had, under Rolf Liebermann's management (1959–73), become a prime venue for new opera, Kagel's piece is a debunking of the whole genre. The full resources of the opera house are put on display—orchestra, *corps de ballet*, soloists, chorus, even props and costumes from the standard repertory—but everything is creatively mishandled, as if by someone who did not know what these things were for: as in Ligeti and Birtwistle, though in yet again a different way, opera is advanced by a startling retreat into a condition of ignorance. Sixteen principals are brought together in a mad ensemble; the dancers are stuck in callisthenic exercises.

Opera (1970) by Luciano Berio (b. 1925) also sees the medium as having entered into desuetude, though its ironies are characteristically more subtle and diffuse, its view of opera as fascinated as disbelieving. The overstacked, toppling state of opera is compared with that of capitalist society, and given another layer of theatrical metaphor in the story of the sinking of the *Titanic*, while Berio's score, in its quizzical examination of operatic history, takes up passages from the libretto of Monteverdi's *Orfeo* and also, as it goes along, reworks fragments of its own past. Each of the three acts begins, for example, with a different version of a soprano aria to words from the prologue from *Orfeo*, and each includes also a new setting of the messenger's solo, the fundamental message of the entire work being that opera is moving unavoidably towards the fate suffered by Euridice, that of irredeemable demise.

It is the message conveyed also by Kagel's anti-opera, by the extra-operatic, vigorous but short-lived existence of music theatre, and by Boulez's strictures, as well as implicitly by the weakness of many of the new works written for the opera house. There were, however, during this complex period also signs of continuing vitality, without the complete overhaul of *Punch and Judy*. One was Dallapiccola's *Ulisse* (1968), a searching portrayal of Dante's Ulysses the eternal wanderer. Another was Nicholas Maw's *The Rising of the Moon* (1970), a surprising achievement in a genre of generous and characterful comedy that might otherwise seem to have been exhausted by *Der Rosenkavalier*. Another came in the decisiveness of Tippett's two operas after *The Midsummer Marriage*: *King Priam* (1962) and *The Knot Garden* (1970), the one a stark kaleidoscope of type characters in an argument on the nature of moral choice, the other a modern myth of personal frictions and changes more akin to *The Midsummer Marriage*, though in a more fragmented style and with allusions now to *The Tempest* and *Così fan tutte*.

Yet another sign of continuity was Britten's last opera, *Death in Venice* (1973). Throughout the operatically perilous 1960s Britten had avoided writing a full-length piece for the theatre, preferring his own genre of church parable and then television in *Owen Wingrave* (1970), though this last work—a second Henry James country-house story, now enabling Britten to press his claims as a pacifist in identifying with the scion of a military family who refuses the course expected of him—has proved viable on the stage. *Death in Venice*, based on the Thomas Mann parable of an established artist in the Dionysiac trap of obsession with a boy, returns to the conflict of order and sensuality in *The Turn of the Screw*, and does so by similar means. Aschenbach's view of the boy is in the glow of tuned percussion, specifically evoking the gong orchestras of Indonesia: the world of hedonistic indulgence is unattainably far away. It is so, too, in the way the central roles are cast. Aschenbach is a tenor (specifically the tenor of Peter Pears), whereas the boy, his family, and his friends are all acted by dancers. Britten thus has the means to show the boy as an embodiment of beauty, and to maintain the essential silence between him and Aschenbach. The work—paradoxically taking more advantage than *Owen Wingrave* had of the fluid changes of locale possible with television—depends much on the central character's recitative monologues, interspersed with action scenes in which the insidious, many-masked lure of the city is realized in the returning arrivals of the same baritone singer in the leading subsidiary roles.

In its view of the errors of self-delusion that open themselves to artists, *Death in Venice* is a contribution to the notable twentieth-century history of the artist as operatic hero, as also is Davies's *Taverner* (1972), concerning the early sixteenth-century English composer John Taverner, who was thought to have abandoned his art to become a Protestant zealot. Extending out from the real Taverner's music, though in a distinctly modernist colliding of Stravinsky with Schoenberg, Davies's music is a metaphor for the workings of his central character's mind, in which alongside real figures—his father, his mistress, the churchmen for whom he composes—are his projections of the self-serving king and cardinal, and of a jester-death character by whom he is persuaded to sign away his artistic soul for the blind certainty that he will be fighting for the truth in persecuting the Old Church. But the meaning of *Taverner* is not only or even primarily religious. Taverner's dilemma is that of Davies, or of any composer in this age of artistic confusion: it is the problem of steering a course between the mere repetition of tradition and the perhaps empty enticement of new forms, new languages. It is the problem that lies behind much of the opera of the 1960s and early 1970s, and also behind much of the work in new genres that briefly seemed an escape, an evolutionary alternative.

There were perhaps two reasons why that alternative failed to take off. One was opera's capacity to embrace new principles, as in the stage musicians and the severe verse-refrain forms of *Punch and Judy*, so that the dichotomy between opera and music theatre ceased to have much meaning. The other was the impossibility of maintaining permanent revolution. As a revolutionary medium, music theatre demanded of its creators perpetual rethinking, an avoidance of duplication: the uniqueness of such works as *Eight Songs for a Mad King* or *Down by the Greenwood Side* is part of the deal, and history has not been kind to imitations. It was therefore inevitable that ideas would be exhausted, and that the anti-conventional urge in music theatre would lead to a world in which there were no taboos left to break, except the taboo against going back to tradition.

That point seems to have been reached around 1972, the year of Berio's *Recital I* (significantly both the first and the last in its series, unsucceeded by any more works of music theatre) and Karlheinz Stockhausen's *Alphabet für Liege*. Berio's concern with new musical-dramatic possibilities went back to two related mime pieces, *Mimusique no. 2* (1955) and *Allez Hop* (1959), and included also the provocative *Passaggio* (1963), in which the female protagonist, unnamed as in Schoenberg's *Erwartung*, is shunted through a sequence of musical-dramatic situations and shown to be not the victim of her own anxieties, as in the Schoenberg, nor the prey of a heartless society, as in Nono's *Intolleranza*, but rather the object of the audience's fantasies: the work ends in disruption brought about by groups planted among the spectators. There are no such interventions in *Recital I*, but again the lone soloist is a woman led through diverse sorts of music (including an early song by Berio himself), and again she is the pawn of the work in which she exists: the piece can be understood as portraying the mental disintegration of a performer who has been called upon to adopt so many different vocal, dramatic, and emotional personae that she has lost track of her self. Unusually defeated in tone, it seems to convey a warning, even a death knell, to the genre in which it was written.

The theatrical engagement of Stockhausen (b. 1928) has been more recent. In 1961 he had created *Originale*, a plethora of more or less defined theatrical incidents unfolding together with a performance of his *Kontakte* for pianist, percussionist, and tape. The model, or at least the stimulus, would seem to have been Cage's unstructured *Theatre Piece* (1960), and Stockhausen continued to avoid any kind of narrative, while profiting from the lesson of other music by Cage (notably his piano pieces of the mid-1950s) that musical performance is of its nature theatrical. For example, even without the additions brought in *Originale*, *Kontakte* is a dramatic work, initiated by a great scrape on a large tam-tam (a gong without a rim), and continuing as a game of answer and allusion in which the two musicians react to what they hear through the loudspeakers. Another manifestly theatrical piece is *Momente* (1962), for an exuberant soprano soloist at the centre of a musical world inhabited by choral groups and instrumentalists. In the light of Stockhausen's subsequent devotion of himself, after 1977, exclusively to a cycle of operas, many of whose constituent scenes can be given as concert pieces, these works of the early 1960s have to be considered at least nascently operatic.

But of course they have very little to do with the tradition of opera from Monteverdi to Britten or even Berio. Stockhausen's understanding of musical theatre was global, particularly after his first visit to Japan in 1966, and it found its roots not in story-telling but in ceremony. There is a link here with Birtwistle, whose theatre pieces also have a ceremonial element, and whose concert works too can have a ritual formality of action and content: in his *Verses for Ensembles* for wind and percussion (1969), for instance, the players have to change their positions in order to project different functions in the abstract drama. The difference is that Birtwistle's works are portraits of rites, rather as Stravinsky's are (*The Rake's Progress* could be seen as a portrait of a Mozart opera), whereas Stockhausen's music is not so explicitly distanced, and increasingly presents itself, from the late 1960s onwards, as giving access to kinds of experience far beyond the musical. An early example was his description of his *Stimmung* for six singers (1968) as 'a fast aircraft to the cosmic and the divine'. Also significant here is his preference, from *Momente* onwards, for musical spans which—like operas, but unlike concert works generally in the Western tradition—occupy a whole performance. Each work becomes a ceremony: a ceremony for several groups of musicians around a park at night in *Sternklang* (1971), an exhibition-ceremony with different stalls displaying the physical and metaphysical properties of sound in *Alphabet für Liège* (1972), a ceremony for a large orchestra supporting mime artists in attitudes of prayer in *Inori* (1974). Such works, although none of them was devised for a normal theatre, belong to the history of opera not only in the light of Stockhausen's subsequent development, but also because they could hardly have been imagined without the disruption of norms that the music-theatre revolution of the 1960s had brought about. The pressure perpetually to find new kinds of musical-dramatic expression—a pressure almost palpable in the works of Birtwistle, Berio, Davies, Pousseur, Kagel, Maderna, and Ligeti—had resulted in the disintegration of opera as a genre.

Opera or 'Opera' Since 1976

And yet operas have continued to be made—if anything, in greater abundance since the mid-1970s than immediately before. Partly this is because many composers have been untouched, or only transiently touched, by the turmoil of the 1960s. Henze, for example, after resuming his operatic career with *We Come to the River*, went on to *The English Cat* (1983), *Das ver-ratene Meer* (1990), and *Venus and Adonis* (1997), while Penderecki's later operas comprise *Paradise Lost* (1978), *Die schwarze Maske* (1987), and *Ubu Rex* (1991). America offers examples of still more prolific opera com-posers, such as Dominick Argento, whose works continue in a direct line from the traditionalism of Moore, Floyd, and Britten. But at the same time other composers, engaged in or sympathetic to the anti-conven-tional trend of the 1960s, have found ways of restoring to opera—as if to a medium that has suffered mortal collapse—ways of writing operas, or at any rate 'operas', in a kind of life after death.

Ligeti has been quite explicit on this point. Feeling that Kagel had written the ultimate anti-opera in *Staatstheater*, an extension of the icon-oclasm of his own *Aventures*, he determined it would now be possible to write an 'anti-anti-opera' (his own term), a work which would take into account the fact that it existed in a world that had been totally disrupted. One could consider *The Rake's Progress*, or maybe even *Mavra*, as the first such post-terminal opera, spatchcocking together bits and pieces from a tradition that had once been alive, and though Ligeti's *Le Grand Macabre* (1978) does not appeal to any particular model, as Stravinsky's works do, it is crammed with allusions and distortions, while dramatically it por-trays an apocalypse which turns out not to be an ending after all. Death here is only a sham. A figure of dread appears on the stage, declaring that he brings the end of the world (he is the 'Grand Macabre' of the title), but he is the only one of the main characters who does not wake to a contin-uing existence after the supposed end of time has come.

But even before this the opera's world was patently artificial, bizarre, and exaggerated, a convolution of theatrical absurdities and musical par-odies (or vice versa). The action unfolds in 'Breughelland', the kingdom of peasants and monsters glimpsed in the Flemish master's paintings, and the cast includes a common man who is drunk throughout the opera, a pair of lovers whose voices (both female) are intertwined in the sensuous manner of the closing duet from *L'incoronazione di Poppea*, another couple whose sexual tastes are more exotic, the boy prince of the country (a treble role) and his coloratura soprano Chief of Secret Police, and two rival bickering politicians (spoken parts). Diverse types of oper-atic possibility and operatic reference are thus set in motion, but the intention does not rest at the anti-operatic level of debunking the reper-tory: wild and weird forms of expression are required by a wild and weird musical drama. But the wildness and the weirdness could only be achieved after a denaturing, a critical deflation of opera's claims to represent human passion, a disbelief such as the works of Stravinsky, Kagel, and the early Ligeti all imply. There can be no going back, Ligeti suggests. 'Both music and speech in my opera', he has said, 'are direct, without psychological undertones, blunt at times and drastic'. The connections are once again—after Busoni, after Birtwistle—with puppet theatre: the librettist and original producer was the director of the Stockholm puppet theatre, Michael Meschke, and puppets appeared physically on the stage, as well as figuratively in the vocal behaviour of the singers. *Le Grand Macabre* is a play with the dry bones of opera and, musically, with the dry bones of tonality, with consonances separated from contexts and yet cranked into a new way of working. As such it confirms that the death of opera—much vaunted in the 1960s, explicitly in Boulez's polemic and implicitly in the music-theatre excursions of so many composers—did in fact take place, but that life after death may be possible.

Ligeti's work is more 'opera' than opera: a contribution to the genre which at the same time firmly places itself on the outside. And it is in this ironic position with regard to the repertory that a great many works since the mid-1970s have been written—have had to be written—though of course the colour of the irony may be something very different from Ligeti's woodcut incisiveness and black humour. It may, for instance, be the warm embrace with which Berio enfolds Verdi, and specifically *Il trovatore*, in *La vera storia* (1982), whose first act is a dismantling of the original into archetypal situations—an execution, the theft of a child, an oath of vengeance, a duel—interleaved with choral tableaux and vernacular ballads bringing in the voices of folk-song and street singing. There is no musical recollection of the Verdi, but the effect is of elements of a partly familiar story being thrown up by the whirlpool of popular celebration suggested by the choruses and the ballads. The second part is then a reordering and reworking of the musical and dramatic materials laid out so far, excluding the ballads, so that the clear outlines are more or less inundated in a musical continuity. As Berio has remarked, 'In Part I, made up of closed numbers, it is the action on stage that dominates; in Part II it is the musical action...Part I is real and concrete, Part II is oneiric. Part I embraces the operatic stage, Part II rejects it.'

Berio's next opera, *Un re in ascolto* (1984), is also concerned with shifts between a drama of action and a drama of listening, but in a more fluid manner, rolling back and forth. This can be so partly because the narrative layers of the piece are so many, but partly because, too, the principal action is itself an act of listening, the 'listening king' of the title being a theatrical producer who is auditioning singers, who is hearing voices of unrest from within his company, who is hearing himself as Prospero in *The Tempest*, and who is trying to shut out voices that come from beyond his theatre. The audience confrontation of *Passaggio* is continued here as it is in *La vera storia*, and expressed in a kind of despair that the real world of action is going on somewhere off-stage: the climax comes with the arrival of a female protagonist from that world, whose criticism of Prospero, and whose usurping of his hitherto sole right to arias in this opera, results in his death, after he had been abandoned by the players and roles he had surrounded himself with. But perhaps his death is made inevitable also by the deepening, gathering texture of the work, which moves, as in *Opera* and *La vera storia*, through different versions of the same musical and dramatic events: three audition scenes, for example, and five arias of introspection for Prospero.

In Berio's work the opera house becomes not so much a theatre of singing—though of course singing remains crucial, and Berio's relish of the voice puts him decisively in the Italian tradition—as a theatre of listening, the emphasis not so much on expression as on understanding, on the ways in which ear and mind grasp and make sense of what is heard. The invitation to listen, though, is still given with an invitation to look, whereas Nono's *Prometeo* (1984) presents itself as a 'tragedy of hearing', an opera for the ears alone. There is not much connection here with radio opera—a genre curiously lacking in major works. Nono's piece was meant for public performance, within a specially constructed wooden shell providing stations for both performers (singers, speakers, instrumentalists, electronics technicians) and listeners: the whole auditorium would thus become a single musical instrument, with the audience within it in darkness, listening rather as the central figure in *Un re in ascolto* listens to what is all around him.

Nono's removal of himself here from the opera house can be understood in the light of his lifelong commitment to challenging the bourgeois commerce of musical production, but in demanding a special ambience *Prometeo* also links itself to patterns of ritual: Nono's working notes suggest connections with the Greek theatre, with the liturgy of San Marco in Venice, with ceremonies in monasteries in Russia or Tibet. It is Stockhausen's work of this period, however, which has least compunction in presenting itself as sacred drama. All the elements were there before, as has been noted: the extension of each work to fill a whole performance span, the appeal to the mystical in sung texts, titles, and programme notes, the prescription of gestures. To these were added costumes in works of the mid-1970s such as *Harlekin* for dancing clarinettist (1976) and *Sirius* (1977), a spectacle for four musicians who arrive as visitors from outer space to teach, guide, and entertain their earthly audience (the unsettling joky-earnest nature of the enterprise is very much characteristic of the later Stockhausen). After this came Stockhausen's entry into the opera house with *Donnerstag* (1981), the first of a projected seven operas designed to be given on the evenings of a week and collectively entitled *Licht*.

The scale of this conception has inevitably invited comparison with the *Ring*, but Stockhausen's means and purposes are very different. For instance, there is no attempt at unity, whether of narrative, of performing forces, of place, of speed, or even perhaps of seriousness. Each opera consists of acts or scenes which often were commissioned for separate occasions, and which may be quite different in all of the above ways. Often, too, these acts and scenes are divided into segments which are entirely distinct. Of course, earlier composers, from Monteverdi onwards, worked in the consciousness that songs and scenes from their operas might be excerpted; the difference is that with Stockhausen each opera is a sequence of free-standing moments with only very loose musical and dramatic links.

These links consist essentially in the presence throughout the cycle of three generative melodies, and of three principal characters associated with those melodies: Michael, the hero, redeemer, and celestial messenger; Eva, who is both his mother and his consort; and Luzifer, his antagonist, the principle of negation. Each of these characters can be represented by a singer (tenor, soprano, bass), an instrumentalist (trumpet, basset horn, trombone) or a dancer, or by any combination or multiplication of these. Stockhausen thus has a great variety of ways of projecting drama on stage, and perhaps his outstanding contribution to the history of opera will be seen as his extension of the possibilities of the mime-instrumentalist, from beginnings perhaps to be placed in *Die Zauberflöte*.

In *Donnerstag*, for example, Michael appears in all three guises in the outer acts, while in the middle act his journey around the world is consigned to the trumpeter, and the whole act is effectively a trumpet concerto. This first part of *Licht* to be completed is a biography of the protagonist, showing his education as a supreme musician, his bringing of a cosmic message to the earth, and his return to heavenly realms in a grand welcome ceremony concluded by a vision in which he recapitulates his life. Two other operas of the cycle similarly concentrate on the other main figures, *Samstag* (1984) belonging to Luzifer and *Montag*

(1988) to Eva. *Samstag* is not a work for the theatre. Its four scenes suggest a progressive expansion of space, from the opening duet for bass and piano, through a long flute solo accompanied by six percussionists with instruments strapped to their bodies, and then a piece for a wind band arrayed on a vertical frame, to a concluding choral ceremony imitated from a mixture of Christian ritual and Japanese temple practice. *Montag*, however, again suggests opera-house performance, and indeed the womb of the auditorium becomes an image in a work dominated by the voices of women and children, and by metaphors of amniotic existence and birth. *Dienstag* (1992), which begins in celebration and ceremonial, has the theatre invaded in its second act, and becomes a battle between the musical forces of Michael and Lucifer.

The absurdity, even the falseness, of projecting a synthetic mythology is something to which *Licht* seems to be responding in its inclusion, along with the awesome, of the charming and the comic. The verbal world of *Montag*, for instance, is grounded—or perhaps 'floated' would be a better word for this aqueous musical environment, engendered so much by electronic sound—in nursery rhymes and baby talk. The first act includes a ballet for pushchairs; the second opens with a procession of singing girls, each dressed as a lily flower and carrying a candle; in this act too a ludicrously extended piano arrives to impregnate with music the colossal seated figure of Eva; and much of the third act is occupied by a version of the Pied Piper story. But it is in this work too that Stockhausen goes furthest in exploring how instrumentalists—especially the flautist and the basset hornist, who are both incarnations of Eva—can be dramatic characters.

Where Stockhausen is most deeply conventional is in his intuition that opera is the forum for myth, as it was for Stravinsky, Schoenberg, Wagner, Mozart, Handel, Purcell, and Monteverdi. That was how other composers, too, arrived at full-scale opera around this time, notably Olivier Messiaen (1908–1992) in *Saint François d'Assise* (1983) and Birtwistle in *The Mask of Orpheus* (1986). Messiaen was even later than Stockhausen in making a start as an opera composer: he began *Saint François* in his late sixties, and he had at first declined the commission on the grounds that opera was not his 'métier'. In saying so he was perhaps thinking of the repertory he most admired—Mozart, Wagner, Musorgsky, Debussy—and acknowledging the gap between such masters of dynamic musical-dramatic continuity and his own way of frankly abutting dissimilar blocks in simple or complex patterns of repetition and alternation. Moreover, at this point he had written no solo vocal music for more than thirty years. His creative development, however, had been one of enlargement rather than moving on, so that all the resources of half a century remained available (and were used in *Saint François*, his biggest work both in its four-hour length and in its musical complement of seven soloists, a chorus of 150 and an orchestra of 120). Meanwhile the development of opera had reached a condition where, half a century after *Oedipus rex*, a theatrical ceremony of a peculiarly static kind was not untoward.

Messiaen's theatre is a theatre of moments rather than of swathes of time. Each of the eight scenes is concerned with a single event, framed and elaborated, rather as a panel in a stained-glass window will show an emblematic figure in an architectural border. Symmetries abound: in verse-refrain forms on both small and large scale, and in the constant recurrence of melodic themes and orchestral signals, the latter usually transcriptions of bird-songs (indeed, a great deal of the work consists of modal chanting in a context of prismatic bird-song imitations in which Messiaen uses his immense orchestra as a great palette of pure colours). The themes and signals are far more rigidly defined than in Wagner, and of course are not subject to alteration in developing musical environments; they have the function, therefore, of a mask or a symbolic gesture, which has to be always the same, and together with the liturgical structuring and sacred subject-matter, they contrive to give the work a hieratic timelessness and to carry it closer to the theatrical and dance-drama forms of Japan, Indonesia, and southern India, say, than to *Le nozze di Figaro*. The case is almost precisely the opposite of *Lakmé* or *Les Pêcheurs de perles*, in that the subject now is Western but in form and function this is a work of the East, or rather it is a portrait of such a work: a rite which has to remain, in a secular ambience and in an age when Messiaen's unquestioning belief is a rarity, across the remove of the footlights. Nor does Messiaen, unlike Stockhausen in this regard, make any claims for the metaphysical efficacity of his work, remarking only that it is intended to show 'different aspects of grace in Saint Francis's soul', and justifying the scale of the enterprise, against the charge that it scarcely accords with the saint's poverty, by saying that 'music richly coloured in timbres, in durations and in sound complexes seems to me perfectly attuned to his real inner nature'.

Birtwistle's *Orpheus* is close to Stockhausen and Messiaen as a work of myth-telling, but distant from them in remaining European: its travels are across time rather than space, though the effect—a drama of showing rather than action, and a ritual severity of form and tone—is to have reached a not dissimilar position. Like Stockhausen, Birtwistle challenges the psychological projection of character by presenting his mythic figures in multiple forms: as different singers and as puppets, all in ostensibly the same role. There is multiplication, too, of event, as in Berio's operas. Key moments in the narrative, including notably the deaths of Euridice and of Orpheus, are enacted in different ways, following different versions of the myth, and there are also windows into parallel stories from Greek mythology, mimed or danced to the accompaniment of electronic music. Like *Punch and Judy*, the work is conceived in small closed numbers, but now in an echoing chamber of reverberations, allusions, and renewals, making for a much more complex form.

In *Yan Tan Tethera* (1986) the dramatic form is again simpler—this is a legend of rival shepherds, told directly and with the use of a straightforward declamatory vocal style—but the orchestral music moves the work on to a different level of sophistication: it is as if what is seen on and heard from the stage is the face of a complicated clock. The disjunction of stage and orchestra may perhaps have been encouraged in the first place by the fact that this was devised as a television opera, but it continues in Birtwistle's second large-scale work for the theatre, *Gawain* (1991), a dramatization of the Middle English romance as a ritual action of death and resurrection, seasonal change, journeying, and self-discovery. Again by contrast with *Orpheus*, the story is given once and straight (though the fact that it is geared, as in the original, to the annual cycle makes it latently repeatable, a story that could be happening in any year, every year, at least for those who are observers, in the audience, and on the stage: only Gawain himself has become something different by the end of the ceremony). There are, however, more intricate and hidden dramas of change and exploration going on in the orchestra.

Contemporary with the works of Birtwistle, Messiaen, and Stockhausen, quite another stream of operatic mythography had its origins in American minimalism. Here the prototype was *Einstein on the Beach* (1976) by the theatre-maker Robert Wilson (who had used the term 'opera' for earlier works with little or no music) and the composer Philip Glass (b. 1937). Wilson's emphasis is on image rather than narrative, which is virtually ruled out by his working only at extremes of mechanical system and free-wheeling intuition. The appearance of Einstein in the opera, as a solo violinist, is almost incidental to a sequence of closely patterned dance and mime scenes, often with voices (singing miscellaneous texts: strings of numbers, bathetic observations and anecdotes, passages with the feel of automatic writing) but with no singing characters. These scenes are supported by constantly repetitive music, consisting of cadences and arpeggios rooted in an ensemble of amplified instruments. The piece is not about anything: it just is. However, Glass's subsequent operas have been very definitely directed to themes, and have restored the conventions of a more normal pit orchestra, soloists representing characters, and a narrative libretto, even while sometimes using languages—Sanskrit in *Satyagraha* (1980), Ancient Egyptian in *Akhnaten* (1982)—limiting comprehension.

Glass's way of giving mythic significance to recent history, by concentrating on a few episodes in Gandhi's life in *Satyagraha*, prepared the ground for the operas of John Adams (b. 1947): *Nixon in China* (1987), on the presidential visit to Chairman Mao, and *The Death of Klinghoffer* (1991), on the hijacking of a Mediterranean cruise ship by Palestinian terrorists. The tone, however, is quite different. Where Glass's is a music of rudiments made plain, Adams is more versatile and ironic: the connections with various kinds of twentieth-century popular music are playfully welcomed, and they work in *Nixon* to suggest how the President and the First Lady are hemmed in by nostalgia and by the banal affective language of show tunes. Nixon is constrained too by the onward rolling of history, which he thinks he is making, but which, in the emphatic pulse and reiteration of the score, insensately carries the whole action and makes him. Another novel feature of the piece is its claim to portray characters still alive (the Nixons, Chou En-lai, Henry Kissinger). The taboo against this, observed hitherto in opera as in the spoken theatre, perhaps acknowledges that stage characters could not seem to be real if they were embodiments of living people, that one could not have, say, two Nixons in the world. The fact that Adams and his colleagues (both his operas were devised in collaboration with the poet Alice Goodman and the stage director Peter Sellars) could break this rule may suggest a relinquishing of the ambition to represent reality.

Now, as this chapter moves towards its close, it practises a deceit, since its subject matter is moving towards the open space of the future. Into that space, obviously, history cannot go, and it even has problems with the present. The operas of Adams, Glass, Birtwistle, Messiaen, Stockhausen, Berio, and Ligeti have all been performed internationally (*Le Grand Macabre*, as is rare for a contemporary opera, in several different productions); some of them have been commercially recorded, at least in audio form; they have entered the public arena. But whether they have entered the living history of the performing repertory is another matter, and equally unknowable is the recognition that may come to other operas of this period which as yet have made little mark (this chapter has included almost nothing from, for instance, the Soviet Union and Scandinavia, and nothing at all from Spain, eastern Europe, Japan, Australia, or South America).

The inherent disorder of the present, from any historical standpoint, is exacerbated in this instance by the sheer volume of operatic activity going on. Quite by contrast with the 1950s and 1960s, when most progressive composers were determined that the genre could not be interesting without radical change, now there are very few (Boulez remains one) who have not committed themselves to opera (of course, this may have less to do with attitudes to opera than with attitudes to being progressive). Works seen within Britain alone during the period of this section have included Judith Weir's *A Night at the Chinese Opera* (1988), *The Vanishing Bridegroom* (1990), and *Blond Eckbert* (1994), telling oriental, Scottish traditional, and German Romantic tales in a brisk, off-beat, clear, and colourful style; David Blake's bending of realist marital drama into and out from recuperative fantasy, including the notable invention of an opera by Mahler, in *The Plumber's Gift* (1989); Oliver Knussen's Ravelian dramatizations of picture books by Sendak in *Where the Wild Things Are* (1980) and *Higglety Pigglety Pop!* (1985); Davies's post-Britten parable *The Martyrdom of Saint Magnus* (1977) and ghost story *The Lighthouse* (1980); numerous operas by Stephen Oliver including *Timon of Athens* (1991); John Casken's energetic retelling of the Jewish robot legend in his chamber opera *Golem* (1989); Tippett's dramas of contemporary alienation in *The Ice Break* (1977) and *New Year* (1989); Jonathan Harvey's parable of death and psychic regeneration in *Inquest of Love* (1993); and Robert Saxton's luminous chamber opera *Caritas* (1991)—all in addition to the works of Birtwistle, to Henze's *We Come to the River*, and to productions of *Le Grand Macabre*, *Un re in ascolto*, *Donnerstag*, and *Akhnaten*, among others. If opera has died, then its afterlife is as vigorous as Ligeti was suggesting.

༥ 10 ༖

THE STAGING OF OPERA

Roger Savage

'Here time becomes space'
Gurnemanz in Act I of
Wagner's *Parsifal*

'The Unique Collaborative Art'

FEW people would suggest that Charles Dickens's greatest claim to fame was as a writer on opera. Yet he did have some vivid things to report about the operas he saw in Paris in the early 1860s, and they are things which helpfully stake out the whole field of 'staging': the art of putting into visible performance the words and music which have come together to make an operatic text, of 'projecting into space what the dramatist has been able only to project into time' (as the influential theatre artist Adolphe Appia put it). For instance, Dickens writes to his friend John Forster in November 1862 about seeing an opera based on a myth which had been treated operatically since the form first began:

Last night I saw Madame Viardot do Gluck's Orphée. It is a most extraordinary performance—pathetic in the highest degree, and full of quite sublime act-ing. . . . When she has received hope from the Gods, and encouragement to go into the other world and seek Eurydice, Viardot's manner of taking the relin-quished lyre from the tomb and becoming radiant again, is most noble. . . . And when, yielding to Eurydice's entreaties she has turned round and slain her with a look, her despair over the body is grand in the extreme. It is worth a journey to Paris to see, for there is no such Art to be otherwise looked upon.

Gluck's *Orfeo ed Euridice*—Dickens saw it in the version made by Berlioz—was a hundred years old in 1862. Three months after writing home about it, he was reporting to another friend, the actor-manager Macready, that he had recently seen something of a novelty, Gounod's three-year-old *Faust*:

A very sad and noble rendering of that sad and noble story. Stage management remarkable for some admirable, and really poetical, effects of light. In the more striking situations, Mephistopheles surrounded by an infernal red atmosphere of his own.... After Marguerite has taken the jewels placed in her way in the garden, a weird evening draws on, and the bloom fades from the flowers, and the leaves of the trees droop and lose their fresh green, and mournful shadows overhang her chamber window, which was innocently bright and gay at first. I couldn't bear it, and gave in completely.

What Dickens was encountering in Paris was the art of staging in its four principal dimensions: the persuasive mounting of new operas, like *Faust*; the telling revival of old ones, like *Orfeo*; the contribution to an opera's power and plausibility made by the movements, gestures, and overall characterization of singer-actors such as the much admired Pauline Viardot; and the contribution to the work's impact and atmosphere of behind-the-scenes specialists of one sort and another (in this case the lighting people, possibly playing with techniques of limelight and electric-arc light which were beginning to supplement the standard theatrical gas-lighting by the 1860s). Happily, Dickens was impressed, touched, and delighted by all this. Gluck and Gounod had been well served.

Not that all distinguished men of letters have been as pleased with the way operas have been served by their stagings. Nearly a century after Dickens went to see *Orfeo* and *Faust*, the poet and librettist W. H. Auden was being wittily sardonic in his 'Metalogue to the Magic Flute' about the misadventures of classic operas such as Mozart's when put into performance.

> A work that lasts two hundred years is tough,
> And operas, God knows, must stand enough:
> What greatness made small vanities abuse.
> What must they not endure? The Diva whose
> Fioriture and climactic note
> The silly old composer never wrote,
> Conductor X, that overrated bore
> Who alters tempi and who cuts the score,
> Director Y who with ingenious wit
> Places his wretched singers in the pit
> While dancers mime their roles, Z the Designer
> Who sets the whole thing on an ocean liner,
> The girls in shorts, the boys in yachting caps;
> Yet genius triumphs over all mishaps,
> Survives a greater obstacle than these,
> Translation into foreign Operese...

Auden is of course painting with a pretty broad brush here, so broad that one is tempted to leap to the defence of his victims. After all, did not certain composers—the composer of *Die Zauberflöte* among them—imply and expect occasional moments of vocal display from their divas which they saw no point in writing down? Should conductors never modify tempos to fit particular theatre acoustics, or make a few pragmatic cuts which allow their audience to catch the last train home? May directors and designers faced with repertory war-horses like *Zauberflöte* never experiment with radical rethinkings? Is opera never to be sung in the language of the audience, even if that involves the occasional—one hopes *very* occasional—anguish/languish-type rhyme? Still, there can be few opera-goers who have not at some time or other felt an irritation like Auden's at something vain, perverse, or malapropos in an opera production.

This is by no means a purely twentieth-century irritation. In fact the classic expression of it is a book-length lampoon dating from around 1720. It was written by Benedetto Marcello, a Venetian lawyer, administrator, poet, and composer who felt he was a cut above the personnel of most of the companies that had been making Venice an operatic boomtown for the previous seventy-five years. His book, *Il teatro alla moda*, is a series of relentlessly ironic recommendations to an *à la mode* company about every aspect of its activities: the writing of libretti, the composing of scores, the balancing of books—and of course the staging. For instance, there is advice for the house poet once his libretto has been written and set:

At the rehearsals of the opera, he will never disclose his intention to any of the actors...If members of the cast ask him on which side they should make their entrances and exits, or in which direction they should make gestures and what they should wear, he will let them enter, exit, make gestures and dress in their own way.... If[he] discovers that the singer enunciates badly, he must not correct him, because if the singer should remedy this fault and speak distinctly, it might hurt the sale of the libretto.

There are suggestions for the décor people too:

The modern stage designer or painter must avoid any familiarity with perspective, architecture, decorating, or lighting. For that reason he should see to it that all architectural sets are designed as if viewed from four or six different points at the same time, and that the horizon is assumed at a different level for each.... Halls, prisons, small rooms, etc., need not have any doors or windows; the singers will climb directly onto the stage out of their boxes anyway. Since they have memorised their parts extremely well there is no need for any lighting either.... The lighting of the centre of the stage is of no great importance; so much more care should be bestowed on the lighting in the wings and backstage.

As for the singer-actors themselves, they must be given a free hand to do all manner of things, the leading man included:

At the performance he should sing with his mouth half-closed and with his teeth firmly pressed together—in short he should do everything to prevent the under-standing of a single word.... While the orchestra plays the introduction to his aria, he should take a stroll backstage, take some snuff, inform his friends that he is not in good voice and has a bad cold.... He should have a few stock gestures for hands, knees and feet; these he should alternate from the beginning to the final curtain of the opera.... In an ensemble scene, when addressed by another character or while the latter might have to sing an arietta, he should wave greetings to some masked lady-friend in one of the boxes.

As for the prima donna, she must be reminded to put first things first. Thus when she is given a part,

she will be particularly concerned about the length of her train, the ballet, the beauty spots, trills, embellishments, cadenzas, protectors, little owls and other equally important paraphernalia.... When she sings during a performance she should beat time with her fan or stamp her foot instead.... She should spit when-ever a rest in the aria provides her with the opportunity.... She also might peek from behind her fan in a most coquettish manner, so that everyone will know that she is Signora Giandussa Pelatutti and not the Empress Filastrocca whose part she is playing.

Marcello here is not just firing off randomly for the fun, or the despair, of it. Beneath all the ironies, a positive, serious ideal for the staging of opera—a basic grammar almost—is implied: one which can only be achieved if the temptations of the *alla moda* people to vanity, self-absorp-tion, laziness, sloppiness, and misplaced ingenuity are overcome. This 'grammar' requires that the verbal and musical values of the libretto and score are respected; that there are proper lines of communication and a good circulation of advice and assistance in an operatic troupe; that the whole show is properly disciplined and controlled; and that the singer-actors collaborate with one another, move on stage with variety and sub-tlety, and always stay in character. And these things are not private to Marcello. A basic grammar of good staging much like his is to be found behind the positive recommendations of many people who have been involved with opera at different times in its 400-year history. For exam-ples of this, we can take some of the practical suggestions in a pair of manuals about the mounting of particular operas, one of the manuals written over a century before Marcello, the other nearly a century and a half after him.

The earlier one dates from 1608 and is a product of the première performances of Marco da Gagliano's opera *Dafne* during festivities that had also included the creation of Monteverdi's *Arianna*. (For his *Dafne*, Gagliano set much the same libretto by Ottavio Rinuccini as had been set by a group of composers about ten years before to make the very first opera of all. In it, Apollo shoots dead the dreaded Python that has been terrorizing the nymphs and shepherds of Delos; but the sun-god is rash enough to brag of his invincibility to the god of love, who promptly sees to it that he should fall for Daphne, a nymph so pure that she will have nothing to do with Apollo, being magically metamorphosed into a laurel-tree the moment he lays hands on her.) Gagliano himself wrote the production manual for *Dafne*, including it in his preface to the published score. The more recent manual—a bigger one for a bigger piece—rose out of the first performances in 1887 at La Scala, Milan, of Verdi's Shakespearian opera *Otello*. This time the manual was assembled, with the approval of Verdi and his librettist Boito, by their publisher Giulio Ricordi as a separate booklet for the use of opera houses ouside Milan that were planning to mount the piece. Naturally there are differences between the two manuals; but their similarities when it comes to a grammar of serious staging are more interesting, especially since Ricordi may very well not even have known of Gagliano's existence. Along with Marcello's *Teatro alla moda*, the pair provide a useful framework for looking at operatic *mise-en-scène* over its first three centuries.

Both manuals make it clear that staging must not cut across the practical vocal needs of the singer-actors. Thus in 1608 Gagliano acknowledges that Apollo's having to sing an aria of victory straight after going through a highly athletic joust in dumbshow with a fire-spitting Python might present the singer with vocal problems; so 'since it would be difficult for him to sing after the fatigue of the combat, two men can be dressed in the same way as Apollo, and the one who sings can enter instead of the other after the death of the Python and sing'. (No one saw through the trick, he claims, when the opera was given at Mantua: perhaps both Apollos were masked.) Similarly, in the 1887 *Otello* manual there are several accommodations to purely musical interests—less radical ones albeit. For instance, Ricordi has a solution to a problem of Desdemona's just after the Willow Song in the last act, when she is kneeling at a prie-dieu and singing the Ave Maria before an image of the Virgin hung far down-right of the stage. 'The actress must set herself on the prie-dieu a little towards the right corner and take a somewhat oblique position. Thus, while seeming fully to face the effigy, she should have a way of seeing the conductor, whenever that is necessary.' Staging, as a collaborator in the total event, must do nothing to hinder musical synchronization. A few minutes later in *Otello* it is stressed that, for the difficult duet of Desdemona's smothering, lengthy rehearsal will be necessary 'before the two actors succeed in playing it with complete theatrical and musical effectiveness, without their being worried about the orchestra or the conductor's baton'. Choruses, however, often require a sight of that baton, as in the big ensemble at the start of the opera: 'Anxiety is shown on everyone's face. Gestures of surprise, of terror, arms raised towards heaven, the Chorus standing in such a way that they appear to look towards the sea, but following the beat of the conductor with their eyes.' A few twentieth-century closed-circuit TV screens would clearly have helped here! Back in the early seventeenth century, there was not only no TV but no baton or conductor to watch either, not even a fixed pit where the band could always be found; yet it was just as important not to neglect synchronization. One should take care, says the *Dafne* manual, 'that those instruments which are to accompany the solo voices are placed where they can be seen by the singers so that they may hear each other better and thus achieve a true ensemble'.

Beyond liaison between staging and musical practicalities, both the 1608 and the 1887 manuals hold that within the staging camp itself there needs to be a good assemblage of various theatre skills so that, as Gagliano says, 'the intellect is moved at the same time by all ... the most delightful arts', among which he includes not only poetry and music but also 'the grace of [an opera's] dancing and gestures, and ... the costumes and the scene-painting'. Ricordi in 1887 takes this further, pressing that all these necessary things should cohere round the central authority of his manual: 'The producer should, in due time, inform the scenic artists, the stage technicians, the costumer, the prop. man, the head of lighting, the director of extras, etc., of the instructions relating to them which are contained in the present book. It is *absolutely* necessary that the artists understand the production book completely and conform to it.' This is 'advice and assistance' with a vengeance! Gagliano in 1608 is less Napoleonic than Ricordi. Still, he does claim to have 'paid diligent attention to all the particulars to be observed in the performance of such a work', so that his manual is a 'little beam of light' by which subsequent stagers are able to 'see the way with less trouble to that utter perfection which is required for the performance of such compositions'.

Some of these 'particulars' involve bits of effective stage trickery with props and scenery, which need to be carried out in a disciplined way. Thus the *Dafne* preface describes in detail how the actor of Apollo can easily but tellingly weave a crown for himself on stage from a branch of laurel plucked from the metamorphosed Daphne ('I wanted to describe this exactly, since it is more important than others may think'); and the *Otello* manual takes ten paragraphs to describe just as exactly the necessary business for stage-crew and chorus-folk in Act I to start the bonfire which celebrates Othello's safe landing on Cyprus, a bonfire managed in such a way that it does not set the chorus, or the theatre, alight. ('The producer is advised to devote special attention and patience to this scenic detail, which should turn out to be very charming, original and effective.')

Other considerations naturally concern acting: matters of general characterization, where the operatic performer is not very different from the actor in spoken drama, and matters of the meshing of movement and gesture to a pre-composed score, where the operatic performer's problems (if not his or her solutions) are closer to a dancer's. Such a meshing is clearly very important, both in 1608 and 1887. In *Dafne*, 'it is imperative ... that each gesture and each step accords with the beat followed by the voice and the accompaniment', though this should be done without dance-like affectation; while for the hero's entry for the murder scene in *Otello* (a moment of especially intricate meshing), 'the actor must memorise the solo of the double-basses well, since all of the action must take place exactly as indicated by the composer on specific beats'. Beyond this aptness and clarity in time, an actor's movements must be legible in space. In *Dafne*, 'the soloists must not be confused with the members of the chorus, but must stand either four or five steps in front of them according to the size of the stage'; and in the *Otello* manual we are given over thirty diagrams to show the legible placing and movement of soloists in relation to the chorus (as well as over 200 for the moves of the soloists alone).

Getting the ladies and gentlemen of the chorus to act in an interesting way—to counteract their tendency to appear mechanical or anonymous or perfunctory—is seen as a priority by both Gagliano and Ricordi. Thus when Apollo in *Dafne* has slain the Python, the nymphs' and shepherds' praises of the god must fill the stage with action which is humanly irregular: 'moving first to the right, then to the left, and then backwards, always however avoiding the use of dance-movements'; and when the shepherd Thyrsis gives them his lengthy account of Apollo's fatal pursuit of Daphne, 'above all, they must be attentive to and show pity at hearing the sad news'. The *Otello* manual is similar, though it gets more emotional on this subject. Ricordi's feelings overflow during his account of the big ensemble of tragic perplexity in Act 3, where the chorus is (or should be) manifestly amazed at Othello's humiliation of Desdemona:

The producer's task is not easy, since we know how difficult it is to succeed in getting the choral masses to identify themselves with the various characters they must represent, and to understand the passions, let alone act them out. . . . That deadly passivity in the facial expressions (typical in choruses, whether it be a tragedy or a comedy that is taking place) must absolutely be banned. . . . [But] a producer who has sufficient authority and clearly explains the dramatic situation and the passions that flow out of it, should obtain miracles.

Finally and crucially, the soloists must also be concerned with the visual potential of the drama, characterizing their roles not only with the voice—which an oratorio, a cantata, or a concert of songs requires quite as much as an opera—but with the whole body as well. They should 'use the gestures suggested by the text', says the *Dafne* manual, while the *Otello* manual states 'that the gestures, the facial expressions, the stage bearing, and the tone of voice must correspond to the words of the text and the musical phrases'. The effective soloist, Gagliano and Ricordi would agree, is the one who respects both verbal and musical values, who finds and maintains the proper character for a particular role, who involves him- or herself deeply in that character so as to do things beyond the scope of external instruction, and yet who is at the same time coolly aware of purely technical matters of stagecraft—as well, of course, as of singing. Thus the soloist in the *Dafne* prologue who takes the part of the poet Ovid, source of the opera's plot, must have an appropriate dignity throughout, and may once in a while use the expressive freedom of interrupting the regular sequence of sung verse and instrumental refrain to show *sprezzatura* (the grace which is beyond the reach of art); yet he must also always remember precisely what beat in that refrain he is to begin his moves on. As for the singer-actor impersonating Desdemona in the last act of *Otello*, she must be inward enough with her role during the Willow Song to 'project that indistinct, sad, almost magnetic impression which is born at the presentiment of an unknown, but great, misfortune'—and this in a scene which is 'one of those musical inspirations that do not allow cold and specific stage directions'. Yet cool technique coexists. Ricordi cannot after all resist prescribing a dozen stage directions for the song; and he is practical enough to suggest that, a few minutes later, while Desdemona is being suffocated by Othello during the orchestra's triple forte, 'the actress should take advantage of this moment, in which she is hidden from the view of the audience, to take the powder puff with her left hand and apply it abundantly to her face'. ('O ill-starred wench! Pale as thy smock!')

A seventeenth-century court theatre presenting a mythological opera for small forces, described in a few pages by its composer only a decade after the beginning of the genre; a nineteenth-century commercial theatre presenting a romantic opera for large forces, described at great length by its publisher when grand opera was at its height: for all the differences of scope and sophistication between the descriptions, both concern themselves with the same sorts of practical issues and take similar attitudes to them. And they are much the same issues and attitudes as are to be found in a solid twentieth-century manual like Walter Volbach's *Problems of Opera Production*, 'a guidebook for people wishing to work in the lyric theatre' (as the blurb has it) which was written in 1953 by a disciple and associate of two of the most significant father-figures of modern staging, Adolphe Appia and Max Reinhardt. In ways that Gagliano and Ricordi would surely have approved, Volbach stresses important general precepts—the need for meticulous planning, for evolving stage-groupings that are easily legible, for making the words of the libretto intelligible, and so on—while also tackling detailed particulars like getting the chorus off the stage within the prescribed two and a half bars in Act 1 of *Le nozze di Figaro*, toting guns properly in *Fidelio* and *Eugene Onegin*, differentiating the smugglers in *Carmen*, and making sure Beckmesser is beaten up with no risk to the baritone playing him in *Die Meistersinger*. Further, Gagliano and Ricordi both work within that grammar of operatic staging which we have seen lies behind the ironies of Benedetto Marcello: the concern with co-operation, communication, concentration, and involvement with the work in hand; and this is something they share with Volbach and with most other serious twentieth-century opera directors as well, however much those directors might differ from them—and from one another—in other ways. Five sentences from five twentieth-century opera people will bear this out:

What matters is the collaboration of all arts.

> (Gustav Mahler, who supervised the stagings of the operas he conducted
> in the 1890s and 1900s)

We shall try to combine the art of living a role with its musical form and the technique of singing.

(Constantin Stanislavski, addressing the students of the Bolshoy Opera Studio in the 1920s)

Once a chorister ceases to feel like a piece of scenery the public also will look on his actions as significant and necessary.

(Günther Rennert, mid-century West German director; Intendant at Hamburg and Munich)

The stage director is only a helper, a mirror to tell [the singer-actor] whether his interpretation is sufficiently clear and intelligible to the spectator, an arranger and co-ordinator who sees the individual in relation to the total effect and puts the details together in a harmonious entity.

(Joachim Herz, East German director, speaking at opening of the new
Leipzig Opera House in 1960)

Theatre isn't about star performances except in a very boring sense, theatre's about doing things together. That's why it has some relevance to society and there's a point to it.... Opera is the unique collaborative art.

(David Freeman, Australian director, and founder between 1973 and 1981 of three Opera
Factories in Sydney, Zurich, and London)

What Gagliano, Marcello, and Ricordi had to say about these things in the seventeenth, eighteenth, and nineteenth centuries is worth bearing in mind since it helps counter the plausible view one sometimes hears that the staging of opera before 1900 is necessarily a closed and irrelevant book to us, that anyway it was always a ramshackle and inadequate affair, and that real staging—staging worthy of the name—did not come into existence until the first stirrings of the newly independent, 'creative' opera director around the beginning of this century. It is certainly true that the rise of a new type of director was a big factor in significant changes in operatic staging since 1900 or thereabouts (and more particularly since 1950)—changes which still affect us today. Yet, as we have seen, serious staging arguably had the same basic grammar both before 1900 and after it. Moreover, it is hard to believe that men like Monteverdi and Lully, Handel and Rameau, Gluck and Mozart, Rossini and Verdi would have gone on and on writing for stages and stagings they considered incurably ramshackle, or indeed that Charles Dickens would have been so moved by Gluck and Gounod in Paris in the 1860s if the contribution of the singer-actors and production team to the *mise-en-scène* of *Orfeo* and *Faust* had not been highly adequate. And in case we are tempted to dismiss Dickens's response to the pathos, nobility, and grandeur of that *Orfeo* performance as uninformed and over-impressionable, there remains someone else's response to a fine staging of the same piece only ten years later: a German staging at Dessau, in which the central characters

were inspired by the most delicate artistic feeling, and so uniformly fine a portrayal of Gluck's creation I never hoped to meet.... Here the operatic mise-en-scène had taken life, and become an active element in the whole performance: each scenic factor, grouping, painting, lighting, every movement, every step, contributed to the ideal illusion which wraps us as it were in twilight, in a dream of truths beyond our ken.

The witness here? That most perfectionist of professionals, Richard Wagner.

Three Operatic Worlds: From the 1590s to the 1890s

Of course, none of this is to imply that, because men like Gagliano, Marcello, and Ricordi shared a basic grammar for operatic staging, they would necessarily have liked the way each other's ideal performances looked and moved, or been at home with the structures of power and decision-making in each other's opera troupes. After all, they came from different operatic worlds.

Gagliano's world was that of late Renaissance Italian courtly spectacle, where operas on mythical and religious subjects were slowly taking their place as fit entertainments for dukes and cardinals, and later for kings and emperors over the Alps, alongside the longer-established spoken tragedies (sometimes with sung choruses), allegorical ballets, part-spoken and part-sung pastoral comedies, and all-spoken intrigue comedies with elaborate, spectacular sung-and-danced intermedi set into them. Because early opera in seventeenth-century Italy had connections with all these forms, its staging was able to creep fairly unobtrusively into existence, tapping theatrical skills the other forms had been developing for years rather than having to fuss over setting up a new art of *mise-en-scène* (though if an opera was thought notable enough to merit revival, some memoranda about how to stage it and shows like it might be set down, as we have seen in the case of Gagliano's printed preface to *Dafne*).

So, how did one get an opera on at court if one was His Highness's master of the revels or supervisor of entertainments? One got together different experts to do different things: to write the poem; to compose the music; to devise the costumes; to design the movable perspective scenery and any supernatural 'machinery' called for (and sometimes to spirit up a temporary stage and proscenium arch for the princely hall as well); to cast the soloists, chorus, and dancers, and the troupe of silent supernumeraries called *comparse*; to arrange and teach any elaborate dances and/or battle scenes; to instruct the cast in acting (first principles or fine details); to light the stage and the auditorium with candles and oil-lamps; and last but not least, to work the scenery, play the instruments—and perform the roles. Where role-playing was concerned, good acting (of a frontally presented, rather rhetorical kind) was asked for and apparently achieved. For instance, the composer Filippo Vitali in 1620 was enthusiastic about the talent in his Roman opera *Aretusa*:

The quality of the actors can easily be imagined when one realises that nowhere on earth is better supplied with eminent singers than Rome. With their gestures they gave the liveliest spirit to the words and ideas. All their movements were graceful, apt and natural; and one could tell from their faces that they were actually experiencing the passions their tongues were uttering.

Twelve years later, another composer, Stefano Landi, is stressing the importance of another element in staging, apropos of his religious piece *Sant'Alessio*:

What shall I say … of the scenic apparatus? The first appearance of the new Rome, the flight of the angel through the clouds, the appearance in the sky of Religion, were all works of ingenuity and machines, but they rivalled nature itself. The scene was most cunningly wrought; the visions of Heaven and Hell marvellous; the changes of the wings and the perspective were ever more beautiful.

Since all this expertise in writing, performing, and decorating grew out of a confident, unified courtly-humanist culture, there was no need for some controlling figure to come up with a personal interpretation of the operatic text in hand in the way a late twentieth-century director faced with a Mantuan opera by Monteverdi or something by Gagliano, Vitali, or Landi would probably feel obliged to. Of course, what was staged then unavoidably *was* an 'interpretation', in that it involved a series of choices as to how the text in hand was to be presented theatrically. But it was an interpretation by convergence of fairly like-minded theatrical talents, though if he was present at rehearsals the opera's librettist might well have a large say in the details of staging. (Giulio Rospigliosi for one, librettist of *Sant'Alessio* and many other operas, seems to have done so; but then he was good enough at directing things generally to end up as director of a large part of Christendom as Pope Clement IX!)

If an early opera's staging needed firm guidance from anyone other than the librettist, this would quite likely be the responsibility of the master of the revels himself. His role would then be a blend of impresario, co-ordinator, instructor in the relevant theatrical techniques, and stage manager. And if he thought that folk away from that particular theatre might benefit from his expertise, he might write a little treatise about it all. Treatises on stagecraft had been put together in the pre-operatic late sixteenth century; but one which places opera very much at the centre of things was written anonymously in Florence around 1630. Called *Il corago*, it is by someone who either was or would dearly like to have been a court 'corago'—the very model of a modern supervisor of entertainments. It recommends a strikingly hands-on approach both to the commissioning and the staging of shows. Apropos of staging, for instance,

It is expected of the *corago* that he will give advice on what gestures accord with the characteristics of the person on stage, and on how these should be shown.... In dances with song, it is one of the *corago*'s duties to see that what the ballet-master devises is suitable to what is being sung.... As choruses appear on stage several times, it is the duty of the *corago* to ensure tht they do not always make the same entry or exit.... I leave it to the judgement of the *corago* to decide where more or less stage light is needed; apropos which, it is necessary to have a rehearsal before the scene is performed.

The author of *Il corago* justifies his office's high profile by being full of good practical advice (keep stage machinery well soaped, check all scenic ropes for sabotage before curtain up, make sure people cannot be seen in the wings, etc.), and also by his searching views on various subjects, not least on operatic acting:

To be a good performer one should above all be a good speaking actor, since we have seen that some who have particular grace in acting have worked wonders when they have also been able to sing.... Since acting in music moves at a slower pace than spoken acting, it is necessary that gesture likewise moves more slowly, so that the hand does not stop before the voice.... From time to time the singing should be broken up by walking, at which point there should be instrumental music.... One should not always stay fixed to the centre, but be now here, now there—in a natural way, though also in good order.

Around the time *Il corago* was being written in Florence, Giovanni Battista Lulli was born there. He was destined to become the hands-on courtly director *par excellence* when, as Jean-Baptiste Lully, he established in the 1670s and 1680s the complex musical and dramatic structure of French opera as the apogee of *à la mode* spectacle at the court of Louis

XIV and at the Académie Royale de Musique (the Paris 'Opéra'). Since he was not only a composer, instrumentalist, and dancer but a canny courtier and a special protégé of the absolutist autocrat on the throne as well, it is not surprising that he should himself become an autocrat in the directing of his own operas, not only in musical matters but in matters of staging too. ('L'opéra, c'est moi.' He may never have said it but he surely must have thought it.) Twenty years after his death, Lully's reign was remembered by an admirer, Lecerf de la Viéville:

He had an extraordinary talent for everything theatrical. . . . He knew how to have an opera performed and how to control the performers as perfectly as he knew how to compose one. . . . [With singers he thought promising] he would himself teach them how to make an entrance, how to bear themselves on stage, how to achieve grace in gesture and movement . . . He would permit only essential personnel—the librettist, the machinist, etc.—to be present [at full rehearsals], so that he could have the freedom to reprove and instruct the actors and actresses, squinting at them with his hand over his eyes to help his short sight.

Lully formed and trained a generation of French singer-actors. One of his stars was Marthe le Rochois, whose portrayal of the passionate sorceress in his *Armide* seems to have been a collector's piece of classic operatic acting, especially in the scene ('Enfin il est en ma puissance') where Armide contemplates her beloved enemy Renaud asleep:

Her looks showed the fury that possessed her; then love seized her heart. Fury and love both shook her in turn. At last pity and tenderness supervened, and love conquered. What beautiful, truthful attitudes! What variety of movements and of expressions in her eyes and on her face!

Le Rochois went on to star in other composers' operas and teach a younger generation of singer-actors, so contributing to the strongly Lullian tradition of staging which was to dominate French opera far into the eighteenth century. The old autocrat himself may have died, but he had set up such an efficient system of *mise-en-scène* in his lifetime, to say nothing of having his operas printed and copyrighted and of starting a long tradition of uncut revivals of them, that his ghost walked the grand machine of the Académie Royale de Musique until at least the time of Gluck in the 1770s, whether it was one of Lully's own pieces which was being given or a new work by Marais, Campra, Rameau, Leclair, or Mondonville which was joining the repertory. Haunted by him, the Opéra was a machine which, without too much grinding of cogs, could mesh together heroic acting from the principals (more piquant and racy acting if it was an opéra-ballet), stirring contributions from the chorus (arranged rather statically in a U-formation around the stage once they had made their spectacular entry), dazzling effects from the designer, chic costumes from the wardrobe, and of course festive *fêtes* and diverting *divertissements* from those great Parisian specialities, the dancers.

Making sure that Parisian operatic wheels went round in the eighteenth century was the responsibility of the *syndic chargé de la régie du théâtre*, the Official Responsible for Theatrical Control. He was one of the two *syndics* of the Opéra (both answerable to a crown-appointed Inspector-General), who were latterly known as *Messieurs les Directeurs*. The *régie* director was clearly something of a *corago* in the old Florentine sense, involved with planning and casting and general supervision. But the holders of the office in the age of Rameau seem by and large to have been hands-*off* in their approach, letting the various experts get on with their specialities in the pious hope that the show at the end of the process would be a benign convergence of excellences. Still, decisions about casting were crucial ones, and a problem aired in *Il corago* itself back in the 1630s—'whether one should cast a tolerable musician who is a perfect actor, or an excellent musician with little or no talent for acting'—must have become ever more pressing as the post-Lullian composers of eighteenth-century France made their music more and more complex and demanding, with the result that some vocally gifted performers might be tempted into thinking that they could get away with being nightingales in costume, songbirds for whom mere acting was neither here nor there. One nightingale of this sort was the tenor Jélyotte, who created some important Rameau roles and whom the librettist Charles Collet described as 'a unique singer, but he has no presence or acting skill, . . . no passions or nobility'. But there were also singer-actors like the baritone Chassé, another Rameau star, whom the musician and philosopher Rousseau cited as an example of the ideal type, the singer with a fine voice who is not that only but the visible inhabitant of a role as well. Such a singer, said Rousseau in the great French *Encyclopédie*,

must not only make us feel what *he* utters but what he leaves to the *symphonie* to utter. The orchestra must not put over any feeling which does not arise from his soul. Steps, looks, gestures and everything must ceaselessly accord with the music, yet without his seeming to give it any thought. He must always be interesting, even when silent; and even in a difficult role, if he drops the character to become merely a singer, he is just a musician on stage and no longer an actor.

Two hundred years later, the stage director Walter Felsenstein was asking the same of his performers and being thought quite radical for it.

If Gagliano's manual on the staging of *Dafne* in 1608 sits comfortably near the beginning of this tradition of Italian and French courtly and court-related opera, *Il teatro alla moda*, Marcello's treatise of around 1720 on how *not* to stage Venetian opera, sits squarely not far from the centre of another major tradition of staging. The operas which it staged were Italian (or Italianate), running roughly from the later operas of Monteverdi in the 1630s and 1640s to the early ones of Giuseppe Verdi 200 years later. They focused on recitative and aria largely at the expense of chorus and dance; the subjects they tackled came in the main not from myth and saints' lives but from secular history (pretty broadly defined and loosely treated) or from modern life (pretty broadly drawn); and their staging was in the hands of commercial operatic troupes run by private-enterprise impresarios who were contracted to independent theatre managers, or to committees of opera-loving worthies, or to the Intendants of princely courts: not only in Italy but in places as far off as Lisbon, London, and St Petersburg.

This tradition made its first big impact in the new-fangled public opera houses of Venice (the first capital of this operatic world) in the mid-seventeenth century. For example, one evening in 1645 the diarist John Evelyn and his friend Lord Bruce reserved seats in advance at the Teatro Novissimo so that they could go

> to the opera, where comedies and other plays are represented in recitative music by the most excellent musicians vocal and instrumental, with a variety of scenes painted and contrived with no less art of perspective, and machines for flying in the air, and other magnificent motions; taken together it is one of the most wonderful and expensive diversions the wit of man can invent. The history was Hercules in Lydia, the scenes changed thirteen times.

In Rovetta's *Ercole in Lidia* that night, the heroine was played by Anna Renzi. She was 'reputed the best treble of women', Evelyn says, though there was a castrato in the cast he thought an even finer treble. Still, Renzi (who created Ottavia in Monteverdi's *L'incoronazione di Poppea*) was clearly a diva; in fact the year before, she had been the subject of one of the first operatic fan-books, the librettist Giulio Strozzi's *Le glorie della Signora Anna Renzi romana*:

> Our Signora Anna was endowed with such lifelike expression that her responses and speeches seem not memorised but born at the very moment. In sum, she transforms herself completely into the person she represents, and seems now a Thalia full of comic gaiety, now a Melpomene rich in tragic majesty.

Strong acting like hers seems to have held its own as a major pleasure in early public opera alongside the brilliance of the singing, the dazzlement of the scenic effects, the teasing intricacy of Venetian-style plot construction—and of course the music of the score. And as the characters' arias towards the end of the century became more and more highly wrought and vocally demanding through the careers of composers such as Cavalli, Cesti, and Alessandro Scarlatti, there were still gifted or conscientious singer-actors who made sure that a telling presentation of character and an elegant, eloquent rhetoric of the body kept pace with their vocal virtuosity. Even the taste-making Englishmen Richard Steele and Joseph Addison, no great lovers of Italian opera generally, had to acknowledge this in 1710 when the castrato Nicolini was in London with Francesco Mancini's *Idaspe fedele*. Nicolini, says Steele in the 115th *Tatler*, 'sets off the character he bears in an opera by his action as much as he does the words of it by his voice.... There is scarce a beautiful posture in an old statue he does not plant himself in, as the different circumstances of the story give occasion for it.' (Steele is thinking of canons of classical beauty like the Apollo Belvedere, the Farnese Hercules, the Dying Gaul.) And Addison in the 13th *Spectator* urges English tragic actors to 'copy after this great master in action. Could they make the same use of their arms and legs, and inform their faces with as significant looks and passions, how glorious would an English tragedy appear!'

Still, the temptations must have been growing to give precious little theatrical characterization to the lengthening, ever-more-brilliant arias, and to assume on going into the profession that all an opera singer needed was outstanding vocal technique and a few stock gestures, especially when the Venetian-style opera of the later seventeenth century sobered down under French neo-classical influence into eighteenth-century opera seria, with its fairly regular alternation of plot-advancing *secco* recitative and time-suspending aria: the arias often elaborate, da capo in form (so raising the issue of how to characterize the 'A'-section's reprise convincingly), and ending with a ritornello which would sweep the singer into the wings. If you let dramatic sense shrivel, if you allowed purely virtuosic concerns to dominate and added a dash of nightingale narcissism, you would be on the primrose path to Marcello's theatrically ungrammatical *Teatro alla moda*, with its pouting prima donnas and strutting castrati whose bad day's work was made worse by incompetent décor-people and uncommunicative theatre-poets.

But clearly it did not have to be like that. The implication underlying Marcello's satire, as we have seen, is that things can go swimmingly with opera seria if there are open lines of communication within the troupe for advice and assistance, a proper respect for musical and dramatic values, and a collaborative involvement in a telling visual demonstration of character in action. That all this was sometimes achieved—in the staging of operas by Handel in London for instance, or in continental houses made momentous by the grand perspectives of décors by Juvarra or the Bibienas—is suggested by accounts of some of opera seria's great singer-actors: people like the Venetian mezzo-soprano Faustina, who was significantly a protégée of Marcello's and whom the composer J. J. Quantz described as 'born for singing and for acting'. ('In her action she was very happy, and as she perfectly possessed that flexibility of muscles and features which constitutes face-playing, she succeeded equally well in furious, amorous and tender parts.') Or like the alto castrato Senesino, as recalled by Roger Pickering in 1755 in his *Reflections upon Theatrical Expression*: 'Eighteen years have not obliterated the full remembrance of that great but natural manner of his deportment in a scene [of a father grieving over his son's self-sacrifice] which called for the exertion of almost every passion.'

Assuming they needed any, what lines of advice and assistance were open to an operatic troupe rehearsing a seria piece? Half a dozen at least. There were instruction manuals in print that anatomized the sculpted, presentative style of baroque acting which was used in both spoken and sung serious drama. There was the spoken drama itself, which in its tirades and tragic soliloquies might provide hints as to effective ways of staging a da capo aria or a *stromentato* recitative. There was the experience of the impresario, who might help the rehearsal process; of the musical director, who might well be the composer too; and of the prompter, who might take a hand in assigning the proper number of *comparse* to each of the principals as pages, honour-guards, waiting-women, and the like. And there was the librettist. If he was not on hand in the building, there were at least the stage directions, often quite detailed, which he had included in his libretto. (When printed for a run of performances, this libretto further served the audience as a cross between twentieth-century programme-book and surtitle system. It would be on sale at the opera house and include the names of the cast as well as a full Italian text, plus, if the opera was being performed outside Italy, a facing translation in the language of the audience. This could be read fairly easily during the show since the house lights were not doused, and in addition there might be libretto-reading candles specially on sale.) Then the absent librettist might be contactable c/o the post-boy. For instance, the formidable Metastasio, whose libretti were set dozens of times in the

eighteenth century, was generous in responding to letters from composers, impresarios, singer-managers, and Intendants about the staging
of his texts over many decades. He might reply with anything from the
lengthy analysis of a protagonist's character to a tactful note accompanying a revised libretto, to the effect that 'you will find [enclosed] on a slip
of paper all the entrances, exits, stage business and situations of the several characters, as I arranged them on my table in writing the
opera.... You need not look at this paper; but if intricacy occurs, it will
save you the trouble of thinking.'

However, the librettist might actually be in the building, or at least
another helpful house-poet much like him. In that case he might, in a
low-profile sense, 'direct' the performance; and not only of opera seria,
but of the saltier opera buffa growing up as younger brother alongside it,
and of the romantic bel canto opera which followed it in Italy in the early
nineteenth century. The great eighteenth-century dramatist Carlo
Goldoni served his time as a house librettist. He tells us that he worked
early in his career for Antonio Vivaldi as word-supplier and stage director; and in 1761 he includes a typical librettist among the opera folk who
appear in his comedy *The Impresario from Smyrna*. ('I instruct the singers
in action, direct the scene, run to the boxes to look after the ladies, attend
to the *comparse* and whistle when the scenery is to be changed.') Later
Italian poets also instruct and direct. We have Lorenzo da Ponte's word
for it that he 'stayed a week in Prague to direct the actors' before the première there of Mozart's *Don Giovanni* in 1787. We have a glimpse of
Bellini's librettist Felice Romani (his wife provides it) training up the
tenor Giovanni Battista Rubini in Milan in 1827 for *Il pirata*: a thankless
task most likely, since Rubini had the reputation of being all voice and no
stagecraft. Still, Romani worked on him: 'Get up, move back, stir yourself, gesticulate....No, no, not like that...you're angry now...a step
backwards...clear words.' And we have a memorandum from Salvadore
Cammarano, Donizetti's librettist at the San Carlo in Naples (where he
was described as 'the poet obliged with the duty of putting operas on the
stage'), which details all sorts of useful things *re* the staging of *Lucia di
Lammermoor* in 1835: stage-sides for entrances and exits, the placing of furniture and props, bits of business and sword-play, and positions for the
comparse and chorus, who were becoming a more consequential race of
people in Italian romantic opera than they had generally been in its seria
and buffa predecessors. Still, whether Cammarano would have had anything like a determining influence on how Fanny Persiani looked and
moved in the Mad Scene of his *Lucia* is hard to say. If he tried to impose on

her, she could always pull financial rank, in which terms she was probably worth about twenty-four of him; at least that is the implication of the
estimates the Neapolitan journalist Vincenzo Torelli offered in 1848,
when he proposed what he saw as a sensible budget for 'our Royal
Theatres'. This included 'one prima donna, of special distinction' with a
monthly salary of 1,200 ducats and 'one poet, responsible for putting
operas on the stage' with a monthly salary of 50...

Within a year of *Lucia*, the young Verdi had written his first opera, the
now lost *Rocester* of 1836; and yet it seems a very long journey from the
world of Cammarano's 750-word *Lucia* memo to the world of that 100-
page production manual of Ricordi's for Verdi's late opera *Otello* of 1887,
with its 250 diagrams, almost obsessive detail and sternly prescriptive
attitude to the opera's *direttore di scena* and cast. The journey in fact
begins further back: in the mid-eighteenth century, when the dissatisfaction of many members of the European Enlightenment with current
things operatic led to a new conception of the making and staging of
opera in houses not tied to traditional-type opera seria, opera buffa,
tragédie lyrique, or opéra-ballet. To those Enlightenment opinion-mak-
ers in an age which valued simplicity, sensibility, and energy, the arias of
serious Italian opera were getting far too long and technically self-
obsessed, thereby chilling the dramatic action, and there was also far too
much mere standing-about-on-stage-in-a-fixed-stance-and-roulading
involved in them. As for French operas, admittedly there the airs were
shorter, but the choruses were too monolithic musically speaking, and
the U-formations in which the choristers stood to deliver them were an
affront to sensitive taste. (They reminded one observer of a row of statues and another of so many organ pipes.) What was more, the dancers in
French operatic divertissements tended to wear outdated neutralizing
masks, and the *comparse* on Italian stages were all too often sloppy and
perfunctory. Everywhere, thought the Enlightenment, there was a loss
of feelingful impersonation, of animation, of focus.

Musical torpor and organizational *laissez-faire* were clearly at the root
of the problem. Operatic music needed a shot in the arm to turn it into
proper action music, or so the Enlighteners believed; and a conscious
effort was needed to make the arts of staging cohere better, since the old
convergences of independent talents seemed not to be working any
more. Gluck and some other composers of his generation provided the
needful action-music. Calzabigi, Gluck's collaborator in two of his most
important scores of the 1760s, *Alceste* and *Orfeo ed Euridice*, describes this
'new species of drama' as one in which 'all depends on the eye of the spec-

tator and consequently on the action', the music being 'exactly fitted to what is happening on the stage'. And an anonymous Parisian tribute in the 1770s turns Gluck into a Titan from Greek mythology to show the revolutionary effect his music seemed to have. At the start of his reforming career, it says, Gluck found

a collection of dummies called a chorus, [and] actors of whom some were as lifeless as the music they sang, while others strove to heat a heavy and dismal droning and a frigid song-style by sheer strength of arms and lungs. [But] Prometheus shook his torch, and the statues came to life.... The actors realised that a music [such as Gluck's] that was both eloquent and expressive needed only to be felt properly to bring with it strong and true acting, and the members of the chorus, put into action by the spirit animating the machine, were amazed to discover that they were actors.

(So begins a motif which has often recurred in the history of operatic staging: the 'thank God we've escaped from those bad old days' motif.)

If this new music called for something of a new stage deportment, then perhaps the contemporary loosening up and dramatic heightening by Jean-Georges Noverre of traditional theatre dancing could be a model for it, or the style in spoken drama of the celebrated Shakespearian actor David Garrick, so much more energetic and (apparently) unstudied than his predecessors'. (It is very apt that Gluck's first Orpheus, Gaetano Guadagni, learnt a lot of his acting from Garrick in London in the 1740s.) But organizational changes in staging were needed too: no more low-profile tinkering by Italian house-poets or arm's-length hoping for the best by *syndics de la régie*! What was needed was an authoritative, properly structured, detailed approach. Noverre himself—a colleague at one time or another of Garrick, Gluck, and Mozart—proposed one model for the new opera in his 1760 *Letters on Dancing*:

Success depends primarily on the poet, since it is he who places, draws and invests the picture with more or less beauty, more or less action, and consequently more or less interest, according to the measure of his genius. The artists who give expression to his imagination are the composer of the music, the *maître de ballet*, the scenic artist, the costume designer and the machinist; all five should equally collaborate for the perfection and beauty of the work by following exactly the basic idea of the poet, who in his turn must watch carefully over everything. The master's eye is imperative: it must supervise every detail.

Late eighteenth-century collaborations of this sort did not always cast the poet as master. Sometimes the role was given to the Intendant of the opera house, as seems to have been the case with Intendant Seeau in the

complex creative collaboration in which Mozart was involved over the
making and staging of *Idomeneo* at the Munich court theatre in the winter of 1780–1. Sometimes at court it could even be the king himself, as
with that enthusiastic drafter of Enlightenment operatic scenarios Gustav III of Sweden (who was not above demonstrating stage-falls at
rehearsals either). Or it could be the composer, as it was at the Stuttgart
Court Theatre. He was another Noverre colleague, Niccolò Jommelli.
An eyewitness, the poet and musician Christian Schubart, described how
he

studied his poet, improved him often,…knew the singers, the orchestra, the
audience with its fancies, and assigned to each his own part in his operas according to the effect of the sound, and fused them together, through the most precise
arrangement with the machinist, the decorator and the ballet master, in a great
totality that moved and uplifted the heart and soul of the coldest listener.

A great totality, supervised in detail by a master: these were ideas with
a future. For the premières of new operas fashioned in this way towards
the end of the eighteenth century, doubtless it was a member of the conceiving team who oversaw the actual stage rehearsals. But what happened when one of these complex works was given a new production
elsewhere with none of that original team present? Then it might be the
musical director at the new house who supervised and controlled
everything on stage. This happened slightly later in the case of Weber,
who liked the idea of great totalities and who was much involved in backstage business during his years at Prague and Dresden in the 1810s and
1820s. His son Max recalled the initial shock for the company he joined at
Dresden when he began to rehearse Méhul's *Joseph*:

Never had so strict a capellmeister been known in the annals of the stage. He had
ears and hands on every side; a rapid glance reprimanded the least note out of
tune.…Now he mounted from the orchestra onto the stage to direct the movements according to his own ideas, and put the singers and choristers into their
places; now he descended from the stage to the orchestra to correct mistakes.…When all was over,…Weber, the indefatigable, held long colloquies
with the wardrobe-keeper over the dresses, with the scene-painter over the new
scenes, with carpenters over new methods of obtaining more order and precision in scene-shifting.

And if a German musical director did not choose to see to the theatrical part of the totality? Then the day could be saved by the creation and
establishment among German theatre companies in the late eighteenth
and early nineteenth centuries of the *régisseur* ('stage manager'/'stage

director'). His role, as one job specification from Stuttgart in the 1780s put it, was to propose casts to the theatre manager, determine scenery and costumes with the relevant experts, see to stage groupings, and correct performers' mistakes. In the decades that followed, the man in a German-speaking house with final say over operatic *mise-en-scène*—as final as the singers on stage would allow, that is—seems sometimes to have been the *régisseur* and sometimes the conductor (who might well in that case have a *régisseur* subordinate to him). Thus in the mid-nineteenth century, Wagner points out in a letter to Liszt that the *régisseur* of a recent production of *Lohengrin*, Eduard Genast, 'remained entirely on the proper standpoint of the stage manager, who arranges things in a general way, and justly leaves it to the individual actors to find out for themselves what concerns them only', but he goes on to suggest that Genast should intervene and interfere more for the good of the opera; and in his 1852 'Address on the Performing of *Tannhäuser*', Wagner urges *régisseurs* to get a thorough knowledge of the stage directions to be found in the score and not just those in the 'book', to collaborate very closely with scene painters, to supervise preliminary 'reading rehearsals' of the libretto (as Weber had done at Dresden thirty years before), thereby correcting the tendency of singer-actors to 'busy themselves with the How of execution before they have learnt to know its What', and at later stage rehearsals to 'pay special heed to the scenic action's synchronizing in the precisest fashion with the various features of the orchestral accompaniment'. On the other hand, later in the century it was Gustav Mahler, musical director in turn of the Budapest, Hamburg, and Vienna Operas, who was clearly also chief stage director at those houses. 'With all the works he produces he dominates the stage, the action, the expression and the motions of actors and chorus with supreme control', said an admirer of his Budapest work, Count Apponyi, while Vienna anecdotes survive of Mahler's demonstrating to the giants Fasolt and Fafner in Wagner's *Rheingold* just how to lift Freya into the air, and of his leaping on to the stage *à la* Weber to manhandle the beefy barons in *Lohengrin* into their proper stage places as if they were so many rubber balls. Clearly Mahler fulfilled one half of his contemporary the conductor Felix Weingartner's prescription (in his book *On Conducting*) for proper production methods at an opera house: 'In my opinion no conductor should be appointed to a theatre who has not proved that he can stage an opera, and no stage director who cannot rehearse the musical part of the work.'

Back in the 1820s, operatic theatre in France (and spoken theatre too) had blended the new *régisseur* with the old *syndic chargé de la régie* to produce a *metteur-en-scène* or *régisseur de la mise-en-scène*. And only just in time, as the early decades of the nineteenth century were seeing the growth in Paris of grand opera: immensely elaborate pieces with music by Meyerbeer, Auber, and the like, where almost aggressively picturesque romantic staging—involving complicated asymmetric sets, big crowds, elaborate stage business, and stunning tableaux—was the order of the day. When Arthur Pougin included an entry on 'Mise-en-scène' in his *Theatre Dictionary* of 1885, he felt called on to hymn the importance of this 'art of directing the theatrical action considered under all its faces and all its aspects', pointing to Meyerbeerian opera as a shop window for it. There one can see clearly, he said,

> what amazing variety and infinite flexibility is brought to the stage in the development, disposition, movement and combination of masses to create the grandest, most charming and most picturesque of effects. In this matter, Act III of *Les Huguenots*, with its succession of episodes so well managed by the librettist, is a veritable masterpiece. One could also cite, for splendour, the great procession in Act I of *La Juive*; for severity, the council scene in Act I of *L'Africaine*; for power, the *tableau* of the ship in the same opera; and for picturesque sentiment, the skaters' divertissement in *Le Prophète*.

These grand operas were mightily labour-intensive pieces to put on; and it would have seemed folly to squander the contributions which all the different on-stage and backstage artists involved had made to the Great Totality on the first night. So the *régisseurs* got it all down on paper—set plans, costumes, props, movements, psychological states, and so on—in a *livret de mise-en-scène*: a production record or model book which could be used to keep subsequent performances in the first run up to scratch and also to provide the blueprint for revivals, in Paris or elsewhere. Many of these *livrets*, for opera and for spoken theatre too, were published by the *régisseur* Louis Palianti. The outstanding grand-opera librettist and well-made playwright Eugène Scribe was delighted with Palianti's work. 'It makes the author's thought clear and intelligible', he wrote in 1842; 'it can stand in for his presence at rehearsals; it can help immensely in the success of dramatic works in the provinces and abroad.'

Of course, at the centre of this mass of minutiae were the stage impersonations of powerful singer-actors such as Meyerbeer's—and Charles Dickens's—favourite Pauline Viardot, who starred in *Le Prophète* and *Les Huguenots* before going on to the Gluck-Berlioz *Orfeo* that Dickens saw in 1862. Wagner too, and Verdi in his mature works, combined musical elaboration and theatrical complexity with a concern for central performances which looked as arresting as they sounded. Both composers were eager to instruct their leading singers in how to act their roles, influencing rehearsals either in person, or through trusted and congenial stage directors, or by letters or printed blueprints (as with Wagner's essays on the *mise-en-scène* of *Tannhäuser* and *Der fliegende Holländer*). They were especially concerned to see an escape from what they regarded as the old, formulaic methods of acting into something more apt and telling (a recurrence of the 'getting away from the Bad Old Days' motif). For instance, in 1847 Verdi writes to the baritone who was to create his Macbeth, 'You'll be able to make much of the death-scene if, together with your singing, your acting is well thought out. You can see very well that Macbeth mustn't die like Edgardo, Gennaro etc. [in Donizetti], therefore it has to be treated in a *new way*.' And in 1882 at the end of his career, Wagner congratulates his troupe in *Parsifal* for getting rid of much of the old histrionic mummery: 'The singer's law for shifting place is commonly an inconsiderate routine, as his most strenuous attention is claimed by the frequently serious difficulties of his purely musical task; but we soon discovered how much was accomplished toward raising our dramatic performance above the operatic level by a careful ordering of his paces and his standing still.'

In later life, both Verdi and Wagner—or valued members of their circles at least—also continued grand operatic practice by moving towards a semblance of 'fixing' the *mise-en-scène* of their pieces, so that these could be taken as models for future stagings. With both of them, the stagings that were fixed—for works like the *Ring, Parsifal, Aida, Otello*—used the full resources of picturesque romantic illusionism: décor that was painterly, detailed, fastidiously historical or archaeological, and acting that matched it. The fixing was done for Verdi by means of printed *disposizioni sceniche*: Italian continuations of the French *livrets de mise-en-scène* (which the composer had seen and enthused over in Paris). Hence, among others, we have the production manual for *Otello* compiled in 1887 by his publisher Ricordi and beginning significantly with a line from *Hamlet*: 'Speak the speech I pray you as I pronounced it to you, trippingly on the tongue', which implies a mixture of studied obedience and natural energy in the performers. These *disposizioni* could be used by a theatre's house-poet and/or stage director if it had one, or by that interesting new species, the Italian opera-*conductor*. Arturo Toscanini was an early specimen of the species; the specification for the opera-house job he got in 1889 when he was 22 stipulated 'a *maestro concertatore* who will also act as a conductor, [directing the scores] exactly as they are written... and the staging as indicated in the respective texts'.

In Wagner's case the fixing was partly a matter of disciples like Heinrich Porges jotting down the Master's ideas as he collaborated with his movement-controller Richard Fricke on rehearsing the stagings of the *Ring* and *Parsifal* at his purpose-built Festspielhaus in Bayreuth, with its hidden orchestra pit. But much more it was those special Bayreuth performances themselves, mounted as they were in a temple to Great Totalities, supervised by Wagner in every detail, encouraging the idea of a pilgrimage to the repository of the Genuine Article, and later revived religiously at the temple-shrine by the Master's widow Cosima. Wagner himself may not have been wholly happy with aspects of the Bayreuth stagings: 'Next year we shall do it all differently', he told Fricke after the first *Ring*; and there were moods when he would say, 'I created the invisible orchestra; now if only I could invent the invisible theatre!' But Cosima certainly felt that the Bayreuth stagings were, to most intents and purposes, fixed. So, when a young Swiss enthusiast, Adolphe Appia, suggested a radically new way of staging Wagnerian opera to Cosima in 1896, thirteen years after the composer's death, she wrote from Bayreuth to a mutual friend that 'Appia does not seem to know that *The Ring* was produced here in 1876, and therefore there is nothing more to be discovered in the field of scenery and production', adding later that 'even as the creator of these works of art constructed his own stage, so also did he determine absolutely their staging'. There was no more to be said—or so it seemed to Cosima...

Continuities and Innovations: 1896–1966

Cosima Wagner was nearly 60 in 1896, Adolphe Appia not quite 35. That generation gap was a significant one in the evolution of operatic staging, for Appia and some of his contemporaries in theatre—people like Max Reinhardt, Edward Gordon Craig, Constantin Stanislavski, and Vsevolod Meyerhold—lived in an operatic world that was quite unlike those of their elders.

Quite unlike, but not wholly unlike. Not everything had changed—nor has it since. The kinds of ineptitudes in staging which Lully and Metastasio, Gluck and Weber, Wagner and Verdi knew all too well did not wholly die out. The inertia that is the occupational hazard of big organizations like opera companies saw to that, as did the tendency of some singer-actors to think of themselves as singers a very great deal and as actors hardly at all. (Thus one of the most celebrated sopranos of the mid-twentieth century, Joan Sutherland, was once heard to say—doubtless under provocation and doing her own abilities less than justice—that 'it is the sound of singing that people want when they come to the opera. If they want a good dramatic performance, they should go to a straight play.') But equally, serious staging, of whatever style and however organized, went on—and has gone on—aspiring to be 'grammatical' in the sense that we have seen was important to Marco da Gagliano in 1608, Benedetto Marcello around 1720, and Giulio Ricordi in 1887: in matters of co-operation, communication, concentration, and involvement with the musico-dramatic values of the role in hand.

Then there were continuities between the nineteenth and twentieth centuries in the organization of operatic staging. As Wagner and others had done, composers continued to stage their own works on occasion: for instance, Leoncavallo, Pfitzner, and Gian Carlo Menotti (who once said 'People often ask me "Why do you want to be a stage director?" My answer is that as long as there is not a Society for the Prevention of Cruelty to Authors, I advise almost any author to become his own stage director'). Or composers might have a 'model book' published for décor and movement which went well beyond the score and libretto in its practical detail and was meant to influence subsequent stagings. Thus in 1911 Richard Strauss got Hugo von Hofmannsthal and Alfred Roller, his librettist and designer for *Der Rosenkavalier*, to collaborate on a prescriptive description of the opera's *mise-en-scène* which was much used (inhibitingly, some said) in the many follow-up productions; and half a century later, Benjamin Britten was asking Colin Graham, who had staged the premières of Britten's stylistically idiosyncratic Parables for Church Performance, to publish *disposizione*-like 'Production Notes' on them (all of 219 notes in the case of *Curlew River*) because, as Graham wrote later, 'Britten was nervous of an "operatic" style of production in other hands, and wanted the notes published not as essential instruction but as an indication of the style in which he felt the operas should be performed'. (It was not the first or the last time that a production style for opera defined itself as anti-'operatic'.)

Then of course the *régisseur* (or *metteur-en-scène* or *direttore di scena* or 'stage director'), who might be a full-time professional or might combine the job with being a librettist or singer, also survived into the twentieth century. In 1885, Arthur Pougin had given him an up-beat job description in his *Theatre Dictionary*:

It is the *metteur en scène* who 'mounts' the pieces jointly with the author, directs the preparation of them, controls the scenic movement, gives the actors all necessary instructions, hints and advice, fixes the place each will occupy on stage, indicates regroupings, entries and exits, arranges the moves for extras and supers—who, in a word, puts the piece into a performable state and is responsible for its good execution. This is no mean task, and a good *metteur en scène* is a precious man in the theatre.

Perceptive turn-of-the-century critics of music and drama like George Bernard Shaw (who became a telling director of his own plays) insisted that modern opera could never do itself justice without proper 'stage management' of this kind: a kind, Shaw felt, that the resident impresario at the Royal Opera House, Covent Garden, seemed all too happy to do without. Shaw defined terms for him in the periodical *The World*:

It must be understood that by a stage manager I do not mean merely a person who arranged the few matters which cannot either be neglected or left to arrange themselves as best they may. I mean rather the man who arranges the stage so as to produce the illusion aimed at by the dramatic poet and musician....I have over and over again pointed out the way in which the heroic expenditure of Sir Augustus Harris gets wasted for want of a stage manager who not only studies the stage picture as it is studied, for instance, at the Savoy Theatre [the home of the Gilbert and Sullivan operettas, which Gilbert directed with a meticulous detail innovatory in British theatre], or at any of our music halls where ballets form part of the entertainment, but who studies the score as well, and orders the stage so that the spectator's eye, ear and dramatic sense shall be appealed to simultaneously.

Such orderings of the stage in the twentieth century might well look much like their nineteenth-century predecessors. For instance, the Wagner stagings at Bayreuth evolved only slowly, and then not very far, in the fifty years after the composer's death: something—indeed about the only thing—they shared with the G & S Savoy Operettas. Then stagings of French and Italian grand operas and verismo pieces until well into the twentieth century could follow the old *livrets* and *disposizioni*—or anyway the last effective production the lead-singers were involved in—quite closely. But perhaps the record for retaining old production styles was held by some Russian companies, which until the break-up of the Soviet Union were still happy to display, preserved in East European aspic, stagings of Musorgsky historical epics which had been made decades earlier, and made in a style with clear roots in the 1830s grand operatic world of Meyerbeer and Scribe.

An efficient stage director in the new century did not necessarily have absolute control over the staging (or even as absolute a control as hallowed tradition, the score, the production book, and the singers' temperaments allowed). He might find himself playing second fiddle to a conductor eager to employ his own staging skills. This seems to have been the case, for example, with *régisseur* Oswald Stoll's career at the Vienna Opera under Mahler in the 1900s, and also to an extent with the *direttore di scena* Giovacchino Forzano at La Scala in Milan under Toscanini in the 1920s. (Forzano, librettist of Puccini's theatrically hyper-active *Gianni Schicchi* and collaborator with Toscanini on the first staging in 1926 of the posthumous *Turandot*, wrote an elaborate *disposizione* for the latter which would doubtless have confirmed the composer's admiration for him as living proof that Italian staging, 'as concerns the movement of masses and fineness of details, can surpass—in agility and genius—what is done in foreign countries'.) Some later conductors, generally with stage directors as assistants, carried on staging up to and beyond the mid-twentieth century. Otto Klemperer was one, though he did not insist on doing so: 'The production side in opera must always be in close touch with the musical director, [though] these two functions need not always be vested in a single person.' Herbert von Karajan was another stager, and in the grandest, most streamlined high-tech. style, especially at Salzburg from the 1960s to the 1980s. According to his chief theatrical assistant, Peter Busse, this was so that he could 'make sure he sees on stage what he sees and feels in the music. The circle is completed. That doesn't happen [in other situations] unless the stage director happens to be right on key with the conductor. Karajan alone has the talent, power, the means to do both.'

However, the talented, powerful, and high-profiled operatic stage director who was neither conductor, singer, nor librettist—the 'creative' director—had become a force to be reckoned with by Karajan's time; and, to go back to that generation gap between Cosima Wagner and Adolphe Appia, the emergence of such a figure had a lot to do with the group of energetic and radical men of a new operatic world who were in their twenties and thirties around 1900: among them Appia himself, Reinhardt, Craig, Stanislavski, and Meyerhold. They were men who came to maturity in a new climate for operatic *mise-en-scène*—or rather in a conjunction of several climates. There was the climate of aesthetics at the turn of the century which put special value on dream, suggestion, symbol, and which warmed to Walter Pater's assertion that 'all art constantly aspires towards the condition of music'. There was the new climate of technology which made possible the total electrification of stage lighting in newly darkened auditoriums, so opening up the potential for spotlights, floods, fades, colour changes, and isolations of small stage areas of a much greater sophistication than could be delivered by the earlier candles, oil-lamps, Argand Light, gaslight, limelight, and electric-arc lighting. There was the new climate of operatic taste (and hence of programming in opera houses) which was less preoccupied than before with 'recent work only and a lot of it' and more concerned with a select, if shiftingly defined, central repertory of masterworks from various lands and times (from Gluck and Mozart to Verdi and Wagner). There was the new climate of opera's next-door neighbour the spoken theatre, where an earnest, would-be-photographic naturalism in writing, décor, and acting was challenging the old romantic melodrama, painted canvas, and histrionics, and where the companies mounting this new drama were in the main being led, not by the actor-managers traditional in spoken theatre, but by charismatic non-playing captains: a new breed of high-profile stage directors who had real power and an ideology to match. And finally there was a new climate of newness itself: of radical reappraisals, of artistic experiment, of modernist 'making it new' (as the arch-modernist poet Ezra Pound put it).

Several of these climates can be felt blowing about the final years of Mahler's reign as conductor and effective stage director of the Vienna Opera in the 1900s, when he took as close collaborator the painter Alfred Roller, whose slogan for décor was 'space, not pictures'. It was the repertory of great German classics, Mozart and Wagner predominantly, that was to be the focus of the company's work; but in new-age stagings which were none the less, according to the conductor Bruno Walter, 'shining examples of *Werktreue*: faithfulness to the work' (a concept which would come to be of considerable importance as the new century wore on). Mahler declared that he was concerned with 'a stage on which everything is only intimated'. He said he wanted 'to make the light'—now electric of course—'serve the theatre in *all* its grades, nuances and degrees of strength.... But the matter does not end with the lighting; the whole of modern art has a part to play on the stage.' Old-timers would probably not be pleased. They were not, for example, in 1904 during Beethoven's *Fidelio*, when Roller rethought the emergence of the prisoners into the courtyard for 'O welche Lust'—it had traditionally been done as rather a brisk mass arrival into a well-lit semicircle for a kind of formal choric aria—by making it a slow, subdued, ragged, naturalistic coming together of 'poor, earthen, suffering worms', singing at first only in small groups. Stoll, the traditionalist *régisseur*, did not like it at all; but Mahler did. Tradition, he held, was generally synonymous with slovenliness: an idea Roller may have recalled at the Dresden Opera in the year of Mahler's death, in connection with rehearsals for *Der Rosenkavalier*.

Strauss and Hofmannsthal were finding that the staging methods of the house *régisseur* Georg Toller—a 'director of the old school', Strauss called him—were getting no life at all into the action. The solution? To import one of the new charismatic director-managers of spoken theatre, Max Reinhardt, the multicompetent virtuoso of *mise-en-scène* to whom the Promethean mission of theatre (as he put it in 1924) was 'to lift the word out of the supulchre of the book, to breathe life into it, to fill it with blood, the blood of today, and thus to bring it into living contact with ourselves, so that we may receive it and let it bear fruit in us'. The result of Reinhardt's *Rosenkavalier* intervention, said Strauss, 'was a new style in opera and a perfect performance'. (A later result was Strauss's affectionate caricature of Reinhardt as the impresario-*régisseur* La Roche in his last opera *Capriccio*: a piece which in part marked the return of the kind of comedy of backstage operatic life which had been quite popular in eighteenth-century intermezzo and opera buffa and which was now used by Strauss as a teasing allegory of the roles in opera of words, music, singing, and staging.)

Adolphe Appia would have agreed that unexamined tradition, even Bayreuth tradition, was slovenliness. He was an obsessive Wagnerite, but he saw no contradiction between an intense reverence for the Master's scores as texts for playing and singing, and a rejection of Bayreuth's as-he-saw-it outdated painted-canvas realisms and pantomimic explicitnesses (a living and breathing horse for Brünnhilde, giant-suits for Fasolt and Fafner, and so on). Staging, Appia felt, should aspire towards the condition of Wagner's music, and the modern arts of highly fluid lighting and functional, three-dimensional set-construction—ramps, rostra, flights of steps, and the like—should have a collaborative part to play on the Wagnerian stage. This stage was to be conceived as a light-taking, semi-symbolic, semi-abstract arrangement of levels honed specifically to the movement needs of the all-important singer-actor: a performer who would practise 'a gymnastic (in the highest sense of the word) which allows him to obey the injunctions of the musical-poetic text'.

Appia saw himself as a new-age director-designer with a mission to conceive and realize whole productions. ('Only a first class *artist* can carry out such a mission.... His influence ought to be magnetic in a way analogous to that of an orchestra conductor of genius.') He even got the personal and quite radical stagings of the *Ring* and *Tristan und Isolde* which he had devised into print in his *Mounting Wagnerian Drama* and *Music and Staging* of 1895 and 1899. In a sense, these books were just latter-day *livrets de mise-en-scène*, but there were crucial differences: there was a lot of explicit and sophisticated theoretical work alongside the blueprinting; there was next to no literalism in the stage actions suggested (no 'swimming' for the Rhinemaidens for instance); and finally— thanks in part to Cosima—when the books came out none of the 'stagings' had actually been staged! (It would be some decades before any of them were.) Appia was to be influential less through his actual productions than through printed visions and theorizings; something which happened also with his near-contemporary and eventual soulmate, the English actor, designer, and director Edward Gordon Craig. Craig too had Wagnerian ambitions around the turn of the century, though as it turned out the only operas he actually contrived to stage— all between 1900 and 1902—were flamboyantly non-repertory pieces by Purcell and Handel. Rather it was as a provocative, polemical, and partisan writer about theatre arts made new and especially about the new 'artist of the theatre' (a figure to whom the old-style stage director related as mere Man related to Nietzschian Superman) that Craig had his influence. Still, the operas he did stage—each one realized as a symbolist dream-vision—were of a piece with the writings. The near-abstract décor, the continuous flow of unearthly movement, the formal patternings of costume, the abolition of footlights, the use of diffused coloured light, gauzes and single-colour backcloths to suggest space and depth, the systematic ignoring of the libretto's stage directions in the name of the higher dream, the treatment of singers and dancers as if they were just puppet-like extensions of the will of the Theatre Artist (who as an *Übermensch* needed, in Craig's word, *Übermarionettes*): all of this would have surprised Handel and Purcell not a little—and Verdi and Wagner too, come to that.

One aspect of Craig's theatre art, his treatment of his performers as puppets, would also have surprised, and rankled with, one of his new-age colleagues, the Russian Constantin Stanislavski. Stanislavski was as reactive as Appia and Craig against what he saw as the bad old stagings of the previous generation, and he was as concerned as they with music as the generator-in-chief of operatic action. But as an influential director of naturalistic spoken drama—he had helped form the Moscow Art Theatre, Chekhov's showcase—he was more concerned to naturalize than to puppetize operatic acting. At the Opera Studio of the Bolshoy Theatre which was set up in 1918 after the Russian Revolution and which later became the Stanislavski Opera Studio, he taught young performers an adaptation to sung theatre of his famous 'method', a major influence on twentieth-century speaking actors internationally:

We shall try to combine the art of living a role with its musical form and the technique of singing.... The whole point is to convert a concert in costume, which is what most opera performances are nowadays, into a genuine dramatic spectacle.... One of the most important aspects in our work [is] the *sub-text*, which enables you to *feel* what the text says in words.... The composer gives you everything: the rhythm for your feelings, the right intonations for each word, and a melody which is the pattern of your emotions. All you have to do is find a true basis for the notes given to you and make them your own.

Stanislavski's younger naturalized-Russian contemporary Vsevolod Meyerhold, another new-style (indeed newer-style) director from spoken drama who made occasional excursions into opera from 1909 to 1939, would have agreed with a lot of this. However, he would have found any very close approximation of the style of the singer-actor to that of the speaking actor in Ibsen or Chekhov wrong-headed. This to him would kill the true rhythm of events on stage. It was rather the dancer, especially the modern dancer as trained by Mikhail Fokine (one of Diaghilev's early choreographers at the Ballets Russes), who was a proper model. Meyerhold's ideal in opera itself was the bass-baritone Fyodor Chaliapin [Shalyapin], famous for his Mephistopheles and Boris Godunov:

Chaliapin's acting is always *true*: not true to life, but theatrically true.... [The singer-actor] will not become a vital element in the Wagnerian synthesis until he learns to see Chaliapin's art not in the light of the Moscow Art Theatre, where actors perform according to the laws of *mimesis* [the copying of actuality], but in the light of omnipotent rhythm.... I tried in *The Queen of Spades* [Tchaikovsky's opera, which Meyerhold staged in 1935] to allow the actor rhythmical freedom within the limits of the musical phrase (like Chaliapin), so that his interpretation, whilst remaining dependent on the music, would have a contrapuntal rather than a metrically precise relationship to it.

Attitudes like those of these pioneers to movement, characterization, lighting, scenery, the role of the *régisseur*, and the status of the text spread among directors with an eye to things 'contemporary' in the first half of the twentieth century. If you put several of the attitudes together, you would be part of a trend towards a making-new of operatic staging which had an edge of controversy to it: something which was to bring in the era of repertory opera in 'progressive, challenging interpretations' (as the admen would soon have it). The trend was taken up, developed, and popularized in different ways in several significant opera houses from the 1920s to the 1960s. Three German theatres provide lively cases in point: the Krolloper in the Berlin of the Weimar Republic under Otto Klemperer, the Komische Oper in Cold-War East Berlin under Walter Felsenstein, and the de-Nazified Bayreuth Festspielhaus of the 1950s and 1960s, hereditarily run by Richard Wagner's grandson Wieland, with his brother Wolfgang.

All three theatres stressed painstaking musical preparation and deep respect for the composers they were staging; but their stagings sparked off controversies of different sorts. Under Klemperer's musical direction and occasional theatrical direction too, the Kroll between 1927 and 1931 was concerned to abolish the operatic star system and to get away at the same time from what was felt to be the tired picturesqueness and irrelevant pomp and circumstance of so much traditional *mise-en-scène*. Stage directors without preconceptions were brought in from spoken theatre, and artists like De Chirico, Schlemmer, and Moholy-Nagy were given shows to design. Along with uncompromising new works like Stravinsky's *Oedipus rex*, the operas staged included much standard repertory in unstandard readings: an anti-rococo *Don Giovanni*; a severely drilled *Fidelio* against Cubistic sets; a modern-dress *Fledermaus*, and a *Falstaff* with the Fat Knight sporting a monocle and young Fenton in plus-fours. Enthusiasts in the press were delighted that 'everything is splendidly new and *sachlich*' ('objective', 'matter of fact', 'functional': a vogue-word of the time); cavillers were outraged by 'the distortions of old masterpieces'. And not all the cavillers were old fogeys. Arnold Schoenberg felt that he was a victim of Kroll 'distortion', and in a 1930 letter to the Intendant lambasted 'producers who look at a work only in order to see how to make it into *something quite different*. Such a wrong could never be greater than if done to *me*, since while I was composing I had all the scenic effects in mind, seeing them with the utmost precision.'

The Kroll's *pièce de résistance* came in 1929 with a demythologized production of *Der fliegende Holländer* which went back to Wagner's first, earthy 1843 version of the score and was promoted as 'a surrealistic penny dreadful': proletarian, immediate, intense, and quite un-Norwegian. 'Nays' in the media claimed that it amounted to 'a total destruction of Wagner's work, a basic falsification of his creative intentions', while the 'Yeas' said it delivered the opera from years of 'metaphorical dust, hollow symbolism, theatrical piety and romantic costuming'.

Delivering opera from itself was to be something of a watchword two decades later with Walter Felsenstein, who from 1947 to 1975 was Intendant and stage director of the Komische Oper in East Berlin (where other operas than the wholly comic were perfectly welcome). Not that Felsenstein was an out-and-out modernist where staging was concerned. 'In this era of the ascendency of the stage director,' he wrote in 1951, we unfortunately attach more importance to a director's interpretation of a work than to the desire to have the work itself perfectly realised. We must reject any interpretation whose primary aim is to produce an interesting performance but which does not carefully explore the intentions of the composer and the author and try to fulfil them as closely as possible. Anyone who thinks he can reshape or modernize a valuable work would do better to have a new work written for him, rather than to misuse the existing one for his own purposes.

In this, Felsenstein seems to be speaking for the type of responsible but low-profile director—skilled enabler rather than creator—who had been encouraged by Wagner, defined by Pougin, promoted by Shaw, and who subsequently circulated fairly quietly round many twentieth-century opera houses. (An example of the breed who did much for opera in Great Britain was Carl Ebert, who went in 1934 from the Charlottenberg Opera in Berlin to the new Glyndebourne Opera in Sussex and was chief stage director there for most of the next thirty years.) Still, when Felsenstein comes to define such a figure positively, the differences between even the quietest member of the tribe and his nineteenth-century forebears are evident:

A stage director must have a forceful personality, first of all to be able to convey unmistakably the original substance of a work by the means that are most likely to reach the audience. Beyond that, he must be able, by his own methods, to help appropriately cast singers, and also the conductor and designer, to become profoundly familiar with the work, and to induce them to bring forth a highly personal interpretation, but one that is completely faithful to the work, according to the laws of the theatre. In no case may the stage director confine himself to spatial and choreographic arrangements, and in no case is he allowed to use the singers as animated marionettes.

Admirers of Gordon Craig's *Übermarionettes* need not apply!

And yet Felsenstein was a modern in a Stanislavskian if not a Craigian way: so much so that he habitually, witheringly, and controversially employed the word 'opera' only in connection with what he held that most *other* companies staged—grand spectacles, boxes of theatrical tricks, concerts in costume, lifeless displays for operatic canary-fanciers—claiming that the Komische Oper was concerned with a different art and a more vital one: 'music theatre'. This did not involve changing the text of the score or libretto. Indeed, they were researched and explored and rehearsed exhaustively: rumours circulated of 157 stage rehearsals for Felsenstein's *Zauberflöte*. What it required was the corporate establishing of a unified, comprehensive, energizing 'subtext' beneath words and notes, which could be drawn on by singer-actors (chorus no less than soloists) in their attempts so completely to identify themselves with the characters they played that their characterizations seemed visibly to motivate—indeed to demand—the music, instrumental as well as vocal. Thus, in Felsenstein's words, 'the duality of music and scenario, of singing and acting [would be] completely eliminated', and the piece performed would turn into 'a theatrical reality that is unconditionally plausible'. Still, canary-fanciers—and other more open-eyed folk occasionally—felt that there was not enough real *singing* in Felsenstein's humane, energetic shows.

With Wieland Wagner's phase of artistic control over the staging of his grandfather's music-dramas at Bayreuth from the theatre's reopening after the Second World War in 1951 until 1966, there was certainly no lack of real singing; but other traditions went by the board as being too implicated with the Bayreuth ethos of the 1930s and early 1940s, when Cosima-style, Nordic, painterly stagings of the operas had come more and more to be associated with a Nazi expropriation of their texts. Wieland revered those texts. In an essay published at the Bayreuth reopening, he announced that 'basically the works of Richard Wagner tolerate no change. Like all elemental works of art, they remain inviolable and sufficient unto themselves.' But there was an important 'but':

The actual staging—and it alone—is subject to change. To avoid change is to transform the virtue of fidelity into the vice of rigidity.... The task before us is to create the essential mood with new means.... The conventional image of bygone days may summon up wistful memories of a notable era to many faithful and deserving veterans, but to the generation which has risen since the quantum theory and atomic science this image has lost its value.

The essential Wagnerian 'mood' for Wieland involved sensing deep structures of universals and archetypes (nothing remotely Nordic, let alone Nazi, about them), and being aware of the clash of complex psyches representative of aspects of all humanity. The new 'image' which was to realize these things in the theatre, where Wieland was designer as well as director of his productions, involved inwardness, depth, a banishing of the literal. The acting was of a subtle, psychoanalytic kind which did not mimic the movement of the music in an overt, carbon-copy way ('Scenic action and musical development do not run parallel to each other in any direct sense'). A spacious, unfussy décor substituted symbolism for traditional landscaping ('My settings abstract essential meanings not from the stage directions but from the scenes themselves'). And a virtuosic, very detailed painting with light was used to locate, focus, and characterize the action ('Illuminated space has replaced the lighted canvas'). In all this, quite a lot of Grandpapa's stage directions fell by the wayside ('What Richard Wagner as a practical man of the theatre laid down as a guide to the production of his operas interests us only in a historical sense'); and some loud protests were heard. Some of the outraged even banded together as the Society for the Faithful Presentation of the Dramas of Richard Wagner. An operatic war was declared which rumbles on still, not only at Bayreuth, not only *re* Wagner.

Though Felsenstein probably had the greater influence on later operatic acting, it is Wieland's modernism that can loosely stand for all midtwentieth-century modernism. There is in it a Reinhardtian concern to fill repertory opera with the blood of today; an Appian use of light, shape, space; a Craigian refusal, in the name of presenting the action as a momentous dream, to treat the stage directions of the opera's text in a fundamentalist way; a Stanislavskian determination to get at the springs of the characters' personalities and actions; and a Meyerholdian inclination to make stage movement in some sense 'contrapuntal' with the music. Yet, as we have seen, Wieland's attempt to create a responsible *mise-en-scène* for Wagner in the post-Atomic age locked horns with a more traditional yet just as committed view of Faithful Presentation, of *werktreue Wiedergabe*. And it could be said that the debate surrounding *Werktreue*—using the word in the broad sense of 'faithfulness to the text' without implying any one definition of 'text' or 'faithfulness'—has gone on dominating the discourse on operatic staging ever since Wieland's death in 1966.

Repertory Opera in the Late Twentieth Century: Faithfulness in One's Fashion

What has given the *Werktreue* debate its importance has been the curious history of the operatic repertory. As we have seen, 'repertory' is a concept which first developed in connection with opera in the later nineteenth century, when a desirable opera season was beginning to be thought of as 'an extended annual course of the masterpieces of the great composers of all nations, and the current productions of contemporary writers for the musical stage', in the words of an 1898 proposal for a new municipal opera house in London. There was doubtless every confidence then that, while the standard repertory's senior citizens would remain Gluck and Mozart, its youngest bloods would move steadily forward in time as opera developed, so that Wagner and Verdi would be replaced as the new boys by equally great composers yet unknown. And indeed this happened—for a while. The composers at the hither end of the repertory did move forwards from Wagner and Verdi; but only for about twenty-five years, as far as Puccini and the early Richard Strauss. There the broad forward movement stopped. True, a few works from after the mid-1920s entered the core repertory: works like Berg's *Wozzeck*, Stravinsky's *Rake's Progress*, Poulenc's *Dialogues of the Carmelites*, and Britten's *Peter Grimes*. But not many; and quite as much growth went on in the other direction, back far beyond Mozart and Gluck to works by Handel and Purcell and Monteverdi, as 'early opera' came to be of more general public interest. As a result, the central repertory—the 'course of masterpieces of the great composers of all nations'—has come to seem like a galaxy moving away from us in time. New scores—'the current productions of contemporary writers for the musical stage'—have of course appeared and occasionally made a strong impact, helped often by their staging, which has sometimes had the close involvement of the composers themselves. (For instance, Benjamin Britten went so far as to check the probable deployment of characters on stage with his director Colin Graham while actually composing his later operas: 'We would discuss the libretto of the passage he was going to write the next day, and he would ask how I would see it being staged.... We did a kind of mock-up of the production.... Then at teatime the next day he would play what he had written, and we'd discuss that.') But in general the late-twentieth-century opera-goer has come to live more and more in a world dominated by revivals where in the nature of things there can be no direct collaboration with the deceased composer: restagings of works from the central repertory, garnished with less-often-done other works by repertory composers and with occasional pickings from beyond the pale. It is rather as if, where spoken drama in English is concerned, four-fifths of what was seen on stage was Shakespeare, Sheridan, and Shaw. So—as indeed is the case with late twentieth-century Shakespeare—*how* those operatic masterpieces from the past are mounted has become a major issue.

Now clearly conductors and singer-actors affect that 'how', not only in a purely audible way but also in their involvement with the stage. The prestige or charisma of a particular stage performer may lead to his or her ideas determining the *mise-en-scène*; the musical textures, pacing, and general characterization of a particular conductor may require a staging to match. But it is the director—collaborating closely with set, costume, and lighting designers, and ideally just as closely with the conductor too—who most obviously ensures that the latest *Figaro*, *Carmen*, or *Madama Butterfly* is 'right for today': interestingly different—a typical late-twentieth-century requirement—from the last one. Interestingly different, yet also in some sense *werktreu*, faithful to the words and music of the *text*; otherwise, how can one say that it is actually *Figaro*, *Carmen*, or *Madama Butterfly* one is seeing? Hence the director (who by now may be full-time in opera or ambidextrous not only with spoken drama but with cinema too) has to answer certain questions about that text and about faithfulness to it. He may have many things laid on for him in the opera house: the willingness of the public relations people to prepare the audience for a show of any complexion; the ability of scenic and lighting technicians to come up with effects in pretty well any style on demand; the connivance—warm or wary—of a conductor; and last but not least the tractability, tolerance, and positive collaborative input of versatile singer-actors. (Tractability most of the time, that is. There is the story, which can stand for many such stories, of the German director Peter Stein, renowned in spoken theatre, abandoning a projected production of *Die Walküre* in Paris because Theo Adam, his Wotan, refused point-blank to wear a dinner jacket in the role.) But the question remains for the director. Just what *is* the operatic text that is being staged? What does it require? How, in a world full of contradictory claims and multiple choices, is a particular staging going to be interestingly faithful to its words and music?

Though in practice they often shade into one another and directors may even pick and mix among them in a production, three separable views have become current in the late twentieth century as to what, from the staging point of view, an operatic text up for revival is: first, that it is the record of an event which deserves repeating; second, that it is a set of instructions asking to be put into effect in the best possible way; and third, that it is a pure, sheer, non-prescriptive stimulus to the free play of theatrical imagination. Being 'faithful' to a text when 'text' is defined in such different ways is clearly going to produce a variety of stagings, a variety compounded by the personalities of the stagers and the characteristics of the revived works themselves, which may be anything from the purely mythical to the highly circumstantial (from *Orfeo ed Euridice* to Britten's *Albert Herring*) and from the bel canto to the *parlando* (from *Lucia di Lammermoor* to Debussy's *Pelléas et Mélisande*). As a result, the sheer variety of staging in the late twentieth century is probably greater than it has been at any other period.

In the first of those three views of a text, the notes, words, stage directions, and any other information that can be found are taken as *the record of a particular event*, generally the première of the opera in question: an event which asks to be repeated. People who take this view tend to hold that a particular libretto and score are to a great extent what they are because of the kind of scenic resources the composer and poet had immediately to hand: the physical stage of their theatre, and the movements and gestures and tableaux they knew they could call on. All the aspects of that operatic event were of a piece, were members one of the other, and there was an intricate primal Rightness about the way they meshed together. So, 'faithfulness' in this definition requires a staging which uses recreations of theatre objects and techniques of the time of the première, and (as far as possible) only those objects and techniques. The Rightness is thus maintained. That way, 'authentic' staging lies: or perhaps one should spell it 'authentick', since any staging of whatever sort that is not authentic in the broader sense of being theatrically alive— a genuine piece of theatre—is *ipso facto* no real staging at all.

This notion of *Werktreue* can be applied to some operas in great and fairly confident detail because so much is known about their original, author-approved stagings (as we have seen with works as different as *Otello* and *Curlew River*). But mostly it has been applied to revivals of pieces from the seventeenth and eighteenth centuries, though with operas of this period—and indeed up to the 1830s—there is the paradox that one can rarely assume that a definitive musical text of the piece was given at the première, or indeed that the piece has such a text at all. Still, stage 'authenticity' has seemed a natural corollary to the new concern for 'period' instruments, voices, and musical techniques which has been such an important factor in late-twentieth-century music-making, especially in the baroque and rococo. And besides, apart from actual candles for stage lighting (which fire regulations are not likely to allow) and the castration of male leads in opera seria (which no one is likely to allow), most of the external aspects of rococo and baroque staging in décor, deportment, and gesture are quite practicable, and are recoverable from paintings, engravings, and treatises of the time. A correct use of the index finger or a correct corset or cloud-machine are arguably on a par with a correct cadential trill. So, the 1970s and 1980s saw (among others) authentick Monteverdi in Italy, Rameau in England, Handel in the USA; and in 1980, meditating at a Vivaldi conference on a less than perfect Vivaldi staging, the Anglo-American critic and libretto-translator Andrew Porter rallied the troops with a set of friendly historicist commandments. Though his collections of music criticism originally written for the *New Yorker* show that he could also be enthusiastic about radically other ways of staging Vivaldi, Handel, and Co., Porter felt on that occasion that wherever possible, one

should go all the way, plunge the audiences straight in at the deep end.... Revive the art of perspective designing and perspective painting and, just as you strive to sing and play so far as possible in the eighteenth-century manner, design in that manner too.... Preserve the original form and organisation of the scenes. Shift the scenery only when the opera calls for changes.... Banish follow spots. Light with footlights and from battens behind the proscenium arch; light from the sides as well as above.... Use a flat floor, or at most just the gentle, regular rake built into some eighteenth-century stages.... On the question of acting, movement and gesture, my confident tone falters just a little.... [But] what I prescribe, I think, is a basis of authentic gesture tempered with a shade of realism, the kind of thing that we read Guadagni learned from Garrick. I am sorry not to sound quite so hardline about this as about everything else. I am waiting, and hoping, to be utterly convinced.

Practical problems bristle, and theoretical ones too. (The antiauthenticks wade in with 'Why do all this for a modern audience which can never *itself* be eighteenth-century?' The authenticks reply with 'Prove to me if you can that visible signs on stage decay in their meaning and need replacing more quickly than musical ones!') Meanwhile, the authentick experiments continue.

The second view of an operatic text is that it is a *set of instructions for carrying out an artistic intention*. What is important in this view is that the librettist and composer have one prime aim: that their audience should get rewardingly involved in a certain story—its shape, its characters, its moods, its issues—through a conglomerate of words, music, singing, playing, and stagecraft. Where the staging is concerned, libretto and score include explicit and implicit recommendations in words and notes as to how that involving should be done: recommendations which may have been highly practical or luminously suggestive in the work's own time, and which may be applicable (with a greater or lesser degree of strictness) to differing stage and audience conditions in later times. So, faithfulness to this definition of a text will lead to a staging which, having a clear conception of the true drift of the piece, realizes it in the way best suited to opera-goers here and now. As Felsenstein put it in 1951, the director's interpretation must 'carefully explore the intentions of the composer and the author and try to fulfill them as closely as possible,... [conveying] the original substance of a work by the means that are most likely to reach the audience'. However, in this view as it is widely held, great operatic masterpieces are (to borrow the pianist Schnabel's phrase) always greater than they can be performed; a production's guiding concept can only be a relative affair; and the here and now changes quickly. In the words of Anthony Besch, who (as if to prove his point) directed two different stagings of *Die Zauberflöte* in the same year, 1975: 'The spectator who rejoices to think he has witnessed a definitive production may find it superseded the following month. The richness of content, of thought and sublimity of aspiration will constantly evoke new approaches and solutions.' And at least one twentieth-century composer-director would agree: Gian Carlo Menotti, who claims that 'when I produce my own operas, I never repeat myself. Every time I stage *The Medium* or *The Consul*, I discover new things to change.'

This second view of the operatic text lies behind a great deal of staging in the later twentieth century, where it has often been fuelled by the Felsensteinian feeling that opera needs saving from itself, and that if vigorous attempts are not made to find and fulfil a revived work's real intentions for now, opera will never fully escape from its Bad Old Days: days filled, or so the demonology has it, with waddling prima donnas, woodenly semaphoring tenors, shambolic choruses, and far too much quite unmotivated warbling. Or it may get sucked overmuch into the Bad *New* Days of jet-setting, globe-hopping artistes carrying their unchangeable characterizations round in their suitcases, much as their eighteenth-century forebears carried around their 'suitcase arias' for insertion into whatever opera their stagecoach took them to. In the face of such things, the modern director concerned with the true intention and meaning of the work has sometimes come to see himself as the keeper of opera's sacred flame. (As the Australian director Elijah Moshinsky puts it, 'the composers had the depth; now that they are dead it is for the producers to keep their moral seriousness alive.')

However, the later twentieth century has seen two different interpretations of what it means to be truly faithful to a text seen in this way as a set of instructions. And the faiths contend and call each other names. One of them holds that an operatic revival should get as close as modern circumstances will allow to the librettist's and composer's vision of the piece as seen in the ideal theatre of their imagination (which does not necessarily correspond to the actual physical theatre they worked in). A strong, unashamed emphasis is placed on the demands of those modern circumstances in matters like the perceived need for vivid and stylish scenery, for subtle high-tech. lighting, for gestures which are not impossibly far away from those of mainstream acting in the spoken theatre of today, and for characterization which seems rounded, unforced, and in a broad sense 'realistic'. But once these essential bridges between here-and-now and the original work are in place, the argument runs, a staging should evoke the ethos—the landscape and styles of dress and move-ment—which composer and librettist probably saw in their mind's eyes (give or take a decade or two to sharpen an image or focus an issue); and it should do everything it can in the way of characterization and use of stage space to integrate itself quite seamlessly with the atmosphere, ideas, and musical idiom of the operatic text.

Much celebrated work in the big houses of Europe and America has been done under this banner; for instance by directors like the German Günther Rennert, who was especially renowned in the 1950s, 1960s, and 1970s. 'An opera producer', he thought, 'translates the artistic form of the work onto the stage in his own language.... The value of his translation is enhanced in proportion to its proximity to the original.... Every oper-atic composition carries itself the style of its presentation, and thus the highest goal of production should be to find the key to this style.' Luchino Visconti and Peter Hall, both of whom also worked in film and spoken theatre, can stand as examples of Mediterranean and Anglo-Saxon directors of broadly this faith. Though still directing in the 1970s, Visconti's most famous work in the opera house was in the 1950s at La Scala, with the creation of the Greek-American soprano Maria Callas as a world-famous singer-actress in Gluck, Spontini, Bellini, Donizetti, and Verdi. Spontini's *La Vestale* of 1809 came first, with Callas as the heroine Giulia. According to Visconti, '*La Vestale* is a difficult opera to stage because it needs great style. This Maria gave it. For me she was a won-derful instrument, which could be played as I wished and which responded in an inspired way. How different from contending with a singer from the old school! As the High Priestess, Ebe Stignani was hope-less with her two stock gestures, worse than a washerwoman on stage. Unbearable!' The style which Callas had and Stignani did not was, among other things, a matter of gestures proper to the piece's Napoleonic period: 'We selected them from the French tragediennes, some from Greek drama, for this was the kind of actress she could be—classical.' The proper modern way to animate the proper period style: this was Visconti's big concern, as in his high-rococo *Iphigénie en Tauride* for Callas; though as it turned out,

we didn't really agree about *Ifigenia*. As always, I conceived my production to make Maria look as glorious as possible. But she didn't understand my idea at all. 'Why are you doing it like this?' she asked. 'It's a Greek story and I'm a Greek woman, so I want to look Greek on stage!' I said, 'My dear, the Greece you are talking about is too far off. This opera must look like a Tiepolo fresco come to life.' But still she fussed, wanting to look Greek.

A similar concern with the right historical *locus*—something which can make sympathetic space for acting of a proper psychological depth—has characterized Peter Hall's operatic work. There is much talk about it in John Higgins's *The Making of an Opera*, a book-length chronicle of the preparation and rehearsals for Hall's Glyndebourne *Don Giovanni* of 1977. (It is a sign of the age's fascination with staging that a book on the subject should have *that* title!) There is much real two-way discussion of character in the book too. As Stafford Dean, Hall's Leporello in 1977, puts it: 'With Peter you come down to the very fundamentals of a work. He invites you to make suggestions so you go along with that. Most producers are very suspicious of other people's ideas and feel that in some way their position might possibly be usurped.... I suppose that I've never discussed an opera in such detail with a producer, but that is simply because I've rarely, if ever, been invited to do so.'

However, a faithfulness of *this* particular sort to the text's instructions and intentions has not been universally accepted by late-twentieth-century directors. Under another banner there are those who believe that a modern audience, whether it knows it or not, needs a more searching and radical approach to their realization. After all (the argument runs), that audience is getting more distant by the minute from the centre of the galaxy of repertory opera and so is unavoidably alienated from it in some ways. The social conventions of an opera's own period may no longer apply. The specific mythology or historical setting the work refers to may, as they stand, now be impossibly obscure to most people. Its original stage visualizations, strong enough no doubt in their day, have become so many clichés to an audience image-saturated by film and television. What is more, long-accepted methods of staging repertory pieces have probably dulled the edge of the works' intentions by making them safe, unimpinging, too implicated with complacent bourgeois commodity culture. So much traditional prettiness, so much comfortable cocooning, so much hollow posturing on the part of the singer-actors obscure the fact that *Figaro, Carmen, Madama Butterfly* were originally *about* something: something immediate, challenging, raw even. This is being lost. Opera as a theatre art has come close to drowning in its own plush.

Indeed, for some observers in the late 1960s, it was an art almost past praying for. The composer-conductor Pierre Boulez hit the headlines by asserting that 'the most elegant solution of the problem of opera was to blow up the opera houses.... Opera is the area before all others in which things have stood still.' And the English director Peter Brook, battle-scarred by a brief period in control of productions at Covent Garden, announced in his influential book of 1968 *The Empty Space* that 'Grand Opera is, of course, the Deadly Theatre carried to absurdity. Opera is a nightmare of vast feuds over tiny details; of surrealist anecdotes that all turn round the same assertion: nothing needs to change. Everything in opera must change.' But change did begin to occur around the time of *The Empty Space* in some unexploded opera houses, through the work of directors who interpreted being faithful to a work's intentions as involving taking radical steps to restore its edge and immediacy, supplying mythical and historical frames which *were* relevant to today, finding décors and acting styles which (post-film, post-TV) would do for now what the originals did for their own time, stripping off the varnish of tradition and brushing away the cobwebs of complacency. Indeed, with the partial blessing from beyond of such modernists as Felsenstein and Wieland Wagner, varnish-stripping and cobweb-brushing have become quite heavy industries in the last twenty-five years.

'Truth to the work' from this point of view has taken various forms (though they have often announced themselves with certain recurrent trademarks, such as the curtain-up overture with mimed action, to underline that the aural and visual are on an equal footing, or the staging of the piece as a fantastic dream, to justify all improbabilities in advance). Sometimes it has been a matter of updating the opera's action to the present day in décor and acting style, so that, arguably, the issues and confrontations are clarified. The drive behind such stagings could be typified in the account by one of Felsenstein's successors at the Komische Oper, Harry Kupfer, of his 1987 production of Gluck's *Orfeo ed Euridice*, its Orpheus leather-jacketed and carrying an electric guitar:

The theme of the piece is the dilemma of the artist in society, how an artist copes, or fails to cope with life and death and how he has the possibility to portray the deepest human conflicts and sufferings. We have staged it as a modern piece naturally, and in pictures which are very close to us today. Every image—and Orpheus himself is an image—must signify from first to last. Otherwise it is no image at all.

Again, this kind of *Werktreue* has sometimes been a matter of relocating the opera in an environment, neither the original nor a modern one, which aims to give the modern audience a more vivid metaphor for the essential action than either of those could. Thus Handel's *Teseo* has been set in a French château requisitioned by the Red Cross near the front line in the First World War; Mozart's *Così fan tutte* on a 1920s luxury cruise vessel (taking a hint perhaps from Auden's designer for *Die Zauberflöte* 'who sets the whole thing on an ocean liner'); and Verdi's *Rigoletto* in the *mafioso* Little Italy of 1950s New York.

Faithfulness of this kind has also involved highlighting an opera's dominant preoccupations with strong visual symbols deriving from one period or more than one, or bringing on to the stage the actual historical grist that fed the work before it had its claws drawn (so to speak) through being 'operatized' into something with a merely picturesque setting. Controversial stagings of Wagner's *Ring* in the 1970s did both of these things, taking their lead from a production at Leipzig by Joachim Herz (one of a group of East German directors known superiorly in some parts of the Western press as the Marx Brothers). 'We decided to play the *Ring*', says Herz, 'as a parable play about conflicts which rose in Wagner's time but are not finished now.' Herz's ultimate mentor in this was George Bernard Shaw, who had urged as early as 1898 in his *Perfect Wagnerite* that the *Ring* was not a piece of Nordic pre-history but essentially a work about capital, labour, and revolution in the nineteenth century. So, arguably, post-Industrial Revolution images must appear, as they did too in Patrice Chéreau's partly Shavian *Ring* at Bayreuth in 1976: hydroelectric dams on the Rhine and a huge fly-wheel at Mime's forge, Victorian mausoleums and twentieth-century tenements, dinner jackets and evening gowns and acting that Ibsen might well have been proud of.

The directors who have been concerned to 'make it new' in this way have naturally differed in style and to an extent in approach. Some have looked for new harmonies, some for stimulating dissonances. The English director and savant Jonathan Miller has looked for harmonies. In his book on the 'afterlife' of works of art, *Subsequent Performances*, he describes his approach to Mozart for Scottish Opera in 1983:

The notion of deep structure helped me to discover how to stage *The Magic Flute*. . . . It had always been an opera that wearied me on stage but moved me very much by its music. . . . I found the staging in the past too literal, as it had simply taken at its face value the setting that Schikaneder and Mozart had written. It may well be that in the period they were writing the genre of the staging realised their intentions, but I found that this genre was no longer satisfactory. . . . I began by asking . . . does it have to be this rather tawdry fairy story to preserve Mozart and Schikaneder's original idea? This led me to wonder about the deep structure that generated that particular surface performance, in the hope that I could find an alternative setting which would be consistent with the deep structure, although quite different in appearance.

The result was a dream-vision involving figures evoking actual historical personages from the whole spectrum of late-eighteenth-century European politics and philosophy, taking place in a fantastic library evoking the Utopian Architecture of the French Enlightenment. A far cry from 'Despina's Diner' at the time of President Reagan's involvement with the *vita militar* in Nicaragua: the creatively discordant setting for the 1984 *Così fan tutte* of the American director Peter Sellars, whose cast, he said, worked at

trying to be simultaneously eighteenth century and twentieth century. See, updating in itself is not interesting, and also equally uninteresting is a so-called 'period' staging. Each is a falsification. . . . The act of theatre is this equation: Whatever you do onstage must = the public at the time you stage it. We may be able to re-create half the equation, the production as it was done in 1790 (though I doubt it), but the other half, the public Mozart did it for, we can never re-create. For me it has to be both. Having set the opera in a coffee shop, we then proceed to violate coffee shop behaviour in the staging. The important thing in theatre is the sense of anachronism.

Sellars is the American cousin of a group of recent British and Continental directors who have been faithful to the text's intentions in their fashion: a fashion which makes a point of avoiding the super-integrated, the seamlessly woven, the highly finished, and which sometimes needles audiences in the process. Another American cousin is David Alden:

I don't like homogeneous things on stage. I think they're boring, and I don't like a production that is a perfectly pasteurized event. . . . I know that Callas said that every gesture is in the score, and she's right in a way, but you have to be extremely intelligent about it and cast a very cold eye on the score, however much you adore it. It's much too easy to make everything of a piece. . . . [The audience at an Alden production] are getting something that is emotionally committed and emotionally daring on the one hand, and they're also getting a completely ironic, 20th-century searchlight thrown on this thing at the same time, and people get angry and confused as well as excited.

Arguably, such stagings can be as 'grammatical' (in our original sense) as those stagings which are more concerned to search for the ideal images in the mind's eye of the composer—and also as ungrammatical. But there has been little love lost between these two faiths to the text as a set of intentions since the more radical one made its presence strongly felt in the 1970s. The radicals (or at least their admirers) have tended to call those of the other faith tame, tired, tory, cosy, dreary, empty, and—worst insult of all—'culinary' (deriving the word from

Bertolt Brecht's dismissal of opera in general as a form in which dynamic ideas are smothered by sensual satisfactions). The 'culinary' ones have retaliated with cries of 'perverse', 'polemical', 'political', 'arrogant', 'interfering', and—the unkindest cut—'*unmusical*'. At least the correspondence columns of the opera magazines have found plenty of copy in the debate!

Finally, there is the third and last view of an operatic text up for revival in the late twentieth century: that it is *a sheer, unprescriptive stimulus* to the free play of theatrical imagination. From this viewpoint, how the text came to be there, what the librettist and composer meant by it, what theatrical and social conventions it drew on, how it was originally designed and performed: these things may well be of some curiosity value and may perhaps be alluded to (probably with irony) in a staging; but they should have no controlling power over that staging. They are not privileged; they cannot compel; they are part of a dead past. To adapt an influential phrase of the critic Roland Barthes: 'The birth of the Director must be at the cost of the death of the Author.' It is the text itself, unshackled by time or authorship, which is alive; and its untrammelled life triggers new responses in the imagination of directors and designers. As a result, *Werktreue*, the keeping of faith with one's view of the text, comes to mean the generating of arresting and significant happenings on stage apropos of all that celebrated language and music.

This may involve devising events which challenge what seem to be the text's drifts and assumptions. Thus Hans Sachs, as (hopefully) a good democrat, may leave the stage with a shrug in the midst of the perhaps faintly fascist rejoicings at the end of Wagner's *Meistersinger*; the Dove at the end of *Parsifal* may feel too sceptical about life in general and the Grail Knights in particular to bring itself to hover over them; Isolde may never really arrive at the end of *Tristan* but only be hallucinated into a phantom existence by the sick hero. Or the drive to generate good happenings may lead to the devising of a quite new scenario which takes off from the operatic text at an intriguing angle. In his book about his collaboration with the illustrator and designer Maurice Sendak on their staging of Prokofiev's 1920s *Love for Three Oranges* in 1982, the American director Frank Corsaro describes in dialogue-form the route the two men took to finding their 'French Revolution' concept of the piece: a concept (involving an *ancien régime* theatre troupe performing for the newly consequential bourgeoisie of a French seaport) which apparently runs quite athwart the Prokofiev text:

FRANK. You know what this means? We'll have to create an entire sub-text so that *it* determines how each and every moment of the opera develops, without changing a single line of the actual text or altering a note of the music.

MAURICE. Frank, are we or are we not being a bit desperate?

FRANK. Maybe, but who cares? If it really works, if it really stimulates us, who cares?

MAURICE. . . . It will be like doing an entirely other opera.

FRANK. In a way, yes. But the piece requires specific focus before it can come to life and take off.

At the end Corsaro was happy with the staging that grew from their 'other opera'. And Prokofiev? Well, Prokofiev was dead. But composers very much alive have had interesting experiences of late-twentieth-century stagings which treat them like repertory composers and seem to build sheer othernesses on their texts. A story of Philip Glass's from his book *Opera on the Beach* points up the paradoxes. When his Gandhi opera *Satyagraha* was to be revived at Stuttgart in 1981, Glass consented to Achim Freyer's staging it though it was clear that the result would be a very different affair from the Rotterdam première Glass himself had been involved in the previous year. 'As long as he followed the settings in the libretto and his interpretation could be supported by the music, he was free to do as he liked', said Glass, who gave his consent for the best liberal reasons: 'Only through reinterpretation of the standard repertory does a true understanding of a work emerge. . . . There is no final version of a work. Nor do the original authors necessarily have the final, or even the best, interpretations.' Still, having stayed away from rehearsals, Glass was deeply surprised when he saw Freyer's production, and hardly recognized anything of his own opera apart from the music. Naturally, Freyer wanted to know what Glass thought:

The fact was, I didn't know what to think. In principle, I believed that what he had done was artistically valid, but actually I didn't understand, at that moment, what he had really done at all.

'That was very interesting, Achim', I began. 'But, tell me. Why did you do it that way?'

At first he seemed surprised by my question. But he recovered quickly and said: 'I did it just the way you wrote it!'

I thought about that for a long time.

If Glass thought for a long time, then doubtless the ghost of Marco da Gagliano might want to do the same when faced with some of the spectrum of possible late twentieth-century productions of that near four-century-old opera of his about Apollo triumphing over the Python, being conquered by love, chasing the chaste nymph Daphne, and crowning himself with the laurel she mysteriously becomes. Gagliano's ghost might perhaps find himself at a staging of *Dafne* which lovingly copied the supposed mood, movement, gestures, costumes, and simulated the candlelight of the opera's Mantuan première in a 'simple' telling of the tale, to match and mix with a period recreation of its music's sonorities and present an arresting challenge to time-travelling eyes as well as ears. Equally he might be at a staging which used modern technology and techniques to open the piece out: to explore the significant lifestyle of the age in which it was written by emphasizing Renaissance Man's pursuits in war and love (the monster, the nymph) and their sublimation in high art (the laurel crown, the opera itself), with the characters dressed as if for a sumptuous masquerade and moving against a golden landscape out of Titian or Rubens. Or he might be at a time-blending production which focused on the perennial psychological issues in the opera and presented a group of quite modern folk coolly exploring its fable in sweatshirts and jeans, perhaps in front of huge back-projections of classic myth, the staging's concern being with the contributions made by emotional rebounds—in this case those resulting from Apollo's encounters with monster, nymph, laurel—to the building of a balanced personality. Or a 'green' staging, set in a rainforest by Howard Hodgkin (say), with a white-colonist Apollo progressing from arrogantly subduing the earth (in the form of the poor old Python, as misunderstood as Shakespeare's Caliban), through acknowledging the growth principle (the power of Cupid), to co-operating with the precious resources of the ecosphere (the laurel). Or a gender-oriented show, played against photo-images of hunter and quarry (from the oldest Lascaux cave to the latest girlie magazine) and mounting a critique of masculine territorial and sexual aggression (bad enough) and masculine sentimentality (worse). All these things when, as we have seen, the living Gagliano had published a preface saying just how *Dafne* ought to be staged! Would his ghost not be tempted to mutter a few curses?

Well perhaps, but hopefully not for long. After some thought, Gagliano would surely remember not only that his manual disclaimed any dictatorial stance—'I am not capable of such downright presumption'—but also that all it really urged on subsequent performers was that their *Dafne*s should have impact, intelligibility, apt design, ensemble of all sorts, discipline married to freshness, and a way of keeping the tread of the performers concordant with the sound of music. (His detailed suggestions for stage business are just means to these ends; and besides almost all of them *could* at a pinch be incorporated in any of our hypothetical modern stagings.) So perhaps, like Philip Glass when he got used to Freyer's staging of *Satyagraha*, Gagliano's ghost would come to accept the new things which had been made out of his text. The two of them could then join with the Beethoven who is memorably imagined by Friedrich Nietzsche in 1879 in the 'Assorted Opinions and Maxims' which eventually found their way into his *Human, All Too Human*. True, Nietzsche is thinking about modern interpretations of Beethoven's instrumental music; but what he has to say could well apply to stagings of *Fidelio* too—and of many other operas besides:

If Beethoven were suddenly to come to life and hear one of his works performed with that modern animation and nervous excitement that bring glory to our masters of execution, he would probably be silent for a long while, uncertain whether he should raise his hand to curse or to bless, but perhaps say at last: 'Well, well! That is neither I nor not-I, but a third thing—it seems to me, too, something right, if not just *the* right thing. But you must know yourselves what to do, as it is in any case you who have to listen. As our Schiller says, "The living man is right". So have it your own way, and let me go down again.'

❦ 11 ❦

OPERA SINGERS

William Ashbrook

A HISTORICAL survey of opera singers and singing is all too apt to end up as an annotated list of names, somewhat less functional than a telephone directory and predictably as notable for its omissions as for its inclusions. To say this is by no means to deny the historical importance of certain names but rather to make the point that the (inevitable) listing can barely hint at the variety and vividness of personality of a Maria Malibran (1808–36) or a Conchita Supervia (1895–1936). The most we can know of Malibran's legendary qualities is at second hand, from reading accounts by those who heard her or knew her, or even from looking at manuscripts of music she sang with her personal embellishments written out; but Supervia, thanks to her many vibrant recordings, we can *hear* for ourselves.

Therefore, thinking about opera singers requires at least two perspectives: one, historical; the other, directly experiential from seeing them in the theatre or on video or from hearing them on disc.

The Historical

Until some other evidence turns up, the earliest surviving example of an opera singer actually singing stems from Copenhagen. On the evening of Peter Schram's 70th birthday, a celebration that occurred in 1889, this bass sang his farewell to the stage as Leporello in Mozart's *Don Giovanni*, and at a party later that night in front of a primitive recording device he was persuaded to sing some of Leporello's music, which he performed in his native Danish. He sings Leporello's first air and the opening of 'Madamina' without accompaniment, ornamenting his music in a way that gives a fascinating glimpse of a mid-nineteenth-century style of singing Mozart. As a young man Schram had studied with Manuel García, jun. in Paris, at the same time Jenny Lind was taking lessons from him. The relatively obscure Schram, at 70 and sounding as though he had been nipping at the aquavit, exists for us in a way that Jenny Lind, for all her celebrity, cannot—unless we could actually hear her, however dimly; but no record of her voice is known to exist.

The term 'opera singers' can have many connotations. It is associated with what can be a quite awesome self-absorption, the sort of thing so deliciously parodied in Fellini's film, *E la nave va* ('And the Ship Sails on'), that ironical salute to the Callas legend. *Divismo*, of the female or male variety, seems old-fashioned in some ways, it is redolent of a distinctly dumpy Tetrazzini in a plumed, half-acre hat waving from a ship's railing, or of Caruso beaming on the boardwalk at Atlantic City, nattily sporting yellow gloves and green spats; yet it exists in other terms today, as at that triumph of promotion, the televised Domingo–Carreras–Pavarotti concert at Rome (1990). Again, the term 'opera' singers is frequently used today as a demarcation of a scarcely crossable line separating them from 'pop' singers. Yet it is well to remember there was a time (before the invention of the microphone) when such a distinction could scarcely be said to exist. Then, serious singers sang all sorts of unserious music.

In days when tastes were less self-consciously pure than they are all too apt to be today, there was a phenomenon known as 'The Lesson Scene' in Rossini's *Barber of Seville*, featuring interpolations which rarely included anything by Rossini. The diva of the evening, let us imagine it would be someone like Adelina Patti (1843–1919) on one of her several trans-American 'farewell' tours, performing in some unlikely place like Cheyenne, Wyoming, back in the mid-1880s. During 'The Lesson Scene' she would sing a favourite aria or other warhorse accompanied by orchestra, but then a piano would be pushed on stage and Patti would accompany herself in 'Home, sweet home'. This was no idle ritual. The combination of piano and home spelled respectability. It suggested Sunday hymn-sings, rather than the 'wicked' stage.

For a woman particularly, the social implications of being an 'opera' singer were once upon a time drastic. When Henriette Sontag (1806–54) married the aristocratic diplomat Count Rossi, she promptly retired from the stage, although she continued to sing as a dilettante, until after the upsets of 1848 when her husband lost his fortune. Then she returned to the boards in what was perceived as an act of self-sacrifice. Indeed it turned out to be one, as she died of cholera in Mexico while on tour. On the other hand, certain prominent singers of the late Victorian period, Nellie Melba (1861–1931) and Emma Eames (1865–1952), for instance, neither one having any use for the other, managed to create sufficient sense that they were socially acceptable for one reason or another that they succeeded through their connections in being 'taken up' in the London of the 1890s, even though each was the wife of a man she was in the process of discarding.

The potential vulnerability of a singer to sexual harassments can be illustrated by the sad case of Giuseppina Strepponi (1815–97). The daughter of a composer who died when she was 17, she took to the stage to help support her widowed mother and siblings; and during the ten years of her active career she bore several illegitimate children, whom she arranged to be raised as discreetly as possible. A wise, compassionate woman as her letters prove her to be, Strepponi went on to become the wife of Verdi, and it seems obvious that her 'past' and the fact they had lived together some years before they were officially married, contributed much to the composer's prickly sense of privacy. Nor were women the only ones at risk: Pol Plançon was dismissed from the Paris Opéra in 1893, after having been caught in his dressing room, compromised by the composer Herman Bemberg.

The phenomenology of opera singing as well as that of those with the capacity to do it can be viewed from a variety of angles. It should be evident, however, that we can scarcely hope to come to terms of understanding merely by projecting present-day expectations back across four centuries. The sound of beautiful singing usually produces a profound physical response, suggesting a shared vibrancy between auditor and singer. It is odd, then, to think that for the space of two centuries the most highly touted opera singers were the so-called castrati, or *evirati*, men whose pre-pubescent soprano or contralto voices had been surgically preserved. This particular phenomenon was actively encouraged in Italy, first in church, there being a papal ban against female participation in *Sei-* and *Settecento* choirs. The power and versatility of these artificially maintained voices, more potent than those of the falsettists, attracted favourable attention, and soon the lucrative tug of secular activity brought them to the opera stage. Indeed, their participation in early opera performances goes back to Peri's *Euridice* of 1600 and to Monteverdi's *La favola d'Orfeo* (1607). Some idea of the vocal capacities of the castrati can be gleaned from such a book as that by the castrato and singing teacher Pier Francesco Tosi (1654–1732), *Observations on the Florid Song*, first published in 1723 as *Opinioni de' cantori antichi e moderni*, or from the music written for these virtuosos by Handel, Hasse, and Gluck. These singing 'machines' can be seen as something quintessentially baroque: elaborate and formal, their participation being confined almost exclusively to opera seria rather than comic works. With the rise of sensibility in the late eighteenth century, their artificiality, the fact that the sounds they produced had little to do with the sexual characteristics of the characters they represented, rendered them less sympathetic. Mozart wrote some important roles for castrati: Idamante (*Idomeneo*) and Sesto (*La clemenza di Tito*), both youthful characters. Although the castrati had almost entirely disappeared from the stage by 1810 (the last one to appear in opera in London was Velluti in 1826), they continued to exert influence in their capacity as teachers of singing.

A good example of such a one is Girolamo Crescentini (1762–1846), who gave up the stage in 1805 upon receiving an appointment in Vienna as singing-master to the Habsburgs. There he was heard by the musically susceptible Napoleon, who lured him to Paris by presenting him with a decoration usually awarded to the military. Reputedly many were offended by this gesture, there being a general prejudice against the castrati among the rational French, but one such discussion was halted when the mezzo-soprano Giuseppina Grassini, the aunt and teacher of Pasta and a seasoned campaigner herself, reminded those who had objected to this honour that Crescentini's career had been rendered possible only by the wound he had sustained. In 1812 Crescentini returned to Italy and eventually took up a position as professor at the Naples conservatory, a whole generation of singers profiting from his instruction. Indeed, the underlying concept of what is loosely termed 'bel canto' refers to the music written for singers who had been trained by the castrati.

They were themselves products of the conservatories, whose original purpose in Italy had been to provide singers and musicians for religious services. An important part of the training they received was in the principles of composition, providing them with skills to invent (as well as execute) the variants they would introduce into the repeated sections of arias. These elaborations or changes were designed to show off the individual expertise of the singer, and therefore were personal rather than general or traditional. Seen from this angle, the castrati reflect the long-standing notion that the executant participates creatively in the work performed, an idea at odds with the current one that preserving the integrity of the composition as first conceived is the sovereign concern.

The earliest female opera singers, among them Francesca and Settimia Caccini, the daughters of the composer Giulio Caccini, author of *Euridice* (1602), received thoroughgoing musical training from their father and have left evidence of their own compositional prowess. As opera performances were only occasional events until the late 1630s, most of the singing the Caccini sisters did was non-operatic. It was not until the time of Anna Renzi (*c*.1620–after 1660) that the concept of a prima donna, a woman whose reputation depended primarily on her appearances in operas, can be said to exist. She was, for instance, the original Ottavia, in Monteverdi's *L'incoronazione di Poppea* (1642) and widely praised for her vocal quality, her affecting declamation. Although the function of prima donna, soon to be associated with notions of vocal virtuosity, was established by the mid-seventeenth century, her dominant emergence did not automatically mean she had exclusive rights to female roles. In Rome and the Papal States, for instance, women were not permitted to participate in stage performances and, consequently, comely young castrati were routinely cast as the heroines in the operas put on there. A sense of dissociation between the character of the role and the sounds produced by the singer performing it produced an ambiguousness that lasted in various forms down to the 1830s. Some notable female opera singers of the eighteenth century were Faustina Bordoni (1697–1781) and Francesca Cuzzoni (*c*.1696–1778), rivals in Handel's operas and neither the first nor the last to resort to fisticuffs, and there were the Germans Gertrud Mara (1749–1833) and Aloysia Lange (*c*.1761–1839), Mozart's sister-in-law, and the English Elizabeth Billington (*c*.1765–1818), whose appearance at the Teatro San Carlo, Naples, was thought by the more superstitious locals to have induced an eruption of Mount Vesuvius, as she was a Protestant.

Since heroic roles had been traditionally assigned to castrati, audiences were used to associating a particular range of sound (usually contralto) with such parts. When their day was over, we find the anomaly of the female contralto-hero (*en travesti*), as reflected by a number of Rossini's roles: among them Tancredi (1813), Falliero in *Bianca e Falliero* (1819), and Arsace in *Semiramide* (1823). Of the singers of such parts one of the earliest and most successful was Benedetta Rosmunda Pisaroni (1793–1872), later succeeded by Rossini's own pupil, Marietta Alboni (1826–1894), whose stage career was interrupted only when she became too stout to stand for more than a brief time. Today these *musico* roles, long in desuetude, have been revivified by Marilyn Horne.

Previously, the casting of an opera depended upon the personnel (rarely more than enough to populate a single cast) engaged by the theatre for which a composer had been contracted to write his opera. And thus we find such a top-heavy work as Rossini's *Armida* (1817), which gives employment to four leading tenors. The tenors of the beginning of the nineteenth century, especially the group engaged by Barbaja in

Naples, such as Andrea Nozzari (1775–1832), Manuel García, sen. (1775–1832), Giovanni Davide (1790–1864), and, most famous of all, Giovanni Battista Rubini (1794–1854), did not sing with the same method as modern tenors. They developed great technical facility, and their vocal production over an extensive compass involved carrying the chest resonance up to the so-called 'passage', usually top-line E or F, above that adopting a mixed-voice (*voce mista*), and, for the topmost notes, 'head' voice or falsetto. Tenors of this type would be cherished for their smooth transition from one kind of resonance to another and for their ability to vary their timbre according to the expressive requirements of the music. In France as well, an equivalent sort of tenor flourished, known as an *haute-contre*; an example of this category would be Joseph Legros (1739–93), who sang the role of Orphée in the Paris revision of Gluck's *Orfeo ed Euridice*, a revision which, among other changes, entailed adapting Orfeo's music, originally for male contralto, for a vocal type more tolerable to a Parisian audience.

There was, however, a vocal revolution a-brewing. In the late 1820s and early 1830s, as Romantic sensibility deepened, the growing vogue in Italy for more overtly tragic subjects, granted that the former (censorial) prejudice against on-stage death scenes was less in evidence, these high Romantic subjects created a demand for more forcible expression. The delicate and virtuosic style of the Rossinian *tenore contraltino* with his effete-sounding top tones was deemed an inadequate medium for more intense, melodramatic sentiments. It is a not particularly surprising anomaly, unfortunately, that most of the tenors involved in the late-twentieth-century Rossini revival sing his music unauthentically, believing that contemporary audiences, so over-indulged with artificially amplified sounds, will not tolerate the delicate tones of mixed resonance shading into falsetto, like those employed by the singers Rossini wrote for. The nearest approximation to them we hear today are the so-called counter-tenors, usually turned loose in eighteenth-century music originally written for castrati, but in fact rather closer in sound to the vocal production of Rubini & Co.

Two consequences of the vocal revolution of the 1830s were the gradual emergence of a more robust type of tenor and the simultaneous development of the baritone persona (either a villain or sympathetic father-figure), the latter a vocal personality quite distinct from the all-purpose basso of the opera seria. As so often happens, the *Zeitgeist* of a particular period will imagine new types of roles while providing the singers to fill them memorably. Two tenors whose influence were central to these developments were Domenico Donzelli (1790–1873), who sang in the *prima* of Bellini's *Norma* (1831), and Gilbert-Louis Duprez (1806–96), the first Edgardo in Donizetti's *Lucia* (1835), who modelled his vocal method on the dramatic style effectively used by Donzelli, but who by dint of hard work managed to extend his so-called chest voice upward to include the high C. The archetypal baritone of this period was Giorgio Ronconi (1810–90), as famous for his high-voltage acting as for his singing.

The tenor Duprez, whose vocal descendants are legion, came to be involved on the very barricades of this vocal revolution. In 1837 he returned to his native France and made his debut at the Opéra as Arnold in *Guillaume Tell*, his brilliant top notes creating a sensation. Rossini himself thought Duprez's high C ugly, likening it to the sound produced by a capon when its throat is being cut. For French audiences, the hero of the losing side of this revolution was the poetic, high-minded Adolphe Nourrit (1802–39), who had been a central figure in the first casts of *Tell*, and of Meyerbeer's *Robert le diable* (1831) and *Les Huguenots* (1836), a tenor whose vocal method depended on the mixed and head resonances. When Nourrit learned that Duprez had been engaged by the Opéra, he felt he could not compete unless he too acquired the new way of singing high notes, and so he betook himself to Italy to learn that skill. He had just embarked on a career as a new-style 'Italian' tenor when his health declined so alarmingly that in a state of deep depression he committed suicide.

'Whom the gods love die young' was a favourite adage in the Romantic era. Nourrit had just turned 37 when he leapt to his death. Even more central to the stereotype was the figure of Maria Malibran, dying at the age of 28 (one year to the day after the death of Vincenzo Bellini at 33). She was the daughter of Rossini's tenor Manuel García, and the elder sister of Pauline Viardot. Ruthlessly trained by her father to a rare degree of vocal agility and gifted with a temperament that could rouse an audience to raptures, Malibran created an indelible impression on her generation during a career that lasted but a dozen years. Defiant, unconventional, and wilful, she was transmuted by her untimely death into a Romantic icon. It is said that Maria Callas always kept Malibran's picture at hand.

At the first performance of *Norma*, the title role was sung by Giuditta Pasta (1797–1865), and that of Adalgisa by Giulia Grisi (1811–69), who shortly would become herself a leading proponent of the role of Norma. Pasta made her debut in 1815 as a mezzo-soprano, achieving great success at the Théâtre-Italien in Paris as much for her acting as for her vocalizing, gradually singing more and more soprano parts. In the carnival season of 1830 at the Teatro Carcano she sang in the *prime* of Donizetti's *Anna Bolena* and Bellini's *La sonnambula*. Hard use of her voice, singing demanding roles three and four times a week, left her a vocal wreck at 40. Grisi, on the other hand, sustained her career more equitably until 1860. She was the prima donna of the leading quartet that sang in Paris during the winter at the Théâtre-Italien and in London from April or May to July. The other members of this quartet were Rubini, who upon his retirement in 1839 was replaced by Giovanni Mario (1810–83), the baritone Antonio Tamburini (1800–76), and the bass Luigi Lablache (1794–1858). This group, with Rubini as tenor, won particular *réclame* for their appearance in the première of Bellini's *I puritani* (1835), and then, with Mario, in the first *Don Pasquale* (1843).

Another important member of this company was Fanny Tacchinardi–Persiani (1812–67), who, along with Duprez, had sung the leading roles in the first cast of *Lucia di Lammermoor*. The daughter of a famous tenor, Nicola Tacchinardi, who taught her all his skills, Persiani was the foremost vocal technician of her generation, if we are to believe what critics such as H. F. Chorley wrote about her. Apparently her voice was rather small (though with an extensive range) and she was by no means a powerful actress, but so vast was her arsenal of vocal witcheries and so prompt her powers of improvisation that she more than overcame her deficiencies. Persiani was in the tradition of Angelica Catalani (1780–1849), another vocal acrobat, whose specialty was airs of parade, particularly a spectacular set of 'Variations in G Major' by the violinist Pierre Rode, but she lacked the inventiveness and the sound musical training to hold her audiences once their original amazement had worn off. Such later 'coloratura' sopranos as Patti, Marcella Sembrich, Melba, Luisa Tetrazzini, and Amelita Galli-Curci can be regarded as epigones of the vein popularized by Persiani.

A pair of imposing German sopranos during the first half of the nineteenth century were Anna Milder-Hauptmann (1785–1838), who sang in both the 1805 and 1814 versions of Beethoven's *Fidelio*, and Wilhelmine Schröder-Devrient (1804–60), whom Beethoven coached as Leonore, whom Weber prized for her performance of Agathe in *Der Freischütz*, and who sang in the premières of Wagner's *Rienzi*, *Der fliegende Holländer*, and *Tannhäuser* (Venus). Milder was more notable as a vocalist (Schubert wrote *Der Hirt auf dem Felsen* for her), but Schröder-Devrient was a singing-actress to the Romantic taste, as popular in London as she was in Dresden, the principal arena of her activities.

The increase in the size and sonority of theatre orchestras in Germany, particularly as the Wagnerian operas made their way into the repertory, created a demand for singers who were more concerned with vocal heft and stamina than with finesse. In the early 1880s, when it was suggested that soprano Therese Vogl and her tenor husband Heinrich, who regularly sang leading Wagnerian roles, should participate in a special performance of Wagner's *Das Liebesverbot* (1836), the sight of the Bellinian *gruppetti* in their voice parts reduced them first to laughter and then to silence. Two important Wagnerian tenors of the first generation were Joseph Aloys Tichatschek (1807–86), the first Rienzi and Tannhäuser, and Ludwig Schnorr von Carolsfeld (1836–65), who died the month following his appearance in the first performances of *Tristan*. More consistent service to the Wagnerian cause came from the giant Albert Niemann (1831–1917), who was Wagner's choice for the ill-fated Paris *Tannhäuser* (1861), Siegmund in the first Bayreuth *Ring* (1876), repeating that role in the first London *Ring* (1882), as well as becoming the first American *Tristan* (1886). Pride of place as the first Brünnhilde goes to Amalie Materna (1844–1918), who was also the first Kundry at Bayreuth in 1882; Materna set something of a record when at the age of 69 she repeated her Kundry in a concert performance in Vienna in 1913 to celebrate the centenary of Wagner's birth. Lilli Lehmann (1848–1929) was also a pre-eminent Wagnerian, singing a Rhinemaiden and one of the Valkyries as well as the Woodbird in the first *Ring* cycle, and later becoming an impressive Brünnhilde and Isolde in her own right. A singer of unusual versatility, her repertory of over a hundred roles included such disparate instances as Queen Marguerite (*Les Huguenots*), Norma, and Carmen. In her late fifties Lehmann made a number of impressive recordings which reveal her no-nonsense approach to Handel, Mozart, Bellini, and Verdi.

While these singers in the German tradition broke new ground, a significant change had taken place in Paris. Instead of the exhibitionistic singing of the Rossini contraltos, a new kind of mezzo-soprano persona was making a place on the stage of the Opéra. First, there had been the ruthlessly ambitious Rosine Stoltz (1815– 1903), who as mistress of Pillet, the director of France's première lyric theatre, would neither tolerate soprano rivals nor permit a major new work into the repertory that had no starring role for her. Thus the mezzo-soprano assumes the functions of heroine and love-interest in such works as Donizetti's *La Favorite* (1840) and *Dom Sébastien* (1843) and in Halévy's *La Reine de Chypre* (1841).

Still another dimension to the mezzo-soprano range was added by the character of Fidès in Meyerbeer's *Le Prophète* (1849). Fidès is the hero's mother but a dominant figure in the plot; her big *scena* in the Act 5 Prison Scene is the ultimate test of a mezzo-soprano's range and technique. The mezzo role of Azucena, the hero's mother, in Verdi's *Il trovatore* exploits analogous dramatic ground to that of Fidès. Meyerbeer had stalled for nearly a decade before releasing his work to the Opéra, deliberately waiting until Stoltz had been banished because of her dictatorial ways and a capable new tenor found to replace Duprez, whose vocal decline had made him a musical liability. Making her triumphant debut as Fidès was Pauline Viardot-García (1821–1910), the younger sister of Malibran. A singer of great resource and a compelling actress, Viardot had pursued a successful career in Italian opera across Europe for a decade before she subdued that bastion of French élitism, the Opéra. The influence of Viardot and her musicianship is difficult to overestimate. Gounod made his debut as a composer for the Opéra with *Sapho*, a work written for her. Berlioz had her in mind as the vocal prototype of Didon in *Les Troyens*, and in 1859 he made his version of Gluck's *Orfeo* for her, providing her with a role that marked the artistic apogee of her stage career. Saint-Saëns composed the role of Dalila to her measure; she helped launch Massenet by appearing in his *Marie-Magdeleine*. Nor was her influence limited to the stage. Schumann dedicated his *Liederkreis* (Op. 24) to her, and she was the soloist in the first performance of Brahms's Alto Rhapsody.

Jenny Lind (1820–87) was the first Swedish Nightingale, but her days as an opera singer were comparatively few, as moral scruples kept her out of the theatre after 1849. The second Swedish Nightingale was Christine Nilsson (1843–1921). After studies first in Sweden and then in Paris, Nilsson made her debut at the Théâtre-Lyrique in the première of the French version of Verdi's *La traviata*. In 1868 she joined the Opéra, making her first appearance there as Ophélie in the première of Thomas's *Hamlet*, and there the following year she was in the first cast of the expanded, five-act version of Gounod's *Faust*. The role of Marguerite further served her when she sang it, now in Italian, in both London and New York; in the latter most memorably in 1883 on the opening night of the Metropolitan Opera House. A brilliant singer as well as a charming actress, she retired in her early forties.

Another singer who made a great impression on the French repertoire was the baritone Jean-Baptiste Faure (1830–1914). A polished singer as well as an imaginative actor, his name is associated with a number of roles that he created: Hoël in Meyerbeer's *Dinorah* (*Le Pardon de Ploërmel*, 1859), Nélusko in *L'Africaine* (1865), Posa in *Don Carlos* (1867), the title role in *Hamlet* (1868). When Gounod's *Faust* moved from the repertory of the Théâtre-Lyrique to the stage of the Opéra, Faure was the elegantly sardonic Méphistophélès. Faure's voice was what the French call a *baryton-noble*, for which such roles as Méphisto, Escamillo, and the High-Priest in *Samson et Dalila* were written; these contain not only high notes to plague a true bass but also ones that a high baritone finds uncomfortably low. Faure is the prototype of such later French baritones as Victor Maurel, Jean Lassalle, Maurice Renaud, and the all-purpose Marcel Journet, who not only sang Méphistophélès, but also Wotan and Hans Sachs and even such disparate roles as Tonio in *Pagliacci* and Athanaël in Massenet's *Thaïs*.

Incidentally, the French have traditionally retained the names of once-popular singers to designate the vocal type associated with them. There is for instance, the *falcon*, a term suggested by the name of Cornélie Falcon (1812–97), whose most memorable creations were Rachel in *La Juive* (1835) and Valentine in *Les Huguenots* (1836). A soprano with a range short on top, she lost her voice irreparably and was obliged to retire at 26, because she forced what had been a sumptuous mezzo-soprano into tessitura too high for it. Another typical French category is the so-called *dugazon*, a term that preserves the name of Louise-Rosalie Dugazon (1755–1821), for years a fixture at the Opéra-Comique. A *dugazon* is a light soprano adept at playing soubrette-like roles, and when the singer became more mature and played elderly but still flirtatious women, a subcategory was christened 'mères *dugazons*'. A particularly French vocal type is that known as a *trial*, which name might seem to come from a different source than Antoine Trial (1737–95) as it refers to a tenor with more acting ability than voice. Some roles associated with this type are Bertrand in Monsigny's *Le Déserteur* and Torquemada in Ravel's *L'Heure espagnole*. And then there is what is known as the *baryton-Martin*, named after Jean-Blaise Martin (1768–1837). Such a voice has a range similar to that of a second tenor. His upper notes shade into falsetto, and he lacks the powerful top tones of a Verdian baritone. Certain roles that can be sung either by a high baritone or tenor, parts like Pelléas and Ramiro in *L'Heure espagnole*, belong to this category. A *baryton-Martin* who made a number of fine records in the 1920s and 1930s is André Baugé (1892–1966), and his performance of the French equivalent of 'Largo al factotum' reveals at once the finesse of this approach to what in an Italian throat is apt to be resounding.

The Experiential

In Italy, the sudden popularity of so-called 'verismo', or naturalistic opera, in the wake of the overnight success of *Cavalleria rusticana* (1890) was to produce a detectable change in the way people sang. Roberto Stagno (1840–97), who along with his wife Gemma Bellincioni (1864–1950) sang the leading roles in that epoch-making performance of *Cavalleria*, can give some idea of the transition. Stagno was a versatile tenor, famous for such lyric roles as Almaviva in *Il barbiere* and Alfredo in *La traviata*, but he became identified with the new movement of naturalistic opera and gave up his former roles. Although just 26 when she sang her first Santuzza, Bellincioni early on ran into vocal problems and maintained her career in terms of her dramatic ability, introducing Strauss's *Salome* to Italy. The depiction of overt passion was seen to demand a more intense, more highly inflected style, sometimes punctuated with ironic laughter or heart-broken sobbing. A case in point is the end of Massenet's *La Navarraise* (1894), which contains the role of Anita written for Emma Calvé. At the end of this one-act opera, instead of singing an elegiac passage over her lover's corpse, Anita breaks into an uncontrollable fit of hysterical laughter.

Emma Calvé (1858–1942) was the most famous Carmen of her generation, appearing in a work that was clearly one of the archetypes of the verismo school. She sang in Italy during the early 1890s, first in *Cavalleria*, and then in the première of Mascagni's *L'amico Fritz* (1891). Significantly, however, she also made her mark in a famous production of *Hamlet* at La Scala, in which she sang the purely lyrical Ophélie to the Dane of Mattia Battistini (1856–1928), one of the great belcantists as his many records testify. (Vladimir Horowitz maintained he studied Battistini's records in order to learn how to imitate the baritone's command of legato.)

In time singers imbued with a taste for veristic effects tended to lose their more lyric qualities. Eugenia Burzio (1872–1922) possessed all the vividness of personality and the exaggerated emphasis associated with a verismo soprano. It is instructive, for instance, to listen to her recorded performance of 'Pace, pace' from Verdi's *La forza del destino*; she makes it sound positively harrowing. This period of transition from more controlled to less controlled singing can be clearly illustrated in the recordings of the Neapolitan tenor Fernando De Lucia (1860–1925). He made his debut in the mid-1880s and established himself as a leading *tenore di grazia*, with all the rhythmic capriciousness, the fine-honed diminuendos, and clean-cut figurations that are such a feature of his early records of *Il barbiere*. De Lucia was one of the first generation of the *veristi* tenors; for instance, he sang Canio in both the London and New York premières of *Pagliacci*. In his early recordings of Loris's confession from Act 2 of Giordano's *Fedora*, a *locus classicus* for veristic effects, De Lucia's diction sounds italicized, his emotionalism is heavy-handed, his tone unsteady.

Enrico Caruso (1873–1921) is for many the Italian tenor *par excellence*. He was gifted with a fine voice and personal magnetism, making him the despair of his rivals and successors. At the outset of his career he had to contend with the problem of unreliable top notes, but his voice developed security and richness, as one can hear in his 1911 recording of 'Io non ho che una povera stanzetta' from Leoncavallo's *La bohème*, where the brazen sheen of the voice takes one's breath away. Later, Caruso turned to heavier roles: Samson, Jean in *Le Prophète*, and Eléazar in *La Juive*; the baritonal colour became more pronounced, and the top B flats no longer seemed effortlesss, but were produced with a palpable muscular push.

What Caruso was to Italian tenors, Titta Ruffo (1877–1953) was to Italian baritones. At its best his voice was inky dark and crowned with a stentorian A flat. Those who heard Ruffo in the flesh speak of tonal impact, and his was such a (dubious) sort of exuberance that when he felt particularly *in vena* he might lavish three huge Gs, instead of one, on 'Incominciate' at the end of the *Pagliacci* prologue. Unfortunately, singing in overdrive, as it were, led to a disastrous vocal decline by the time he was 50. Ruffo's style, aggressive and bombastic, is quite different from that of the baritones of a generation earlier, from that of Battistini, for instance, whose seamless legato, elegance of phrasing, and mastery of those pianissimo effects the Italians call *sfumature* are present in his many records. Significantly, Battistini retained his voice and continued to sing past 70.

There was something approaching a glut of fine Italian baritones who were more or less contemporaries of Ruffo. Slightly older was Antonio Scotti (1866–1936), whose voice lost its flexibility early, but so riveting were his dramatic skills, particularly as Scarpia in *Tosca*, that he remained a fixture at the Metropolitan for thirty years. Mario Sammarco (1868–1930) was a great favourite in London and also in New York, where he appeared at Oscar Hammerstein's Manhattan Opera House, and the fine duet recordings he made with John McCormack amply justify his popularity. Pasquale Amato (1878–1942) appeared only briefly in London, but Toscanini brought him to the Met, where his healthy voice and dramatic perception earned him a decade of success. His recording of 'Eri tu' from Verdi's *Un ballo in maschera*, a memento of the Toscanini 1913 revival at the Met, is particularly expressive. Less obviously impressive than these was Giuseppe De Luca (1876–1950), but he proved a more durable artist: his vocal good breeding preserved his voice at an age when his rivals were in ignominious retirement.

The Czech soprano Emmy Destinn (1878–1930) made her mark in Berlin and London before she embarked on a brief but memorable career in New York. Artur Rubinstein reported in his memoirs that she had had a snake tattooed the length of one of her legs. Handsome, possessed of a powerful temperament, and gifted with a burnished dramatic soprano, Destinn is spoken of with awe by those who heard her at her best. Unfortunately she is rather like Maria Jeritza, one of those fabled singers whose records rarely reproduce the impression they are known to have made upon a knowledgeable audience. Then there is also the other kind of singer, who for one reason or another pursued a generally undistinguished career but left a series of striking recordings: such a one is Celestina Boninsegna (1877–1947).

During the interwar years there was a great galaxy of singers who shone particularly in the Wagnerian repertory. Frida Leider (1888–1975) combined vocal splendour with a trenchant sense of text and dramatic purpose. Kirsten Flagstad (1895–1962) had a radiance in her seemingly indefatigable voice that set it apart. Lauritz Melchior (1890–1973) was the Heldentenor who long eclipsed the efforts of others who tackled the same daunting repertory. Of their excellence as singers of Wagner there is abundant recorded testimony. Nor is it confined to these three but extends to their regular colleagues—the eloquent baritone Friedrich Schorr (1888–1953), a non-pareil Hans Sachs, and such sterling mezzos as Karin Branzell (1891–1974), Kerstin Thorborg (1896–1970), and Margarete Klose (1902–68). Among basses of this epoch, two whose records are well worth seeking out are Ivar Andresen (1896–1940) and Ludwig Weber (1899–1974).

This was also a fine period for the works of Richard Strauss. Maria Jeritza (1887–1982) was a striking personality as Octavian and Salome, although her voice was no longer reliable by the early 1930s. Too much Turandot in the opinion of some. Elisabeth Schumann (1888–1952) and Adele Kern (1901–80) were adorable Sophies in *Der Rosenkavalier*, and the latter had the upper extension, as had Erna Berger (1900–90), to dazzle in the parodic coloratura of Zerbinetta in *Ariadne auf Naxos*. The Marschallin of Lotte Lehmann (1888–1976) attracted many almost fanatical adherents for her flavoursome projection of text coupled with a sexy-sounding voice, but there are those who found her in some respects too short-breathed, altogether thick-wristed and bourgeoise. It would be a dull world if everyone shared the same fanaticisms. Of the various Baron Ochs who flourished in this time, there was the gamey if sometimes vocally tremulous Emanuel List (1891–1967), and Ludwig Weber (1899–1974) sounded resplendent in this part, but the palm for all-around excellence in this role belonged to Richard Mayr (1877–1935), whose interpretation survives in the abridged *Rosenkavalier* of 1933 conducted by Robert Heger, with a cast that includes Lotte Lehmann and Elisabeth Schumann.

The interwar years were memorable ones for Verdi interpretations, as well. There was Rosa Ponselle (1894–1981), whose accomplishments included the title role in Spontini's *La Vestale* and her noble, if rather drastically transposed, Norma, as well as a sizeable list of Verdi heroines. Ponselle was really a *falcon*; she had lost her topmost notes by the age of 40, but her lower octave was sumptuous. Karin Branzell is reported to have declared that she hated to sing the *Gioconda* duet with Ponselle because the soprano's low notes sounded so much more contralto-ish than hers. Ponselle's nearest rival was not Rosa Raisa (1893–1963), although their repertories were similar, but Claudia Muzio (1889–1936), whose fine-grained soprano and dynamic versatility were combined with a degree of dramatic involvement that Ponselle, for all the sheer beauty of her voice, never quite attained. Two other fine sopranos in much the same repertory were the classical Giannina Arangi-Lombardi (1890–1951) and the less even, but more exciting, Gina Cigna (born 1900), whose interpolated high D in the Act 1 finale of *Norma* was a tone of extraordinary size and impact. The tenors Giovanni Martinelli (1885–1969), Aureliano Pertile (1885–1952), and Giacomo Lauri-Volpi (1892–1979) were stalwart performers in the middle-weight and dramatic Italian roles. Beniamino Gigli (1890–1957) began as a lyric tenor with a remarkably appealing sound and in time graduated to heavier roles, while the lighter-voiced Tito Schipa (1889–1965) was faithful to a limited repertory and made artistic capital out of comparatively slender resources. Among the Italian-style bassos of this epoch were the imposing Spaniard José Mardones (1869–1932), the huge-voiced Nazzareno De Angelis (1881–1962), who recorded a complete *Mefistofele* of awesome malignity, and the suave Ezio Pinza (1892–1957), who developed a special affinity for Mozart roles, and Tancredi Pasero (1890–1980), with his keen sense of style and impeccable legato.

The most remarkable bass of this generation was the Russian Fyodor Shalyapin (1873–1938). A towering personality, he was an actor of extraordinary conviction, a master of make-up and costume. His voice combined aspects of bass and baritone, and he could sing pianissimi of extraordinary delicacy. His greatest role was that of Boris Godunov, being particularly impressive in the guilt-ridden Hallucination and the Death Scenes. His instinct for emotive drama shines through his recording of Act 5 of Massenet's *Don Quichotte* (1910), the title role written for him, but on which he sings both the parts of the dying Quichotte and the grieving Sancho Panza.

These were the years of some distinguished singing of Puccini's music. Lucrezia Bori (1887–1960), whose lyric voice was deployed with an irresistible amalgam of artistry and charm, made an unforgettable Mimì and Magda (*La rondine*). Three Italian sopranos who understood the art of singing well and at the same time delivered text with vivid dramatic flavour were Gilda Dalla Rizza (1892–1975), although later her voice became stiff and unwieldy from singing roles too heavy for her essentially lyric organ, Mafalda Favero (1905–81), exceptionally vivid, and Pia Tassinari (b. 1903), although the latter concluded her career singing mezzo-soprano parts with her husband Ferrucio Tagliavini. In Italian and French roles the Swedish tenor Jussi Björling (1910–60) sang extremely well. Although his acting produced little impression in the theatre, his posthumous reputation has been well served by his many brilliant-sounding recordings.

The nearest equivalent to the sort of impact on the public made by Shalyapin has been produced by Maria Callas (1923–77), who has become a cult figure. She was able to exploit a keen musical sensibility by applying it to an instrument that was well equipped technically, and at the same time she possessed a shrewd sense of herself as a character impersonating a role. With her you never got a singer lost in her part, immersed in being Lucia or Violetta, for example, but instead a very calculating Callas playing Lucia or Violetta. There is no doubt that damage was inflicted on her voice by the ill-considered range of roles that she threw herself into too soon. Kundry (even in Italian), Gioconda, and Elvira (in *I puritani*) are parts with contradictory requirements even for a healthy natural voice, and in a very real sense Callas's voice was to some extent manufactured. In a few years the loss of steadiness at the top could no longer be disguised. Her heyday was tragically short, and unfortunately her later recordings do her an injustice. In retrospect, she seems like a meteor left over from the nineteenth century.

Renata Tebaldi (b. 1922) was a very different kind of singer, gifted with a most beautiful natural voice. As sheer sound, it was something to take a bath in. The purposes to which that ravishing sound was put, however, were rarely stimulating for a whole evening's opera. Hers was a kind of rhythmic lethargy that proved, ultimately, unriveting. Her handsome presence and an innate dignity were attractive in themselves, but dramatic insight was not her shining strength. It was much easier to be grateful to her than enthusiastic over her. No such qualifications need be made about the galvanic performances of Birgit Nilsson (b. 1918) in major works by Wagner and Strauss.

While this survey, diplomatically, is confined to singers no longer active before the public, it cannot come to an end without a salute to a number of extraordinary English and Australian singers. Malibran thought highly of the tenor John Braham (1774–1856), who was in the original cast of Weber's *Oberon* (1826). Sir Charles Santley (1834–1922) had a career fifty-four years in length, and held his own against some eminent competition, both as a cultivated singer and as a convincing actor. Nellie Melba (1861–1931) sang her Covent Garden farewell in 1926, at the age of 65, with her excellently placed voice still very much its recognizable self. Alfred Piccaver (1884–1958), born in Lincolnshire, pursued his career primarily singing Italian roles on German-speaking stages and was all but idolized by the Viennese. Eva Turner (1892–1990), the fresh-voiced *Turandot* of many seasons, came to seem as much an institution as the lions in Trafalgar Square. Peter Pears (1910–86) left an indelible series of impressions in Britten's operas with his impersonations of Peter Grimes, Captain Vere, and Aschenbach. The contralto Kathleen Ferrier (1912–53) was more a recitalist than a frequent performer of operas, but her noble simplicity left its imprint on all she touched. Janet Baker (b. 1933) is another singer who illuminated a large and unorthodox repertory. At her best, for the size of voice and adroitness of execution, Joan Sutherland (b. 1926) made herself a place that few can hope to fill.

In reading about singers since the beginning of opera back in 1600, one cannot help but be struck by the fact that almost every generation at some point has wrung its collective hands over what was perceived as a decline in singing. Nostalgia is an ever-recurring emotion, and *ubi sunt?* a universal cry. Recently certain aspects of opera singing have changed radically, but change need not be automatically equated with decline. In a time when more people can see a televised performance of an opera at one time than may have attended all the performances inside theatres that that work has ever received, it seems likely that direct interaction between performer and audience is more apt to decrease than increase in the years ahead. Even when the public is physically present, communica-

tion between singer and audience is diluted by the intervention of sur-
titles, which, while they may explain the plot, continue to deflect the
attention from the potential expressiveness of the performer. And is it
too much to hope that there may be a reaction against technological
interference? That singers may long to play to their fellows in spaces of
more human dimension than some of the vastnesses now masquerading
as opera houses? The legitimate function of the singer as participant in
the creative work, contributing to a composition with the ornamentation of melodies, is already recognized in certain specialized areas of
'period' revivals. The day when all operas were sung in the style currently popular, regardless of when they were composed, has finally set,
and the diversities of approach now acceptable have opened up possibilities still to be explored. Perhaps the pendulum may even swing so far as
to return singers to something like the prominence they once enjoyed,
before they began to be tyrannized by the *maestri* and victimized by producers hell-bent on being taken as original.

OPERA AS A SOCIAL OCCASION

John Rosselli

The Popularity of Opera

AMONG Western musical forms, only opera demands more bodies in the audience than are needed to perform it. A song or an instrumental work can be a solo in the full meaning of the word. Chamber music was originally, and may still be, a matter for the players alone. Even an orchestral work, if the orchestra is small, can be performed for an audience of one, like Wagner's *Siegfried Idyll*, a birthday present for his wife. But when King Ludwig II of Bavaria commanded performances of Wagner's operas at which he was the only spectator this was held to be evidence of his madness. Opera, a multi-media entertainment, requires so many people to produce it—singers, orchestral players, stage-hands, painters, seamstresses, maybe dancers and extras besides the composer and librettist—that it can be justified only if the audience is large or is made up of important people, preferably both.

This is not a personal opinion; it sets out what most people have taken for granted since the genre began. As a social occasion opera wants a crowd. True, an early court opera like Monteverdi's *Orfeo* of 1607 was probably given in a smallish room, but that room seems likely to have been packed with the duke of Mantua's courtiers and servants. Again, many performances in public opera houses down to the late nineteenth century were ill attended; though partly disguised (for reasons to be explained) by the layout of theatres and by audience habits, a thin house still seemed disappointing. With the rise of the middle class and of democracy, audiences grew larger, requiring bigger theatres. Modern attempts at small-scale opera often take refuge in some other term, like Britten's 'parables' for church performance, or 'music theatre'. Opera is inescapably larger than life.

It has also been addressed to important people. These need not always be high-born or rich: Wagner meant *Der Ring des Nibelungen* as a great national occasion for an audience drawn from the people at large, though economic necessity made him settle for the cosmopolitan and well-heeled. Under the late communist regimes, you got to hear the equivalent of Domingo or Sutherland not by paying a vast sum but by knowing the right party official. Through most of its history opera has been an affair of the ruling classes, however defined, with a fringe of less eminent hearers getting in besides. It is still the thing to take a visiting head of state to, even though he might prefer dancing girls, or *Cats*.

Truly popular opera, attended by many blacksmiths, butchers, petty clerks, commercial travellers, market stallholders, and their families down to children in arms, did exist, but it was both limited in time (from about 1860 to sometime between 1920 and 1950) and confined to cities with a large Italian population: it flourished in Buenos Aires and Brooklyn as well as in Genoa and Naples. Popular opera then gave way to cinema and broadcasting; the recent revival of huge arena stagings looks so far like an offshoot of television, especially since 'Nessun dorma' at the World Cup.

Whether in a pompous or a seedy house, at no time before the late nineteenth century was the audience chiefly concerned with the performance of an opera as a complete work of art. You were not necessarily expected to arrive on time, sit still, keep quiet, concentrate on the stage action, or stay to the end. At most, some of the earliest operas may have held people's attention through their sheer novelty: gasps, swoons, and tears were recorded at Lully's works. But once opera moved into public theatres and people got used to it, new conditions set in.

In Italian towns and at the Paris Opéra the same people were likely to hear the same work many times over—twenty times in a row in an Italian season, forty or fifty times in Paris in the early years. Towns were compact, potential audiences (those with the money to spare) were small: if you went to the opera at all you might well go most nights as long as the season was on.

The cheaper theatres that grew up from the mid-eighteenth century, on the other hand, fed their public a rapidly changing diet, often of mixed plays and operas. In twelve years' management of a Viennese suburban theatre, Emanuel Schikaneder put on 404 productions, most of them far more ephemeral than Mozart's *Die Zauberflöte*. At Béziers in the south of France the theatre in the 1840s gave each year some 115 performances of eighty-five separate programmes, including thirty-five operas (up to ten of them new to the town). Even in Paris the Opéra-Comique in 1825 gave ninety-nine different operas. Here too people came again and again, but such helter-skelter productions clearly were semi-improvised, with much help from the prompter and many off moments.

The Audience

In these conditions no audience could have behaved as ours do. Audiences at concerts and spoken plays, for that matter, chatted and let their attention wander in ways that would not now be tolerated. All this explains how people could cope with the five-hour opera and ballet evenings, the three- to four-hour concerts, the tragedy-and-farce double bills that were the norm. Wagner, followed by Mahler and Toscanini, put an end to the old opera-house manners by darkening the theatre and requiring complete attention for an art which to many people, in the German-speaking lands above all, was increasingly a substitute for religious worship.

Early opera-goers, then, expected to have plenty to look at and wonder at, not just on stage but among their own ranks, and plenty to do on their own account, sometimes away from the auditorium. Where they looked and how they behaved depended on whether they were attending a court opera in the strict sense of the word or a public theatre.

The Vienna court opera in the seventeenth and early eighteenth centuries shows the first type at its purest. The Emperor Leopold I (reigned 1658–1705) was himself an opera composer and took a keen interest in the genre. Yet the way the audience was set out (not always in the same part of the palace) tells us that the point was to show off, first, the monarch, secondly the court, and thirdly the opera; this—generally put on to celebrate an imperial birthday, name day, or wedding, or a great victory— might itself be a vehicle for propaganda, with a title like *La monarchia latina trionfante*.

The audience sat on the long sides of a rectangle—one engraving shows a line of soldiers behind each side, for display rather than for protection or intimidation—with the emperor on a throne in the middle of the short side. This was an old renaissance layout, which in pre-operatic court entertainments such as Florentine intermedi and English masques had sometimes allowed performers to occupy the middle of the rectangle; it ensured that the monarch was the focal point of the spectacle, which ideally was to be witnessed from where he sat. With opera confined to a stage at one end of the rectangle, some of the audience must have had a better view of the emperor and of one another than of the spectacular scenery that was a main point of the entertainment.

This perhaps did not matter too much. Only nobles were allowed into the court opera; when the ladies who sang in an amateur performance were allowed two tickets each to give away, they were limited to their noble acquaintances. Respectable Vienna lawyers or shopkeepers could witness a cavalry ballet given in the palace square (from a space under the stands) but not opera. There, courtiers would be looking at other courtiers, or else at their master—to a courtier, a satisfying sight. They could also thrash out points of etiquette; the seating of ambassadors could just be coped with—not without disputes—but visiting royalty such as Peter the Great raised such problems that they had to be tucked away incognito in a box hidden behind a grille.

Were there really no commoners present? It would be surprising if there had not been, hovering around the edges of the crowd, the courtiers' liveried servants. These were seen as an extension of their masters' personality, part of the family (understood as the household). If they behaved as we know they did in other royal palaces such as Versailles, and at other performances, they must have added a good deal to the sanitary problem facing all opera audiences before 1800 or thereabouts. Besides cloud machines on stage, and panniered skirts in the auditorium, we must imagine an aura of chamber pots and worse.

Opera Houses

These seventeenth-century Vienna operas were representative of much that went on in other German courts, as well as in Warsaw and St Petersburg and at the stiff Franco-Italian court of Turin. In some of these, non-nobles—hand-picked by court officials—were let in. Sometime in the eighteenth century—as late as 1789 in Berlin, half a century earlier in Vienna—part of the opera house was thrown open to anyone who could pay the price of admission. This might amount to no more than the pit (the back of the stalls or orchestra area) and gallery; down to the French Revolution period and sometimes beyond, the monarch might still vet the list of boxholders and reserve the best boxes for nobles.

Italy was somewhat different. Its courts, where opera had begun, included the palaces of great cardinals and nobles as well as those of petty rulers. Venice, the republican city, had invented the public opera house to which anyone with the entrance money (several times a labourer's daily wage) could gain admittance. Opera became so fashionable that by the last quarter of the seventeenth century Italian rulers were encouraging their nobles to set up town theatres on the Venetian model. They themselves might keep on a court theatre for occasional performances but spend most evenings in the new town theatre. Towns without a ruler's court, like Bologna, saw the founding of two or more opera houses of Venetian type, again the property of leading families—usually, to begin with, of a single family, but increasingly as time went on of an association.

The layout of Italian opera houses, like Italian opera itself, came to dominate the genre everywhere outside France down to the late nineteenth century. The important people sat in boxes piled up in tiers, as many as six, and arrayed in horseshoe, bell, or U shape. In many theatres a family owned its own box or part of a box, which it could sell, let, lend, or mortgage. Though the ruler or his representative still sat in the middle of the best tier (usually the second), the design ensured that the people in the boxes were most of the time looking either at the stage or at one another. The theatre was an assembly room for the élite rather than a court.

Because the boxes were partitioned off, their occupants could also spend much of their time looking in rather than out; at La Scala, Milan, before 1830 they could even close the box off from the auditorium by drawing a curtain. Though governments might suspect the worst, banning curtains and (at one time in Rome) cutting down partitions for morality's sake, the point of drawing the curtain—anyhow at fashionable opera performances—was to make possible cosy drawing-room conversation or even a hand of cards.

Not everyone could let a mirror into the back of the box, as the king did in Turin—it enabled him to follow the action while playing cards with his back to the stage—but, unless stopped by government order, people could and did bring in their own coats of arms, furniture, and hangings. They also had a dressing-room across the passage from the box, where their servants could prepare drinks and meals; in the eighteenth century their majordomo or chief clerk might have privileged access to the stalls, their footmen to the gallery or the pit or both, not to mention the corridors; in the foyers they had plenty of room for gambling (allowed at various times up to 1814), for more innocuous games, or for refreshments. To such people the opera house was a home from home; warmer, too—though inadequately heated by wood-burning stoves, it outdid a looming, stone-built Italian palazzo that could scarcely be heated at all.

The French model differed from the Italian in having fewer boxes— only two tiers in Lully's Académie Royale de Musique—and more 'amphitheatres' (raked, unpartitioned balconies) distributed here and there; Lully's theatre even had an area where you could hear but not see the stage. French theatres remained fragmented and far less dominated by boxes and boxholders than those inspired by the Italian model.

In the early part of the century in London, and up to the Revolution in Paris, opera houses allowed part of the audience the expensive privilege of sitting on stage, so that they could at once be seen and ogle, compliment, or proposition the women singers as they squeezed past to go on or off (see above). Further sexism was manifested in the stalls area of Paris opera houses, reserved for men (standees at most times up to the early nineteenth century), whereas in most Italian theatres the stalls came rather earlier to be mixed and at least partly seated; true, army officers there often had the first three rows reserved for them, and did their share of ogling, not to mention talking in parade-ground voices and on occasion standing so as to block everyone else's view.

An unpartitioned top gallery, open to many people besides the servants of the nobility, was in many places a late development, not seen till the late eighteenth or even the late nineteenth century. It usually had a separate entrance and no access to the rest of the house—something still found today in older theatres.

The Opera Experience

Let us suppose that we are going to the opera, in London, Paris, Hamburg, or any North Italian town, at any time between about 1700 and 1860; from about 1800 we could also imagine that we are in any large French- or German-speaking town, or in Barcelona, Cadiz, Amsterdam, Stockholm, Odessa, or (a little later) New York, Buenos Aires, or Constantinople. In other words, we are in a place where opera is not the preserve of a court.

Before we go, we are likely to have heard or read a good deal about the forthcoming opera season. The arrival of the company, whether hired by the year (as in many places outside Italy) or by the season (as in nearly all Italian theatres), has given rise to plenty of gossip. This concerns not just singers' rumoured love affairs but their voices: in this pre-recording age, scarcely anyone in town has heard any of them before; much of their potential appeal lies in their novelty, and the management may take a singer to court for letting himself be heard ahead of the season in somebody's drawing-room or in church. Newspapers echo this gossip; even where there is no periodical press, as in Rome in the early years, handwritten newsletters give details, for instance of the forty-seven entertainments (operas and plays, public and semi-private) planned for the Rome carnival of 1696. By the early nineteenth century many lightweight magazines aimed at women as well as men centre on opera news and gossip, above all in the despotic Italian states (where politics are unmentionable) but in Paris too.

If we belong to the élite of the town this preliminary chatter has helped to make up our minds on an important question: shall we subscribe for the season? If we own a box, shall we use it? (This as a rule means contributing a sum to the management expenses, or, more precisely, undertaking to pay it and then—often—waiting to be dunned for it). Or shall we, on the contrary, let the box for the season, or even night by night? The answer depends a good deal on what we make of the prospectus: not only the singers but the works announced are likely to be new to us. But it also depends on how well-off we feel—during an agricultural depression our incomes go down steeply and we are even shorter of cash than usual—and perhaps on political circumstances such as revolution or war.

We now set off for the opera house, and run into a traffic jam. This is just as likely to be true if we are in Paris in the late seventeenth century as anywhere else, possibly truer: there are few surer recipes for a jam than cramming into narrow streets a lot of heavy coaches drawn by four or six horses and owned by aristocrats with a keen nose for precedence. If we want to catch the beginning of Lully's opera we may have to reach the approaches to the theatre an hour ahead. Jams are likely to be just as bad after the performance: in Naples about 1820 we cool our heels under the San Carlo canopy while a princess's horses block the way.

This traffic problem, though often the subject of police regulations, has never been solved for the sort of opera performance that draws the carriage trade. Before the Covent Garden fruit and vegetable market moved out of central London in 1974 the worst jams came on Wagner nights, when the late curtain ran into the first cabbage lorries. The coming of efficient public transport in the nineteenth century was some help, but last trains to the suburbs meant anxious moments for part of the audience and, in 1860s' Paris, cuts in long works such as Verdi's *Don Carlos*.

We reach the opera house. If all we can afford is 'the gods' we find a crowd waiting at the bottom of the stairs for the arrival of the subcontractors who have bought the right to sell the gallery tickets: two shabbily dressed men, perhaps, with a lantern, a key, and a rough box. They take our money; we then join a collective dash up many flights of stairs, for the gallery (like the theatre as a whole but for the boxes) is unnumbered: first come, first seated on what are no more than steps or backless benches.

In the stalls the principle is the same but the procedure is more complicated. You are unlikely to find a crush to get in unless on a particularly fashionable first or last night—in which case you may well be borne in on a tide of distraught people, losing a hat or a shoe on the way. But such evenings are rare.

You do not always pay for a seat: in an Italian opera house you are likely to pay something just to get into the building, and may well have a subscription ticket for the purpose; then, if you choose, you need not bother to go into the auditorium, but may content yourself with gambling, eating, drinking, chatting, and possibly visiting friends in their boxes. If you do go into the stalls (which may cost an extra sum) you will find nearly everywhere that besides a number of benches there is plenty of room to stand or to walk about, and a number of people, mainly men, are doing so—with their hats on.

In France, as we have seen, everyone stands, though the Revolution for a time brings all-seated stalls as a mark of popular dignity—in curious harmony with the San Carlo in Naples, an ultra-monarchical house where, likewise, everyone sits from its opening in 1737. In London, the standing space is known as Fops' Alley, and the perambulating fops try to defend it against whittling down in the nineteenth century. In many theatres there are a few locked stalls seats with arm rests; if you want one you again pay a flunkey to unlock it.

These flunkeys, by the way, in eighteenth-century Italy are masked. Like much else in opera, this is a Venetian invention. Venice, ruled by a discreet aristocracy that held power for a thousand years, found a useful way to keep revelling crowds in order was to exploit the fashion for wearing masks. If a croupier was masked, no one could tell who he might be. A masked usher at the opera house shared in this anonymity, and might hope to outface a truculent member of the upper classes. In Italy to this day a theatre or cinema usher is called a *maschera*, though the mask has long since gone.

All this coming and going—and standing—means that a thin house does not look as thin as the same numbers would today. Like the House of Commons, it may empty for boring bits and fill up for exciting bits. At the New York Academy of Music in 1865, the bulk of the audience makes for the foyers when a notoriously poor tenor is announced as an emergency replacement in *Il trovatore*, but when he suddenly manages a loud high C many of them come back.

There are also plenty of people with free entry who can help to fill up parts of the house. Before a date close to one of the French revolutions (1789 or 1830) many of these freeloaders are hangers on of authority, down to such a personage as the apothecary by appointment to a ducal court. After the revolutions the free list is shorter, though in Paris especially it still includes many journalists. The management is also happy to give out free entrance tickets to its own employees: in times when the house is unlikely to be full they might as well have something to eke out their wages and please their friends. Just occasionally something goes wrong and, touts aiding, more people turn up than there is room for: hence a riot, as at the first night of Donizetti's *Adelia*, in Rome in 1841, which has to be stopped.

What you see once you are in the auditorium varies a good deal with time and with the kind of opera on offer. The light you see it in changes. We cannot picture an auditorium wholly lit by candles or by oil-lamps; the best help is the candlelit Venetian gambling casino in Stanley Kubrick's film *Barry Lyndon*, a wonderful evocation of a soft bloom of light now unknown. Gaslight, in contrast, is harsh, though the fussiness of Victorian dress and decoration may do something to absorb and refract, and people used to gas-lamps in everyday life may adjust their eyes to it.

Do you at once see an audience glittering with silks and diamonds, as in a Hollywood costume film of the 1930s? Sometimes you do—at court; on any well-attended night in London, where full evening dress is required in the stalls and boxes and, for much of the eighteenth century, men glitter as much as women; in the more fashionable seasons elsewhere. In English-speaking countries, where opera is a foreign import, a long tradition of dressing the house with exotic or exciting visitors goes back to 1710, when four men alleged to be 'Red Indian kings' are put on display in the stage boxes. But there are plenty of occasions when the audience is dowdy or even *louche*.

We are again helped by a marvellous historical reconstruction on film, the Russian version of Chekhov's *Lady with a Little Dog*. The hero pursues a married woman to the provincial town of Saratov and eventually to the opera house. Most people in the audience look jaded, their clothes none too spruce or well chosen; they have all seen one another too often; the theatre could do with refurbishing; the evening barely improves on staying at home. There have been many evenings like that, not only in Russia but all over the Western world.

Another fictional account, in Flaubert's *Madame Bovary*, has Emma and her small-town doctor husband attending a performance at Rouen of *Lucie de Lammermoor* (the French-language version of Donizetti's opera). The audience, drawn from the surrounding mill-town area, talks cottons and dyes; dandies parade in pink or apple-green cravats; painted trees on stage shake whenever a singer takes a step; Dr Bovary tries to follow the plot and announces, 'Her hair is down: it looks like ending badly.' Yet for Emma the opera works an emotional trigger—she meets again the young clerk Léon and embarks on a love affair—as it will, half a century later, for the repressed English visitors to Tuscany in E. M. Forster's *Where Angels Fear to Tread*.

The widest range of brilliance or dowdiness can be found in Italy and Germany between about 1750 and 1914. So much opera goes on that there is bound to be a hierarchy of theatres and seasons. At the top stands the fashionable season of serious opera in the leading theatre in the town, attended night after night by virtually the whole of the élite. In Italy, and in some German towns such as Munich, the season is usually carnival (from Boxing Day to Shrove Tuesday). Then come seasons of comic opera or Singspiel at other times, seasons of serious opera in lesser theatres, and so on down to puppet operas or mixed bills of spoken plays and sung intermezzi or farces such as the novelist Lady Morgan witnesses in Rome in 1820: at the 'smoky and time-stricken' Teatro Pace, the boxes are packed with groups of tradespeople, every one worthy of a Flemish genre painter:

The prompter, with his head popped over the stage lights, talked to the girls in the pit; the violoncello flirted with a handsome [woman from the wrong side of the Tiber] in the boxes; and a lady in a stage box blew out the lamplighter's candle as often as he attempted to light it, to the infinite amusement of the audience.

Even to such a house the upper classes go slumming once a season, for fun, but for regular visits they stick to 'their' theatre and season. And even in the leading Rome opera house in the off season, late-eighteenth-century programmes of plays and intermezzi bring out the shopkeeping and artisan audience: this means much eating and lovemaking in the boxes, sometimes with prostitutes, and quarrels breaking out in the gallery, to be subdued when the soldier on duty there calls the patrol by banging the butt of his musket on the floor.

There are indeed—at least in Italy and Germany—soldiers wherever we look save in the boxes: soldiers outside the main entrance and the stage door, soldiers in the main foyer, and soldiers or police all over the auditorium. At the seventeenth-century imperial court—we have seen—

they were decorative; they still are, for soldiers before the Boer War wear scarlet, bright blue, white and gold, froggings, braid, plumes. Even in countries that do not set a military guard on theatres, officers off duty go to the opera and, by the late nineteenth century, stand out against the penguin get-up of civilian men.

When a state does set a guard on a public opera house the motive is fear of riot. Let us say that on this particular night nothing holds out the prospect of disturbance; we note the soldiers as we walk in, feeling, according to our political outlook, a shiver of apprehension or satisfaction.

Are we, at this point, hungry or well fed? But for the early years, when performances may start in the early afternoon, the curtain goes up more or less as now—about 7 p.m. or a little later. (An exception is the Ascension Fair in late-eighteenth-century Venice, a fortnight's social whirl in late May or June, when performances start at 11 p.m. and go on till 3; fashionables then walk in St Mark's Square, or take a gondola to a private pavilion where they watch the sun rise). This means that a mid-Victorian high civil servant or banker who, like Trollope, spends 'six hours a day at the shop' from 10 till 4 and then dines at 5, still has time to dress and get to the opera without a rush. There isn't the question, a live one since the upper and upper-middle classes started dining at 7 or later, whether to eat before or after the performance or just grab a sandwich.

Opera-goers none the less develop an appetite: hence supper, which can take many forms from the ices served gratis by a seventeenth-century cardinal to the brown bread and sausage an artisan chews on in the gallery. Italian boxholders with their dressing-rooms have the resources to enjoy complete meals, but others in all countries can take advantage of refreshment rooms, often more spacious in continental Europe than the well-named crush bars in Anglo-Saxon theatres built for profit. What the refreshment rooms serve is seldom recorded: chocolate (in the eighteenth century), wines and liqueurs, ices, some kind of food. Eating and drinking, and then sitting in a stuffy theatre, tends to put one to sleep, but to this day people of normally sober habits find that an outing to Glyndebourne or Salzburg, or even to Covent Garden, calls for smoked salmon and champagne as an outing to Stratford-upon-Avon, say, does not. Nor is this just a crass northern trait: Parma boxholders still do themselves well on the local superfine ham, salami, and wine.

After eating and drinking one may need a lavatory. What if anything early opera houses provide is seldom clear. Pepys's diary shows that seventeenth-century wooden theatres have nothing: when a woman he is with urgently needs to go he has to escort her to a nearby inn. Internal sanitary regulations of 1789 at La Scala, Milan, record large buckets meant for urine only; experience, they state, shows that 'on unusually crowded nights many pass water elsewhere than into the buckets', while the buckets themselves 'sometimes fill up rapidly because servants attending on boxholders furtively empty into them not just water but all kinds of ordure'. Men and women in the boxes—this suggests—can meet all their needs thanks to their dressing-rooms and to chamber pots (dealt with, one way or another, by servants); men in other parts of the house can use a *pissoir* of sorts; women not in a box have no resource.

These regulations, however, show La Scala striving to join the movement towards better public hygiene, already pioneered in Britain with the invention of the water-closet. La Scala is usually the first Italian opera house to bring in new devices: we may assume a fairly rapid spread of modern lavatories, there and elsewhere, in the early nineteenth century. By 1850, when Mrs Gladstone—wife of the future prime minister—has to leave the Teatro Nuovo, Naples, because of the stink, it comes as a surprise; but then the Nuovo ('new' in 1724) is a second-rank opera house in a city not known for hygiene. Not that many opera houses even today have solved the problem of the queue for the ladies' room.

We also know curiously little of what goes on in the gaming rooms, except in nineteenth-century Baden-Baden and Monte Carlo where the opera house is an annexe of the casino rather than—as in eighteenth-century Italy and in parts of Napoleonic Europe—the other way round. The few contemporaneous comments dwell, perhaps inevitably, on the man of good family who loses a fortune, goes home, and shoots himself: happy gamblers have no history.

The climax of all this eating, drinking, and gambling in the opera house is the masked ball, held usually after one of the last performances of the carnival season, but sometimes on its own; the stalls are emptied or covered over for dancing, while the stage may house a banquet. At the height of its popularity in Italy, from about 1748 to 1848, some opera houses give as many as twelve balls in a row—the high spot of the social year. When imitated in Paris and London, however, the masked ball may be denounced as immoral: 'very commonly the ruin of ladies of the first quality' runs one early comment in London, where the bishop bans it in 1724. By the early nineteenth century the opera ball (no longer necessarily masked, but perhaps costumed) has an aura of low life and drunkenness: the burning down of Covent Garden in 1856 during one such ball leads to much moralistic head-shaking, even though the fire started in the roof.

In Italy, its first home, the masked ball bothers governments: the mask, originally imposed (like the accompanying black cloak) to stop Venetian nobles from competing to display their wealth, might be used to hide not just misconduct but conspiracy. After 1792, no one can forget that King Gustav III of Sweden was assassinated at a masked ball in his own opera house (not exactly as shown in Verdi's opera). At sensitive moments, governments forbid masking; at most times they demand that maskers in the opera house should be 'decently dressed', which rules out most of the population and ensures that any unaccustomed social mixing will be discreet. Only in disturbed times, like the early years of the Napoleonic regime, do some maskers assume the freedom to go where they like: in 1803, the governor of Parma has to issue a decree empowering boxholders to keep some maskers out of their boxes.

The requirement of 'decent dress' is only one among several bars on who is allowed in, where they may sit, and what they may do. The 'noble parterre' (part of the stalls) at the rebuilt Kärntertortheater in Vienna (1761) earns the nickname 'the ox corral'; it is probably one of a number of areas set aside for the aristocracy in German opera houses, apart from the boxes, especially the first two tiers, which *ancien régime* nobles in any case tend to monopolize. In some places the government controls ambassadors' seating, just as it did at court, to avoid disputes over precedence. Until the Napoleonic regime puts an end to such distinctions, some Italian governments forbid 'mechanics' (people whose trade involves manual labour) or Jews to take boxes in the first two tiers. Worse prohibitions face Jews in some central European towns: at Prague in 1738 they may attend the opera only by special arrangement, in a place other than the theatre attended by the gentile population, and must then be escorted back to the ghetto by the watch—to 'guard against any untoward event', presumably an attack by hostile townspeople.

Social distinction, visible and invisible, is altogether the mark of *ancien régime* opera, with some carry-over into recent times. Until a date somewhere between 1789 and the mid-nineteenth century, many opera houses charge nobles more than commoners, men more than women; in pre-revolutionary Turin only noblewomen may have a torchbearer to light their way, while in Parma only the first two tiers of boxes may have their own candles. All this strengthens the role of the opera house as a meeting-place of the élite, hierarchically arrayed. Hence the power of a scene such as that in which the adulterous Anna Karenina, back in St

Petersburg, goes to the opera and is insulted by a woman acquaintance in the next box: her lover (who goes on his own) has already recognized 'some forty of the *real* people'—those who are it; Anna's flight marks her banishment.

In places smaller than the Russian capital the audience are most of them acquainted not only with one another but, for good or ill, with the representative of authority—there he is in his box—and with some of the singers: the prima donna at least has had many upper-class visitors and invitations, both to people's houses and (during the ballet) to their boxes. This can make the performance into a social drama more absorbing than the opera itself.

Are we to applaud? *Ancien régime* etiquette forbids it if the monarch is present and does not choose to lead the applause: hence some eerily glacial first nights. Dare we demand an encore? Or boo or (in Latin countries where it is equivalent to hissing) whistle? Official regulations, in the Italian states especially, forbid all that as well. But audience enthusiasm or discontent knows no such bounds. Many incidents show a contest between the audience and the powers that be, ending sometimes in riot and arrests (with the theatre cleared by soldiers), sometimes in concessions.

Audience and singer may be at odds not because of a bad performance but because an admired artist's social relations with the élite have gone sour. This is the likely explanation of what happens at La Scala in 1780 to the soprano Caterina Gabrielli, near the end of a glorious career. Despite frantic applause, she refuses an encore at the end of Act 1; the ballet begins but, in the face of continuing hubbub, is cut short; Gabrielli appears and starts her encore, only for the audience to take 'revenge' by all coughing or blowing their noses at once; she flees into the wings, at which the theatre explodes in a torrent of insults; she then, according to report, faints, vomits, and goes into convulsions. Yet Gabrielli is a seasoned veteran. On a milder note, many Buenos Aires boxholders troop to Maddalena Mariani Masi's dressing-room when, on a night in 1875, she loses her voice and has to cry off the mad scene in *Lucia*: they have met her socially and wish to commiserate.

The good side is the creative part an audience plays when all goes well. This is reported of Italians in particular: in the 1880s, as the tradition nears its end, a visitor finds that the Genoa audience still chatters unconcernedly through the choruses; when a brilliant passage comes round, however, it gives the singers and musicians its unanimous 'straightforward sympathy and... tangible, though subtle, help'. This probably means—as we know from other witness—not just a rapt hush but an occasional intake of breath or short sharp 'bravo!', 'very encouraging to the singers'. At such moments it is not too much to speak of communion between audience and cast.

We are now, however, entering the period around the turn of the nineteenth and twentieth centuries when the old order in the opera house begins to give way to the new. By the end of the First World War opera as a social occasion has undergone a marked change. It has become at once more demanding, more orderly, and more impersonal.

Wagner in 1876 darkened the Bayreuth theatre. No one was to attend to anything other than the work; the theatre in its original state—a structure meant to be temporary—in any case did away with boxes, foyers, refreshment rooms, and all such distractions, as well as with gold leaf and plush. Long rows of seats set on a shallow rake enabled each member of the audience to see and hear as well as every other. No question of arriving late or leaving early: there were no aisles. You were there for the opera and for nothing else: it started in mid-afternoon and went on till late, with a long dinner interval; all you could do the rest of the time was walk or drive in the hills and prepare for the main rite. In the darkened Festspielhaus, all were worshippers—known, at the height of the Wagner craze in the 1880s and 1890s, as 'pilgrims'.

Like other revolutions, Wagner's was extreme; other theatres and opera-goers did not literally copy its extremism, yet they were powerfully influenced by it, as we are to this day. Its influence worked alongside other trends in late-nineteenth-century society. Cities were now much larger, the professional and business classes much more numerous and more varied, communications more rapid; only in a small town could a narrow élite, all known to one another, go on dominating the opera house. Rising incomes and the spread of modern comforts led more and more theatres by the 1880s to take benches out of the stalls, fill them with chairs with arm rests, and cut standing room down to almost nothing; promenading was out. New theatres had fewer boxes and more open balconies, and some older theatres followed suit by taking down partitions.

By the late 1890s the leading conductors of the day, Arturo Toscanini and Gustav Mahler, were setting out to darken the opera house and discourage late-comers. Toscanini did not succeed at the first attempt—to his disgust, the management yielded to audience protests and turned the lights half on again—but that battle was soon won. Keeping out late-comers took a good deal longer. Shaw in 1891 could still record an 'unusually copious influx of young barbarians' into the Covent Garden boxes, chattering and laughing through the *Fidelio* overture. Mahler in Vienna would at first turn round and glare at stragglers, pince-nez lenses flashing; later he provided a box, a kind of 'sin bin', where they had to sit until the interval.

When the Emperor Francis Joseph heard of Mahler's disciplinary measures he is said to have remarked 'But after all, the theatre is meant to be a pleasure.' This was the time when some people began to feel that going to the opera was a penance. Many in earlier audiences had disliked particular operas; many no doubt were unmusical. But this mattered little when you could talk to your companions, observe other people's clothes, notice who was with whom, or take a turn in the foyer, perhaps joining in a card game. Now you were trapped; all was dark; you must keep quiet. No wonder *Parsifal*—to some people—seemed interminable, while for others even *Aida* perked up only when the ballet came on.

Early warning of this state of things came in a Parisian boulevard comedy of 1861, Labiche's *La Poudre aux yeux*. Two young people wish to get engaged; their crassly bourgeois families compete in pretending to be much grander than they are. To keep up with the Duponts, each rents an expensive box at the fashionable, all-singing Théâtre-Italien, whereas their sort would normally go, if at all, to the Opéra-Comique with its spoken French dialogue. None of them likes it; one of the wives goes to sleep, and one of the fathers complains: 'They're always giving the same work. Four times we've been to it already—four times to *Rigoletto*! For a start, it's in Italian—you can't make out a thing!' And as they bow to each other from their boxes they have visions of 'an infinity of *Rigolettos*' to be endured.

If the denouement had not saved them from such a fate they would shortly have found relief in the spread of repertory opera, which was setting in about that time. Fewer and fewer new operas were being created; opera-goers were now content to hear the same dozen or two old works again and again, with a novelty once in a while. But they did not, as before, hear an opera twenty times in a season; instead they might hear it ten times in forty years, each time with a different cast that had come together specially, often with minimal rehearsal or none. In Germany and Italy this came to mean that subscribers were entitled to go once to each opera in the season's programme.

The new system, together with the anonymity of a metropolis and, nowadays, the spread of tourism, has broken up the cohesion of audiences where people once saw one another night after night. In London, Paris, or New York one can now go without meeting a single acquaintance; the person next to you has probably dropped in from Tokyo.

Change has been slower in a place like Milan, where something of the old centrality of opera lingers on. La Scala met great resistance a few years ago when it tried to reshuffle some subscribers, for instance from *turno B* (the third performance of every opera) to *turno C* (the fourth). 'I can't give up *turno B*', one woman told me, 'it's where I meet most of my friends.' The persistence of the subscription system in Italy and Germany explains why visitors may be told at the box-office that only the worst seats are available, and then find great gaps in the best parts of the house: for one reason or another—word may have got about that the performance is poor—some regulars have not bothered to turn up.

Outside Glyndebourne, Salzburg, and one or two other such festive places audiences no longer feel the old urge to dress up. This is particularly true of the last twenty-five years; it marks not so much a change in the social make-up of opera-goers as wider changes in dress habits making for informality (the displacement of long gowns by short, of jackets by blousons). In the dressiest of countries, Italy, politics does come in: after years of La Scala first nights awash in diamonds and furs, the 1968 students' revolt saw the season in with a riot of egg- and tomato-throwing. Since then, dress has been subdued—relatively. (A Venetian woman explained to me in about 1980 how she reached La Fenice unscathed. As is the way in Venice, she had to walk; she pinned up her long dress, put on wellingtons and a raincoat, then, when safely inside the doors of the theatre, let down her dress and put on the smart evening shoes she had brought in her handbag.)

Throwing eggs at opera-goers at least implies that the occasion matters. With present-day means of communication, opera in the theatre seems more and more subordinate to records and television. We live in what Kierkegaard, a century and a half ago, called an 'age of publicity' when no event is deemed to have happened unless it is announced, discussed, and consecrated in the media.

A new opera—rare bird—is preceded by a barrage of colour supplement articles. Only in places like Leeds and Krefeld are audiences likely to discover a new voice—and even then it has probably been heard already in some televised prize competition. In a leading opera house the performance is no longer a collective act of discovery and mutual agreement or disagreement, still less of moment-by-moment exchange of feeling between auditorium and stage; it ratifies what nearly everyone in the audience has been taught by hearing Pavarotti—or somewhat less famous singers—on records or on the air.

Live voices and instruments still communicate something that the most advanced technology does not: opera-goers may still go through an unconvenanted emotional experience that seems for the moment to unite them. But the occasion can no longer represent them to themselves as a social entity. Men and women at the opera are now like passengers on an inter-city train: bodies sitting side by side for a particular purpose, who do not know one another and will soon part.

FURTHER READING

INTRODUCTION

HISTORIES of opera go back at least to the nineteenth century, with H. S. Edwards' *History of Opera from Monteverdi to Donizetti* (London, 1862) and R. A. Streatfield's *The Opera* (London, 1897) still occasionally turning up in antiquarian shops. Of twentieth-century histories, Donald Jay Grout's *A Short History of Opera* (New York, 1947; 3rd edn., rev. W. H. Williams, 1988) remains the most thoroughgoing; the *History of Opera*, ed. Stanley Sadie (London, 1989) has many interesting contributions; Leslie Orrey's *Opera: A Concise History* (London, 1972; rev. R. Milnes, 1987) is brief and accessible; the *Storia dell'opera italiana*, ed. Lorenzo Bianconi and Giorgio Pestelli (Turin, 1987–), three volumes of which have so far appeared, is ground-breaking in the cultural breadth of its coverage.

A number of important reference books have appeared in the last years. *The Oxford Dictionary of Opera*, ed. John Warrack and Ewan West (Oxford, 1992) is a conveniently concise one-volume dictionary. Larger and more exhaustive is *The Viking Opera Guide*, ed. Amanda Holden (Harmondsworth, 1993). The ultimate reference work, probably for many years to come, is *The New Grove Dictionary of Opera*, ed. Stanley Sadie, 4 vols. (London, 1992). Of earlier dictionaries, *Kobbé's Complete Opera Book*, rev. Earl of Harewood (London, 1987) is still used by many, in particular for its lengthy synopses, and Alfred Loewenberg's *Annals of Opera 1597–1940* (1947; rev. H. Rosenthal, London, 1978) offers details of the local premières of many operas.

On the nature of opera, Joseph Kerman's *Opera as Drama* (1956; rev. edn., Berkeley, 1988) remains controversial and stimulating; Herbert Lindenberger's *Opera: The Extravagant Art* (Ithaca, NY, 1984) and Paul Robinson's *Opera and Ideas: From Mozart to Strauss* (New York, 1985) are valuable contributions from non-specialists. Michel Poizat's *The Angel's Cry: Beyond the Pleasure Principle in Opera* (Ithaca, NY, 1992) offers a highly idiosyncratic interpretation deriving from French psychoanalytic models. Carolyn Abbate's *Unsung Voices: Opera and Musical Narrative in the Nineteenth Century* (Princeton, 1991) is a brilliantly argued lyrical search for opera's true voice.

I. THE SEVENTEENTH CENTURY

The period is well covered in the literature: the following are only the most obvious sources, from which further reading can be gleaned. In terms of broad surveys, Donald Jay Grout's *A Short History of Opera* (New York, 1947; 3rd edn., rev. W. H. Williams, 1988) is still useful, if now somewhat dated; Robert Donington's *The Rise of Opera* (London, 1981) is more focused on philosophical issues; and Lorenzo Bianconi's *Music in the Seventeenth Century* (Cambridge, 1987) covers social, economic, and ideological issues in new and often revealing ways.

For the first part of the seventeenth century (as well as sixteenth-century precedents), Nino Pirrotta's splendid *Music and Theatre from Poliziano to Monteverdi* (Cambridge, 1982) is indispensable; and Oliver Strunk's *Source Readings in Music History: From Classical Antiquity to the Romantic Era* (London, 1952) gives translations of much relevant material. Early Florentine opera and other entertainments are discussed in Tim Carter, *Jacopo Peri (1561–1633): His Life and Works* (New York and London, 1989), and Frederick W. Sternfeld, *The Birth of Opera* (Oxford, 1993); contemporary accounts can be found in Aloys M. Nagler, *Theatre Festivals of the Medici, 1539–1637* (repr. New York, 1976); Robert L. and Norma W. Weaver's *A Chronology of Music in the Florentine Theater, 1590–1750: Operas, Prologues, Finales, Intermezzos and Plays with Incidental Music* (Detroit, 1978) gives some useful listings. The standard text for Monteverdi is Paolo Fabbri's *Monteverdi* (Turin, 1985; an English translation is forthcoming from Cambridge University Press); Denis Arnold's *Monteverdi* in the 'Master Musicians' series (3rd edn., London, 1990) is still useful; John Whenham (ed.), *Claudio Monteverdi: 'Orfeo'*, published in the series of Cambridge Opera Handbooks (1986), and Iain Fenlon's and Peter Miller's *The Song of the Soul: Understanding 'Poppea'* (London, 1992) are the main introductions to Monteverdi's first and last operas; Gary Tomlinson's *Monteverdi and the End of the Renaissance* (Oxford, 1987) offers some important, if slightly idiosyncratic, ideas on the period.

For Roman opera, see Margaret Murata, *Operas for the Papal Court, 1631–1668* (Ann Arbor, Mich., 1981). Venetian opera is the subject of Ellen Rosand's impressive *Opera in Seventeenth-Century Venice: The Creation of a Genre* (Berkeley, 1991), which is the source of a number of the quotations in translation here: this supersedes Simon Townley Worsthorne's *Venetian Opera in the Seventeenth Century* (rev. edn., Oxford, 1968) and Jane Glover's *Cavalli* (London, 1978). Touring companies are discussed in Lorenzo Bianconi and Thomas Walker, 'Dalla *Finta pazza* alla *Veremonda*: storie di Febiarmonici', *Rivista Italiana di Musicologia*, 10 (1975), 379–454, and economic and other issues in id., 'Production, Consumption and Political Function of Seventeenth-Century [Italian] Opera', *Early Music History*, 4 (1984), 209–96. Paolo Fabbri's *Il secolo cantante: per una storia del libretto d'opera nel Seicento* (Bologna, 1990) is an important first step towards a history of the seventeenth-century libretto; other useful details can be culled from Renate Döring, *Ariostos 'Orlando furioso' im italienischen Theater des Seicento und Settecento* (Hamburg, 1973), and Maria Antonella Balsano and Thomas Walker (eds.), *Tasso, la musica, i musicisti* (Florence, 1988). The essays in Michael Collins and Elise K. Kirk (eds.), *Opera & Vivaldi* (Austin, 1984), provide useful coverage of the seventeenth and eighteenth centuries; and the series *Drammaturgia musicale veneta* (Milan, 1983–) is an important collection of facsimiles of contemporary scores.

For France, the standard text remains James R. Anthony's *French Baroque Music: From Beaujoyeaulx to Rameau* (2nd edn., London, 1978), although Robert M. Isherwood's *Music in the Service of the King: France in the Seventeenth Century* (Ithaca, NY, 1973) is still useful. More detailed studies are provided by Joyce E.

Newman, *Jean-Baptiste de Lully and his Tragédies lyriques* (Ann Arbor, 1979), and Cuthbert Girdlestone, *La Tragédie en musique (1673–1750) considérée comme genre littéraire* (Geneva, 1972). England in this period is best covered by Curtis A. Price, *Music in the Restoration Theatre, with a Catalogue of Instrumental Music in the Plays 1665–1713* (Ann Arbor, 1979), and id., *Henry Purcell and the London Stage* (Cambridge, 1984); there is also some useful material in the Norton Critical Score of Purcell's *Dido and Aeneas* (New York, 1986).

2. THE EIGHTEENTH CENTURY: SERIOUS OPERA

For richness and immediacy of commentary and detail, nothing will ever surpass the travel notes of Charles Burney, *The Present State of Music in France and Italy* (London, 1773), and the *Lettres historiques et critiques sur l'Italie* of Charles de Brosses (Paris, 1799). Among modern works, Vernon Lee's *Studies of the Eighteenth Century in Italy* (London, 1880; 2nd edn. 1907) remains one of the most elegant introductions to the world of opera seria in Italy, although Michael Robinson's *Naples and Neapolitan Opera* (Oxford, 1972) and Dennis Libby's superb chapter 'Italy: Two Opera Centres' in *Man & Music: The Classical Style* (London, 1989) now provide the most comprehensive and authoritative introduction to the field. The literary aspects of the Arcadian reform of seventeenth-century opera are still well served by Nathaniel Burt's 'Opera in Arcadia', *Musical Quarterly*, 41 (1955), 145–70. Alan Yorke-Long offers richly detailed vignettes of the genre at four courts in *Music at Court* (London, 1954).

On individual composers, Edward Dent's classic study *Alessandro Scarlatti* (London, 1905) was updated by Thomas Walker in 1960, and Winton Dean has examined Handel's opera both in breadth—*Handel and the Opera seria* (Berkeley, 1969)—and (with J. Merrill Knapp) in depth—*Handel's Operas 1704–26* (Oxford, 1987). On Rameau and French opera, most useful is James R. Anthony's *French Baroque Music* (2nd edn., London, 1978; 2nd edn. 1978). I discuss serious opera in German in Thomas Bauman, *North German Opera in the Age of Goethe* (Cambridge, 1985).

Daniel Heartz's essays 'From Garrick to Gluck', *Proceedings of the Royal Musical Association*, 94 (1967/8), 111–27, and 'Hasse, Galuppi and Metastasio', *Venezia e il melodramma nel Settecento* (Florence, 1981), 309–39, are unsurpassed as broad-ranging portraits of Italian serious opera's situation around mid-century. His essays on Mozart's serious operas in *Mozart's Operas* (Berkeley, 1990) supersede the rather cursory treatment Dent gave them in his own *Mozart's Operas* (London, 1913; 2nd edn. 1947, reissued 1991), illustrating the radical revision of the genre's standing in recent scholarship. See on this score both the symposium proceedings edited by Don Neville in *Studies in Music from the University of Western Ontario*, 7 (1982), and Marita McClymonds's article 'Opera seria' in *The New Grove Dictionary of Opera* (London, 1992), iii, 698–707, including the most recent literature cited there.

3. THE EIGHTEENTH CENTURY: COMIC OPERA

The rather complex situation of Italian comic opera during the first half of the eighteenth century is addressed by Michael Robinson in *Naples and Neapolitan Opera* (Oxford, 1972). Path-breaking essays on the creation of opera buffa proper are Daniel Heartz's 'The Creation of the Buffo Finale in Italian Opera', *Proceedings of the Royal Musical Association*, 104 (1977–8), 67–78, and especially 'Vis comica: Goldoni, Galuppi, and L'Arcadia in Brenta (Venice, 1749)', *Venezia e il melodramma nel Settecento* (Florence, 1981), ii, 33–69.

The vernacular traditions of comic opera with spoken dialogue in France, England, and Germany are best studied in David Charlton's *Grétry and the Growth of Opéra Comique* (Cambridge, 1986), Roger Fiske's comprehensive *English Theatre Music in the Eighteenth Century* (London, 1973; 2nd edn. 1987) and my *North German Opera in the Age of Goethe* (Cambridge, 1985).

The second half of the century is quite naturally dominated by work on Mozart's comic operas. (Good studies in English on Mozart's contemporaries remain distressingly few.) The monographs of Edward Dent, *Mozart's Operas* (London, 1913; 2nd edn. 1947, reissued 1991), and Daniel Heartz, *Mozart's Operas* (Berkeley, 1990), offer companion perspectives by two of our century's most eminent Mozarteans. One must include here as well Wye J. Allanbrook's rich and thoughtful study, *Rhythmic Gesture in Mozart: Le nozze di Figaro and Don Giovanni* (Chicago, 1983). Andrew Steptoe provides an excellent social background to the major comic operas in *The Mozart–Da Ponte Operas* (Oxford, 1988). More idiosyncratic interpretations are offered in William Mann's survey, *The Operas of Mozart* (London, 1977), Brigid Brophy's psychoanalytic study *Mozart the Dramatist* (London, 1964; 2nd edn. 1988), and Ivan Nagel's political-philosophical ramble *Autonomy and Mercy* (Cambridge, Mass., 1991).

4. THE NINETEENTH CENTURY: FRANCE

Many thematic articles, dealing with cities, genres, staging practice, and literary matters, will be found in *The New Grove Dictionary of Opera* (London, 1992). For different overviews of the many-sided cultural picture during this period, four studies will be of interest: *Neo-Classicism* and *Romanticism*, both by Hugh Honour (Harmondsworth, 1968 and 1979); *A Cultural History of the French Revolution* by Emmet Kennedy (New Haven, Conn., 1989); and the authoritative survey of *The French Romantics*, edited by D. G. Charlton (2 vols., Cambridge, 1984). In a period rich in autobiographical revelation, letters and memoirs are an indispensable source of information. English observers include the Second Viscount Palmerston, a selection of whose papers are in *Portrait of a Whig Peer*, ed. Brian Connell (London, 1957); and John Moore, in *A Journal during a Residence in France...1792* (London, 1793). Translated documents include *The Memoirs of Hector Berlioz*, ed. David Cairns (London, 1969, and several subsequent edns.); *The Journal of Eugène Delacroix*, ed. Walter Pach (New York, 1937, and subsequent edns.); and *Giacomo Meyerbeer: His Life as Seen through his Letters*, ed. Heinz and Gudrun Becker (Portland, Or., 1989). Berlioz's *Evenings with the Orchestra*, ed. Jacques Barzun (Chicago, 1956) is a uniquely Romantic combination of musical critique and fiction, centred on opera. For readers of French, composers' letters have been edited by Julien Tiersot (*Lettres de musiciens écrites en français*; Turin, 1924, and Milan, 1936) and by Marc Pincherle (*Musiciens peints par eux-mêmes*; Paris, 1939).

Histories of theatre and drama now regularly include information about opera, acknowledging its major status in the nineteenth-century panorama. Conversely, opera histories can emphasize political and literary matters. Marvin Carlson's *The Theater of the French Revolution* (New York, 1966) and Herbert Lindenberger's *Historical Drama* (Chicago, 1975) fall into the first category; T. J. Walsh's *Second Empire Opera: The Théâtre Lyrique, Paris, 1851–1879* (London, 1981), Lindenberger's *Opera: The Extravagant Art* (Ithaca, NY, 1984), and Jane Fulcher's *The Nation's Image: French Grand Opera as Politics and Politicized Art* (Cambridge, 1987) fall into the second. Valuable chapters on *grand opéra*, the Théâtre-Italien, and the boulevard theatres are in Peter Bloom's lively compendium *Music in Paris in the Eighteen-Thirties* (New York, 1987). The pervasive influence of the novel is explored in Jerome Mitchell's *The Walter Scott Operas* (Birmingham, Ala., 1977) and in several newer books, including Gary Schmidgall's *Literature as Opera* (New York, 1977). Fascinating documentary material has been edited by H. Robert Cohen in *The Original Staging Manuals for Twelve Parisian Operatic Premières* (New York, 1991).

Monographs in English about French composers are not abundant. Berlioz fares better than most, for example in David Cairns's *Berlioz: The Making of an Artist* (London, 1989), D. Kern Holoman's *Berlioz* (London, 1989) and in Ian Kemp's wide-ranging handbook on *Les Troyens* (Cambridge, 1988). Winton Dean's *Bizet* is a classic study (London, rev. edn. 1975). Recent research is available on two other composers: in *Jacques Offenbach*, by Alexander Faris (London, 1980), and *The Operas of Charles Gounod* by Steven Huebner (Oxford, 1990). The unique case of Chabrier is explored in the affectionate *Emmanuel Chabrier and his Circle* by Rollo Myers (London, 1969). Harder to find are Wagner's articles on Halévy and Auber, buried within *Richard Wagner's Prose Works*, ed. W. A. Ellis (vol. v (1896), 35–55, and vol. viii (1899), 175–200).

5. THE NINETEENTH CENTURY: ITALY

A recent survey of nineteenth-century Italian opera may be found in David Kimbell's *Italian Opera* (Cambridge, 1991), chs. 21–32. He deals adequately with Rossini, Bellini, and Verdi, rather skimpily with Donizetti, and somewhat slightingly with Puccini. A better-balanced summary of this period, along with many illustrations, is found in William Weaver's *The Golden Century of Italian Opera: From Rossini to Puccini* (New York, 1988).

A sense of the excitement generated in Rossini's own day may be gleaned from Stendhal's sometimes unreliable *Life of Rossini*, helpfully translated and annotated by Richard N. Coe (Seattle, 1970). Stronger for biography than for discussion of the music is Herbert Weinstock's *Rossini* (New York, 1968). A most readable book, if somewhat old-fashioned, is Radiciotti's three-volume *Gioacchino Rossini, vita documentata, opere ed influenza su l'arte* (Tivoli, 1927–9). A good summary of life and works is Richard Osborne's *Rossini* (revd. edn. London, 1993).

The most comprehensive work on Donizetti is William Ashbrook's *Donizetti and his Operas* (Cambridge, 1982), totally rewritten after his earlier *Donizetti* (London, 1965). Additional material may be found in Herbert Weinstock's *Donizetti and the World of Opera in Italy, Paris and Vienna* (London, 1964). The end-materials of Robert Steiner-Isenmann's *Gaetano Donizetti: Sein Leben und seine Opern* (Bern, 1982) helpfully include a chronology, details of plots, a discography, and a discussion of various stylistic details.

Of all the composers covered in this survey, none stands in greater need of a modern comprehensive examination in English than does Bellini. In the meantime, the handiest is Leslie Orrey's *Bellini*, a part of the Master Musicians series (London, 1969). For those at home in Italian, Adamo's and Lippmann's *Vincenzo Bellini* (Turin, 1981) sheds much light.

One of the high watermarks of recent scholarship on Verdi is Julian Budden's three-volume *The Operas of Verdi* (London, 1973, 1979, and 1981; rev. edn., Oxford, 1992). Other useful books are *The Verdi Companion*, ed. William Weaver and Martin Chusid (New York, 1979), David Kimbell's *Verdi in the Age of Italian Romanticism* (Cambridge, 1981), and Frank Walker's *The Man Verdi* (London, 1962). One of the most frustrating books in the huge Verdi literature is Franco Abbiati's *Giuseppe Verdi*, 4 vols. (Milan, 1959), which is filled with inaccuracies but contains invaluable documentation. Mary Jane Phillips-Matz's *Verdi: A Biography* (Oxford, 1993) is a detailed account of Verdi's life with much new information.

'Quixotic though helpful' describes Mosco Carner's *Puccini: A Critical Biography* (London 1958, rev. 1974). Limiting itself to the stage works, William Ashbrook's *The Operas of Puccini* (Ithaca, NY, 1985) gives a general background. Containing many, but not all, of Puccini's letters is *Carteggi pucciniani*, ed. Eugenio Gara (Milan, 1958); others are to be found in Giuseppe Adami's *Giacomo Puccini: Epistolario* (in an English translation: New York, 1974); still more in Vincent Seligman's *Puccini among Friends* (New York, 1938).

Full bibliographies of these and other figures may be found in *The New Grove Dictionary of Opera* (London, 1992).

6. THE NINETEENTH CENTURY: GERMANY

The general reader in search of further broad overviews of German Romantic opera could do no better than John Warrack's masterly survey 'Germany and Austria' in the New Grove Handbook *History of Opera* (London, 1989) or that of Winton Dean, 'German Opera', in the *New Oxford History of Music*, viii (Oxford,

1982). Warrack is also Britain's leading authority on Weber, whose operas are fully discussed in his *Carl Maria von Weber* (London, 1968; 2nd edn. 1976), while in 'Richard Wagner and Weber's *Euryanthe*', *19th-Century Music*, 9 (1985–6), Michael C. Tusa draws attention to some striking parallels between Weber's work and Wagner's *Tannhäuser* and *Lohengrin*. The major study of Spohr in English remains Clive Brown's *Louis Spohr* (Cambridge, 1984), and the other major figure of emergent German Romantic opera is dealt with by A. Dean Palmer in *Heinrich August Marschner: His Life and Stage Works* (Ann Arbor, 1980).

If few of the second-rank composers who feature in this chapter have received the attention they deserve in critical studies, that is true in particular of Lortzing and Nicolai. Entries on these composers and their works (and indeed on all the figures discussed here) can, however, be read in *The New Grove Dictionary of Opera* (London, 1992). One other significant contemporary of Wagner's is treated by John Warrack in 'Mendelssohn's Operas', in *Essays in Honour of Winton Dean*, ed. Nigel Fortune (Cambridge, 1987).

The Sorcerer of Bayreuth himself, along with his works, is discussed by the present author in Barry Millington, *Wagner* (2nd edn., London, 1992), and again in *The Wagner Compendium*, ed. Millington (London, 1992). The latter volume contains a comprehensive survey of the musical background to, and influences on, Wagner's operas by Thomas S. Grey, as well as studies of the works from various points of view by Arnold Whittall, Stewart Spencer, and others. General studies of Wagner's works from the musical point of view are surprisingly uncommon, but Ernest Newman's classic *Wagner Nights* (London, 1949) remains the most detailed commentary. *The Wagner Companion*, ed. Peter Burbidge and Richard Sutton (London, 1979), has several useful chapters, as does *The Wagner Handbook*, ed. John Deathridge (London, 1992), while for the specialist *Analyzing Opera: Verdi and Wagner*, ed. Carolyn Abbate and Roger Parker (Berkeley, 1989), contains much of interest.

With one exception, there are no full-scale studies in the English language relating to the life or works of any of the post-Wagnerian school of composers; Hugo Wolf alone has received the accolade of a proper biography—that by Frank Walker (London, 1951). In German, there is a comprehensive volume devoted to Cornelius—*Peter Cornelius als Komponist, Dichter, Kritiker und Essayist*, ed. Helmut Federhofer (Regensburg, 1977)—and Humperdinck is dealt with in a pair of studies: E. Thamm, *Stilkritische Bemerkungen zum Schaffen Engelbert Humperdincks* (Cologne, 1974), and H. J. Irmen, *Die Odyssee des Engelbert Humperdinck: eine biographische Dokumentation* (Siegburg, 1975). Peter P. Pachl's *Siegfried Wagner: Genie im Schatten* (Munich, 1988) is a valuable guide to the life and works of the Bayreuth master's son and heir.

7. RUSSIAN, CZECH, POLISH, AND HUNGARIAN OPERA TO 1900

There are no studies of opera in the region as a whole but Jim Samson's 'East Central Europe: The Struggle for National Identity' in the volume he edited in the 'Man & Music' series *The Late Romantic Era* (London, 1991) provides an excellent introduction to the historical and cultural background and its implications. Of the individual operatic traditions Russian opera is by far the best served as far as literature in English is concerned. The only monographic treatment of the subject, Rosa Newmarch's *The Russian Opera* (London, n.d.), is outdated and often little more than plot summaries. Gerald Seaman's *History of Russian Music* (Oxford, 1967) includes material on the early period of Russian opera up to Dargomïzhsky. There are detailed treatments of opera in composer monographs such as David Brown's *Mikhail Glinka: A Biographical and Critical Study* (London, 1974), and his four-volume study *Tchaikovsky: A Biographical and Critical Study* (London, 1978–92). Rimsky-Korsakov is less well treated but he has left his own memoirs (*My Musical Life*) which deal very fully with his operas and which are available in an English translation (New York, 1923, rev. 1942; many later reprints). Musorgsky's operas are usefully handled in '*Khovanschchina*' *Modest Musorgsky*, ed. Jenny Batchelor and Nicholas John (ENO Opera Guide, London, 1994), and in Caryl Emerson and Robert Oldani's *Modest Musorgsky and 'Boris Godunov'* (Cambridge, 1994).

Two writers in particular dominate the literature in English on Russian opera: Gerald Abraham and Richard Taruskin. Although he has published general summaries in *The New Oxford History of Music*, vols. viii (1982) and ix (1990), Abraham's most valuable writings on Russian opera are short articles on particular works or topics, published in a variety of journals. Many have been collected and can be found in the following publications by Abraham: *On Russian Music* (London, 1939, repr. 1980); *Slavonic and Romantic Music: Essays and Studies* (London, 1968); *Essays on Russian and East European Music* (Oxford, 1985). These last two volumes also include articles on Polish and Czech opera.

Taruskin's dissertation *Opera and Drama in Russia as Preached and Practiced in the 1860s* (Ann Arbor, 1981) centres on the now almost forgotten figure of Serov but he also provides comprehensive before-and-after essays which illuminate the influence of Glinka and Dargomïzhsky. Taruskin's penetrating Musorgsky essays have been collected in *Musorgsky: Eight Essays and an Epilogue* (Princeton, 1992).

Information on Polish and Hungarian opera is scanty in English but useful up-to-date material can be found on the CD sets which have come out of Erkel's *Hunyadi László* and Moniuszko's *Halka*. There are two slighter English-language books on Moniuszko: B. M. Maciejewski's *Moniuszko: Father of Polish Opera* (London, 1979) and Jan Prosnak's pictorially engaging *Moniuszko* (Cracow, 1980). One German-language book is recommended to fill out information on Erkel, Gyula Véber's *Ungarische Elemente in der Opernmusik Ferenc Erkels* (Bilthoven, 1976), providing useful historical background and detailed analyses of all the operas.

There are monographs in English on the two major Czech opera composers of the nineteenth century, Smetana and Dvořák, with sections on their operas: John Clapham's *Antonín Dvořák: Musician and Craftsman* (London, 1966) and

Smetana (London, 1972), and Brian Large's more detailed *Smetana* (London, 1970). John Tyrrell's *Czech Opera* (Cambridge, 1988) tackles the subject in chapters on theatres, composers, librettists, subject-matter, voice types, use of folk music, and word-setting.

8. THE TWENTIETH CENTURY: TO 1945

Further information about twentieth-century opera has to be sought in studies of particular composers and particular works. The classic English-language composer monographs relevant to this period include Halsey Stevens's *The Life and Music of Béla Bartók* (New York, 1953; 3rd edn. rev. Gillies, 1993), George Perle's two volumes *The Operas of Alban Berg* (Berkeley, 1980 and 1984), Edward Lockspeiser's two volumes *Debussy, his Life and Mind* (London, 1962 and 1965), Antony Beaumont's *Busoni* (London, 1985), Jaroslav Vogel's *Leoš Janáček* (London, 1962; 2nd edn. 1980), John Tyrrell's *Janáček's Operas: A Documentary Account* (London, 1992), William Mann's *Richard Strauss: A Critical Study of the Operas* (London, 1964) and Norman Del Mar's three-volume *Richard Strauss* (London, 1962–72), Michael Kennedy's *Richard Strauss* (London, 1976; 2nd edn. 1988), Eric Walter White's *Stravinsky* (London, 1966; 2nd edn. 1979), and Stephen Walsh's *The Music of Stravinsky* (London, 1988).

The series of Cambridge Opera Handbooks includes volumes on *Kát'a Kabanová* by John Tyrrell (1982), *Der Rosenkavalier* by Alan Jefferson (1981), *Pelléas et Mélisande* by Roger Nichols and Richard Langham Smith (1989), *Wozzeck* (1989) and *Lulu* (1991) by Douglas Jarman, *Arabella* by Kenneth Birkin (1989), *Salome* (1989) and *Elektra* (1989) by Derrick Puffett, and *The Threepenny Opera* by Stephen Hinton (1990). The Opera Guides published in London and New York in association with English National Opera cover *Der Rosenkavalier* (1982), *Pelléas et Mélisande* (1982), *Arabella* (1985), *Jenůfa* and *Katya Kabanova* (1985), *Salome* and *Elektra* (1988), *Wozzeck* (1990), *Oedipus rex* and *The Rake's Progress* (1991), and *The Stage Works of Béla Bartók* (1991). For a consideration of Schreker and Pfitzner see Peter Franklin's *The Idea of Music* (London, 1985) and John Williamson's *The Music of Hans Pfitzner* (Oxford, 1992).

9. THE TWENTIETH CENTURY: 1945 TO THE PRESENT DAY

There is a rich English-language bibliography of Britten and Tippett, including Arnold Whittall's *Britten and Tippett* (London, 1982; 2nd edn. 1990). Other books on the former include Peter Evans's *The Music of Benjamin Britten* (London, 1979), Patricia Howard's *The Operas of Benjamin Britten* (London, 1969), *The Britten Companion* edited by Christopher Palmer (London, 1984), and Eric Walter White's *Benjamin Britten* (London, 1970; 2nd edn. 1983). There are Cambridge Opera Handbooks on *Peter Grimes* by Philip Brett (1983), *The Turn of the Screw* by Patricia Howard (1985), and *Death in Venice* by Donald Mitchell (1987). The Opera Guides published in London and New York in association with English National

Opera cover *Peter Grimes* and *Gloriana* (1983), and *The Operas of Michael Tippett* (1985). Also on Tippett see his own collections of essays *Moving into Aquarius* (London, 1958; 2nd edn. 1974) and *Music of the Angels* (London, 1980), and Ian Kemp's *Tippett* (London, 1984).

The only other composer of this period comparably well treated is of course Stravinsky: see the bibliography to the preceding chapter and also the Cambridge Opera Handbook on *The Rake's Progress* by Paul Griffiths (1982). Monographs on later composers include David Osmond-Smith's *Berio* (Oxford, 1991), Michael Hall's *Harrison Birtwistle* (London, 1984), Paul Griffiths's *Peter Maxwell Davies* (London, 1982), *György Ligeti* (London, 1983) and *Olivier Messiaen* (London, 1985), and Robin Maconie's *The Works of Karlheinz Stockhausen* (Oxford, 1976; 2nd edn. 1990). Composers' own collections of essays include Glass's *Opera on the Beach* (London, 1988) and Henze's *Music and Politics* (London, 1982).

10. THE STAGING OF OPERA

As yet there is no full-length comprehensive history of operatic staging across Europe and America. Indeed, only one country has been treated with any real thoroughness from the staging angle: Italy, in volumes iv and v of L. Bianconi and G. Pestelli (eds.), *Storia dell'opera italiana* (Turin, 1987–8). Still, many aspects of the subject have been investigated in scattered books, essays, and interviews. The most comprehensive listings of these for the English reader (the material itself is in many languages) are the bibliography to S. Sadie (ed.), *History of Opera* (London, 1989)—see under 'Staging' in its four period sections—and the bibliographies under 'Production', 'Stage Design', and 'Costume' in *The New Grove Dictionary of Opera* (London, 1992). The essays in both publications to which these bibliographies are appended are worth consulting as broad introductions to the subject.

As one way of cutting through the jungle of material on staging, the recommendations which follow are, with one exception, all in English. (Most of the quotations to be found in the staging chapter in this book can be located in one or other of them.) The recommendations are mainly grouped under five historical periods. First, however, some books spanning more than one period, beginning with the one non-English text: H. C. Wolff, *Oper: Szene und Darstellung von 1600 bis 1900* (Leipzig, 1968)—a well-documented book of pictures in the series *Musikgeschichte in Bildern*; R. and H. Leacroft, *Theatre and Playhouse: An Illustrated Survey of Theatre Building from Ancient Greece to the Present Day* (London, 1984); G. Bergman, *Lighting in the Theatre* (Stockholm, 1977); H. Pleasants, *The Great Singers: From the Dawn of Opera to our own Time* (London, 1967); M. Baur-Heinhold, *Baroque Theatre* (London, 1967); and J. Rosselli, *The Opera Industry from Cimarosa to Verdi: The Role of the Impresario* (Cambridge, 1984). There are also some lavish documentations of operas in performance over the years: R. Angermüller, *Mozart's Operas* (New York, 1988); O. G. Bauer, *Richard Wagner: The Stage Designs and Productions from the Premières to the Present* (New York, 1982); and R.

Hartmann, *Richard Strauss: The Staging of his Operas and Ballets* (New York, 1981). The Wagner volume should be supplemented with G. Skelton, *Wagner at Bayreuth* (2nd edn., London, 1976), and B. Millington and S. Spencer (eds.), *Wagner in Performance* (New Haven, 1992).

Translations and studies of Italian material from the seventeenth century include B. Hewitt (ed.), *The Renaissance Stage: Documents of Serlio, Sabbattini and Furttenbach* (Coral Gables, Fla., 1958), on décor, etc.; A. M. Nagler, *Theatre Festivals of the Medici 1539–1637* (New Haven, 1964); versions of Gagliano's preface to *Dafne* in J. Erber's edn. of the opera (London, 1978) and in C. MacClintock (ed.), *Readings in the History of Music in Performance* (Bloomington, Ind., 1979); R. Savage and M. Sansone, '*Il Corago* and the Staging of Early Opera: Four Chapters from an Anonymous Treatise *circa* 1630', *Early Music*, 17 (1989); M. Murata, *Operas for the Papal Court, 1631–1668* (Ann Arbor, 1981); S. T. Worsthorne, *Venetian Opera in the Seventeenth Century*, 2nd edn. (London, 1968); E. Rosand, *Opera in Seventeenth-Century Venice* (Berkeley, 1991). For England in the later seventeenth century, see J. Powell, *Restoration Theatre Production* (London, 1984), and J. Milhous, 'The Multimedia Spectacular on the Restoration Stage', in S. S. Kenny, *British Theatre and the Other Arts, 1660–1800* (Washington, DC, 1984).

Basic texts for the eighteenth century include Marcello's *Teatro alla moda*, trans. R. Pauly in *Musical Quarterly*, 24–5 (1948–9), and Noverre's *Letters on Dancing and Ballets*, trans. C. W. Beaumont (London, 1930). See also the study-cum-anthology by Dene Barnett, *The Art of Gesture: The Practices and Principles of 18th Century Acting* (Heidelberg, 1987). The stage for opera seria is discussed in W. Dean, *Handel and the Opera Seria* (London, 1970), and L. Lindgren, 'The Staging of Handel's Operas in London' in S. Sadie and A. Hicks (eds.), *Handel Tercentenary Collection* (London, 1987). For developments later in the century see D. Heartz, 'From Garrick to Gluck: The Reform of Theatre and Opera in the Mid-18th Century', *Proceedings of the Royal Musical Association*, 94 (1967–8), M. McClymonds, *Niccolò Jommelli: The Last Years, 1769–1774* (Ann Arbor, 1980), and M. Horányi, *The Magnificence of Esterháza* (London, 1962). An interesting recent discovery is described in A. Banducci, 'Staging a *tragédie en musique*: a 1748 promptbook of Campra's *Tancrède*', *Early Music*, 21 (1993).

J. Warrack's *Carl Maria von Weber* (2nd edn., Cambridge, 1976) is valuable for operatic theatre in the earlier nineteenth century, as are J. Black's essay 'Cammarano's Notes for the Staging of *Lucia di Lammermoor*' in the *Donizetti Society Journal*, 4 (1980) and his book *The Italian Romantic Libretto: A Study of Salvadore Cammarano* (Edinburgh, 1984). For the grand-operatic *livret de mise-en-scène*, see H. R. Cohen, *The Original Staging Manuals for 12 Parisian Operatic Premières* (New York, 1991), and for its Italian equivalent, see D. Rosen, 'The Staging of Verdi's Operas: An Introduction to the Ricordi *Disposizioni sceniche*', in D. Heartz and B. Wade (eds.), *International Musicological Society: Report of the Twelfth Congress* (Kassel, 1981). H. Busch has translated two useful collections: *Verdi's 'Aida': The History of an Opera in Letters and Documents* (Minneapolis, 1978) and *Verdi's 'Otello' and*

'*Simon Boccanegra*'... in *Letters and Documents* (Oxford, 1988). For Wagner, see the three books mentioned earlier in this note; also R. Fricke's memories of 1870s Bayreuth translated in the journal *Wagner*, 11–12 (1990–1).

The 1890s to the 1960s: there is an introductory essay on some of the fathers of modern staging in W. Volbach, *Problems of Opera Production* (2nd edn., New York, 1967), and the whole of Volbach's book is instructive on practicalities. Useful works by or on individual directors include R. Beacham, *Adolphe Appia: Theatre Artist* (Cambridge, 1987); C. Innes, *Edward Gordon Craig* (Cambridge, 1983); C. Stanislavski and P. Rumyantsev, *Stanislavski on Opera* (New York, 1975); E. Braun (ed.), *Meyerhold on Theatre* (London, 1969); P. Heyworth, *Otto Klemperer: His Life and Times*, i (Cambridge, 1983), on the Krolloper; P. P. Fuchs (ed.), *The Music Theatre of Walter Felsenstein* (London, 1991); G. Skelton, *Wieland Wagner: The Positive Sceptic* (London, 1971); J. Ardoin and G. Fitzgerald, *Callas* (London, 1974), especially on her relations with Visconti; D. Herbert (ed.), *The Operas of Benjamin Britten* (London, 1979), which includes essays by three directors of Britten premières.

For staging since the 1960s, M. and S. Harries, *Opera Today* (London, 1986) is illuminating, as is the account of the return of 'early opera' in H. Haskell, *The Early Music Revival: A History* (London, 1988). Then there are vivid accounts of Karajan in operation as director in R. Vaughan, *Herbert von Karajan: A Biographical Portrait* (London, 1986), and of Peter Hall in J. Higgins, *The Making of an Opera* (London, 1978). But in the main it is best to go to the horse's mouth: to published interviews, reminiscences, and manifestos by notable directors. Interviews can sometimes be found in the magazine *Opera*, e.g. with G. Friedrich in vol. 36 (1985), D. Alden in 39 (1988), H. Kupfer and D. Freeman in 40 (1989), and N. Hytner in 42 (1991). See also the interview with P. Sellars in A. Bartow (ed.), *The Director's Voice: Twenty One Interviews* (New York, 1988). Directors' published accounts of their own productions include A. Besch in P. Branscombe (ed.), *W. A. Mozart: 'Die Zauberflöte'* (Cambridge, 1991); F. Corsaro, *The Love for Three Oranges: The Glyndebourne Version* (London, 1984); D. Freeman in J. Whenham (ed.), *Claudio Monteverdi: 'Orfeo'* (Cambridge, 1986); and J. Miller, *Subsequent Performances* (London, 1986). Modern composers' attitudes to being staged are exemplified by P. Glass, *Opera on the Beach* (London, 1988), and M. Tippett, *Those Twentieth Century Blues* (London, 1991).

II. OPERA SINGERS

A general introduction to this subject is Henry Pleasants's informed discussion in *The Great Singers* (New York, 1966; rev. 1981). More specialized, but engrossing, is Heriot's *The Castrati in Opera* (London, 1956). Also limited, but this time to singers who made recordings, is John Steane's *The Grand Tradition* (London, 1974), which offers an acute and far-reaching panorama. Limited to a series of interviews with retired singers, Lanfranco Rasponi's *The Last Prima Donnas* (New York, 1982) is entertaining, although it harps, not unsurprisingly, on the theme that their day was superior to the one that follows.

As a literary sub-species the memoirs of singers, all too often self-serving and apt to be idiosyncratically selective in what they choose to include or omit, constitute for most an acquired taste. A handy, fully (and sometimes wickedly) annotated guide to the field may be found in Andrew Farkas's *Opera and Concert Singers* (New York, 1985).

Some worthwhile biographies that can be recommended without reservation are April Fitzlyon's lives of the García sisters, *Maria Malibran* (London, 1987) and *The Price of Genius: A Biography of Pauline Viardot* (London, 1964). Well balanced and researched is Michael Henstock's *Fernando De Lucia* (London, 1990). Much original material turns up in *Enrico Caruso: My Father and his Family* by Enrico Caruso, jun., and Andrew Farkas (Portland, Or., 1990). An account of an amazing life is to be found in Ira Glackens's *Yankee Diva: Lillian Nordica and the Golden Days of Opera* (New York, 1963). A circumspect account of her great contemporary may be sought in John Hetherington's *Melba* (New York, 1967), more reliable than her own ghost-written memoirs. A series of provocative comparisons of the singers active 1900–50 whom he heard or sang with is provided by Giacomo Lauri-Volpi's *Voci parallele* (Milan, 1955).

For those interested in tracing the details of singers' actual careers, a basic source of information is to be found in the chronologies, or *cronistorie*, of various theatres. Two sound ones to start with are Harold Rosenthal's *Two Centuries of Opera at Covent Garden* (London, 1958) and the even more compendious *Annals of the Metropolitan Opera*, ed. Gerald Fitzgerald (Boston, 1989), two volumes.

12. OPERA AS A SOCIAL OCCASION

As a social event, opera has figured in many novels. Those of Flaubert, Tolstoy, and E. M. Forster are quoted in the text; another novelist, Stendhal, has most to say in his non-fiction works, especially his *Life of Rossini*, ed. and trans. R. N. Coe (London, 1956), and *Rome, Naples et Florence* (1826). Historians and sociologists, however, have only recently shown an interest in the subject.

Among early efforts are J. Rosselli, *The Opera Industry in Italy from Cimarosa to Verdi* (Cambridge, 1984), J. Mongrédien, *La Musique en France des Lumières au Romantisme* (Paris, 1986), and P. Barbier, *La Vie quotidienne à l'Opéra au temps de Rossini et de Balzac* (Paris, 1987). The earliest phase of French opera is dealt with by R. M. Isherwood, *Music in the Service of the King* (Ithaca, NY, 1973). We lack studies of opera as a social phenomenon in Germany and Russia.

The many histories of individual opera houses are the most profitable source. Because of strong local patriotism in Italy and Germany, allied to opera-mindedness, some of the best appeared in those countries in the late nineteenth century; the great philosopher Benedetto Croce wrote a full history of *I teatri di Napoli* (first version, 1891). For London, the richest sources are the many publications of J. Milhous and R. D. Hume, especially *Vice-Chamberlain Coke's Theatrical Papers 1706–15* (Carbondale, Ill., 1982), (with C. Price) *The Impresario's Ten Commandments* (1972), and *Italian Opera in London in the Eighteenth Century* (vol. 1, Oxford,

1995; vol. II, forthcoming) and H. Rosenthal, *Two Centuries of Opera at Covent Garden* (London, 1958). Opera in the United States has been studied city by city.

Travellers' accounts are not always reliable; one of the liveliest is Lady Morgan, *Italy* (1821). Among autobiographies that of the baritone Charles Santley, *Student and Singer* (London, 1892), is revealing, as is the criticism of George Bernard Shaw (several volumes, now collected as *Shaw's Music*, ed. Dan H. Laurence, London, 1989). Periodicals can be helpful; one of the best is the *Gaceta Musical* of the operatically important city of Buenos Aires.

CHRONOLOGY

MARY ANN SMART

c.1480   Angelo Poliziano, *Orfeo*, Mantua

1589   intermedi organized in Florence by Giovanni Bardi for wedding of
         Ferdinando I de' Medici and Christine of Lorraine; music by Luca
         Marenzio, Jacopo Peri, and Giulio Caccini

1598   Peri, *Dafne*, Florence

1600   Emilio de' Cavalieri, *Rappresentatione di anima e di corpo*, Rome
         Peri, *Euridice*, Florence
         Caccini, *Il rapimento di Cefalo*, Florence

1601   Caccini, *Euridice* (first performed Florence 1602)

1607   Claudio Monteverdi, *Orfeo*, Mantua

1608   Marco da Gagliano, *Dafne*, Mantua
         Monteverdi, *Arianna*, Mantua (lost, except for 'Lamento')

1619   Stefano Landi, *La morte d'Orfeo*, Venice

1627   Heinrich Schütz, *Dafne*, Torgau

c.1630   *Il corago*, anonymous Florentine treatise on operatic staging

1632   Landi, *Sant'Alessio*, Rome

1637   opening of first ever public opera house, the Teatro Tron in Venice

1639   Marco Marazzoli, *Chi soffre speri*, Rome

1640   Monteverdi, *Il ritorno d'Ulisse in patria*, Venice

1641   Francesco Sacrati, *La finta pazza*, Venice

1643   Monteverdi, *L'incoronazione di Poppea*, Venice
         Francesco Cavalli, *Egisto*, Venice

1649   Cavalli, *Giasone*, Venice

1651   Cavalli, *Calisto*, Venice

1671   inauguration of Académie de l'Opéra, Paris

1672   Jean-Baptiste Lully, *Les Fêtes de l'Amour et de Bacchus*, Paris

1674   Lully, *Alceste*, Paris

1676   Lully, *Atys*, St Germain-en-Laye

c.1683   John Blow, *Venus and Adonis*, London

1685   Lully, *Roland*, Versailles

1686   Lully, *Armide*, Paris

Lully, *Acis et Galatée*, Paris

1689   Henry Purcell, *Dido and Aeneas*, London

1690   Purcell, *Dioclesian*, London

1691   Purcell, *King Arthur*, London

1692   Purcell, *The Fairy Queen*, London

1695   Purcell, *The Indian Queen*, London

1697   André Campra, *L'Europe galante*, Paris

1699   André Cardinal Destouches, *Amadis de Grèce*, Paris

1702   Campra, *Tancrède*, Paris

1707   Reinhard Keiser, *Der Carneval von Venedig*, Hamburg

1710   Campra, *Les Fêtes vénitiennes*, Paris

1711   George Frideric Handel, *Rinaldo*, London

1712   Campra, *Idomenée*, Paris

1718   Handel, *Acis and Galatea*, Cannons, Edgware
        Alessandro Scarlatti, *Il trionfo dell'onore*, Naples

c.1720 Benedetto Marcello, *Il teatro alla moda*, satirical manual of operatic
        production

1721   Scarlatti, *Griselda*, Rome
        Destouches, *Les Éléments*, Paris

1724   Handel, *Giulio Cesare in Egitto*, London

1726   Leonardo Vinci, *Didone abbandonata*, Rome

1728   John Gay and Johann Christian Pepusch, *The Beggar's Opera*, London

1730   Johann Adolf Hasse, *Artaserse*, Venice

1731   Charles Coffey and Mr Seedo, *The Devil to Pay*, London
        Hasse, *Cleofide*, Dresden

1732   Giovanni Battista Pergolesi, *Lo frate 'nnamorato*, Naples
        opening of first opera house on the site of Covent Garden

1733   Handel, *Orlando*, London
        Jean-Philippe Rameau, *Hippolyte et Aricie*, Paris
        Pergolesi, *La serva padrona*, Naples

1735   Pergolesi, *L'olimpiade*, Rome
        Handel, *Alcina*, London

1737   opening of Teatro San Carlo, Naples
        Rameau, *Castor et Pollux*, Paris

1738   Thomas Arne, *Comus*, London
        Handel, *Serse*, London

1744   Handel, *Semele*, London

Piccinni, *Roland*, Paris

1779   Gluck, *Iphigénie en Tauride*, Paris

1781   Mozart, *Idomeneo*, Munich

1782   Mozart, *Die Entführung aus dem Serail*, Vienna
Giovanni Paisiello, *Il barbiere di Siviglia*, St Petersburg
Haydn, *Orlando paladino*, Eszterháza

1783   opening of Théâtre-Italien, Paris

1784   André-Ernest-Modeste Grétry, *Richard Cœur-de-Lion*, Paris

1786   Mozart, *Der Schauspieldirektor*, Vienna
Nicholas-Marie Dalayrac, *Nina, ou La folle pour amour*, Paris
Mozart, *Le nozze di Figaro*, Vienna

1787   Giuseppe Gazzaniga, *Don Giovanni, o sia il Convitato di pietra*, Venice
Mozart, *Don Giovanni*, Prague

1787   Antonio Sacchini, *Œdipe à Colone*, Versailles

1788   Dalayrac, *Sargines, ou L'élève de l'amour*, Paris

1789   Paisiello, *Nina, o sia la pazza per amore*, Belvedere, nr Caserta

1790   Mozart, *Così fan tutte*, Vienna
Joseph Quesnel, *Colas et Colinette*, Montreal

1791   Grétry, *Guillaume Tell*, Paris
Luigi Cherubini, *Lodoïska*, Paris
Rodolphe Kreutzer, *Lodoiska, ou Les Tartares*, Paris
Mozart, *La clemenza di Tito*, Prague
Mozart, *Die Zauberflöte*, Vienna

1792   Domenico Cimarosa, *Il matrimonio segreto*, Vienna
opening of Teatro La Fenice, Venice

1793   Jean-François Le Sueur, *La Caverne*, Paris

1794   Etienne-Nicolas Méhul, *Mélidore et Phrosine*
Cherubini, *Elisa, ou Le voyage aux glaciers du Mont St-Bernard*, Paris

1796   Cherubini, *Médée*, Paris
Niccolò Zingarelli, *Giulietta e Romeo*, Milan
Cimarosa, *Gli Orazi e Curiazi*, Venice

1799   Ferdinando Paer, *Camilla, ossia Il sotteraneo*, Vienna
Méhul, *Ariodant*, Paris

1807   Gaspare Spontini, *La Vestale*, Paris

1809   Paer, *Agnese*, Parma
Spontini, *Fernand Cortez*, Paris

1813   Gioachino Rossini, *Tancredi*, Venice
Rossini, *L'italiana in Algeri*, Venice

Johann Simon Mayr, *La rosa bianca e la rosa rossa*, Genoa

1813–14   E. T. A. Hoffmann, *Undine* (first performed Berlin 1816)

1814   Ludwig van Beethoven, *Fidelio*, Vienna (first version 1805)

1816   Rossini, *Il barbiere di Siviglia*, Rome
Rossini, *Otello*, Naples
Louis Spohr, *Faust*, Prague

1817   Rossini, *La Cenerentola*, Rome

1819   Rossini, *La donna del lago*, Naples

1821   Carl Maria von Weber, *Der Freischütz*, Berlin

1822   Franz Schubert, *Alfonso und Estrella* (first performed Weimar 1854)

1823   Rossini, *Semiramide*, Naples
Henry Bishop, *Clari, or The Maid of Milan*, London
Spohr, *Jessonda*, Kassel
Weber, *Euryanthe*, Vienna
Schubert, *Fierrabras* (first performed Karlsruhe 1897)

1825   François-Adrien Boïeldieu, *La Dame blanche*, Paris

1826   Bishop, *Aladdin*, London
Rossini, *Le Siège de Corinthe*, Paris (French version of *Maometto II*, Naples 1820)

1827   Rossini, *Moïse et Pharaon*, Paris (French version of *Mosè in Egitto*, Naples 1818)

Vincenzo Bellini, *Il pirata*, Milan

1828   Daniel-François-Esprit Auber, *La Muette de Portici*, Paris
Heinrich Marschner, *Der Vampyr*, Leipzig

1829   Bellini, *La straniera*, Milan
Rossini, *Guillaume Tell*, Paris
Marschner, *Der Templer und die Jüdin*, Leipzig

1830   Auber, *Fra Diavolo*, Paris
Bellini, *I Capuleti e i Montecchi*, Milan
Gaetano Donizetti, *Anna Bolena*, Milan

1831   Bellini, *La sonnambula*, Milan
Ferdinand Hérold, *Zampa*, Paris
Giacomo Meyerbeer, *Robert le diable*, Paris
Bellini, *Norma*, Milan

1833   Auber, *Gustave III, ou Le bal masqué*, Paris
Bellini, *Beatrice di Tenda*, Venice
Donizetti, *L'elisir d'amore*, Milan
Marschner, *Hans Heiling*, Berlin
Donizetti, *Lucrezia Borgia*, Milan
Richard Wagner, *Die Feen* (first performed Munich 1888)

1835   Bellini, *I puritani*, Paris
Fromental Halévy, *La Juive*, Paris
Donizetti, *Lucia di Lammermoor*, Naples

1836   Saverio Mercadante, *I briganti*, Paris
Meyerbeer, *Les Huguenots*, Paris
Michael Balfe, *The Maid of Artois*, London
Wagner, *Das Liebesverbot*, Magdeburg
Mikhail Ivanovich Glinka, *A Life for the Tsar*, St Petersburg

1837   Mercadante, *Il giuramento*, Milan
Lortzing, *Zar und Zimmermann*, Leipzig

1838   Hector Berlioz, *Benvenuto Cellini*, Paris

1839   Mercadante, *Il bravo, ossia La veneziana*, Milan
Giuseppe Verdi, *Oberto, conte di San Bonifacio*, Milan

1840   Donizetti, *La Fille du régiment*, Paris
Donizetti, *La Favorite*, Paris

1842   Verdi, *Nabucodonosor [Nabucco]*, Milan
Lortzing, *Der Wildschütz*, Leipzig
Wagner, *Rienzi*, Dresden
Glinka, *Ruslan and Lyudmila*, St Petersburg

1843   Donizetti, *Don Pasquale*, Paris
Balfe, *The Bohemian Girl*, London
Donizetti, *Dom Sébastien*, Paris
Wagner, *Der fliegende Holländer*, Dresden

1844   Verdi, *Ernani*, Venice
Ferenc Erkel, *Hunyadi László*, Budapest
Edward Geoghagen, *The Currency Lass*, Sydney

1845   Wagner, *Tannhäuser*, Dresden (revised 1847, Paris 1861, Munich 1867)

1846   Berlioz, *La Damnation de Faust*, Paris

1847   Friedrich Flotow, *Martha*, Vienna
Verdi, *Macbeth*, Florence (revised Paris 1865)

1847   Isaac Nathan, *Don John of Austria*, Sydney

1848   Stanisław Moniuszko, *Halka* (final version Warsaw 1858)

1849   Verdi, *Luisa Miller*, Naples
Meyerbeer, *Le Prophète*, Paris
Otto Nicolai, *Die lustigen Weiber von Windsor*, Berlin

1850   Verdi, *Stiffelio*, Trieste (revised as *Aroldo*, Rimini 1857)
Robert Schumann, *Genoveva*, Leipzig
Wagner, *Lohengrin*, Weimar

1851   Wagner, *Oper und Drama*, theoretical work on opera

Verdi, *Rigoletto*, Venice

1853   Verdi, *Il trovatore*, Rome
Verdi, *La traviata*, Venice

1854   Gounod, *La Nonne sanglante*, Paris
Wagner, *Das Rheingold* (first performed Munich 1869)

1855   Verdi, *Les Vêpres siciliennes*, Paris

1856   Auber, *Manon Lescaut*, Paris
Alexander Sergeyevich Dargomïzsky, *Rusalka*, St Petersburg
Wagner, *Die Walküre* (first performed Munich 1870)

1857   Verdi, *Simon Boccanegra*, Venice (revised version Milan 1881)
Balfe, *The Rose of Castille*, London

1858   Berlioz, *Les Troyens* (first performed Paris 1863; first complete
performance Karlsruhe 1890)
Jacques Offenbach, *Orphée aux Enfers*, Paris
opening of Royal Opera House, Covent Garden

1859   Verdi, *Un ballo in maschera*, Rome
Gounod, *Faust*, Paris
Wagner, *Tristan und Isolde* (first performed Munich 1865)

1861   Erkel, *Bánk bán*, Budapest

1862   Verdi, *La forza del destino*, St Petersburg
Berlioz, *Béatrice et Bénédict*, Baden-Baden

1863   Georges Bizet, *Les Pêcheurs de perles*, Paris

1864   Gounod, *Mireille*, Paris
Jacques Offenbach, *La Belle Hélène*, Paris

1865   Meyerbeer, *L'Africaine*, Paris

1866   Bedřich Smetana, *The Brandenburgers in Bohemia*, Prague
Smetana, *The Bartered Bride*, Prague (final version 1870)
Ambroise Thomas, *Mignon*, Paris

1867   Gounod, *Roméo et Juliette*, Paris
Bizet, *La Jolie Fille de Perth*, Paris
Verdi, *Don Carlos*, Paris (revised four-act version Milan 1884)

1868   Thomas, *Hamlet*, Paris
Arrigo Boito, *Mefistofele*, Milan
Wagner, *Die Meistersinger von Nürnberg*, Munich

1869   Dargomïzhsky, *The Stone Guest* (first performed St Petersburg 1872)
opening of Staatsoper (called Hofoper until 1919), Vienna

1871   Verdi, *Aida*, Cairo
Wagner, *Siegfried* (first performed Bayreuth 1876)

1872   opening of Festspielhaus, Bayreuth

1874 Smetana, *The Two Widows*, Prague
      Modest Musorgsky, *Boris Godunov* (composed and revised St
          Petersburg 1868–9, 1871–2, 1873)
      Wagner, *Götterdämmerung* (first performed Bayreuth 1876)

1875 opening of Palais Garnier, Paris
      Bizet, *Carmen*, Paris

1876 *Der Ring des Nibelungen* (*Das Rheingold, Die Walküre, Siegfried,
          Götterdämmerung*), first complete cycle, Bayreuth
      Amilcare Ponchielli, *La gioconda*, Milan

1877 Emmanuel Chabrier, *L'Étoile*
      Camille Saint-Saëns, *Samson et Dalila*, Weimar

1879 Pyotr Il'yich Tchaikovsky, *Eugene Onegin*, Moscow

1872–80 Musorgsky, *Khovanshchina* (first performed St Petersburg 1886)

1881 Offenbach, *Les Contes d'Hoffmann*, Paris

1882 Wagner, *Parsifal*, Bayreuth
      Calixa Lavallée, *The Widow*, Hamilton, Canada

1883 Léo Delibes, *Lakmé*, Paris

1884 Jules Massenet, *Manon*, Paris
      Giacomo Puccini, *Le villi*, Milan

1887 Chabrier, *Le Roi malgré lui*, Paris
      Verdi, *Otello*, Milan

1888 Edouard Lalo, *Le Roi d'Ys*, Paris

1889 Puccini, *Edgar*, Milan

1890 Alexander Porfir'yevich Borodin, *Prince Igor*, St Petersburg
      Pietro Mascagni, *Cavalleria rusticana*, Rome
      Tchaikovsky, *The Queen of Spades*, St Petersburg

1892 Ruggero Leoncavallo, *Pagliacci*, Milan
      Massenet, *Werther*, Vienna

1893 Puccini, *Manon Lescaut*, Turin
      Verdi, *Falstaff*, Milan
      Engelbert Humperdinck, *Hansel und Gretel*, Weimar

1894 Massenet, *Thaïs*, Paris
      Richard Strauss, *Guntram*, Weimar

1896 Puccini, *La bohème*, Turin
      Umberto Giordano, *Andrea Chenier*, Milan
      Hugo Wolf, *Der Corregidor*, Mannheim

1897 Massenet, *Sapho*, Paris
      Nikolay Andreyevich Rimsky-Korsakov, *Sadko*, Moscow

1899 Massenet, *Cendrillon*, Paris
      Antonín Dvořák, *Kate and the Devil*, Prague

1900	Puccini, *Tosca*, Rome
	Gustave Charpentier, *Louise*, Paris
1900	Rimsky-Korsakov, *The Tale of Tsar Saltan*, Moscow
1901	Dvořák, *Rusalka*, Prague
1902	Claude Debussy, *Pelléas et Mélisande*, Paris
	Francesco Cilea, *Adriana Lecouvreur*, Milan
1904	Leoš Janáček, *Jenůfa*, Brno
	Puccini, *Madama Butterfly*, Milan
1905	Strauss, *Salome*, Dresden
1907	Paul Dukas, *Ariane et Barbe-Bleue*, Paris
	Frederick Delius, *A Village Romeo and Juliet*, Berlin
1909	Rimsky-Korsakov, *The Golden Cockerel*, Moscow
	Strauss, *Elektra*, Dresden
	Ermanno Wolf-Ferrari, *Il segreto di Susanna*, Munich
	Maurice Ravel, *L'Heure espagnole* (first performed Paris 1911)
	Arnold Schoenberg, *Erwartung* (first performed Prague 1924)
1910	Puccini, *La fanciulla del West*, New York
1911	Strauss, *Der Rosenkavalier*, Dresden
	Béla Bartók, *Bluebeard's Castle* (first performed Budapest 1918)
1912	Franz Schreker, *Der ferne Klang*, Frankfurt
1914	Igor Stravinsky, *The Nightingale*, Paris
	Rutland Boughton, *The Immortal Hour*, Glastonbury
1916	Strauss, *Ariadne auf Naxos*, Vienna (first version in one act 1912)
1917	Sergey Prokofiev, *The Gambler* (first performed Brussels 1929)
	Hans Pfitzner, *Palestrina*, Munich
1918	Puccini, *La rondine*, Monte Carlo
	Puccini, *Il trittico*, New York (*Il tabarro*, *Suor Angelica*, *Gianni Schicchi*)
1919	Strauss, *Die Frau ohne Schatten*, Vienna
1919–23	Prokofiev, *The Fiery Angel* (first performed Venice 1955)
1921	Janáček, *Káťa Kabanová*, Brno
	Prokofiev, *The Love for Three Oranges*, Chicago
1922	Alexander von Zemlinsky, *Der Zwerg*, Cologne
1923	Alban Berg, *Wozzeck* (first performed Berlin 1925)
1924	Strauss, *Intermezzo*, Dresden
	Janáček, *The Cunning Little Vixen*, Brno
1925	Ravel, *L'Enfant et les sortilèges*, Monte Carlo
	Ferruccio Busoni, *Doktor Faust*, Dresden
1926	Karol Szymanowski, *King Roger*, Warsaw
	Puccini, *Turandot*, Milan

Paul Hindemith, *Cardillac*, Dresden
Janáček, *The Makropulos Case*, Brno

1927   Ernst Krenek, *Jonny spielt auf*, Leipzig
       Stravinsky, *Oedipus rex*, Paris

1928   Kurt Weill, *Die Dreigroschenoper*, Berlin

1929   Ralph Vaughan Williams, *Sir John in Love*, London

1930   Weill, *Aufstieg und Fall der Stadt Mahagonny*, Leipzig
1930   Janáček, *From the House of the Dead*, Brno
       Dmitry Shostakovich, *The Nose*, Leningrad

1930–2 Schoenberg, *Moses und Aron* (first performed Hamburg 1954)

1933   Strauss, *Arabella*, Dresden

1934   Dmitry Shostakovich, *Lady Macbeth of Mtsensk District*, Leningrad

1935   George Gershwin, *Porgy and Bess*, New York
       Berg, *Lulu* (three-act version completed by Friedrich Cerha; first
         performed Paris 1979)

1937   Marc Blitzstein, *The Cradle Will Rock*, New York
       Vaughan Williams, *Riders to the Sea*, London

1938   Hindemith, *Mathis der Maler*, Zurich

1941   Benjamin Britten, *Paul Bunyan*, New York

1942   Strauss, *Capriccio*, Munich

1945   Britten, *Peter Grimes*, London

1946   Gian Carlo Menotti, *The Medium*, New York
       Britten, *The Rape of Lucretia*, Glyndebourne

1947   Menotti, *The Telephone*, New York
       Britten, *Albert Herring*, Glyndebourne

1949   Luigi Dallapiccola, *Il prigioniero*, Italian radio

1950   Menotti, *The Consul*, Philadelphia

1951   Stravinsky, *The Rake's Progress*, Venice
       Menotti, *Amahl and the Night Visitors*, US television
       Britten, *Billy Budd*, London
       Vaughan Williams, *The Pilgrim's Progress*, London

1952   Leonard Bernstein, *Trouble in Tahiti*, Waltham, Massachussetts

1953   Britten, *Gloriana*, London

1954   Britten, *The Turn of the Screw*, Venice
       William Walton, *Troilus and Cressida*, London

1955   Michael Tippett, *The Midsummer Marriage*, London

1956   Bernstein, *Candide*, Boston
       Douglas Moore, *The Ballad of Baby Doe*, Central City, Colorado

1957   Bernstein, *West Side Story*, Washington

1958   Samuel Barber, *Vanessa*, New York

1960   Britten, *A Midsummer Night's Dream*, Aldeburgh

1961   Hans Werner Henze, *Elegy for Young Lovers*, Schwetzingen
        Luigi Nono, *Intolleranza*, Venice

1965   György Ligeti, *Aventures* (1962) and *Nouvelles Aventures*, Hamburg
        Bernd-Alois Zimmermann, *Die Soldaten*, Cologne
        Henze, *Der junge Lord*, Berlin
        Healey Willan, *Deirdre of the Sorrows*, Toronto

1966   Henze, *The Bassarids*, Salzburg
        Barber, *Antony and Cleopatra*, New York

1967   Harry Somers, *Louis Riel*, Toronto
        Pierre Boulez announces the decline of opera since Berg and
            advocates blowing up the world's opera houses

1968   Harrison Birtwistle, *Punch and Judy*, Aldeburgh
        Britten, *The Prodigal Son*, Orford
        Dallapiccola, *Ulisse*, Berlin
        Peter Maxwell Davies, *Taverner* (first performed London 1972)

1969   Davies, *Eight Songs for a Mad King*, London
        Krzysztof Penderecki, *The Devils of Loudun*, Hamburg

1970   Luciano Berio, *Opera*, Santa Fe

1971   Mauricio Kagel, *Staatstheater*, Hamburg

1973   Britten, *Death in Venice*, Snape, Maltings
        opening of Sydney Opera House

1974   Peter Sculthorpe, *Rites of Passage*, Sydney

1976   Henze, *We Come to the River*, London
        Philip Glass, *Einstein on the Beach*, Avignon

1978   Penderecki, *Paradise Lost*, Chicago
        Ligeti, *Le Grand Macabre*, Stockholm

1980   Glass, *Satyagraha*, Rotterdam
        Davies, *The Lighthouse*, Edinburgh
        Oliver Knussen, *Where the Wild Things Are*, Brussels

1981   Karlheinz Stockhausen, *Donnerstag aus Licht*, Milan (first in a
            projected seven-opera cycle, *Licht*)

1982   Berio, *La vera storia*, Florence
        Sculthorpe, *Quiros*, Australian television

1983   Bernstein, *A Quiet Place*, Houston (revised version, including *Trouble
            in Tahiti*, Milan 1984)
        Olivier Messiaen, *Saint François d'Assise*, Paris

R. Murray Schafer, *Ra*, Toronto (Part 6 of a six-part cycle entitled *Patria*, performed in various venues, Ontario and Liège 1972–92)

1984 Nono, *Promoteo*, Venice
Glass, *Akhnaten*, Stuttgart
Berio, *Un re in ascolto*, Salzburg

1986 Birtwistle, *The Mask of Orpheus*, London
Richard Meale, *Voss*, Adelaide

1987 John Adams, *Nixon in China*, Houston
Penderecki, *Die schwarze Maske*, Salzburg
Cage, *Europeras 1 and 2*, Frankfurt
Judith Weir, *A Night at the Chinese Opera*, Cheltenham

1989 John Casken, *Golem*, London

1990 Weir, *The Vanishing Bridegroom*, Glasgow
opening of Opéra Bastille, Paris

1991 Penderecki, *Ubu Rex*, Munich
Adams, *The Death of Klinghoffer*, Brussels
Cage, *Europera 5*, Buffalo
Birtwistle, *Gawain*, London

1992 Somers, *Mario and the Magician*, Toronto
Glass, *The Voyage*, New York

1993 Jonathan Harvey, *Inquest of Love*, London

1994 Weir, *Blond Eckbert*, London
Birtwistle, *The Second Mrs Kong*, Glyndebourne

1995 Alfred Schnittke, *Gesualdo*, Vienna
Schnittke, *Faust*, Hamburg

1996 Berio, *Outis*, Milan
Davies, *The Doctor of Myddfai*, Cardiff
Tan Dun, *Marco Polo*, Munich

1997 Henze, *Venus and Adonis*, Munich

NOTES ON THE CONTRIBUTORS

WILLIAM ASHBROOK is Distinguished Professor of Humanities (Emeritus) at Indiana State University, and editor of *The Opera Quarterly*. His many books include *Donizetti* (Cassell, 1965), *The Operas of Puccini* (Cassell, 1969; revised Oxford, 1985), *Donizetti and His Operas* (Cambridge, 1982), and, with Harold S. Powers, *Puccini's 'Turandot': The End of the Great Tradition* (Princeton, 1991).

THOMAS BAUMAN, Professor of Music at the University of Washington, has published articles and monographs on German opera during the Enlightenment, including *North German Opera in the Age of Goethe* (Cambridge, 1985), the Cambridge Opera Handbook on Mozart's *Entführung aus dem Serail* (1987), in addition to studies of Venetian opera and the reception of Mozart's Requiem.

TIM CARTER is Reader in Music at Royal Holloway and Bedford New College, University of London, and joint editor of *Music & Letters*. He has published widely on music and patronage in late sixteenth- and early seventeenth-century Italy, including a revised edition of Denis Arnold's *Monteverdi* in the Master Musicians series (London, 1990), and *Music in Late Renaissance and Early Baroque Italy* (London, 1992). He is the author of the Cambridge Opera Handbook on Mozart's *Le nozze di Figaro* (1987), and has contributed extensively to *The New Grove Dictionary of Opera*.

DAVID CHARLTON is Reader in Music, University of East Anglia. He is the author of *Grétry and the Growth of Opéra-Comique* (Cambridge, 1986) and editor of *E. T. A. Hoffmann's Musical Writings* (Cambridge, 1989). He wrote on French Opera, 1830–1890, in Volume IX of The New Oxford History of Music, edited by Gerald Abraham, and was an Area Advisor to *The New Grove Dictionary of Opera*.

PAUL GRIFFITHS is music critic of *The New Yorker* and a writer of fiction. He has written a number of books on music, including studies of Boulez, Cage, and Messiaen, the Master Musicians volumes on Bartók and Stravinsky, and the Cambridge Opera Handbook on Stravinsky's *The Rake's Progress* (1982). The fiction includes two novels and the libretto of an opera with music by Mozart, *The Jewel Box* (1991).

BARRY MILLINGTON is a music critic for *The Times*. He is the author of *Wagner* in the Master Musicians series, wrote the entries on Wagner for *The New Grove Dictionary of Opera*, is editor of *The Wagner Compendium* (London, 1992), and co-editor (with Stewart Spencer) of *Selected Letters of Richard Wagner* (London, 1987), *Wagner in Performance* (Yale, 1992), and *Wagner's 'Ring of the Nibelung': A Companion* (London, 1993). He is also Reviews Editor of the *BBC Music Magazine*.

ROGER PARKER, until recently Associate Professor of Music at Cornell University, is now Lecturer in Music, University of Oxford, and Fellow of St Hugh's College. He has published extensively on Verdi and on nineteenth-century Italian opera in general, including the entries on Verdi for *The New Grove Dictionary of Opera* and the Cambridge Opera Handbook on Puccini's *La bohème* (with Arthur Groos, 1986). His critical edition of Verdi's *Nabucco* appeared in 1987 and he is co-ordinating editor (with Gabriele Dotto) of the Donizetti critical edition. He is founding co-editor of the *Cambridge Opera Journal*.

JOHN ROSSELLI is a historian who for the past fifteen years has concentrated on the social history of opera. His books include *The Opera Industry in Italy from Cimarosa to Verdi* (Cambridge, 1984), *Music and Musicians in Nineteenth-Century Italy* (London, 1991), and *Singers of Italian Opera: The History of a Profession* (Cambridge, 1992). He has reviewed opera for the *Guardian* and the *Times Literary Supplement*.

ROGER SAVAGE is Senior Lecturer in English Literature at the University of Edinburgh and much involved with the teaching of drama there. He has directed numerous productions of the Edinburgh University Opera Club and a couple for the Scottish Early Music Consort. He has made English performing versions of libretti for operas by Handel, Chabrier, and others, published essays on theatre-music by Purcell, Rameau, and Stravinsky (also on aspects of early operatic staging), contributed to *The New Grove Dictionary of Opera*, and made a number of broadcasts for the BBC.

MARY ANN SMART is Assistant Professor of Music at SUNY, Stony Brook, and has published several articles on nineteenth-century Italian and French opera. She is currently working on a critical edition of Donizetti's *Dom Sébastien*.

JOHN TYRRELL is Professor of Music at the University of Nottingham. He has written extensively on Czech opera in *The New Grove Dictionary of Opera* and the *Penguin Dictionary of Opera*. His book *Czech Opera* (Cambridge, 1988) appeared in a Czech translation in 1992. He is well known for his work on Janáček, writing the notes accompanying the celebrated Decca series of Janáček opera recordings, and, with Sir Charles Mackerras, reconstructing the original version of *Jenůfa* (published in full score and study score in 1996). His *Janáček's Operas: A Documentary Account* appeared in 1992; his translation of Janáček's letters to Kamila Stösslová (*Intimate Letters*) was published by Faber in 1994.

INDEX

Composers' works are organized alphabetically without reference to the definite and indefinite articles of the languages in which they are given, i.e. according to the first major word. Works with extensive page references are indexed separately; others are listed under the name of the composer.

Slovakia 158
Slovenia 157, 158
small-scale opera 208
Smetana, Bedřich 161, 169, 180, 203, 210
   works: *The Bartered Bride* 163, 166, 167–8,
    173, 174, 175; *The Brandenburgers in*
    Bohemia 166, 173; *Dalibor* 173, 174, 180;
    The Devil's Wall 168; *The Kiss* 167, 175,
    178; *Libuše* 162, 166, 167, 184; *The Secret*
    178; *The Two Widows* 168, 174
Soane, George 99, 100
social occasion of opera 95, 304–21
social issues 116; criticism 64, 69, 199–200,
   209; socio-political statements 74, 79
Society for the Faithful Presentation of the
   Dramas of Richard Wagner 271
Sografi, Antonio 55
soldiers 313–14
Soler, *see* Martín y Soler
soliloquy 132
solos / soloists 115, 119, 154, 220, 221, 230, 295;
   based on double-aria principle 174;
   brief, homophonic ensemble sung by
   all 61; combining passages with choral
   interjections 117; dance 192;
   instrumental 104; large orchestra, with
   chorus and 219; main character
   established by 93; self-contained songs
   143; set-piece, rationed 93; singing
   together 207; soprano 224; substantial
   passages 189
song 131, 183, 189; bird- 231; formal, excuse
   for 17; French-style 29; German,
   militantly simple 51; love, triple-time
   17; off-stage 119; patter 118; popular
   style 202; self-contained 143, 154;
   simple folk-like 144; solo 154; type used
   in Greek and Roman plays 5–6;
   Ukrainian hero 169
   see also folk music
Sontag, Henriette, Countess Rossi 287
Sophia Eleonora, princess of Saxony 23
Sophocles 2, 206
sopranos 74, 121, 128, 136, 222, 224, 229;
   baritone and 128, 129; breeches part for
   164; coloratura 194, 226, 293; dramatic
   89; fearless use of the voice 192; fine-
   grained 300; first-rate, absence of 73;
   pentatonic music featuring 197; Italian
   301; low notes 300; most demanding
   aria 171; prepubescent voices 288;
   range short on top 296; rival 294; to

sing the role of a boy 204 untrained 79;
   verismo 297
   see also mezzo-sopranos; *also under*
    individual names, e.g. Boninsegna;
    Branchu; Callas; Calvé; Dalla Rizza;
    Destinn; Ehrenbergů; Favero; Flagstad;
    Gabrielli; Jeritza; Leider; Lind; Melba;
    Novello; Sutherland; Tassinari
soubrette-like roles 296
sound: electronic 230; music richly coloured
   in 231; physical and metaphysical
   properties 225
sousedská (Czech dance) 167, 168
South Africa 209
South America x, 234
Soviet Union 204, 205, 209, 217, 234, 262;
   administration 164; rebaptism of *Tosca*
   as *The Battle for the Commune* 204
Spain 7, 12, 18, 96, 234
spectacle 28, 29, 124, 148, 190, 267; *à la mode*,
   French opera as apogee of 247–8; desire
   for more 45; enduring popular appeal
   at Vienna of operas mixing farce,
   supernatural, and 81; fluid interchange
   of singing, declamation, dance, and 42;
   grand 269; introduced by a new
   generation of librettists 55; religious,
   multi-media 244; visually compelling,
   of scant literary merit 82
Spectator (periodical) 251
speech: natural, rhythms and melodies of
   203; over music 194, 219; realistic setting
   of 182; sung stylization of 183
speech-melody theory 184
speech-song 198
speeches 189
Spohr, Louis 144, 146; *Faust* 139, 140, 141, 147;
   Jessonda 140–1, 144
spoken dialogue 67, 87, 140, 173–4; enhanced
   by *frissons* of supernatural 85; French
   319; instead of recitative 54, 63, 71;
   interspersed 140, 144; recitative could
   replace 108; self-contained musical
   numbers interspersed with 138;
   substitution of recitative for 72, 141;
   witty 90
spoken drama 16, 252, 255, 267, 273;
   historical, detail typical of 99;
   naturalistic 266
spoken theatre 257, 258, 273; charismatic
   director-managers 265; mainstream
   acting in 276–7; new verse drama in
   216

Index compiled by Frank Pert